Communications in Computer and Information Science 2668

Rationale

The CCIS series is devoted to the publication of proceedings of computer science conferences. Its aim is to efficiently disseminate original research results in informatics in printed and electronic form. While the focus is on publication of peer-reviewed full papers presenting mature work, inclusion of reviewed short papers reporting on work in progress is welcome, too. Besides globally relevant meetings with internationally representative program committees guaranteeing a strict peer-reviewing and paper selection process, conferences run by societies or of high regional or national relevance are also considered for publication.

Topics

The topical scope of CCIS spans the entire spectrum of informatics ranging from foundational topics in the theory of computing to information and communications science and technology and a broad variety of interdisciplinary application fields.

Information for Volume Editors and Authors

Publication in CCIS is free of charge. No royalties are paid, however, we offer registered conference participants temporary free access to the online version of the conference proceedings on SpringerLink (http://link.springer.com) by means of an http referrer from the conference website and/or a number of complimentary printed copies, as specified in the official acceptance email of the event.

CCIS proceedings can be published in time for distribution at conferences or as post-proceedings, and delivered in the form of printed books and/or electronically as USBs and/or e-content licenses for accessing proceedings at SpringerLink. Furthermore, CCIS proceedings are included in the CCIS electronic book series hosted in the SpringerLink digital library at http://link.springer.com/bookseries/7899. Conferences publishing in CCIS are allowed to use our online conference service (Meteor) for managing the whole proceedings lifecycle (from submission and reviewing to preparing for publication) free of charge.

Publication process

The language of publication is exclusively English. Authors publishing in CCIS have to sign the Springer CCIS copyright transfer form, however, they are free to use their material published in CCIS for substantially changed, more elaborate subsequent publications elsewhere. For the preparation of the camera-ready papers/files, authors have to strictly adhere to the Springer CCIS Authors' Instructions and are strongly encouraged to use the CCIS LaTeX style files or templates.

Abstracting/Indexing

CCIS is abstracted/indexed in DBLP, Google Scholar, EI-Compendex, Mathematical Reviews, SCImago, Scopus. CCIS volumes are also submitted for the inclusion in ISI Proceedings.

How to start

To start the evaluation of your proposal for inclusion in the CCIS series, please send an e-mail to ccis@springer.com

Marcello Bonsangue · Yixiang Chen
Editors

Artificial Intelligence Logic and Applications

5th International Conference, AILA 2025
Xi'an, China, August 16–17, 2025
Proceedings

Editors
Marcello Bonsangue
Leiden University
Leiden, Zuid-Holland, The Netherlands

Yixiang Chen
East China Normal University
Shanghai, China

ISSN 1865-0929 ISSN 1865-0937 (electronic)
Communications in Computer and Information Science
ISBN 978-981-95-8261-7 ISBN 978-981-95-8262-4 (eBook)
https://doi.org/10.1007/978-981-95-8262-4

This Springer imprint is published by the registered company Springer Nature Singapore Pte Ltd.
The registered company address is: 152 Beach Road, #21-01/04 Gateway East, Singapore 189721, Singapore

Preface

This volume contains the proceedings of the 2025 International Conference on *Artificial Intelligence Logic and Applications (AILA 2025)*, the fifth edition in the AILA conference series dedicated to advancing research in classical and non-classical logics and their applications in artificial intelligence. Hosted by Xi'an Shiyou University, AILA 2025 was held in the historic city of Xi'an, Shaanxi Province, China, on August 16–17, 2025.

Since the beginning of AI research, logic has served as a fundamental pillar for knowledge representation and reasoning, playing an important role in automated decision-making, formal verification, and intelligent systems. As the field of AI continues to advance, the integration of logical frameworks with emerging technologies such as machine learning, reinforcement learning, and hybrid systems has become more important. The AILA conference series provides an international forum for researchers to present and discuss cutting-edge developments at the intersection of logic and AI, fostering interdisciplinary collaboration that bridges theoretical foundations with practical applications.

The AILA conference series originated in 2019, when it began as a special session within the *IEEE 14th International Conference on Intelligent Systems and Knowledge Engineering (ISKE 2019)*. Following its successful start, AILA evolved into a standalone event, with a virtual second edition in 2022. Subsequent editions were hosted by Jilin University (2023) and Lanzhou Jiaotong University (2024). This year marked a special milestone as we brought AILA to Xi'an, a city famous for its cultural heritage and academic community.

The conference received 34 high-quality submissions from researchers across the globe. Each submission underwent a rigorous single-blind peer-review process, evaluated by at least three Program Committee members or external experts. After careful deliberation, the committee selected 12 full papers and 6 short papers for inclusion in these proceedings, representing a diverse range of innovative research in the field. The technical program also included five distinguished keynote lectures:

- Natasha Alechina (Open University of the Netherlands and Flanders) on "Logic for Reinforcement Learning"
- Yongming Li (Shaanxi Normal University) on "Possibilistic Temporal Logic: Decidability and Complete Axiomatization"
- Naijun Zhan (Peking University) on "Extending Hoare Logic to Hybrid Systems"
- Guo-Qiang Zhang (University of Texas Health Science Center at Houston) on "Ensemble Logic: A Unified Framework for Temporal, Spatial, and Spatial-Temporal Reasoning"
- Beihai Zhou (Shanxi University) on "A Formal Semantics for Generic Sentences and Metaphorical Sentences"

AILA 2025 presented a Best Paper Award during its closing ceremony. The winner was selected by an independent panel of three judges, who evaluated papers nominated by the Program Committee for their technical excellence and their presentation quality at the conference.

The success of AILA 2025 was made possible through the collective efforts of many individuals and organizations. We extend our deepest gratitude to the Steering Committee and Honorary Chairs for their leadership in shaping the AILA conference series. Special thanks are due to the Conference Chairs, Jinfu Wang, Guo-Qiang Zhang, and Songmao Zhang, for their guidance throughout the planning process. We are particularly grateful to the Program Committee members and reviewers for their work in evaluating submissions and ensuring the high quality of the accepted papers. Our sincere appreciation also goes to Organization Chairs Yanhong She and Yong Zhang, along with Publicity Chairs Yangyang Li and Yiming Tang, for their efforts in coordinating all conference operations. Special thanks go to the volunteers and staff from Xi'an Shiyou University who ensured the smooth execution of the event.

We used the EasyChair conference management system to streamline the submission, review, and proceedings preparation processes. Finally, we express our sincere appreciation to Springer for their support in publishing the AILA 2025 proceedings as part of the esteemed Communications in Computer and Information Science (CCIS) series.

We hope this collection of papers will inspire further research and innovation in artificial intelligence logic and its applications.

August 2025

Marcello Bonsangue
Yixiang Chen

Organization

Program Committee

Michal Baczynski	Faculty of Science and Technology, University of Silesia in Katowice, Poland
Marcello Bonsangue	Leiden University, Netherlands
Shuwei Chen	Southwest Jiaotong University, China
Yixiang Chen	Software Engineering Institute, East China Normal University, China
Shifei Ding	China University of Mining and Technology; Key Laboratory of Intelligent Information Processing, Chinese Academy of Sciences, China
Xiaoxuan Fu	China University of Political Science and Law, China
Leandro Gomes	INESC TEC, Portugal
Jiahong Guo	Beijing Normal University, China
Hans-Dieter Hiep	CWI, Netherlands
Guoqiang Li	Shanghai Jiao Tong University, China
Kaixuan Li	Nanyang Technological University, Singapore
Yangyang Li	Academy of Mathematics and Systems Science, Chinese Academy of Sciences, China
Fenrong Liu	Tsinghua University, China
Han Liu	Hong Kong University of Science and Technology, China
Alexandre Madeira	University of Aveiro, Portugal
Wenji Mao	Institute of Automation, Chinese Academy of Sciences, China
Jihong Pei	Shenzhen University, China
Rosa M. Rodríguez	University of Jaén, Spain
Yun Shang	Academy of Mathematics and System Sciences, China
Yabin Shao	Chongqing University of Posts and Telecommunications, China
Yong SuSuzhou	University of Science and Technology, China
Meng Sun	Peking University, China
Hongwei Tao	Zhengzhou University of Light Industry, China
Hui Wang	Queen's University Belfast, UK
Kaiyun Wang	Shaanxi Normal University, China

Zhu Wang	Law School of Sichuan University, China
Bin Wei	Guanghua Law School, Zhejiang University, China
Maonian Wu	Huzhou University, China
Zhongdong Wu	Lanzhou Jiaotong University, China
Yuxin Ye	Jilin University, China
Guo-Qiang Zhang	University of Texas Health Science Center at Houston, USA
Min Zhang	East China Normal University, China
Songmao Zhang	Chinese Academy of Sciences, China
Yong Zhang	ATR National Defense Science and Technology Key Lab, College of Information Engineering, Shenzhen University, China
Yuanrui Zhang	Nanjing University of Aeronautics and Astronautics, China
Yang Zhao	Shenzhen University, China
Hongjun Zhou	Shaanxi Normal University, China

Additional Reviewers

Fei, Chaoqun
Gomes, Leandro
Gu, Zhenzhen
Li, Weizhuo
Wei, Zeming

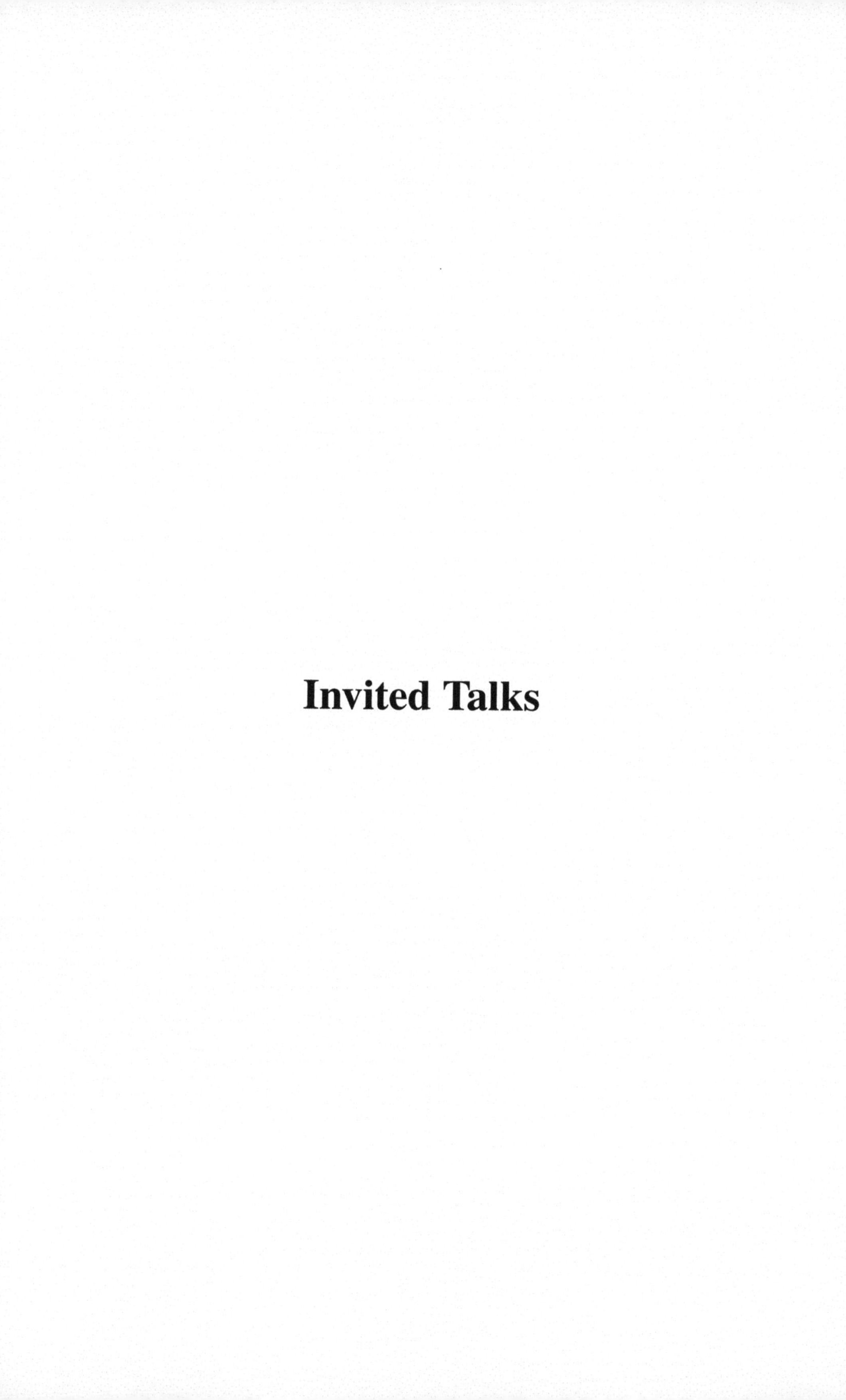

Invited Talks

Logic for Reinforcement Learning

Natasha Alechina

Open University of Netherlands and Flanders, Netherlands

Abstract. Temporal logic is increasingly used in Reinforcement Learning to give a declarative specification of a task to be learned (and avoid problems with reward gaming and other challenges of reward functions) and to specify declarative constraints on agents' behaviour (in particular, safety constraints). In this talk I will present recent work in this area.

Possibilistic Temporal Logic: Decidability and Complete Axiomatization

Yongming Li

Shaanxi Normal University, China

Abstract. Possibilistic computation tree Logic (PoCTL) is one kind of branching temporal logic combined with uncertain information in possibility theory, which was introduced in order to cope with the systematic verification on systems with uncertain information in possibility theory. There are two decision problems related to PoCTL: the model checking problem and the satisfiability problem. The model checking problem of PoCTL has been studied, while the satisfiability problem of PoCTL was not tackled. One of the purposes of this talk is to study the satisfiability problem of PoCTL. We show that the satisfiability problem of PoCTL is decidable in exponential time. Furthermore, we give a complete axiomatization of PoCTL, which is another important inference problem of PoCTL.

Extending Hoare Logic to Hybrid Systems

Naijun Zhan

School of Computer Science, Peking University, China

Abstract. In this talk, I will present our efforts on extending Hoare logic to hybrid systems, named hybrid Hoare logic, including two versions: a DC-based version and a generalized version without DC. I will briefly introduce the DC-based version and mainly focus on the second version. I will explain why we need a generalized version, and present its proof system, the soundness and discrete and continuous relative completeness of the proof system, the implementation of an interactive theorem prover based on Isabelle/HLL called HHLProver, the automation of HHLProver, and finally introduce some applications with the logic and its prover.

Ensemble Logic: A Unified Framework for Temporal, Spatial, and Spatial-Temporal Reasoning

Guo-Qiang Zhang

The University of Texas Health Science Center at Houston, USA

Abstract. I introduced Temporal ensemble logic (TEL) a year ago to fill a gap in formal languages for capturing phenotypes in biomedicine. TEL combines first-order logic and modal logic constructs as primitives in a novel setup that is more expressive than existing linear-time temporal logic. In this presentation I will cover the latest development in this area, with motivating examples and expressiveness results in terms of language classes and undecidability properties, and introduce Ensemble Logic (EL) as a generalized, unified framework for (1) temporal, (2) spatial, and (3) spatial-temporal reasoning on any mathematical space consisting of a monoid with a distance measure or an order relation, such as real numbers ($\mathbb{R}$), integers ($\mathbb{N}$), and Euclidian spaces ($\mathbb{R}^n$).

A Formal Semantics for Generic Sentences and Metaphorical Sentences

Beihai Zhou

School of Philosophy, Shanxi University, China

Abstract. Generic sentences are sentences such as "Birds can fly". Generic sentences are sentences that express the characteristic attributes of things. They are universal and at the same time tolerate exceptions. This characteristic is one of the fundamental reasons for the non-monotonicity of reasoning. Therefore, the logic of generic sentences is also a non-monotonic logic. The formal characterization of the reasoning of generic sentences was first proposed by default logic. There are different understandings of generic sentences, and multiple formal characterization schemes have also emerged. These understandings and characterizations all have their own problems. This study argues that generic sentences are sentences that express the connotations of everyday concepts, and based on this, a formal semantics for generic sentences is provided. The formal semantics of generic sentences has two aspects of significance: on the one hand, it is an intermediary connecting intuitive analysis and formal characterization. Starting from the basic understanding of generic sentences, through this intermediary, one can then move on to the formal characterization of the logic of generic sentences; on the other hand, there is a natural connection between generic sentences and metaphorical sentences. If a formal semantics correctly characterizes generic sentences, then it should be able to be extended to metaphorical sentences. It is precisely based on this view that the formal semantics of generic sentences provided in this study are then extended to metaphorical sentences. The success of this extension in turn confirms the rationality of understanding generic sentences based on everyday concepts.

Contents

Probabilistic and Fuzzy Systems

Optimization and Efficiency

Specification and Verification

Explainable AI

Formal Semantics in XAI: A Categorical Diagrammatic Framework

Yidan Li[1], Jianying Cui[1(✉)], and Minghui Xiong[2]

[1] Institute of Logic and Cognition, Department of Philosophy, Sun Yat-sen University, Guangzhou, China
liyd66@mail2.sysu.edu.cn, cuijiany@mail.sysu.edu.cn
[2] Guanghua Law School, Zhejiang University, Hangzhou, China
xiongminghui@zju.edu.cn

Abstract. Machine learning-based AI systems, despite their widespread success, suffer from limited trust and deployment in critical domains due to their black-box nature. In response, this paper introduces a semantic framework of category-theoretic diagrammatic formalism, which focuses on diagrammatization of model components and formal semantic mapping: translating intuition into mathematical derivations. Our analysis proceeds in three stages: (1) structural decomposition, where string diagrams visually represent model components and their interactions; (2) semantic mapping, where semantic interpretations are assigned to each component, particularly, unlike existing DisCoCat frameworks, our work offers a higher-order extension using typed lambda calculus to systematically capture complex semantics like negation and quantification; and (3) compositional reasoning and verification, where categorical morphisms enable traceability and behavioral transparency through diagrammatic transformation rules that ensure formal uniqueness of interpretations. This semantic framework supports interpretable validation of AI models by leveraging string diagrams to intuitively visualize component interactions and compositional information flow.

Keywords: Compositional Reasoning · Formal Semantics · Explainability · Category Theory · String Diagrams · Diagrammatic Semantics

1 Introduction

With the widespread application of machine learning (ML) models in high-risk fields such as healthcare and finance, model interpretability is critical to addressing the core issues of transparency and ethics in decision-making for AI systems. According to the differences in the stages of model intervention, interpretability can be classified into intrinsic and post-hoc interpretability [2]. The rapidly evolving field of explainable artificial intelligence (XAI) primarily focuses on post-hoc explanation techniques which take a trained AI model and aim to give

M. Bonsangue and Y. Chen (Eds.): AILA 2025, CCIS 2668, pp. 3–16, 2026.
https://doi.org/10.1007/978-981-95-8262-4_1

explanations for either its overall behaviour, or individual outputs [14]. Rudin has highlighted that post-hoc explanations may be untrustworthy for two facts. Firstly, they rely on approximations of the original model, which are inherently unfaithful, and secondly, such explanations are often non-unique and might even seem adjustable at will [6,7].

Unlike post-hoc interpretability techniques, intrinsic interpretability refers to enable transparency and self-interpretation of the model's decision-making process through structural design. Current research on intrinsic interpretability unfolds along two dimensions. The first is modifying model components, which modifies the 'black-box' components and their associated structures [2]. For example, reasoning transparency is implemented through architectural modifications (e.g., sparse attention mechanisms [17]), the introduction of interpretable components (e.g., dynamic weights [5]), or modifying the middle layer [10]. These works ensure that intermediate states can be interpreted using human language due to the modular design and through component-verifiable arithmetic units, but to some extent increase model complexity at the expense of representational flexibility [8,12]. The second dimension is mechanistic investigation for intrinsic interpretability. Introducing knowledge distillation mechanisms [11]can partially enhance model interpretability. Especially in handling complex tasks, the distilled knowledge may still be difficult to interpret [15]. The chain-of-thought (CoT) generation methods [19]narrow the performance gap between interpretable and frontier models by relying on heuristic rules in language models. However, these methods lack formal guarantees [1,9].

To address the limitations of current intrinsic interpretability methods, we introduce a novel paradigm grounded in category theory. This framework provides a mathematically rigorous foundation for modeling how meaning is composed, enabling intrinsic interpretability through formal verification. We leverage string diagrams, a powerful visual calculus from category theory. These diagrams can be seen as a powerful evolution of the intuitive flowcharts common in machine learning papers [16]. However, unlike traditional flowcharts, string diagrams are not mere visual aids; they are a rigorous mathematical language where the visual structure and transformation rules directly correspond to formal, provable derivations of a system's behavior. Specifically, we achieve this "combinatorial interpretability" through the following steps: 1) defining the structure of the Categorical Compositional Distributional models (DisCoCat) with a category-theoretic framework; 2) employing string diagrams to represent the way the model is combined; 3) deriving the overall behavior through the rules of combination; and 4) parsing the contributions of each module to improve the transparency and interpretability of the model.

The rest of this article is organised as follows. Section 2, we introduce the basic mathematical theory, including categories ,string diagrams and the definition of a compositional model. Section 3, taking DisCoCat model as an example, the linguistic structure is mapped to a "computable" category. The functor transfers objects and morphisms between categories while preserving their compositional structures. Section 4, We combine specific text, which involves complex semantics such as negation, disjunction, and universal quantification, and these are assigned higher-order types; Sect. 5 presents the future research directions.

2 Formal Semantics for Compositional Models

To formally describe compositionality, we employ the mathematics of category theory and its associated graphical language of string diagrams to examine the composition of systems and morphisms [13]. These diagrams provide a rigorous yet visually intuitive framework, where in structural constraints guide abstract reasoning.

2.1 Categories and String Diagrams

The semantics of diagrams are defined within the cartesian monoidal category [16] whose objects are Euclidean spaces (viewed as real finite-dimensional vector spaces) and whose morphisms are continuous functions between them. The most powerful feature of these categories is that they admit a purely diagrammatic calculus, in which wires denote spaces and boxes denote morphisms. The two ways to compose processes, namely sequential composite($\circ$) and parallel composition ($\otimes$) in a symmetric monoidal category (SMC).[1]For all spaces, the basic diagrammatic vocabulary are given in Fig. 1.

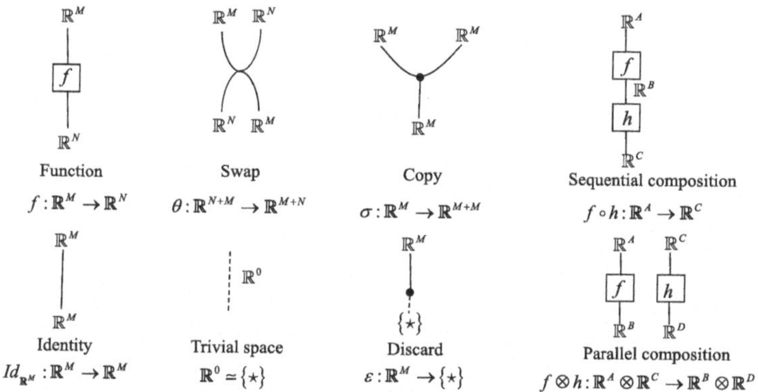

Fig. 1. The Syntax of String Diagrams for Cartesian Categories.

String diagrams, grounded in SMCs, offer geometric syntax for model architectures. The visually intuitive equivalences in the information flow of string diagrams correspond directly to equivalent symbolic derivations of system behavior.

[1] An SMC is a category $\mathcal{C}$ equipped with a bifunctor $\otimes\colon \mathcal{C} \times \mathcal{C} \rightarrow \mathcal{C}$, a unit object I, and natural isomorphisms satisfying coherence conditions for associativity and symmetry.

As an example, functoriality of $\otimes$ means that we always have:

$$(f \otimes g) \circ (f' \otimes g') = (f \circ f') \otimes (g \circ g') \tag{1}$$

In diagrams this is automatic, the 'interchange law' which lets us freely slide boxes along wires. This means that the cumbersome algebraic proofs are naturally handled by diagram isotopies.

String diagrams, grounded in SMCs, represent Euclidean spaces as wires, providing a geometric syntax for tensor operations. For instance, a morphism $f : \mathbb{R}^M \to \mathbb{R}^N$ corresponds to a map between N-dimensional and M-dimensional vector spaces over the scalar field $\mathbb{R}$. To simplify notation, parallel iterations of such maps are indicated by labelled ticks on wires.

Just as $\mathbb{R}^M$ denotes the space of length-M vectors taking values in $\mathbb{R}$, the Cartesian product space $\mathbb{R}^{A\times C}$ corresponds to the space of $\mathbb{R}$-valued A-by-C matrices. Generalizing this formalism, ticks on wires extend to higher-dimensional tensor spaces by indicating indices of arbitrary rank. For example, a tensor in $\mathbb{R}^{A\times B\times C}$ can be decomposed into a sequence of tensor product factors, each represented by a wire with ticks annotating its index structure. This visual encoding not only aligns with algebraic definitions but also enables functions between $\mathbb{R}$-valued tensor spaces to be naturally expressed through diagrammatic compositions, such as in Fig. 2.

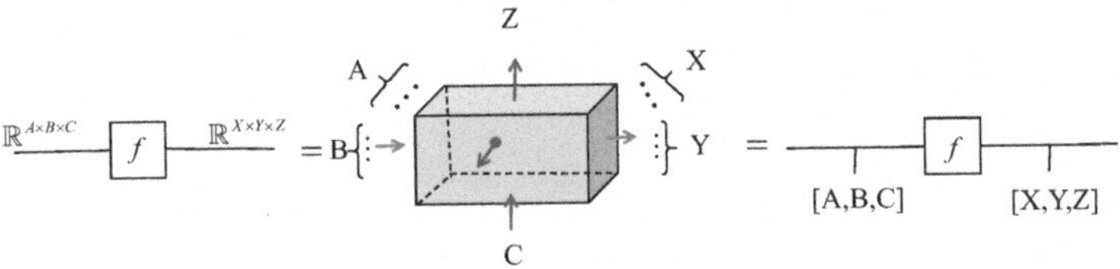

Fig. 2. String diagram representation of tensor operations in SMCs.

2.2 Compositional Models Based on String Diagrams

In this section, we introduce the formal definitions of two core concepts: compositional models and their interpretability [16]. These definitions are grounded in categorical structures, including object categories, morphisms, string diagrams, and representation functor. Specifically, a categorical model is characterized as a functor mapping from a structural category to a semantic category.

Definition 1. *A (monoidal) signature G consists of:*

- *a set G_{ob} of 'objects', which are called variables.*
- *a set G_{mor} of 'morphisms' called generators, whose inputs and outputs are lists of objects*[2].

[2] Formally, these come with functions $\text{in}, \text{out} : G_{mor} \to G_{ob}^*$ that send each generator to a list of input variables and output variables, respectively. All possible morphisms can be generated by composing generators and tensor products. For example, if $\text{in}(f) = [A, B]$ and $\text{out}(f) = [C]$, then f represents the morphism from $A \otimes B$ to C.

- *a set G_{eq} of equations of the form $D_1 = D_2$,where D_1, D_2 are string diagrams constructed from the generators.*

Typically, a signature G consists of basic objects and processes, which combine to generate a category. Given a class of string diagrams (e.g., monoidal diagrams), we define Free(G): objects are lists of variables $(X_i)_{i=1}^{n}$ from G_{ob} , and a morphism D constructed from G_{mor} with inputs and outputs as corresponding lists. Two morphisms $f \cong g$ are deemed equivalent in Free(G)if and only if there exists a finite sequence of diagrammatic isotopies (such as sliding boxes along wires, bending wires downward, and performing swap operations) and equational rewrites, such that homotopy chain preserves topological equivalence of the string diagrams.

A combinatorial model integrates basic variables and generators through composition rules (e.g., sequential or parallel), thereby characterizing complex processes.

Definition 2. *A compositional model M=(S,C,F) consists of:*

- *a structure category S=Free(G);*
- *a semantics category C;*
- *a representation functor:*

$$F : S \to C$$

A *compositional model* is a triple $M = (S, C, F)$, where $S = \text{Free}(G)$ is a structure category freely generated from a graph G, C is a semantics category, and $F : S \to C$ is a functor assigning semantic interpretations to objects and morphisms of S. String diagrams serve as natural representations of such models, with wires and boxes corresponding to variables and generators, respectively. Such as in Fig. 3 The pair (D, M), where D is a diagram of a specific shape and M provides its interpretation, defines a diagram in C[3].

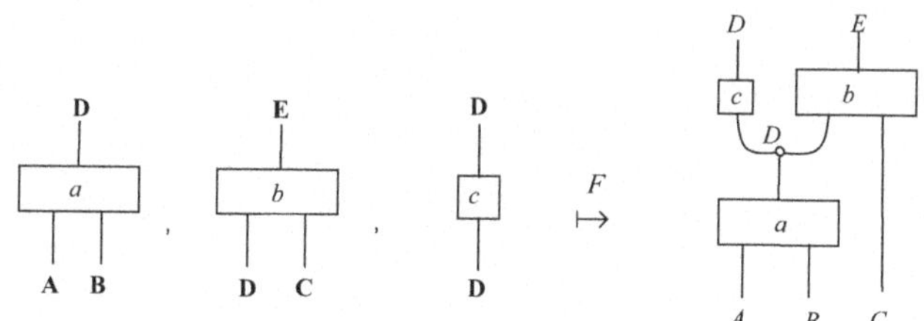

Fig. 3. Compositional model architecture and string diagram semantics.

[3] we distinguish objects and morphisms in S from their representation in C by using different fonts.

This means that the signature G consists of variables **A**, **B** , **C**, **D**, **E** and generators a ,b ,c. The structure category $S = Free(G)$ is generated by all possible cd-diagrams constructible from the given variables and generators in Fig. 4.

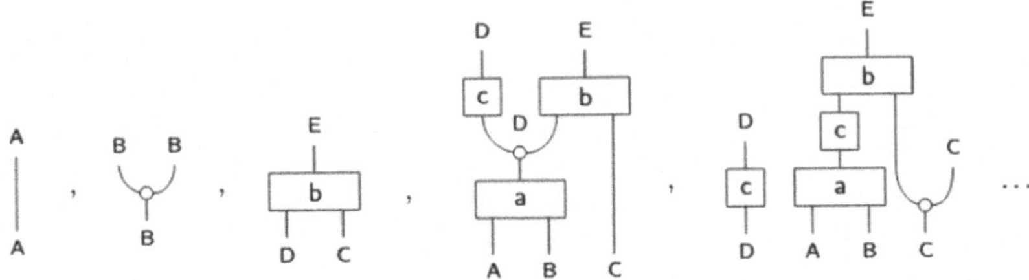

Fig. 4. Signature G and the construction of the free category S.

3 CCG as a Pipeline for DisCoCat

The compositionality of language systems manifests as the ability of discrete symbols to form "multi-word constructions". As a paradigm of compositional reasoning, finds a powerful mathematical realization in the DisCoCat model. Different from the traditional version of DisCoCat that is bound to pregroups, we offer a version of DisCoCat whose domain is Combinatory Categorial Grammar (CCG) [20]. This reformulation offers two key advantages. First, as CCG is a mildly context-sensitive grammar [18], it enhances the generative power of DisCoCat beyond that of pregroup-based systems; and second, the availability of robust CCG parsers —such as the one developed by Clark and Curran [3]— enables the automatic derivation of syntactic structures from large-scale corpora. This section details the formal machinery for this CCG-based DisCoCat model, establishing a clear and theoretically sound pathway from syntactic structure to semantic representation.

3.1 CCG as a Biclosed Category

This paper illustrates, with CCG as an example, how categorical migration enables linguistically meaningful compositionality in structured language representations. DisCoCat models are structure-preserving maps, which can be formalised as functors $F : \mathbf{G} \rightarrow \mathbf{FdVect}$ from the category generated by a formal grammar **G** to the monoidal category **FdVect** of finite-dimensional vector spaces and linear maps equipped with the tensor product [4].

CCG is a syntactic framework based on typed functional application. Its structure encompasses two-layered syntax: one is a rule set for constructing complex types from primitive types and the other is a rule set for combining terms according to these types.

Definition 3. *A categorial grammar is formally defined as a quadruple* $G = (V, X, \Sigma, s)$*, where:*

- V *is the set of lexical items.*
- X *is the set of basic type.Type is the set of type expressions generated from* X*,* $T(X)$ *is the set of all formal expressions, recursively generated from* X *using the following operations:* $x \otimes y$*,* $x \backslash y$*,* $x/y \in T(X)$*, for all* $x, y \in T(X)$
- Σ *is a lexicon ,defined as a set of pairs* $[w : t]$*, where* $w \in V$ *and* $t \in T(X)$*.*
- $s \in X$ *represents the sentence type.*

Formalizing the term-combination rules mathematically, CCG can be modeled as a proof system that naturally forms a *biclosed category* $\mathcal{B}$. In this categorical structure:

- Objects of $\mathcal{B}$ correspond to CCG types in T(X).
- Morphisms of $\mathcal{B}$ represent valid syntactic derivations or proofs: a morphism $f : X \to Y$ encodes a proof that type X can be combined (via CCG rules) to yield type Y. Function application rules determine the number, type, and direction of arguments, as well as the new types generated by applying these rules. The CCG rules such as in Table 1

Table 1. Category Composition Rules in CCG

Category Composition Rule (Rule B)		**Category Lifting Rule (T-Rule)**	
FA	$X/Y \quad Y \to X$	BA	$Y \quad X\backslash Y \to X$
$FC(> B)$	$X/Y \quad Y/Z \to X/Z$	$FTR(> T)$	$X \to T/(T/X)$
$BC(< B)$	$Z\backslash Y \quad Y\backslash X \to Z\backslash X$	$BTR(< T)$	$X \to T\backslash(T/X)$

The key structural property is the existence of two natural isomorphisms for left/right-currying (for any objects A, B, C):

$$\kappa^L_{A,B,C} : \mathcal{B}(A \otimes B, C) \cong \mathcal{B}(B, A\backslash C)$$

$$\kappa^R_{A,B,C} : \mathcal{B}(A \otimes B, C) \cong \mathcal{B}(A, C/B)$$

where:

- $A \otimes B$ denotes the sequential composition of types.
- $A\backslash C$ (left-accepting) and C/B (right-accepting) are standard CCG function types

The CCG combination rules are converted into string diagrams through currying/uncurrying.

This structure provides formal foundations for *type-term-rule* relationships. The fundamental insight is that CCG's application rules are not ad hoc, but emerge naturally from these isomorphisms via (un)currying of identity morphisms[4].

[4] The backward application rule $A \otimes (A\backslash B) \to B$ arises from uncurrying $Id_{A\backslash B} : A\backslash B \to A\backslash B$. Likewise, forward application ($(C/B) \otimes B \to C$) is the uncurrying of $Id_{C\backslash B}$.

3.2 The Functorial Passage to Semantic Tensors

To now give semantics to this syntactic structure, we must define a **closed monoidal functor** $F\colon \mathcal{B} \to \mathcal{C}$, as follows.

Definition 4. *Let Σ be a CCG lexicon. a DisCoCat model based on CCG consists of:*

- *S=FreeBi(Σ) is a free biclosed category,which generated from Σ;*
- *a semantic biclosed categorie $\mathcal{B}$;*
- *a biclosed monoidal functor F.*

where $\mathcal{C}$ is a compact-closed category (e.g., FdVect) that serves as the semantic domain. This functor F preserves the compositional structure of $\mathcal{B}$ while mapping syntactic types and derivations to semantic objects and operations. Let $\{N, S\}$ denote the set of CCG atomic categories representing a noun phrase and a sentence, respectively, and T denote a word type. $\mathcal{C}$ like FdVect, the functor maps:

- Basic type mapping:
$$F(NP) = \mathbf{n},\ \ F(S) = \mathbf{s}$$
where $\mathbf{n}, \mathbf{s}, \mathbf{p}$ are vector spaces for noun phrases, sentences, and prepositional phrases respectively.
- Lexical mapping: A word morphism $w\colon I \to t$ in $\mathcal{B}$ is mapped to $F(w)\colon I \to F(t)$ in $\mathcal{C}$, e.g.,
$$F(\text{Alice})\colon I \to \mathbf{n} \text{ (a vector in } \mathbf{n}\text{)},$$
$$F(\text{likes})\colon I \to \mathbf{n}^* \otimes \mathbf{s} \otimes \mathbf{n}^* \text{ (a 3rd-order tensor)}.$$
- Slash operator preservation:
$$F(X\backslash Y) = F(X)^* \otimes F(Y), \quad F(X/Y) = F(Y) \otimes F(X)^*$$
- Functorial laws:
$$\begin{aligned} &F(f \circ g) = F(f) \circ F(g) \\ &F(\mathrm{Id}_X) = \mathrm{Id}_{F(X)} \\ &F(X \otimes Y) = F(X) \otimes F(Y) \\ &F(I_{\mathcal{B}}) = I_{\mathcal{C}} \end{aligned}$$

In that case, any CCG lexicon Σ generates a free bi-closed category **FreeBi(Σ)** and the DisCoCat models F : **FreeBi**(Σ) $\to$ **FdVect** map grammatical structures to the closed structure of $Vect$ in a canonical way.

Encoding CCG in this way makes every order-preserving grammatical rule appear as a canonical biclosed diagram, while rules that relax word order or introduce cross-serial dependencies are realised by additional morphisms. Because the target category **FdVect** is symmetric monoidal, these permutation morphisms can be implemented graphically by simply swapping wires.

Overall, viewing CCG as a biclosed category $\mathcal{B}$ and interpreting it through the functor F into a compact-closed semantic category $\mathcal{C}$ provides a mathematically rigorous account of linguistic compositionality: syntactic combinations correspond exactly to semantic operations such as tensor contraction, allowing sentence meaning to emerge systematically and transparently from word meaning and syntactic structure.

4 Explanations from Diagrams

To summarize the current situation, on the one hand, DisCoCat models defined in terms of tensor representations can be trained from data and allow for efficient semantic comparison (with e.g. inner products), The meaning of a sentence is given by composing these terms together to get a diagram which can be interpreted in Vect, as in a DisCoCat model, or in fact in any monoidal category C.DisCoPy[5] is a string diagram modelling tool, but it is very powerful in one way - each diagram can be mapped to a specific tensor representation using a functor.

A commonly used semantics category for DisCoCat models is the category $C = FVec$ of finite-dimensional real vector spaces and linear maps $F : V \to W$. This category is compact, meaning that it is symmetric monoidal and that its left and right adjoints coincide. For a space V we have that $V^l = V^r = FVec(V, \mathbb{R})$. In such a DisCoCat model, a word such as *likes* corresponds to a vector of the tensor product $n \otimes s \otimes n$, also simply called a tensor. For example, the sentence *Alice likes Bob* is mapped to a vector of s given by the tensor contraction:

$$|\text{Alice likes Bob}\rangle_k = \sum_{i=1}^{n}\sum_{j=1}^{n} |\text{Alice}\rangle_i |\text{likes}\rangle_{i,k,j} |\text{Bob}\rangle_j \tag{2}$$

Our analysis of the DisCoCat compositional model and its interpretability raises a key question: How can the model's internal diagrammatic structure explain its specific outputs? To address this, we demonstrate how interpreted diagrams enable reasoning about the model's behavior. Consider a DisCoCat model where a verb, such as *likes* in the sentence *Alice likes Bob*, is represented as a channel. The word *likes* acts only on the wires corresponding to *Alice* and *Bob*, while behaving as the identity on all other discourse referents. Consequently, the resulting channel permits signaling exclusively between the *Alice* and *Bob* wires, with all other wires signaling only to themselves.

The string diagram representation of the logical structure of the sentence *Alice does not like Bob*. Among them, *like* is regarded as a functional word. In the string diagram, *does* being entirely made up of wires, while *not* also involving a ¬-labeled box which represents negation of the meaning. The sentence's logical structure through diagrammatic rewriting becomes clear when we yank them:

In standard DisCoCat models, the meaning of a sentence is constructed by mapping the meanings of individual words to tensors, which are then composed

[5] https://github.com/oxford-quantum-group/discopy.

according to the grammatical structure of the sentence. This framework allows meanings to be compared efficiently via operations such as inner products and supports data-driven learning. However, when dealing with sentences involving complex semantic phenomena—such as negation and quantification, as illustrated by the example *"no fish can swim here, but some are swimming"*—the type structures assigned to words become significantly more complicated. As a result, the number of parameters that must be learned increases rapidly, leading to scalability issues in practical applications. Higher-Order DisCoCat improves the efficiency of reduces parameter count, as shown in Table 2.

Table 2. Word Types and Their Categorical Semantics

Word	Type	Meaning $F(w \to t)$
no	$n \leftarrow n$	$\lambda f.\ \mathrm{cut}(f)$
fish	n	$\lambda x.\ \mathrm{fish}(x)$
can	$(n \to s) \leftarrow (n \to s)$	$\lambda P.\ P$
swim	$n \to s$	$\lambda x.\ \mathrm{swim}(x)$
here	$(n \to s) \to (n \to s)$	$\lambda Px.\ \mathrm{here}(P(x))$
some	$n \leftarrow n$	$\lambda PQ.\ \exists x.\ P(x) \wedge Q(x)$
are	$(n \to s) \leftarrow n$	$\lambda PQ.Q(P(\mathrm{id}_N)^T)$

Thus, higher-order DisCoCat model[6] is needed to extend the composition functionality of the original framework. This approach combines the strengths of both the DisCoCat and Montague semantics paradigms. Specifically, we assign to each word a simply-typed lambda term, capturing higher-order semantic phenomena in a systematic way. Unlike in traditional Montague semantics, where the resulting logical forms are computationally intractable for machine learning (e.g., equivalence of first-order logic formulas is undecidable), our lambda terms operate over diagrammatic primitives. The meaning of a sentence is obtained by composing these lambda terms into a diagram, which can be interpreted in a vector space, as in a standard DisCoCat model, or more generally in any monoidal category. Of course, when using the Web tool-DisCoCat diagram generator[7] to generate DisCoCat diagrams, we find that due to the NP-ellipsis on the right side of the quantifier *some* in the sentence, its type is inconsistent with that of the quantifier *no*.

We implement a formal categorical framework for logical semantic derivation, with complete computational details provided in Appendix A. Large Language Models (e.g., GPT) spontaneously acquire combinatorial rules and categorical structures within their high-dimensional latent spaces during training. Analyzing diagram representations aims to identify specific regions or directions cor-

[6] https://docs.discopy.org/en/main/notebooks/higher-order-discocat.html.
[7] https://qnlp.cambridgequantum.com/generate.html.

responding to linguistic features, including syntactic categories, logical operations, and semantic roles. The DisCoCat framework enables parallel syntactic and semantic inference by mapping formal linguistic structures to the model's implicit representation space.

5 Conclusion and Future Work

This study addresses the interpretability challenges of deploying machine learning models in high-risk domains by proposing a category-theoretic diagrammatic semantic framework. Through a three-stage methodology of structural decomposition, semantic mapping, and compositional verification, our framework tries to explain AI models' generated behaviours. Unlike existing post-hoc interpretability methods that rely on model approximations and lack credibility, our intrinsic interpretability approach embeds verifiable semantic traceability during model design through rigorous preservation of compositional structures via categorical morphisms.

At the theoretical level, we demonstrate the potential of integrating formal semantic structures with contemporary model architectures to enhance interpretability and compositional reasoning, providing novel formal tools for analyzing the emergence mechanisms of hierarchical semantic structures. The visual encoding of model components and information flow through string diagrams not only enables interpretable validation of compositional reasoning processes, but also establishes strict mathematical correspondences at the syntax-semantics interface. While the current study focuses on some tractable subsets of grammatical phenomena, it lays the groundwork for more comprehensive formal-semantic integration in language understanding systems. This formal framework can be effectively applied to quantum natural language processing (QNLP), which employs categorical compositional semantics. The lambeq toolkit[8] orchestrates this workflow, integrating readers for multimodal input processing while supporting both knowledge-driven parameter initialization and data-driven optimization. This unified architecture bridges formal linguistics with quantum-native representations, enabling systematic evaluation of compositional models' expressivity across classical and quantum paradigms.

Future efforts will aim to extend the framework along several dimensions. One avenue involves refining hierarchical diagrammatic representations to retain expressivity in large-scale architectures such as Transformers while improving their structural transparency. Another direction explores compositional semantics in multimodal settings, with a focus on constructing unified semantic representations across modalities like text-image pairs. Finally, expanding the formal implementation to cover more complex syntactic phenomena—such as nested clauses and ellipsis—will be crucial to improving both the coverage and generalization of the approach, bringing formal theoretical insights closer to practical language understanding.

[8] https://github.com/CQCL/lambeq.

Acknowledgement. The paper is supported by Major Project of the National Social Science Foundation of China (No.19ZDA042) and Philosophy and Social Science Planning Projects of Guangdong Province(No.GD24CZX02)

A Appendix

Listing 1.1. DisCoPy Implementation

```
# Step 1: Define Formula as a subclass of frobenius.Diagram
from discopy import frobenius
from discopy.balanced import Diagram
from discopy.tensor import Dim, Tensor
from discopy.cat import Category, factory

@factory
class Formula(frobenius.Diagram):
    ty_factory = frobenius.PRO # Natural numbers as objects

    def eval(self, size):
        return frobenius.Functor(
            ob=lambda _: Dim(size),
            ar=lambda box: box.data,
            cod=Category(Dim, Tensor[bool]))(self)

class Cut(frobenius.Bubble, Formula): pass
class Ligature(frobenius.Spider, Formula): pass
class Predicate(frobenius.Box, Formula): pass

Id, Formula.bubble_factory = Formula.id, Cut
Tensor[bool].bubble = lambda self, **_: self.map(lambda x: not x)

# Step 2: Parse natural language sentences
from discopy.grammar.categorial import Ty, Word, BA, FA
from discopy import Cup, Id
n, s = Ty('n'), Ty('s') # Noun and sentence types

# Lexicon definitions
no = Word("no", n << n)
fish = Word("fish", n)
can = Word("can", (n >> s) << (n >> s))
swim = Word("swim", n >> s)here = Word("here", (n >> s) >> (n >> s))
Some = Word("Some", n << n)
are = Word("are", (n >> s) << n)
swimming = Word("swimming", n >> s)
but = Word("but", (s << s) >> s)

# Sentence composition
no_fish = no @ fish >> BA(n)
```

```
can_swim_here = can @ (swim @ here) >> FA((n >> s), (n >> s))
first_clause = no_fish @ can_swim_here >> FA(n, n >> s) >> Cup(n, s)

some_fish = Some @ fish >> BA(n)
are_swimming = are @ swimming >> FA(n, n >> s)
second_clause = some_fish @ are_swimming >> FA(n, n >> s) >> Cup(n, s)

full_sentence = but @ (first_clause @ second_clause) >> FA(s, s << s) >>
    Cup(s, s)

# Step 3: Random interpretations
from random import choice
size = 42
random_bits = lambda n=size: [choice([True, False]) for _ in range(n)]

# Predicate definitions
is_fish = random_bits()
is_swimming = random_bits()
can_swim_here_pred = [[choice([True, False]) for _ in range(size)]
                      for _ in range(size)]

# Step 4: Higher-order DisCoCat functor
from discopy import closed
from discopy.python import Function

F = closed.Functor(
    cod=Category(tuple[type, ...], Function),
    ob={s: Diagram, n: Diagram},
    ar={
        fish: lambda: frobenius.Box('fish', Ty(), n),
        swim: lambda: frobenius.Box('swim', n, s),
        no: lambda P: (P >> frobenius.Cup(n, n.r)).bubble(),
        Some: lambda P: P,
        but: lambda x, y: x @ y >> frobenius.Swap(s, s)
    })

evaluate = lambda sentence: bool(F(sentence)().eval(size))
assert evaluate(full_sentence) == (
    all(not is_fish[x] or not can_swim_here_pred[x][x]
        for x in range(size)) # "no fish can swim here"
    and any(is_fish[x] and is_swimming[x]
            for x in range(size)) # "some are swimming"
)
```

References

1. Alvarez Melis, D., Jaakkola, T.: Towards robust interpretability with self-explaining neural networks. In: Advances in Neural Information Processing Systems, vol. 31 (2018)
2. Carvalho, D.V., Pereira, E.M., Cardoso, J.S.: Machine learning interpretability: a survey on methods and metrics. Electronics **8**(8), 832 (2019)
3. Clark, S., Curran, J.R.: Wide-coverage efficient statistical parsing with CCG and log-linear models. Comput. Linguist. **33**(4), 493–552 (2007)
4. de Felice, G.: Categorical Tools for Natural Language Processing. Ph.D. Thesis, University of Oxford (2022)
5. Foerster, J.N., Gilmer, J., Sohl-Dickstein, J., Chorowski, J., Sussillo, D.: Input switched affine networks: an RNN architecture designed for interpretability. In: International Conference on Machine Learning, pp. 1136–1145 (2017)
6. Freiesleben, T., König, G.: Dear XAI community, we need to talk! Fundamental misconceptions in current XAI research (2023)
7. Graziani, M., et al.: A global taxonomy of interpretable AI: unifying the terminology for the technical and social sciences. Artif. Intell. Rev. **56**(4), 3473–3504 (2023)
8. Hudson, D.A., Manning, C.D.: Compositional attention networks for machine reasoning. In: International Conference on Learning Representations (2018)
9. Ji, J., et al.: AI alignment: A comprehensive survey (2024)
10. Li, C., Yao, K., Wang, J., Diao, B., Xu, Y., Zhang, Q.: Interpretable generative adversarial networks. In: Proceedings of the AAAI Conference on Artificial Intelligence, vol. 36, pp. 1280–1288 (2022a)
11. Li, J., Li, Y., Xiang, X., Xia, S.T., Dong, S., Cai, Y.: TNT: an interpretable tree-network-tree learning framework using knowledge distillation. Entropy **22**(11), 1203 (2020)
12. Mascharka, D., Tran, P., Soklaski, R., Majumdar, A.: Transparency by design: closing the gap between performance and interpretability in visual reasoning. In: Proceedings of the IEEE Conference on Computer Vision and Pattern Recognition, pp. 4942–4950 (2018)
13. Piedeleu, R., Zanasi, F.: An Introduction to String Diagrams for Computer Scientists (2023)
14. Räuker, T., Ho, A., Casper, S., et al.: Toward transparent AI: a survey on interpreting the inner structures of deep neural networks. In: IEEE Conference on Secure and Trustworthy Machine Learning (SaTML) (2023)
15. Sachdeva, N., McAuley, J.: Data distillation: A survey. Transactions on Machine Learning Research (2023)
16. Selinger, P.: A survey of graphical languages for monoidal categories. In: New structures for physics, pp. 289–355 (2010)
17. Vaswani, A., et al.: Attention is all you need. In: Advances in Neural Information Processing Systems, vol. 30 (2017)
18. Vijay-Shanker, K., Weir, D.J.: The equivalence of four extensions of contextfree grammars. Math. Syst. Theory **27**(6), 511–546 (1994)
19. Wei, J., et al.: Chain-of-thought prompting elicits reasoning in large language models. Adv. Neural. Inf. Process. Syst. **35**, 24824–24837 (2022)
20. Yeung, R., Kartsaklis, D.: A CCG-based version of the DisCoCat framework. In: Proceedings of the Workshop on Semantic Spaces at the Intersection of NLP, Physics, and Cognitive Science (SemSpace), pp. 20–31. Association for Computational Linguistics, Groningen, The Netherlands (2021)

The Interpretability Analysis of DCNN Models Based on Structured Pruning Compression

Kai Wang[1,2], Mingjie Xie[1], Yang Zhao[3], and Jihong Pei[1,2](✉)

[1] College of Electronics and Information Engineering, Shenzhen University, Shenzhen, China
{2310433042,xiemingjie2021}@email.szu.edu.cn

[2] Guangdong Key Laboratory of Intelligent Information Processing, Shenzhen, Guangdong, China
jhpei@szu.edu.cn

[3] College of Computer Science and Software Engineering, Shenzhen University, Shenzhen, China
zhaoyang1990@szu.edu.cn

Abstract. Structured pruning systematically removes redundant structural components (such as convolution kernels and filters) to compress deep convolutional neural network (DCNN) models and accelerate inference, with its efficiency optimization value being extensively studied. However, the potential of structured pruning in enhancing model interpretability remains underexplored. In this study, leveraging the advantage that structured pruning simplifies networks, we propose a progressive multi-scale sparse pruning algorithm and conduct an interpretability analysis on DCNN models. First, we quantify the intersection of union (IoU) using network dissection methods to compare the semantic purity characterized by filters (neurons) before and after pruning. Subsequently, we design a heuristic key neuron scoring strategy that focuses on contextual interaction information among neurons, thereby obtaining the global-level key decision pathway of the model for a specific category of image input, which provides a more intuitive semantic understanding of model decisions. Experimental results demonstrate that structured pruning can effectively strip away chaotic parts from model neurons, thereby improving the semantic purity of neurons. Moreover, based on the sparse connections of the pruned model, we are able to extract a clear key decision pathway with high semantic purity, revealing the hierarchical knowledge structure during decision-making.

Keywords: Structured Pruning · Model Interpretability · Semantic Purity · Key Decision Pathway

1 Introduction

With the continuous advancement of deep learning, deep convolutional neural networks (DCNN) have demonstrated exceptional performance across various

M. Bonsangue and Y. Chen (Eds.): AILA 2025, CCIS 2668, pp. 17–31, 2026.
https://doi.org/10.1007/978-981-95-8262-4_2

computer vision tasks. However, from AlexNet [1] to VGG [2], and subsequently the residual connection innovation in ResNet [3], the number of model parameters has steadily increased, leading to a significant rise in model complexity. Consequently, the "Black-Box" nature of these models has become more pronounced, severely limiting their application in scenarios with stringent interpretability requirements, such as medical diagnosis and autonomous driving.

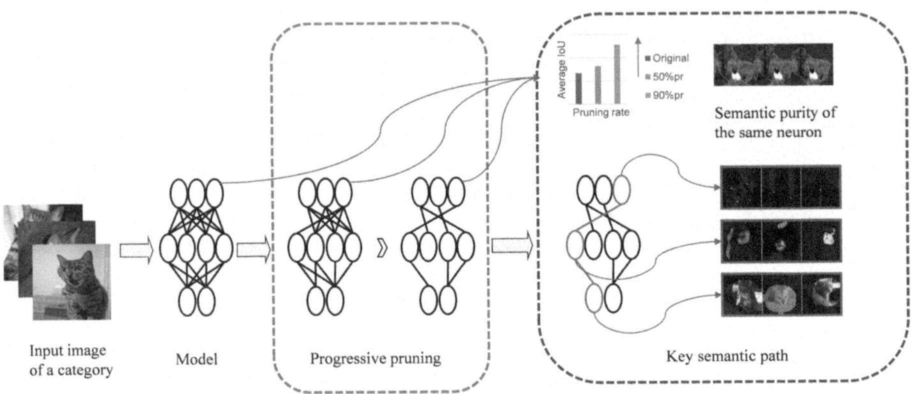

Fig. 1. Interpretability framework of the DCNN model based on structured pruning. The semantic purity of the original model neuron is relatively low. Structured pruning can remove the chaotic parts of the model, enhance the semantic purity of neuron, and obtain a clear pathway.

For the aforementioned challenges, researchers have proposed a variety of interpretability methods. For instance, Zhou et al. introduced Class Activation Mapping (CAM) [4] in 2016, which generates category-sensitive heatmaps by leveraging the weights of the global average pooling layer. In the same year, Selvaraju proposed Gradient-weighted Class Activation Mapping (Grad-CAM) [5], an extension of CAM that utilizes gradient information to compute the importance weights of feature maps. Subsequent methods, such as ablation-CAM [6], layer-CAM [7], and group-CAM [8], represent further refinements of CAM. Additionally, there exist local interpretation methods based on occlusion. These methods assess the impact on model output by systematically occluding different regions of the input image. For example, Zeiler et al. [9] employed fixed-size gray pixel blocks to sequentially occlude local regions of the input image and observed the resulting model predictions. Petsiuk et al. [10] utilized Monte Carlo algorithms to generate random occlusions. However, the aforementioned methods are all local interpretation techniques, whose explanations rely on the attention distribution of model outputs, representing indirect inference rather than direct analysis of the model's internal decision-making mechanism.

To gain a deeper understanding of the model internal structure, Zhou et al. proposed Network Dissection [11], which establishes semantic associations for the internal components of the model. Mu and Andreas extended these ideas in

Composition Explanation [12], aiming to generate more complex and detailed explanations. Ahn et al. further explained the internal neurons of the model through the "WWW" framework [13], namely "What, Where, Why." However, these methods also exhibit several limitations. First, since these methods are generally based on the original model for analysis, they fail to account for the potential interference of a large number of model parameters and chaotic components on the interpretation results. For instance, some kernels may encode a significant amount of noise response, thereby contaminating the interpretability results with chaotic signals. Secondly, these methods predominantly focus on the internal neurons of the model while neglecting the model's decision-making process. Therefore, we propose analyzing the interpretability of DCNN models through the simplified network obtained after structured pruning.

Structured pruning significantly simplifies the network by removing unimportant structures within the model. This not only enables us to exclude noise interference caused by chaotic components of the model but also facilitates analyzing the internal decision-making process of the neural network through the simplified architecture. Our overall research process is illustrated in Fig. 1. In Sect. 2, we propose a progressive multi-scale pruning and compression method. Subsequently, in Sect. 3, we quantify the IoU values of neurons and compare the semantic purity of neuron interpretability before and after structured pruning. Finally, in Sect. 4, we identify the key decision pathway for a specific category based on the pruned model, thereby providing a more intuitive semantic interpretation of model decisions.

In summary, our contributions are as follows:

1. To the best of our knowledge, this is the first study to leverage structured pruning for investigating the interpretability of DCNN models.

2. A progressive multi-scale sparse pruning method is proposed. By gradually constructing models with different levels of sparsity, redundant connections are effectively removed, enabling the activation of neurons to focus more on key semantic features. Experimental results on models such as ResNet18 and VGG16 show that the average IoU value of pruned neurons is significantly higher than that before pruning, significantly improving the purity of semantic representation.

3. We devised a series of heuristic key neuron scoring strategies to extract the global-level key semantic decision pathway of the pruned model for a specific category of image input. This provides a more intuitive understanding of interpretability and reveals the hierarchical knowledge structure during model decision-making.

2 Progressive Multi-scale Sparse Pruning Compression for DCNN Model Explanation

Typical structured pruning methods can be categorized into filter pruning and kernel pruning based on the pruning granularity, ranging from coarse to fine. RNF [14] and DepGraph [15] fall under filter pruning methods. PKPSMIO [16]

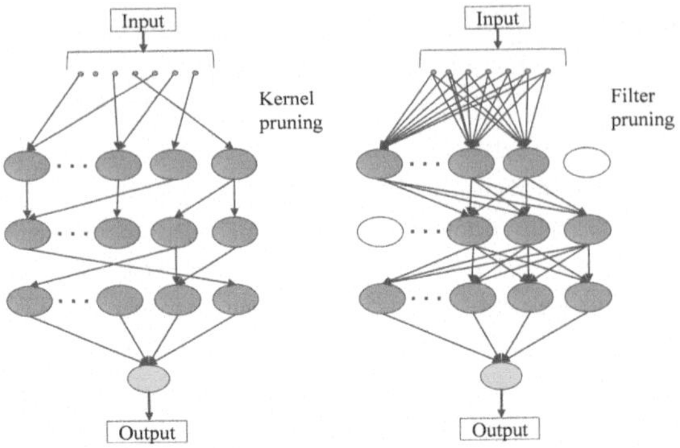

Fig. 2. Comparison chart of different structured pruning methods.

and KSE [17] belong to convolution kernel pruning methods. Structured pruning can significantly simplify the network while preserving its original functionality by removing unimportant structures within the model. We compare the two different structured pruning methods of filter pruning and kernel pruning, as shown in Fig. 2.

Although the granularity of filter pruning is relatively coarse, it does not alter the fully connected mode between neurons. Furthermore, an excessively high pruning rate in filter pruning can lead to a significant decline in model accuracy, which is detrimental to our interpretability research on the model. Kernel pruning simplifies the model by sparsifying the connections between neurons, thereby not only eliminating redundancy within neurons but also substantially reducing the complexity of analyzing subsequent model decision pathways. Consequently, we constructed a progressively sparse network via kernel pruning to facilitate our subsequent interpretability research.

Previous kernel pruning methods, such as PKPSMIO, rely on the norm values of kernels within filters and groups. However, this method necessitates re-evaluating kernels in each epoch, resulting in frequent reversals of importance for kernels deemed redundant in earlier epoch during subsequent epoch. This dynamic pruning approach renders the model structure under the same pruning rate highly unpredictable, further exacerbating the interpretability dilemma. Therefore, as illustrated in Fig. 3, we propose a progressive kernel pruning algorithm to construct a progressively sparse network.

Considering a pre-trained DCNN model with L layers, we denote the kernel of the l-th layer as K^l. A filter is defined as a set of kernels associated with all channels of the previous layer, and a set of kernels sharing the same channel is referred to as a group. Suppose M^{t-1} represents the kernel-level mask obtained from the previous pruning epoch (where 0 indicates that the corresponding kernel needs to be pruned, and 1 indicates retention). Let C^t denote the intermediate mask obtained in the current pruning epoch. Then, the final mask M^t is obtained

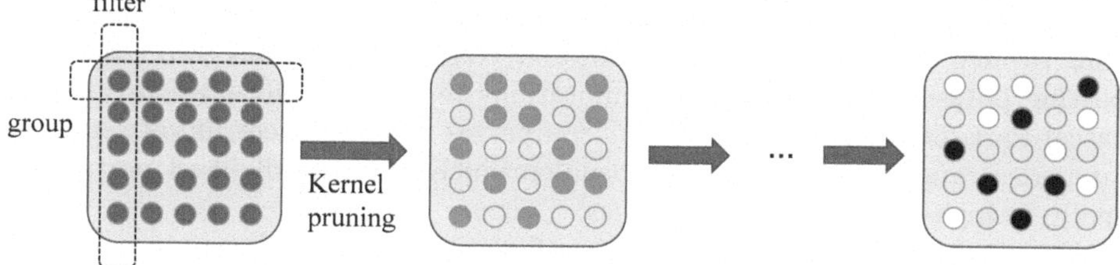

Fig. 3. Progressive kernel pruning.

by Equation (1), $\odot$ denotes the Hadamard product.

$$M^t = M^{t-1} \odot C^t \tag{1}$$

Our entire pruning process is shown in Algorithm 1.

Algorithm 1: Progressive kernel pruning for DCNN

Input: 1. A pre-trained L-layer DCNN 2. Target pruning rate p_t
Output: A pruned network with mask $\mathbf{M}^t$
Initialize mask $\mathbf{M}^t \leftarrow \mathbf{0}$,*epoch* $\leftarrow 1$;
while $p \leq p_t$ **do**
  for *each layer* $l \in \{1, 2, \ldots, L\}$ **do**
    Calculate 2-norm of each kernel in groups;
    Get Top-k retained kernels $C^{l,t}_{\text{group}}$;
    Calculate 2-norm of each kernel in filters;
    Get Top-k retained kernels $C^{l,t}_{\text{filter}}$;
    $C^{l,t} \leftarrow C^{l,t}_{\text{group}} \bigvee C^{l,t}_{\text{filter}}$;
  end
  Set elements in $\mathbf{M}^t$ (retained kernels) via Equation (1);
  Get $\mathbf{M}^t$;
  Calculate current pruning rate p;
  epoch $\leftarrow$ *epoch* $+ 1$;
end
Apply mask and fine-tune pruned model;

---

3 Semantic Purity Measurement of Progressive Multi-scale Sparse Neuron Interpretability

Semantics play an indispensable role in enabling people to interpret DCNN models. Here, we adopt the method proposed by Zhou et al. in Network Dissection for semantic representation and evaluate its semantic purity using the IoU value of neurons. First, we introduce the Broden dataset utilized in Network Dissection. Broden is a hierarchically annotated collection that integrates multiple existing datasets with pixel-level annotations (e.g., ADE20K, Pascal-Context, Pascal-Part, OpenSurfaces), which encompasses a broad spectrum of semantic categories ranging from low-level visual primitives to middle-level parts, and finally to high-level objects and scenes.

For a given deep learning model, we first identify the neurons in a specific layer of the neural network. Subsequently, we input all annotated image data from the Broden dataset and record the activation map $A_i(x)$ generated by neuron i for each image x in the dataset. Then, based on $P(a_i > T_k) = 0.005$, we determine the highest quantile T_k to establish the threshold for defining the activation region. At the same time, we should upsample the $A_i(x)$ to the same resolution as the semantic annotation mask L_c through bilinear interpolation to obtain the $S_i(x)$. Finally, $S_i(x)$ is binary segmented using threshold T_k to derive the final mask $M_i(x)$.

After completing these steps, it is essential to calculate the IoU between each neuron i and each semantic concept c in the semantic annotation dataset. The calculation method is presented in Equation (2).

$$IoU_{i,c} = \frac{\sum |M_i(x) \cap L_c(x)|}{\sum |M_i(x) \cup L_c(x)|} \tag{2}$$

By employing this method, we can quantify the degree to which each unit represents each semantic concept. If the IoU value between neuron i and the corresponding concept c is the highest, the semantic concept characterized by neuron i is concept c. A higher IoU score indicates a higher semantic purity of the neuron, thereby enabling more accurate representation of the corresponding semantic concept. Generally, directly calculating the IoU for neurons in the original model leads to inaccurate results due to the significant redundancy in the original model, which may encode substantial noise or features irrelevant to decision-making. Neurons obtained after convolution kernel pruning and compression effectively eliminate redundancy while retaining the core functionality of the model. Here, we conduct pruning experiments on the original model, and the experimental results strongly validate the effectiveness of our progressive multi-scale sparse pruning method. Specific experimental details will be elaborated in Sect. 5.2.

4 Key Neuron and Pathway Discovery in Model Decision-Making

In this section, we propose a novel measurement method for neuron activation. By combining this measurement method with the frequency of neuron occurrences, we identify the key neurons that contribute to the model decision-making for a specific category. Subsequently, based on the connectivity status of these key neurons after model pruning, we construct the critical decision pathways of the model. The following subsections will elaborate on the proposed neuron measurement method and the identification of key decision pathways.

In complex deep neural networks, directly identifying which neurons are most critical for specific tasks poses a significant challenge. Consequently, we developed a heuristic-based comprehensive scoring approach to assess the importance of neurons. This method systematically evaluates the importance S_i of neurons by integrating three key indicators, as presented in Eq. (3).

$$S_i = \alpha \cdot S_{\text{prev },i} + \beta \cdot S_{\text{input },i} + \gamma \cdot G_i \tag{3}$$

Among them, α, β, γ are non-negative weight coefficients utilized to balance the relative importance of the three indicators, and their sum is typically set to 1 . $S_{\text{prev },i}$ denotes the degree to which the activation $a_{L,i}$ of neuron i inherits information from the previous layer neurons set P . $S_{\text{input },i}$ measures the similarity between the activation $a_{L,i}$ of and the original input x_0', with both being calculated using cosine similarity $\text{sim}(\cdot)$. $S_{\text{prev },i}$ and $S_{\text{input },i}$ can be represented by Equation (4) and (5), respectively.

$$S_{\text{prev },i} = \max\left(0, \max_{j \in P}\left[\left(\text{sim}\left(a_{L,i}, a_{L-1,j}'\right)\right)\right]\right) \tag{4}$$

$$S_{\text{input },i} = \text{sim}\left(a_{L,i}, x_0'\right) \tag{5}$$

The average absolute value of the gradient G_i indicates the influence of small changes in the activation value of neuron i on the score of a specific category. Let the loss function to be cross-entropy loss. Then, G_i can be expressed as the

Algorithm 2: Get key neurons for a category

```
Input:  1. Pruned DCNN (L layers)   2. Training images x'_n
        3. Threshold T               4. Frequency M
Output: Key neurons set K_l
Initialize neuron frequency f_i and important neurons set I_l for each layer;
for each image x'_p ∈ x'_n do
    for each layer l ∈ {1, 2, ..., L} do
        Calculate neuron score S_i using Equation (3);
        if S_i > T then
            I_l ← I_l ∪ {i} , f_i ← f_i + 1;
        end
    end
end
for each neuron i ∈ I_l do
    if f_i > M then
        K_l ← K_l ∪ {i};
    end
end
```

average gradient of each element n in the activation $a_{L,i}$. G_i can be represented by Eq. (6)

$$G_i = \frac{1}{N} \sum_{n=1}^{N} |(\nabla_{a_i} L_c)_n| \tag{6}$$

Algorithm 2 illustrates the procedure for obtaining key neurons. Here, to further mitigate the potential influence of individual sample variability, we aggregated results across multiple samples and selected neurons whose importance was observed more than M times as key neurons.

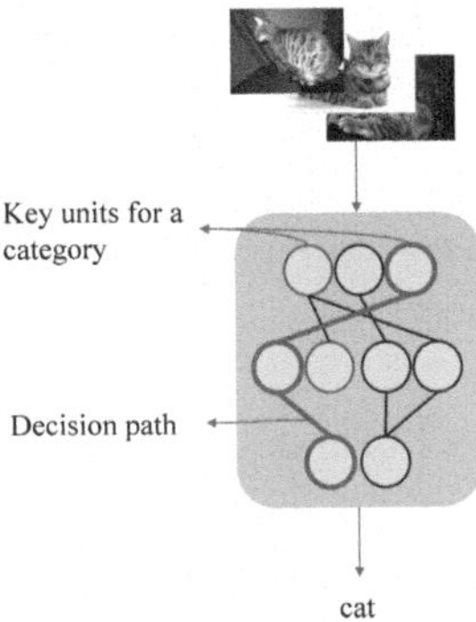

Fig. 4. Key neurons and decision path for a category.

Subsequently, based on the original connection constraints of the pruned model, we establish connections among the key neurons by incorporating the inter-layer relationships, while discarding neurons with no connections or only single-end connections. Through this process, we are able to extract the model decision pathway for a specific category, as illustrated in Fig. 4. Based on the analysis of the neuron semantic representation presented in Sect. 3, we can further elucidate the decision-making process of the model across the entire neural network.

5 Experiments

5.1 Progressive Multi-scale Sparse Pruning Experiment

Pruning Details: The dataset employed in this study is the ILSVRC 2012 (ImageNet Large-Scale Visual Recognition Challenge 2012) Each baseline model is a pretrained model provided by official library. All pruning experiments were conducted on PyTorch 1.12.1, utilizing two NVIDIA 3090 GPUs for parallel training. The optimization method adopted was the SGD optimizer, with momentum set to 0.9, batch size set to 256, and weight decay set to 0.0001. Upon reaching the scheduled pruning rate, the process transitioned to the fine-tuning stage. We performed 100 epochs of fine-tuning for each pruned network, with a weight decay of 1e-4 and an initial learning rate of 0.01, which was respectively decayed to 0.001 after 40 epochs and to 0.0001 after 70 epochs.

Pruning Results: We conducted experiments on multiple DCNN models, and the results are presented in Table 1. As our progressive pruning method proceeds (original → 35% pruned → 50% pruned → ...), the reduction in model accuracy between consecutive pruning stages remains largely within an acceptable range. Notably, at a 35% pruning rate, the model performance surpasses that of the original model, further demonstrating the reliability of our progressive pruning method. Moreover, since the comparison method PKPSMIO does not involve progressive pruning, we only applied the first-stage pruning operation to it.

Table 1. Pruning results on ImageNet. (35%pr represent pruning rate of 35%).

Model	Progressive pruning rate	PKPSMIO	Ours	Acc ↓ (Ours)
ResNet18	Original	69.76%	69.76%	/
	Original → 35%pr	69.93%	69.99%	+0.23%
	35%pr → 50%pr	/	69.58%	0.41%
	50%pr → 70%pr	/	65.83%	3.75%
	70%pr → 90%pr	/	57.02%	8.81%
ResNet34	Original	74.44%	74.44%	/
	Original → 35%pr	74.51%	74.47%	+0.03%
	35%pr → 50%pr	/	73.55%	0.92%
	50%pr → 70%pr	/	70.91%	2.64%
	70%pr → 90%pr	/	65.78%	5.13%
VGG16	Original	71.59%	71.59%	/
	Original → 35%pr	71.79%	71.76%	0.17%
	35%pr → 50%pr	/	70.74%	1.02%
AlexNet	Original	56.52%	56.52%	/
	Original → 35%pr	55.78%	55.74%	0.78%
	35%pr → 50%pr	/	55.14%	0.60%

5.2 Sematic Purity Experiment

In this section, we conducted semantic purity comparison experiments of various models, including ResNet18, ResNet34, VGG16, and AlexNet. Additionally, we visualized the activation patterns of selected neurons.

Semantic Purity Comparison: Figure 5 illustrates the average IoU values of neurons across all categories in the ResNet18 model under different pruning rates, while Fig. 6 depicts the average IoU values of neurons in four specific categories under varying pruning rates. The result showed that as the pruning rate increases, the average IoU value of neurons also continues to rise. This experimental result further validates our conclusion that structured pruning enhances the semantic purity characterized by neurons. However, when the pruning rate becomes excessively high (e.g., at 95%), the average IoU value not only fails to improve but also experiences a significant decline. Upon examining the internal neurons of the model, we discovered that the reduction in average IoU was attributed to an insufficient number of internal kernels, which severely compromised the model's feature extraction capabilities.

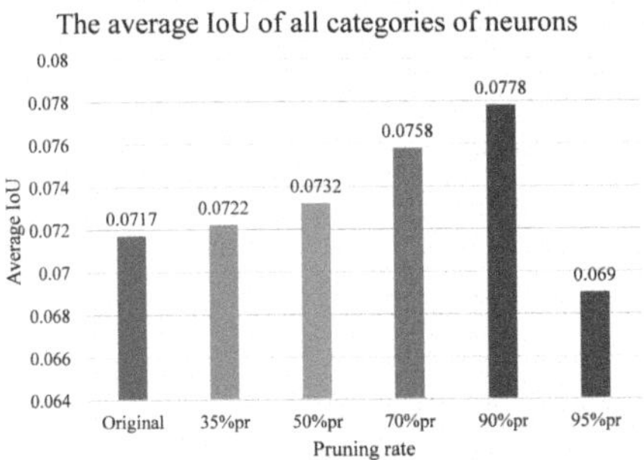

Fig. 5. Comparison of the average IoU of all categories with ResNet18 model.

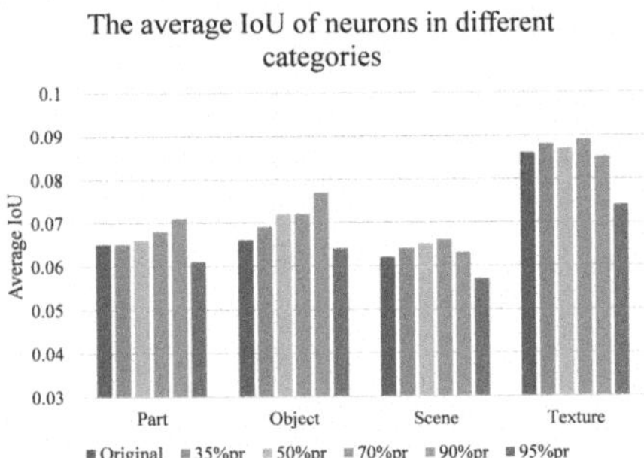

Fig. 6. Comparison of the average IoU in different categories with ResNet18 model.

In addition, experiments were also conducted on various models. The results in Table 2 indicate that the average IoU values of neurons in the four categories after pruning are higher than those before pruning. Furthermore, as the pruning rate increases, the average IoU value also continues to rise.

Activation Visualization: For more intuitive illustration, we visualized the activation maps of selected neurons in the ResNet18 model under varying pruning rates, as depicted in Fig. 7. It can be observed that the activation maps in the pruned model are more object-focused compared to those in the original model, effectively eliminating the background regions present in the original model. This indirectly substantiates that structured model pruning removes redundant and chaotic components, thereby enhancing the semantic purity represented by model neurons.

5.3 Analysis of Key Pathways in Model Decision-Making

Key Neuron Acquisition: We set the hyperparameters α,β,γ in Eq. (5) to 0.2, 0.1, and 0.7, respectively. The important neuron screening threshold T is

Table 2. Comparison of average IoU of different models

Model	Pruning rate	All	Part	Object	Scene	Texture
ResNet18	Original	0.0717	0.0650	0.0667	0.0621	0.0861
	35%pr	0.0722	0.0654	0.0690	0.0644	0.0876
	50%pr	0.0732	0.0655	0.0717	0.0648	0.0869
	70%pr	0.0758	0.0684	0.0715	0.0656	0.0893
ResNet34	Original	0.0658	0.0605	0.0645	0.0605	0.0784
	35%pr	0.0662	0.0611	0.0668	0.0628	0.0791
	50%pr	0.0669	0.0614	0.0678	0.0631	0.0793
VGG16	Original	0.0769	0.0724	0.0760	0.0729	0.0877
	35%pr	0.0772	0.0725	0.0766	0.0732	0.0878
	50%pr	0.0776	0.0728	0.0762	0.0743	0.0885
AlexNet	Original	0.0763	0.0753	0.0672	0.0479	0.0806
	35%pr	0.0770	0.0755	0.0696	0.0670	0.0802
	50%pr	0.0781	0.0762	0.0718	0.0676	0.0813

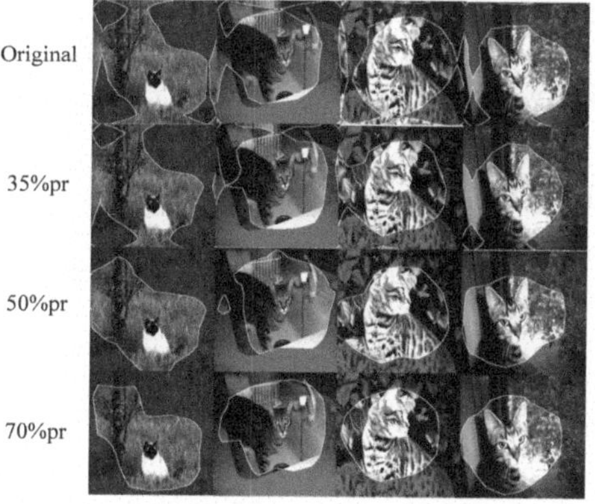

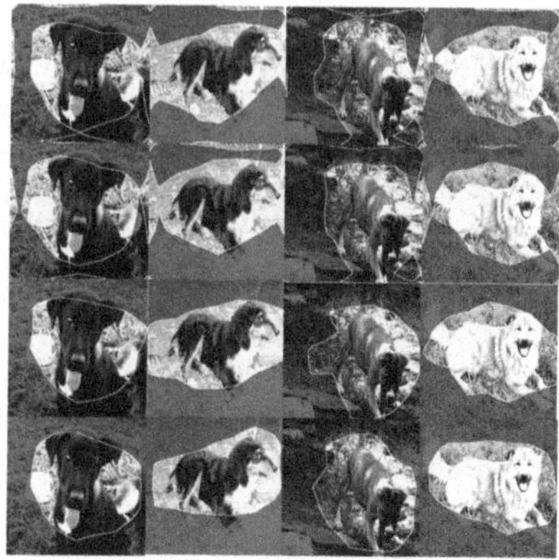

Fig. 7. Activation visualization of the cat and dog neuron under different pruning rates.

set to 0.2. We selected all 50 images labeled as "Tabby cat" from the Imagenet validation set and identified the key class-related neurons of the 90%pr ResNet-18 model, as shown on the left side of Fig. 8. Compared with the original model, the decision path of the pruned model is more streamlined. Furthermore, as demonstrated by the experiments in Sect. 5.2, the pruned neurons exhibit higher semantic purity, thereby enhancing the reliability of the semantic analysis of the subsequent model decision path.

Validity Verification: To validate the effectiveness of the key neurons, we masked neurons and measured the classification accuracy for the tabby cat class (a single category) as well as the overall accuracy across all categories. The results

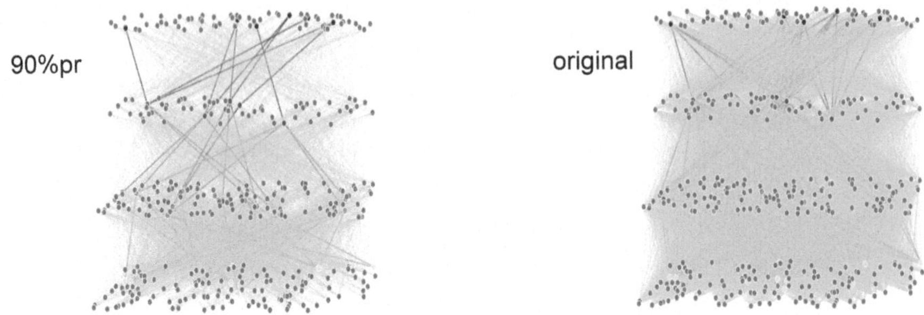

Fig. 8. Visualization of key class-related neurons and their connections in four layers (high-lighted in color) for the Tabby cat category in 90%pr ResNet18 and original ResNet18.

are presented in Table 3. It can be observed that masking only the top 50% of neurons with the highest scores on the pathway reduces the pruned model's accuracy in distinguishing tabby cats from 78.4% to 63.3%. When the top 80% of high-scoring neurons are masked, the classification accuracy for tabby cats further decreases to 54.8%, approaching chance level (50%). In contrast, the overall classification accuracy across all categories remains largely unaffected, changing minimally from 57.02% to 56.83%.

Table 3. Validation accuracy when neurons as a set

Model	Sigle-class Accuracy	All-class accuracy
Unchaged ResNet18 with 90%pr	78.4%	57.02%
50% most important neurons removed	63.3%	56.98%
80% most important neurons removed	54.8%	56.83%

Semantic Analysis of Model Decision Pathway: After identifying the key neurons, we extracted a tabby cat decision pathway with the highest average score based on the connection pattern of the 90%-pruned ResNet18 model, as illustrated in Fig. 9. By analyzing the semantics of this decision chain, we observe that when recognizing a tabby cat, the model initially focuses on color information, specifically "black," followed by attention to numerous underlying textures such as parallel stripes and spots. This aligns with the black stripes characteristic of the tabby cat body. Subsequently, the model identifies local features of the tabby cat, including its "arm" and "nose." As the model progresses through deeper layers, it learns increasingly abstract representations, culminating in the recognition of the entire object as a "cat." This step-by-step learning process—from color and texture to local structures and finally the whole object—mirrors the human cognitive process of progressing from simple to complex concepts.

Regarding the residual path unique to the ResNet architecture, we find that it primarily conveys underlying texture details of the tabby cat fur. This suggests that the residual path serves to supplement semantic information and enhance low-level visual details. Furthermore, given that tabby cat recognition heavily depends on distinctive fur textures and other low-level features, the residual path effectively assists the main pathway by preserving and transmitting these fundamental texture characteristics, thereby improving the accuracy of the tabby cat visual representation.

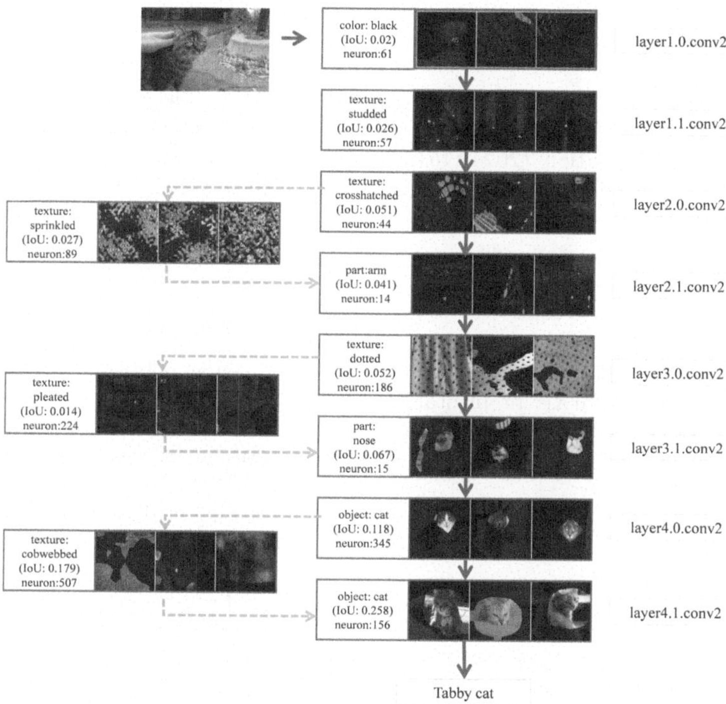

Fig. 9. The decision path with the highest average score for the tabby cat on the ResNet18 model with 90% pruning rate.

6 Conclusion and Discussions

In this study, we first introduced structured pruning technology into the interpretability research of DCNN models. We designed a progressive multi-scale pruning method to gradually eliminate unimportant structures within the model. Subsequently, by measuring the IoU value, we quantitatively compared the semantic purity characterized by model neurons before and after pruning, revealing that pruning enhances the semantic purity represented by neurons. Furthermore, the sparse connections of the pruned model enable us to clearly identify key decision pathways with high semantic purity, thereby uncovering the knowledge hierarchy during decision-making and providing a more intuitive approach to explain DCNN models.

However, it should be noted that while structured pruning enhances the interpretability of general object classification, it may compromise some models that require complex feature interactions (for example, fine-grained classification models). Moreover, for certain models that require semantic alignment, pruning may also disrupt these relatively fragile alignment patterns, causing the models to deviate from the alignment behavior. For these models, if we need to conduct interpretability analysis of the model through pruning, we need to be more cautious when performing the pruning.

Acknowledgments. This work was supported in part by the National Natural Science Foundation of China (Grant No. 62201355), Guangdong Basic and Applied Basic Research Foundation (2024A1515010977), Shenzhen Science and Technology Projection (JCYJ20220531102407018), Guangdong Provincial Key Laboratory (Grant 2023B1212060076).

References

1. Simonyan, K., Zisserman, A.: Very deep convolutional networks for large-scale image recognition. arXiv preprintarXiv:1409.1556 (2014)
2. Krizhevsky, A., Sutskever, I., Hinton, G.E.: Imagenet classification with deep convolutional neural networks. In: Advances in Neural Information Processing Systems, vol. 25 (2012)
3. He, K., Zhang, X., Ren, S., et al.: Deep residual learning for image recognition. In: Proceedings of the IEEE Conference on Computer Vision and Pattern Recognition, pp. 770–778 (2016)
4. Oquab, M., Bottou, L., Laptev, I., et al.: Is object localization for free?-Weakly-supervised learning with convolutional neural networks. In: Proceedings of the IEEE Conference on Computer Vision and Pattern Recognition, pp. 685–694 (2015)
5. Selvaraju, R.R., Cogswell, M., Das, A., et al.: Grad-CAM: visual explanations from deep networks via gradient-based localization. In: Proceedings of the IEEE International Conference on Computer Vision, pp. 618–626 (2017)
6. Guruprasad Ramaswamy, H., et al.: Ablation-CAM: visual explanations for deep convolutional network via gradient-free localization. In: Proceedings of the IEEE/CVF Winter Conference on Applications of Computer Vision, pp. 983–991 (2020)
7. Jiang, P.T., Zhang, C.B., Hou, Q., et al.: LayerCAM: exploring hierarchical class activation maps for localization. IEEE Trans. Image Process. **30**, 5875–5888 (2021)
8. Zhang, Q., Rao, L., Yang, Y.: Group-CAM: group score-weighted visual explanations for deep convolutional networks. arXiv preprint arXiv:2103.13859 (2021)
9. Zeiler, M.D., Fergus, R.: Visualizing and understanding convolutional networks. In: Fleet, D., Pajdla, T., Schiele, B., Tuytelaars, T. (eds.) ECCV 2014. LNCS, vol. 8689, pp. 818–833. Springer, Cham (2014). https://doi.org/10.1007/978-3-319-10590-1_53
10. Petsiuk, V., Das, A., Saenko, K.: Rise: randomized input sampling for explanation of black-box models. arXiv preprint arXiv:1806.07421 (2018)

11. Zhou, B., Bau, D., Oliva, A., et al.: Interpreting deep visual representations via network dissection. IEEE Trans. Pattern Anal. Mach. Intell. **41**(9), 2131–2145 (2018)
12. Jesse, M., Andreas, J.: Compositional explanations of neurons. Adv. Neural. Inf. Process. Syst. **33**, 17153–17163 (2020)
13. Ahn, Y.H., Kim, H.B., Kim, S.T.: Www: a unified framework for explaining what where and why of neural networks by interpretation of neuron concepts. In: Proceedings of the IEEE/CVF Conference on Computer Vision and Pattern Recognition, pp. 10968–10977 (2024)
14. Lin, M., Cao, L., Zhang, Y., et al.: Pruning networks with cross-layer ranking & k-reciprocal nearest filters. IEEE Trans. Neural Netw. Learn. Syst. **34**(11), 9139–9148 (2022)
15. Fang, G., Ma, X., Song, M., et al.: DepGraph: towards any structural pruning. In: Proceedings of the IEEE/CVF Conference on Computer Vision and Pattern Recognition, pp. 16091–16101 (2023)
16. Zhu, J., Pei, J.: Progressive kernel pruning with saliency mapping of input-output channels. Neurocomputing **467**, 360–378 (2022)
17. Li, Y., Lin, S., Zhang, B., et al.: Exploiting kernel sparsity and entropy for interpretable CNN compression. In: Proceedings of the IEEE/CVF Conference on Computer Vision and Pattern Recognition, pp. 2800–2809 (2019)

FairShap: A Fairness Framework Based Explainable Machine Learning

Xikuan Wang(✉), Min Zhang, and Jie Li

East China Normal University, Shanghai, China
wang117687@gmail.com, mzhang@sei.ecnu.edu.cn

Abstract. With the increasing application of machine learning in real-world decision-making systems, the fairness and interpretability of tasks involving humans have not yet been fully guaranteed. In order to solve the above problems, we propose an interpretable fairness framework based on feature contributions, which aims to improve the degree of interpretability of fairness in binary classification tasks. First, the fairness contribution is explained by the importance of interpretable features and quantified by the Shapley value in Game Theory; then, groups are divided according to different protective attributes, and discrimination detection and debiasing algorithms are applied to specific groups to mitigate the bias in the original samples. The experimental results show that the proposed method significantly outperforms the existing methods in terms of interpretability and demonstrates wide applicability to different classifiers and fairness metrics.

Keywords: Machine Learning · Trustworthy AI · Fairness · Interpretability

1 Introduction

Machine Learning(ML) is increasingly used across various real-world decision-making systems, including autonomous driving [1], financial risk assessment [2], traffic control [3], medical diagnostics [4], resume recruitment [5], credit assessment [6], and criminal justice [7]. However, machine learning are susceptible to biases, which can lead to potentially discriminatory outcomes. While machine learning are fundamentally data-driven, the data itself may embody statistical or societal biases. [8] Such biases can be exacerbated during the machine learning process, particularly when sensitive attributes such as gender and race are involved, resulting in significant adverse effects on vulnerable populations (Fig. 1).

In this paper, we propose FairShap, which aims to improve the fairness and interpretability of machine learning models. For the classification task, an interpretable fairness method is proposed, which combines group classification, discrimination detection and mitigation to process the dataset, and then combines

M. Bonsangue and Y. Chen (Eds.): AILA 2025, CCIS 2668, pp. 32–46, 2026.
https://doi.org/10.1007/978-981-95-8262-4_3

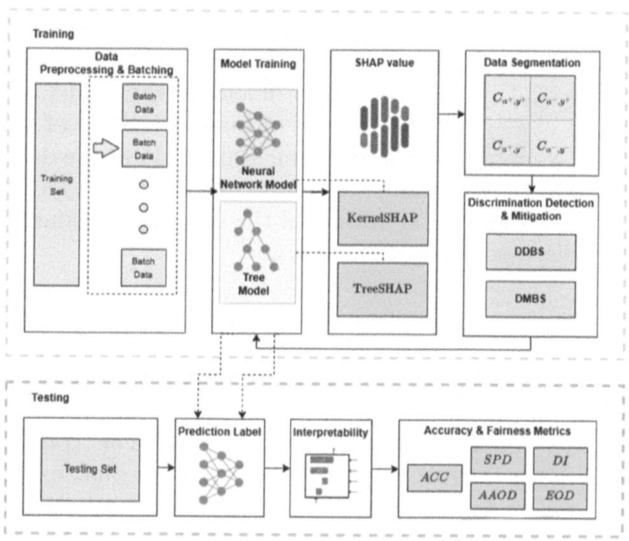

Fig. 1. FairShap Framework.

the interpretable methods in the test and evaluation part to achieve the balance between classification fairness and accuracy populations (Fig. 2).

Since there are many ways to quantify contributions in the interpretable domain [9], a model-independent and interpretable method for quantitatively calculating contributions is needed. In this paper, we will choose the Shapley value [10] to quantify contributions, which ensures that contributions can be calculated more efficiently in the following process, and achieves a balance between fairness and accuracy. While previous studies usually classify groups based on protective attributes [11], this paper uses a more detailed classification method, i.e., group classification based on the combination of protective attributes and labels, which can more accurately generate a candidate set and provide a basis for subsequent discrimination detection.

Traditional methods often use clustering techniques to recognize the fairness intuition that "similar individuals should be treated similarly" [12]. On this basis, this paper introduces the extended assumption that "similar individuals should have similar contributions", where contributions have been quantified by Shapley values. By calculating the Shapley value and filtering the samples, it is possible to identify the samples with mismatched contributions in the same group, and then label these samples as discriminatory or preferential samples.

Since the model is targeting discriminatory samples, this paper proposes an innovative discrimination mitigation algorithm. The algorithm is based on the perturbation of the protected attributes and the Shapley value for the identified discriminated or favored samples to alleviate the imbalance problem within the dataset.

We perform experiments on three datasets for the protection attribute and compared with two other fairness methods. From the perspective of fairness and interpretability, we explore the potential problems of the model, the correctness and fairness of the model, and the degree of interpretability of the visual analytic model. Then, we interpret the experimental effects at the dataset level and analyze the effects of the experimental results on different models and different protection attributes. Finally, the results of the experiments and the framework are analyzed and discussed in the conclusion.

2 Definition

2.1 Problem Formulation

We consider general binary classification problems. The training dataset is denoted as (X, A, Y), where X represents a sample set that excludes sensitive attributes. The variable A denotes a predefined protective attribute, such as race, gender and age, or marital status, while Y denotes the corresponding label. In this study, we assume that both A and Y are binary variables.

Specifically, we denote a complete sample, inclusive of labels, as (x_i, a_i, y_i), where $x_i = (x_i^1, x_i^2, ..., x_i^n) \in Rn$. The sample labels are categorized into two classes: $y_i \in \{y^+, y^-\}$, where y^+ signifies the positive class and y^- signifies the negative class. The protective attributes are similarly classified as $a_i \in \{a^+, a^-\}$, with a^+ representing advantageous protective attributes and a^- representing disadvantageous protective attributes.

2.2 Fairness Metrics

Four principal guidelines define fairness within the context of machine learning: Statistical Parity Difference, Equal Opportunity Differences, Demographic Parity Difference, and Average Absolute Odds Difference. [13–15]

Statistical Parity Difference (SPD). A classifier h trained on a data distribution (X, A, Y) satisfies Statistical Parity Difference if the prediction $\hat{Y} = h(X)$ independent of the protective attribute A. The Statistical Parity Difference can be articulated as follows:

$$SPD = Pr\{\hat{Y} = y^+|A = a^-\} - Pr\{\hat{Y} = y^+|A = a^+\} \leq \tau$$

Here, τ serves as the threshold for the fairness constraint. Smaller values of SPD indicate fairer models.

Disparate Impact (DI). Also based on statistical parity, defined as follows:

$$DI = \frac{Pr\{\hat{Y} = y^+|A = a^-\}}{Pr\{\hat{Y} = y^+|A = a^+\}} \leq \tau$$

The closer the value of DI is to 1, the fairer the model is. The difference between DI and SPD is that SPD focuses more on absolute differences, and is suitable for scenarios where there is a need to look at the equality of outcomes between different groups. DI focuses on proportional comparisons and is used in scenarios where the degree of relative fairness is important, especially when there are large differences in group bases.

Equal Opportunity Differences (EOD). Based on equal opportunity, outputs from different groups are required to have the same True Positive Rate(TPR), defined as follows:

$$EOD = Pr\{\hat{Y} = y^+|A = a^-, Y = y^+\} - Pr\{\hat{Y} = y^+|A = a^+, Y = y^+\} \leq \tau$$

This metric is assessed by calculating the predicted difference in positive class samples between different groups, with smaller values of EOD indicating a fairer model.

Average Absolute Odds Difference (AAOD). Both True Positive Rate(TPR) and False Positive Rate(FPR) are considered, defined as follows:

$$AAOD = \frac{1}{2}(|FPR_{a^+} - FPR_{a^-}| + |TPR_{a^+} - TPR_{a^-}|) \leq \tau$$

2.3 Interpretability Assessment

The main focus of the interpretability assessment is the change of the model on the protection attribute A. By analyzing the contribution of the protection attribute A before and after the optimization of the model, the decision-making process of the model can be deeply understood.

Global Interpretability Assessment [16] is designed to provide a holistic view of the contribution of model features to the output. By visualizing the overall contribution of each feature to the model output, special attention is given to the changes in the protective attribute A before and after model optimization. This approach helps to fully understand the decision-making mechanism of the model under the influence of different features.

Comparative Interpretability Assessment [17] is the evaluation of the protective attribute A between different debiasing algorithms. It analyzes the effectiveness of different methods by comparing the distribution of protective attributes of each model. This evaluation method can not only reveal the differences in the processing of protective attributes among different algorithms, but also provide empirical evidence for the selection of the optimal debiasing strategy.

SHAP. In cooperative Game Theory, Shapley values are used to distribute the benefits of cooperative outcomes. Based on this theory, the Shapley value is widely used in the field of machine learning to explain the prediction results of models, especially in interpretability assessment. The core idea is to calculate the overall contribution of each feature by considering its marginal contribution in all possible combinations.

Consider a model f that receives M features as inputs, and suppose we want to interpret the output of the model f with input x. Since there is no origin for the scale of the model output, we can only explain the difference between the observed model output and the chosen origin, which can be either the output value of a function of some arbitrary record or the average output value over a set of records D, and if the latter is used, the computation is expressed as follows:

$$\sum_{i=1}^{M} \phi_i = f(x) - \mathbb{E}_{y \sim \mathcal{D}}\left[f(y)\right]$$

Define F to be the set having M attributes, i.e., $F = \{F_1, ..., F_M\}$, and define S to be an arbitrary subset of $F \backslash \{F_i\}$, i.e. $S \subseteq F \backslash \{F_i\}$, then the Shapley value ϕ_i can be calculated according to the following equation:

$$\phi_i = \frac{1}{M} \sum_{S \subseteq F \backslash \{F_i\}} \frac{1}{\binom{M-1}{|S|}} \left(f(S \cup \{F_i\}) - f(S)\right)$$

where $f(S)$ are computed by treating S as a missing input.Thus the process of computing SHAP interpretations can be viewed as starting with S that does not contain F_i, adding F_i, and then observing the differences in the output values. For nonlinear functions, the values obtained will depend on which features are already in S, so we are interested in selecting a subset of the set size $|S|$ and then averaging the contributions of all subset sizes.

3 Dataset

ADULT dataset. The ADULT dataset is a publicly available dataset that is widely used in classification and machine learning research. It was originally derived from the 1994 U.S. Census and is used to predict whether an individual's annual income exceeds \$50,000. The dataset has 14 characteristics, including gender, marital status, and nationality, with the protected attributes being gender and race. This dataset suffers from data imbalance.

COMPAS dataset. The COMPAS dataset is a public dataset used for risk assessment and is widely used to study fairness and bias in machine learning models. It is derived from defendant records in Broward County, Florida, USA, and is used to predict whether a defendant will reoffend within two years. The dataset has 12 characteristics, including the number of prior offenses, race, and age, with the protected attributes being gender and race.

DEFAULT dataset. The DEFAULT dataset is a classic dataset used to study credit risk and default prediction, and is often used in finance and credit rating to predict whether a customer will default on a loan at some point in the future. The dataset has 25 characteristics, including age, gender, and income, with the protected attribute being gender.

4 Methodology

4.1 Candidate Set Generation

Algorithm 1. Candidate Set Generation Algorithm

Input: Dataset $\mathcal{D}(X, Y)$, Protected attributes A, Model M, Interpreter E
Output: Shapley value Φ_X, Candidate Set $\mathcal{C}_{\text{candi}}$

```
Φ_X ← ∅                                        ▷ Init Φ_X Set
if Model M is Tree-Model then
    Φ_X ← E(TreeSHAP, M)                        ▷ Using TreeSHAP Model
else
    Γ ← Sample(min(λ|D|, ν))                    ▷ Using shap lib samples as background data
    Φ_X ← E(KernelSHAP, M, Γ)                   ▷ Using KernelSHAP Model
end if
C_{a+,y+} ← ∅                                   ▷ Init C_{a+,y+} Set
C_{a−,y−} ← ∅                                   ▷ Init C_{a−,y−} Set
for all (x, y) ∈ D(X, Y) do
    if X[A] = a+ and y = y+ then
        C_{a+,y+} ← C_{a+,y+} ∪ {(x, y)}        ▷ For the dominant group, add to C_{a+,y+}
    end if
    if X[A] = a− and y = y− then
        C_{a−,y−} ← C_{a−,y−} ∪ {(x, y)}        ▷ For protected groups, add to C_{a−,y−}
    end if
end for
C_candi ← C_{a+,y+} ∪ C_{a−,y−}
return Φ_X, C_candi
```

The pseudo-code for the computation of the Shapley values and the population segmentation of the data is shown in Algorithm 1. The algorithm describes the specific steps of FairShap candidate set generation. The inputs include the dataset $D(X, Y)$, the protected attribute A, the model M, and the interpreter E; the outputs are the Shapley value Φ_X and the candidate set $\mathcal{C}_{\text{candi}}$.

Specific steps are as follows: 1. Initialize the candidate set: First, initialize the set of Shapley values Φ_X. 2. Select the interpreter: Use different interpretation methods according to the model type. If the model is a tree model, use TreeSHAP for interpretation; Otherwise, use KernelSHAP. Construct Candidate Sets: Iterate through each sample (x, y) in the dataset, and based on the values and labels of the protected attributes, add the eligible samples to the dominant group candidate set $\mathcal{C}_{a^+,y^+}$ or to the protected group candidate set $\mathcal{C}_{a^-,y^-}$ 4. Return results: Finally, the computed Shapley value set Φ_X and the candidate set $\mathcal{C}_{\text{candi}}$ are returned.

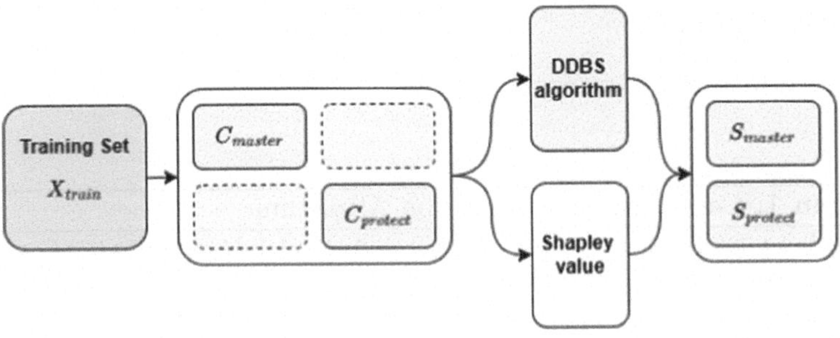

Fig. 2. The process of group segmentation to generate candidate and target sets.

4.2 Discrimination Detection Based Shapley Value Algorithm

Algorithm 2. DDBS Algorithm

Input: Shapley Value Φ_X, Candidate Set $\mathcal{C}_{\text{candi}}$, Thresholds τ
Output: Dominant group set $\mathcal{S}_{\text{master}}$, Protected group set $\mathcal{S}_{\text{protect}}$

$\mathcal{S}_{\text{master}} \leftarrow \emptyset$ ▷ Init $\mathcal{S}_{\text{master}}$
$\mathcal{S}_{\text{protect}} \leftarrow \emptyset$ ▷ Init $\mathcal{S}_{\text{protect}}$
for $(x, y) \in C_{candi}$ **and** $i \in |C_{candi}|$ **do**
  $\varphi \leftarrow \Phi_{X[i]}$
  if $y = y^+$ **and** $\varphi \geq \tau$ **then**
    $\mathcal{S}_{\text{master}} \leftarrow \mathcal{S}_{\text{master}} \cup (x, y)$
  end if
  if $y = y^-$ **and** $\varphi \leq -\tau$ **then**
    $\mathcal{S}_{\text{protect}} \leftarrow \mathcal{S}_{\text{protect}} \cup (x, y)$
  end if
end for
return $\mathcal{S}_{\text{master}}, \mathcal{S}_{\text{protect}}$ ▷ Return group set

The pseudo-code for the Discrimination Detection Based Shapley Value Algorithm is shown in Algorithm 2. The algorithm describes the specific implementation process of DDBS. Based on the input Shapley values and candidate sets, it identifies and adjusts the performance of the model in different groups to achieve fairness.

Inputs include Shapley value Φ_X, which is used to evaluate the contribution of each feature to the model prediction; Candidate set $\mathcal{C}_{\text{candi}}$, a set that contains the sample features and labels to be analyzed; and Threshold τ: a threshold of importance for determining the influence of features. Outputs include Dominant group set $\mathcal{S}_{\text{master}}$, which contains the set of samples that positively influence the model decision; Protect group target set $\mathcal{S}_{\text{protect}}$, which contains the set of samples that negatively influence the model decision.

Specific steps are as follows: 1. Initialize target sets: first, the algorithm initializes two empty target sets $\mathcal{S}_{\text{master}}$ and $\mathcal{S}_{\text{protect}}$, which will be used to store the eligible samples. 2. Iterate over the candidate sets: For each sample (x, y) in the candidate set $\mathcal{C}_{\text{candi}}$, the algorithm extracts the Shapley-valued feature φ of the sample. 3. Judge and classify the samples: For each sample, if its true label y is a positive class and the Shapley-valued feature φ is greater than the threshold τ, the sample is added to the dominant group target set $\mathcal{S}_{\text{master}}$. This step ensures that a sample is included in the dominant group set only if it contributes significantly to the model predictions. Similarly, if the true label y is a negative class and the Shapley value feature φ is less than the negative threshold, that sample is added to the protected group set $\mathcal{S}_{\text{protect}}$, which ensures that the sample from the protected group reflects potential bias of the model The algorithm is then used to generate a sample of the protected group. 4. Return results: Finally, the algorithm returns the combination of the dominant group set and the protected group set $\mathcal{S}_{\text{master}}$ and $\mathcal{S}_{\text{protect}}$. this is done to further analyze and adjust the model's performance across different groups to ensure fairness.

Algorithm 3. DMBS Algorithm

Input: Dataset $\mathcal{D}(X, Y)$, Dominant group set $\mathcal{S}_{\text{master}}$, Protected group set $\mathcal{S}_{\text{protect}}$
Output: Generated Dataset $\mathcal{D}_{\text{gen}}(X_{\text{gen}}, Y_{\text{gen}})$

function MODIFYSENSITIVEATTR(C, ξ, π)
  $X_t \leftarrow \emptyset$ ▷ Init X_t
  $Y_t \leftarrow \emptyset$ ▷ Init Y_t
  for $i \in C$ **do**
    $x \leftarrow X_i$
    if $y_i = \pi$ **then**
      $x[A] \leftarrow \xi$ ▷ Modifying Protected Attributes
    end if
    $X_t \leftarrow X_t \cup \{x\}$
    $Y_t \leftarrow Y_t \cup \{y_i\}$
  end for
return X_t, Y_t
end function
$X_{a^+}, Y_{a^+} \leftarrow \text{ModifySensitiveAttr}(\mathcal{S}_{\text{master}}, a^-, y^+)$
$X_{a^-}, Y_{a^-} \leftarrow \text{ModifySensitiveAttr}(\mathcal{S}_{\text{protect}}, a^+, y^-)$
$X_{\text{gen}} \leftarrow X \cup X_{a^+} \cup X_{a^-}$ ▷ Construct X_{gen}
$Y_{\text{gen}} \leftarrow Y \cup Y_{a^+} \cup Y_{a^-}$ ▷ Construct Y_{gen}
$D_{\text{gen}} \leftarrow (X_{\text{gen}}, Y_{\text{gen}})$
return D_{gen} ▷ Return Generation Dataset

4.3 Discrimination Mitigation Based Shapley Value Algorithm

Algorithm 3 describes the specific implementation of DMBS. The main objective is to mitigate model bias by modifying sensitive features in order to generate a fair dataset. Inputs include Dataset $\mathcal{D}(X, Y)$: a dataset containing the features X and labels Y; Dominant group set $\mathcal{S}_{\text{master}}$: a collection of samples that represent the dominant group; Protection group set $\mathcal{S}_{\text{protect}}$: the set of samples representing the protected group. The output consists of the generated dataset $\mathcal{D}_{\text{gen}}(X_{\text{gen}},$ modified to mitigate model bias.

Specific steps are as follows: 1. Define the function: Firstly, define the auxiliary function ModifySensitiveAttr, whose parameters are the set C, the value of the protection attribute ξ, and the label value π. The method mainly uses π to judge and modify the value of the protection attribute to ξ, in order to mitigate or eliminate the bias of the data. 2. Initialize Collections: Initialize two empty collections X_t and Y_t to store the modified features and labels. 3. Iterate over the sensitive features: for each sample i in the input set assign the sample feature to x. Check the label of the sample y_i. If the label is equal to the target label π, then modify the sensitive attributes: replace the sensitive attributes in the feature x with a specified modified value. Update the set of features X_t and the set of labels Y_t. 4. Call the function: For the dominant group set $\mathcal{S}_{\text{master}}$ and the protected group set $\mathcal{S}_{\text{protect}}$, respectively, call the ModifySensitiveAttr function to modify the sensitive attributes. For the dominant group, modify its sensitive attributes to a^- and target label y^+. For the protected group, modify its sensitive attributes to a^+ and the target label y^-. 5. Construct the generated dataset: The modified dataset is merged and a new feature set X_{gen} and label set Y_{gen} are constructed by aggregating the modifications of the dominant and protected groups. 6. Return results: Finally, the generated dataset D_{gen} is returned, which has been modified with sensitive features aimed at reducing the bias of the model on specific groups.

5 Experiments and Results

5.1 Experimental Models and Methods

In this paper, we will use the XGBoost and Random Forest RF models from the Tree Integration Model, both of which are based on the aspect of tree integration in calculating the Shapley values and are more advantageous in terms of computational complexity. Also we chosen MLP.

Experiment uses two comparison methods, one is the MARGIN-KNN [18], which uses KNN combined with a classification interval-based fairness algorithm, the MARGIN-KNN method looks for similar data points from the training data, and based on the principle of the maximum interval, the samples will be projected and the target set will be selected to eliminate the discrimination algorithm. The second is the FAIR-SMOTE [19], the core idea of which is an algorithm that removes bias labels and rebalances the internal distribution using SMOTE oversampling technique.

5.2 ADULT Results

Interpretability Assessment. From Fig. 3a, it is observed that the Shapley value of the experimental model on the protective attribute SEX is significantly

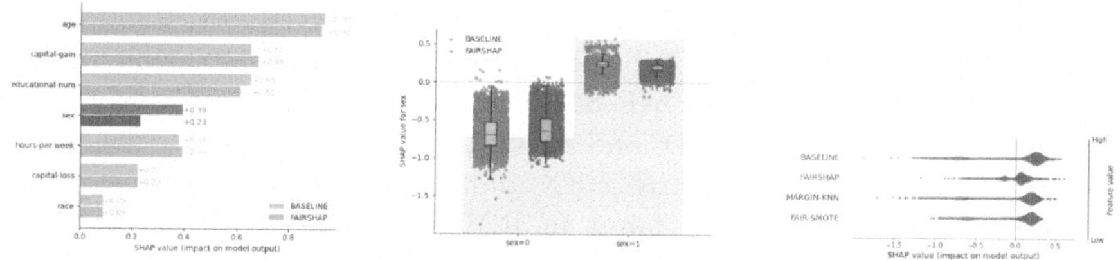

(a) Global absolute values of Shapley values before and after characterization experiments (b) Distribution of Shapley values before and after experiments on protected attributes (c) Comparison of Shapley value distribution of different methods

Fig. 3. ADULT Interpretability Assessment (with SEX as the protected attribute).

changed, and the global Shapley value of SEX is reduced by 39.5%. This shows that the FairShap correction significantly mitigates the gender bias of the model.

From Fig. 3b, we can analyze that the distribution of outliers for gender groups is reduced and converges close to zero.

Through the comparative analysis in Fig. 3c, it can be observed that in terms of SEX-related Shapley values, although both the MARGIN-KNN and FAIR-SMOTE methods improve fairness, the Shapley values generated by FairShap are more concentrated in the overall distribution, which suggests that the model is able to reflect the contribution of different groups in a more balanced way when dealing with the protective attribute of gender.

Table 1. ADULT Dataset Fairness Assessment with SEX as Protected Attribute

Model	Method	ACC	DI	SPD	EOD	AAOD
XG	BASELINE	0.8556	0.1664	0.1931	0.2503	0.1639
	MARKNN	0.8554	0.1831	0.1839	0.2248	0.1482
	FAIRSMOTE	0.8540	0.2002	0.1770	0.2085	0.1356
	FAIRSHAP	0.8551	**0.2269**	**0.1729**	**0.2063**	**0.1354**
RF	BASELINE	0.8433	0.1537	0.1577	0.2326	0.1448
	MARKNN	0.8410	0.1554	0.1479	0.2159	0.1339
	FAIRSMOTE	0.8450	0.1960	0.1505	0.1985	0.1250
	FAIRSHAP	0.8395	**0.2234**	**0.1268**	**0.1722**	**0.1042**
MLP	BASELINE	0.8057	0.3768	0.1514	0.1925	0.1262
	MARKNN	0.8056	0.3633	0.1684	0.2141	0.1428
	FAIRSMOTE	0.8052	0.2469	0.1722	0.2047	0.1374
	FAIRSHAP	0.8053	**0.4113**	**0.1322**	**0.1544**	**0.1088**

Fairness Assessment. Table 1 shows the results using XGBoost, Random Forest, and MLP models on the ADULT dataset, and the related debiasing methods FairShap, MARGIN-KNN, and FAIR-SMOTE results for the ACC and the four fairness indicators DI, SPD, EOD, and AAOD.

Of the two protection attributes, SEX and RACE, the fairness metrics DI, SPD, EOD, and AAOD are all fairer in RACE than SEX. Since the model itself discriminates more deeply against SEX, the effect of FairShap on SEX is obviously better than that of RACE, so here we mainly show the results when the protected attribute is SEX.

As can be seen from Table 1, the FairShap method is better than the MARGIN-KNN method. On some metrics such as SPD and EOD, FairShap and FAIR-SMOTE perform equally well on some models, with reductions of 17.6% and 16.7% on SPD, respectively.

Overall, when dealing with the main protected attributes of the dataset, FairShap is effective in improving the fairness metrics without a significant impact on correctness, and achieves better results than the other two compared methods in most cases.

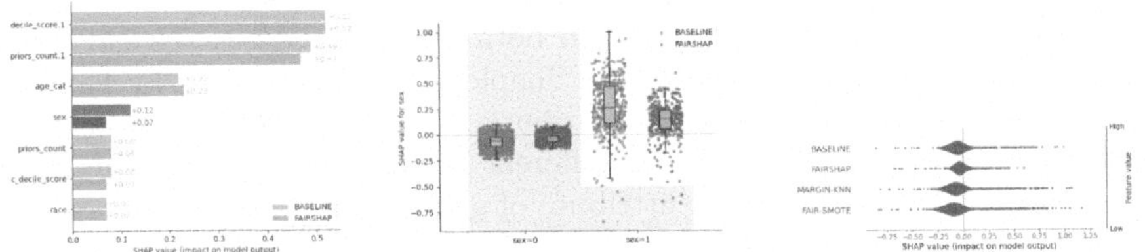

(a) Global absolute values of Shapley values before and after characterization experiments

(b) Distribution of Shapley values before and after experiments on protected attributes

(c) Comparison of Shapley value distribution of different methods

Fig. 4. COMPAS Interpretability Assessment (with SEX as the protected attribute).

5.3 COMPAS Results

Interpretability Assessment. Fig. 4a shows significant change in Shapley value on the protection attribute SEX for the model after the experiment. The global Shapley value for SEX is reduced by 41.6%, indicating that the FairShap correction significantly mitigates the gender bias of the model.

Analyzing Fig. 4b, we can see that the data converges for all gender groups and the extreme outliers are reduced.

Figure 4c shows the distribution of Shapley values on SEX for the three methods and the base method. Through the comparative analysis in Fig. 4c, it can be observed that in terms of SEX-related Shapley values, although both the

MARGIN-KNN and FAIR-SMOTE methods improve fairness, the Shapley values generated by FairShap are more concentrated in the overall distribution, which suggests that the model is able to reflect the contribution of different groups in a more balanced way when dealing with the protected attribute of gender.

Table 2. COMPAS Dataset Fairness Assessment with SEX as Protected Attribute

Model	Method	ACC	DI	SPD	EOD	AAOD
XG	BASELINE	0.6734	0.7342	0.2035	0.1095	0.1865
	MARKNN	0.6662	0.7320	0.2079	0.1137	0.1904
	FAIRSMOTE	0.6699	0.7009	0.2358	0.1407	0.2173
	FAIRSHAP	0.6693	**0.7894**	**0.1533**	**0.0616**	**0.1364**
RF	BASELINE	0.6896	0.7509	0.1913	0.1111	0.1642
	MARKNN	0.6901	0.7294	0.2140	0.1304	0.1884
	FAIRSMOTE	0.6933	0.7348	0.2084	0.1174	0.1844
	FAIRSHAP	0.6878	**0.7734**	**0.1684**	**0.0814**	**0.1439**
MLP	BASELINE	0.6970	0.7445	0.2163	0.1318	0.1928
	MARKNN	0.6965	0.7462	0.2133	0.1333	0.1840
	FAIRSMOTE	0.6928	0.7413	0.2113	0.1307	0.1848
	FAIRSHAP	0.6965	**0.7471**	**0.2026**	**0.1302**	**0.1713**

Fairness Assessment. Table 2 shows the results using XGBoost, Random Forest, and MLP models on the COMPAS dataset, and the related debiasing methods FairShap, MARGIN-KNN, and FAIR-SMOTE results for the ACC and the four fairness indicators DI, SPD, EOD, and AAOD.

Of the two protection attributes, SEX and RACE, the fairness metrics DI, SPD, EOD, and AAOD are all fairer in RACE than SEX. Since the model itself discriminates more deeply against SEX, the effect of FairShap on SEX is obviously better than that of RACE, so here we mainly show the results when the protected attribute is SEX.

As can be seen from Table 2, FairShap reduces 25.3% on the SPD on the XGBoost model, while FAIR-SMOTE and MARGIN-KNN exacerbate discrimination on some metrics, suggesting that the FairShap method is significantly better than the other two.

Overall, as with the ADULT dataset, when dealing with the protective attributes of the main discrimination of the dataset, FairShap can be effective in improving the fairness metrics without a significant impact on correctness and achieves better results than the other two compared methods in most cases.

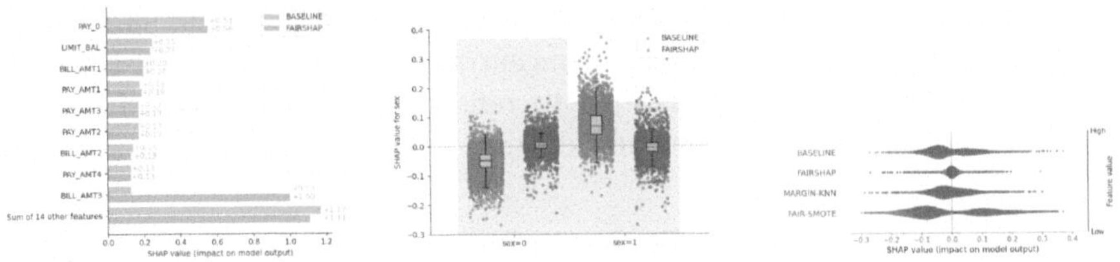

(a) Global absolute values of Shapley values before and after characterization experiments (b) Distribution of Shapley values before and after experiments on protected attributes (c) Comparison of Shapley value distribution of different methods

Fig. 5. DEFAULT Interpretability Assessment (with SEX as the protected attribute).

5.4 DEFAULT Results

Interpretability Assessment. In Fig. 5a, we cannot observe any specific change in SEX, mainly because its contribution is not high compared to other attributes, so it is not a major factor influencing the decision.

Figure 5b shows the global characteristic Shapley absolute value plots of SEX for the protected attribute in the DEFAULT dataset before and after FairShap's experiments.

Through the comparative analysis in Fig. 5c, it can be observed that in the distribution of Shapley values of attribute SEX among different methods, FairShap is significantly better than the other two methods, in which FAIR-SMOTE exacerbates the discrimination.

Table 3. DEFAULT Dataset Fairness Assessment with SEX as Protected Attribute

Model	Method	ACC	DI	SPD	EOD	AAOD
XG	BASELINE	0.8131	0.8259	0.0254	0.0083	0.0163
	MARKNN	0.8129	0.8157	0.0285	0.0155	0.0185
	FAIRSMOTE	0.8127	0.8372	0.0223	0.0385	0.0355
	FAIRSHAP	0.8122	**0.8888**	**0.0151**	**0.0133**	**0.0131**
RF	BASELINE	0.8199	0.9063	0.0107	0.0186	0.0138
	MARKNN	0.8182	0.8989	0.0112	0.0212	0.0160
	FAIRSMOTE	0.8188	0.8604	0.0170	0.0337	0.0195
	FAIRSHAP	0.8196	**0.9605**	**0.0041**	**0.0041**	**0.0085**
MLP	BASELINE	0.7821	0.7458	0.0001	0.0012	0.0008
	MARKNN	0.7819	0.7301	0.0012	0.0010	0.0001
	FAIRSMOTE	0.7756	0.7482	0.0304	0.0029	0.0183
	FAIRSHAP	0.7813	**0.7981**	0.0012	0.0017	0.0013

Fairness Assessment. Table 3 shows the results using XGBoost, Random Forest, and MLP models on the DEFAULT dataset, and the related debiasing methods FairShap, MARGIN-KNN, and FAIR-SMOTE results for the ACC and the four fairness indicators DI, SPD, EOD, and AAOD.

As can be seen from Table 3, after using the FairShap method, except for DI, which will improve slightly, the rest of the indicators are already relatively fair on BASELINE, so the effect of the three debiasing methods is not particularly significant, and the bias is aggravated in FAIR-SMOTE on the fairness indexes EOD and AAOD on the XGBoost model, which reduces fairness.

6 Conclusion

This paper focuses on improving the fairness and interpretability of machine learning models, especially in dealing with human-related decision-making tasks. With the widespread use of machine learning in real-world decision-making systems, it is important to understand and mitigate unfair decisions caused by data discrimination and algorithmic biases that have a profound impact on individual opportunities.

We propose FairShap, an interpretable fairness framework based on feature contributions, which aims to improve the fairness and interpretability of models in binary classification tasks. Based on the assumption that "the protective attributes of individuals within the same group should have similar contributions to their outcomes", and combining with the concept of Shapley value in cooperative Game Theory, the framework performs debiasing in the preprocessing stage of the model to effectively alleviate the unfairness in the dataset, and provides an explanation for the unfairness in the dataset. This can effectively alleviate the unfair phenomenon in the dataset and provide an explainable explanation.

Through the experiments on the datasets ADULT, COMPAS and DEFAULT, this paper verifies that the proposed discrimination detection algorithm DDBS and discrimination elimination algorithm DMBS effectively balance the classification fairness and accuracy, and satisfy the fairness criteria DI, SPD, EOD, AAOD. In the research process, we explore several key issues, including the interpretability effect under different protection attributes, the fairness performance on different datasets, and the comparison with other methods, and discuss the key issues with the experimental results. Finally, the experimental results show that the method outperforms existing algorithms in terms of interpretability and provides an interpretable account of fairness, and demonstrates wide applicability to different classifiers and fairness metrics.

References

1. Bojarski, M., et al.: End to end learning for self-driving cars (2016)
2. Aseervatham, V., Lex, C., Spindler, M.: How do unisex rating regulations affect gender differences in insurance premiums? Geneva Papers Risk Insur. Issues Pract. **41**(1), 128–160 (2016)

3. Julian, K. D., Lopez, J., Brush, J. S., Owen, M. P., Kochenderfer, M. J.: Policy compression for aircraft collision avoidance systems. In: 2016 IEEE/AIAA 35th Digital Avionics Systems Conference (DASC), pp. 1–10, IEEE (2016)
4. Obermeyer, Z., Powers, B., Vogeli, C., Mullainathan, S.: Dissecting racial bias in an algorithm used to manage the health of populations. Science **366**(6464), 447–453 (2019)
5. Chan, J., Wang, J.: Hiring preferences in online labor markets: evidence of a female hiring bias. Manage. Sci. **64**(7), 2973–2994 (2018)
6. Bono, T., Croxson, K., Giles, A.: Algorithmic fairness in credit scoring. Oxf. Rev. Econ. Policy **37**(3), 585–617 (2021)
7. Berk, R., Heidari, H., Jabbari, S., Kearns, M., Roth, A.: Fairness in criminal justice risk assessments: the state of the art. Sociol. Meth. Res. **50**(1), 3–44 (2021)
8. Mavrogiorgos, K., Kiourtis, A., Mavrogiorgou, A., Menychtas, A., Kyriazis, D.: Bias in machine learning: a literature review. Appl. Sci. **14**(19), 8860 (2024)
9. Bach, S., Binder, A., Montavon, G., Klauschen, F., Müller, K.-R., Samek, W.: On pixel-wise explanations for non-linear classifier decisions by layer-wise relevance propagation. PLoS ONE **10**(7), e0130140 (2015)
10. Lundberg, S. M., Lee, S.-I.: A unified approach to interpreting model predictions,. In: Advances in Neural Information Processing Systems, vol. 30 (2017)
11. Zafar, M. B., Valera, I., Rogriguez, M. G., Gummadi, K. P.: Fairness constraints: mechanisms for fair classification. In: Artificial Intelligence and Statistics, pp. 962–970, PMLR (2017)
12. Anderson, N., Bera, S. K., Das, S., Liu, Y.: Distributional individual fairness in clustering. arXiv preprint arXiv:2006.12589 (2020)
13. Madras, D., Creager, E., Pitassi, T., Zemel, R.: Learning adversarially fair and transferable representations. In: International Conference on Machine Learning, pp. 3384–3393, PMLR (2018)
14. Kurakin, A., Goodfellow, I., Bengio, S.: Adversarial machine learning at scale. arXiv preprint arXiv:1611.01236 (2016)
15. Lahoti, P., Gummadi, K. P., Weikum, G.: IFair: learning individually fair data representations for algorithmic decision making. In: 2019 IEEE 35th International Conference on DATA ENGINEERING (ICDE), pp. 1334–1345, IEEE (2019)
16. Hakkoum, H., Idri, A., Abnane, I.: Global and local interpretability techniques of supervised machine learning black box models for numerical medical data. Eng. Appl. Artif. Intell. **131**, 107829 (2024)
17. Chan, C. S., Kong, H., Liang, G.: A comparative study of faithfulness metrics for model interpretability methods. arXiv preprint arXiv:2204.05514 (2022)
18. Shi, X., Li, Y.: Discrimination sample discovery and elimination algorithm based on categorization interval in fairness machine learning. Sci. China: Info. Sci. **50**(8), 1255–1266 (2020)
19. Chakraborty, J., Majumder, S., Menzies, T.: Bias in machine learning software: why? how? what to do?. In: Proceedings of the 29th ACM Joint Meeting on European Software Engineering Conference and Symposium on the Foundations of Software Engineering, pp. 429–440 (2021)

Knowledge Systems

Improving the Agent's Formalization of Relevance: An Epistemic Logic Grounded in Possible Knowledge Bases

Haoxuan Luo[1(✉)] and Mengqin Ning[2]

[1] Department of Philosophy, School of Humanities, Tsinghua University, Beijing, China
luohx24@mails.tsinghua.edu.cn

[2] Institute of Logic, School of Philosophy, Beijing Normal University, Beijing, China

Abstract. When faced with complex epistemic-combinatorial situations, agents struggle to formally differentiate between relational patterns, creating gaps in formal models. To address this, we introduce strictly relevant operators ($(\phi \mid \psi)$, $(\phi \parallel \psi)$, $(\phi \nmid \psi)$) and construct an Epistemic Logic based on Possible Knowledge Bases (EL_{PKB}). Among these, these new operators require not only the absence of counterexample situations but also every truth case must exist, ensuring a precise representation. To this end, we introduce a non-Kripke model that incorporates PKBs to define the semantics. In this context, a PKB refers to the knowledge combinations that an agent might possess in a given state. Then we explore the correspondence between PKBs and Global Modal Logic models within the proposed framework, while also providing variants of RN for EL_{PKB}. Finally, we also explore the cognitive attributes of agents, particularly focusing on two distinct levels of facticity and positive introspection within agent cognition. This capability to identify logical relevance is also a critical step toward enabling AI to approach human-level cognition.

Keywords: Logical relevance between propositions · Strictly relevant sufficient condition · Possible Knowledge Bases · Epistemic logic

1 Introduction

Current generative AI systems fundamentally rely on the correlation degrees between tokens of large language models[1], which excel in question-answering tasks. However, when confronted with cognitively relevant scenarios beyond their trained memory, these AI systems struggle with performing cognitive combinatorial judgments on the relation of relevance between uncertain propositions [2,3].

[1] They are automatically extractable language traces that reflect human language habits, and have the context-sensitive statistical property [1].

M. Bonsangue and Y. Chen (Eds.): AILA 2025, CCIS 2668, pp. 49–63, 2026.
https://doi.org/10.1007/978-981-95-8262-4_4

This capability represents a key step toward enabling AI to approach human-level cognition. It directly contributes to the field of AI cognitive modeling and facilitates research on explainable frameworks for AI uncertainty reasoning. Therefore, the first task is to capture the logical structures (knowledge-driven) that humans employ to address such problems.

In the real world, information is characterized by its complexity and diversity. From the epistemic perspective of the agent, there exists information that remains uncertain, driven by intellectual curiosity, we seek to deepen our understanding of these uncertainties. One pathway to achieve this is by determining the logical relevance among uncertain propositions within the agent' s cognitive system.

The characterization of logical relevance between propositions has always been a central concern of formal logic. For example, the formalization of sufficient conditions pays particular attention to implication relations, such as classical material implication ($p \rightarrow q$) primarily focuses on the truth-value in conditional statements [4,5], but this approach encounters paradoxes of implication. Strict implication ($\Box(p \rightarrow q)$) introduces a necessity modal operator requiring $p \rightarrow q$ to hold in all possible worlds [6,7]. Relevance logic emphasizes the requirement of content-relatedness between premises and conclusions (e.g., shared propositional variables) [8], some research also introduced epistemic contexts [9,10]. Modal dependence logic [11] provides another method to characterize propositional relation by integrating dependence logic [12,13] into Kripke models. It employs $=(p, q)$ to denote dependency and introduces $p_1 \perp_q p_2$ for independence [14], thereby enhancing its expressiveness.

Gerhard Lakemeyer(1997) explored relevance from an epistemological perspective, conducting a series of analytical reflections that integrated epistemic logic [15].In recent years, some studies have also focused on characterizing 'propositional relations' from a cognitive perspective. Xuefeng Wen (2024) discussed the influence of indicative terms and epistemic modalities on conditional reasoning, proposing a novel context-sensitive semantics [16]. David Makinson (2009) proposed that the relation of relevance was considered modulo the choice of a background belief set [17]. Jarmużek, T.(2020) formulated a logic based on relating semantics to evaluate both the extensional conditions and sufficiently relevant intensional conditions of propositional formulas [18].

Within relevant cognitive contexts, agents can already distinguish different types of propositional relationships (e.g., sufficient condition relations, equivalence relations, and irrelevance) to some extent using existing logical tools. However, when faced with complex epistemic combinations, agents struggle to formally distinguish different relational patterns, creating gaps in formal models.

We now present two intuitive examples to illustrate the existing issues and the stricter propositional relationships we aim to capture within epistemic contexts.

1.1 Example 1: The Barber Shop

In 1894, Lewis Carroll proposed a celebrated logical paradox [19]. Three barbers, Allen, Brown, and Carr, operate a barber shop. (1) The shop is always open, which means at least one barber is present. (2) After Allen developed a fever, he became anxious and never leaves the shop unless Brown accompanies him when he goes out.

Now we use a to denote "Allen is in the shop", b to denote "Brown is in the shop", c to denote "Carr is in the shop". We can derive two key pieces of information:(1)$a \vee b \vee c$ (2) $\neg a \rightarrow \neg b$. According to Modus Tollens[2], we now have the following inference.

(α) If Carr is out then if Allen is out then Brown is in.

(β) It is not the case that if Allen is out then Brown is in.

(γ) Therefore, it is not the case that Carr is out.

Based on (1) and (2), we can conclude that both (α) $\neg c \rightarrow (\neg a \rightarrow b)$ and (β) $\neg(\neg a \rightarrow b)$ are true. However, (γ) is clearly false because when Brown is in the shop and Carr is out, both (1) (2) regarding the barber shop are satisfied.

Why do we get different results? The critical issue lies in the different number of truth-value cases required for $(\neg a \rightarrow b)$ in (α) and (β).

In (α), when Carr is absent (i.e.,$\neg c$), the truth-values of a and b in $(\neg a \rightarrow b)$ are restricted to two possibilities: $a \wedge b$ and $a \wedge \neg b$. This satisfies the notice (1) and (2). However, (β) aims to express that the situation "Allen went out alone without Brown" is impossible, that is, we only negate $\neg a \wedge b$. However, $(\neg a \rightarrow b)$ can hold in other truth situations.

Therefore, (β) is incorrect. If we want to retain the original meaning, we must introduce a "weaker" formulation than (β)[3], thereby avoiding the structure of Modus Tollens. Consequently, we no longer get the contradictory result (γ).

1.2 Example 2: The Candy House

This is an original example we developed. On the first day, the child entered the Candy House, where there was a candy box (denoted as Box 1) on the table. The shopkeeper described its properties: "This candy box contains only two types of candies: milk candies(m) and fruit candies(f). When you press the button on top, one of three outcomes will occur randomly[4] :① *both m and f* ② *no candies* or ③ *only f*. The case of ④ *only m* is impossible."

The shopkeeper then asked a question to the child: "Let's denote proposition p as 'milk candy appears when you press the button'[5], and proposition q as 'fruit candy appears when you press the button'. Based on this information, what relation do you perceive between p and q?" The child replied: "First, I think that the situations $p \wedge q$, $\neg p \wedge \neg q$, and $\neg p \wedge q$ are all possible, while $p \wedge \neg q$ is impossible. From this, I conclude that p is a sufficient condition for q."

The shopkeeper nodded and invited the child to return the next day.

The next day, the child returned to find two identical-looking candy boxes on the table. The shopkeeper explained: "In addition to yesterday's candy box

---

[2] Modus Tollens means form $\phi \rightarrow \psi$ and $\neg\psi$, we can get $\neg\phi$.

[3] i.e., a stronger formal expression than $(\neg a \rightarrow b)$.

[4] It is guaranteed that all possible cases occur.

[5] $\neg\, p$ as 'milk candy does not appear when you press the button'.

Fig. 1. The three scenarios in the Candy House.

(Box 1), we've added another box (Box 2). The new box also contains only two types of candies, but differs in that pressing the button will randomly result in one of three outcomes: ① *both m and f* ② *no candies* or ④ *only m*. The case of ③ *only f* is impossible."

The shopkeeper asked the child to randomly stand in front of one of the boxes and questioned: "You don't know which box you're facing. Under this uncertainty, what relation do you perceive between p and q?" The child responded: "If I'm facing yesterday's box (Box 1), analysis shows that p could be a sufficient condition for q. Similarly, if I'm facing the new box (Box 2), then q could be a sufficient condition for p. Therefore, both $p \rightarrow q$ and $q \rightarrow p$ are possible."

The shopkeeper replied: "While 'both $p \rightarrow q$ and $q \rightarrow p$ are possible' describes your cognition in the above situation, it could also apply to other situation–for instance, if there were two boxes, one box ③ *only appears f* after pressing the button and the other ④ *only m*. Although the formal representation remains the same, your judgment of the relationship between p and q in this situation is different from before. Do we have a stricter formulation to respond this?"

The child thought for a moment and answered: "I'll revert to the initial analysis. Since I might be facing Box 1, I consider $p \wedge q$, $\neg p \wedge \neg q$, and $\neg p \wedge q$ as possible. If it's Box 2, then $p \wedge \neg q$ is also possible. Combining both possibilities, the outcomes $p \wedge q$, $\neg p \wedge \neg q$, $\neg p \wedge q$, and $p \wedge \neg q$ are all possible." The shopkeeper noted: "This is indeed stricter, but could it also apply to other situations?"

The shopkeeper then led the child to another table with two identical boxes, and explained: "These new boxes also contain only two types of candies. One box (Box3) will, upon pressing the button, randomly result in one of the two outcomes: either ① *both m and f*, or ② *no candies*; the other box (Box 4) will randomly result in one of the four outcomes: ① *both m and f* ② *no candies* ③ *only f*, or④ *only m*." The shopkeeper again asked about the relation between p and q. The child replied: "Analyzing each box separately and then combining the possibilities, the outcomes $p \wedge q$, $\neg p \wedge \neg q$, $\neg p \wedge q$, and $p \wedge \neg q$ remain possible."

The epistemic judgment of the relation between propositions p and q remains same when confronted with two distinct candy box combinations (1+2 vs. 3+4). Therefore, we need a strictly relationship to describe the difference between (Box 1,Box,2) and (Box 3,Box,4).

1.3 Research Objectives

This paper focuses on distinguishing the logical relevance between propositions from an epistemic perspective. By introducing strictly relevant operators, we construct an "Epistemic Logic based on possible knowledge bases (EL_{PKB})" to characterize agents' epistemic differentiation of the logical relevance, thereby effectively addressing the above complex combination in cognition.

Building upon the above examples: Candy Box 1 formally captures the intuition that "when pressing the button, the appearance of a milk candy (p) strictly relevantly guarantees the appearance of fruit candy (q), while the converse does not hold." This indicates that p is a ***strictly relevant sufficient condition*** for q. Similarly, Candy Box 2 expresses that q is a strictly relevant sufficient condition for p. Candy Box 3 shows that "pressing the button always results in both milk (p) and fruit candies (q) appearing at the same time," which corresponds to p ***strictly relevant equivalent*** to q. Candy Box 4 illustrates that "the appearance of milk (p) and fruit candies (q) are no connection when pressing the button," meaning p and q are ***strictly irrelevant*** in this context.

The concept of strict relevance here involves three key aspects:

First, these strictly relevant operators require not only the absence of counterexample situation but also that every truth situations must exist, ensuring a precise representation. Crucially, in complex cognitive situations, these operators can capture distinct combinations of propositional relations, which distinguishes them from material implication and strict implication. And such semantics can avoid the "one-to-many"[6] problems in the Candy House example.

Second, this semantics cannot be captured by Kripke possible-world models, necessitating the introduction of the ***Possible Knowledge Bases*** in Sect. 2 of this paper. In this context, a PKB refers to the knowledge combinations that an agent might possess in a given state. When defining the PKBs, we first established atomic cases, then defined cases for K (representing knowledge operator), and finally formalized cases for the strict relevance operators. This process is also an inherent manifestation of our logical relevance.

Third, it is important to note that when an agent considers p to be a strictly relevant sufficient condition for q, this requires that both p and q are propositions whose truth-values are epistemically uncertain to the agent[7]. For example, consider the statement: "If 1+1=3, then x>3". Since the antecedent "1+1 = 3" is cognitively necessarily false, the strictly relevant sufficient condition proposed above should not apply here[8].

The paper considers that an agent's epistemic judgment of propositional relevance inherently constitutes a manifestation of cognitive capacity. Additionally,

---

[6] This refers to the example where the child's epistemic judgment of propositional relevance between p and q yields identical conclusions across different candy box combinations (e.g., 1+2, 3+4).

[7] Laplace (1820) posited that the laws of nature are deterministic, and randomness arises solely from our ignorance of underlying factors [20].

[8] This concept excludes propositions that are tautologies and contradictions, thereby avoiding paradoxes of material implication.

this paper distinguishes the cognitive levels of agents through cognitive attributes (such as "facticity", "positive self-reflectivity" and so on), thereby enriching the modeling of higher-order cognitive abilities [21]. In Sect. 4, this hierarchical distinction is mapped through knowledge bases defined under different definitions, enabling the differentiation of agents with distinct degrees of higher-order cognitive capabilities. Meanwhile, this also provides significant insights into enhancing the cognitive capabilities of AI agents.

The present paper is structured as follows. Section 2 provides the language, models and semantics of EL_{PKB}, Sect. 3 discusses some properties of Possible Knowledge Bases, and Sect. 4 elaborate on model properties and corresponding definitions.

2 Language, Models and Semantics

Definition 1 (Language $\mathcal{L}$). *The formulas ϕ of Epistemic Logic grounded in Possible Knowledge Bases (EL_{PKB}) are given by the rule*

$$\phi ::= \bot \mid p \mid \phi \to \phi \mid \phi|\psi \mid \phi||\psi \mid \phi \nmid \psi \mid K\phi,$$

where p is a propositional variable.

Extending the standard symbolism of basic epistemic modal logic, we formalize propositional relevance through three novel operators:$\phi|\psi$ (strictly relevant sufficient condition), $\phi||\psi$ (strictly relevant equivalence), and $\phi \nmid \psi$ (strict irrelevance). The epistemic constructions should be interpreted as: $K(\phi|\psi)$ denotes that ϕ being a strictly relevant sufficient condition for ψ is the agent's knowledge; $K(\phi||\psi)$ denotes that ϕ and ψ are being strictly relevant equivalence is the agent's knowledge; $K(\phi \nmid \psi)$ denotes that ϕ and ψ are being strict irrelevance is the agent's knowledge.

In the Candy House example, the agent's knowledge is partitioned based on different possible combinations. Therefore, when constructing the model, we allow an agent to possess distinct possible knowledge bases at the same state and determine their ultimate knowledge by evaluating each knowledge base they hold.

We define the model of EL_{PKB} as follows:

Definition 2 (Models). $\mathcal{M} = (W, V, B, F)$, *$W$ is a non-empty set, regarded as a set of possible worlds. V is an assignment on W (from a set of propositional letters Φ to $\mathcal{P}(W)$), B is a collection of formula sets(will be defined later), regarded as the set of possible knowledge bases. F is a function from W to $\mathcal{P}(B)$.*

In contrast to conventional epistemic models, this novel frame eliminates epistemic accessibility relations defined over state points. Instead, B is regarded as a set of possible knowledge bases, and through the function F, the possible knowledge base possessed by the agent at the state point is given. Next, we define the conditions of the possible knowledge base B:

Generally speaking, a possible knowledge base is regarded as a combination of some cognitive states of the agent, needs to satisfy the following properties:

1. Maximality and closure property of propositional formulas: maximality requires that for any proposition and its negation at least one must be epistemically possible within the possible knowledge base. Closure property ensures that the possible knowledge base is closed under Modus Ponens[9].
2. Higher-order knowledge: we assume that each agent has the ability of higher-order cognition.
3. Relevant condition: with the help of the relevant operator, agents can recognize the relevance of different propositions.

Definition 3. *To ensure those properties are satisfied in possible knowledge base, the following conditions are required:*

For each $s \in B$, s is a set of $\mathcal{L}$-formulas, meeting the following conditions:

1. Maximality and closure property of propositional formulas:[10]

1.1 $\bot \notin s$.

1.2 for any formula ϕ. if $\neg\phi \notin s$, then $\phi \in s$.

1.3 $\phi_1 \wedge \phi_2 \wedge ... \wedge \phi_n \in s$ *if and only if with* $\phi_{a_1} \wedge \phi_{a_2} \wedge ... \wedge \phi_{a_n} \in s$, *where* $a_1, a_2, ..., a_n$ *is a permutation of* $1, 2, ..., n$.

1.4 Let ψ be such a formula, in the form of replacing $\neg\neg\alpha$ anywhere in ψ with α, then $\phi \in s$ if and only if $\psi \in s$.

1.5 If $\phi \in s$, then $\phi \wedge \psi \in s$ or $\phi \wedge \neg\psi \in s$.

1.6 $\phi \wedge \neg(\psi_1 \wedge \psi_2) \in s$ *if and only if* $\phi \wedge \neg\psi_1 \in s$ *or* $\phi \wedge \neg\psi_2 \in s$.

1.7 If $\phi \wedge \psi \in s$, then $\phi \neq \neg\psi$ and $\phi \in s$, $\psi \in s$ ("=" means the equivalence about string).

2.Higher-order knowledge:

2.1 If $\neg K\neg\phi \in s$, then $\phi \in s$.

2.2 If $K\phi_1 \wedge ... \wedge K\phi_n \wedge \neg K\neg\psi \in s$, *then* $\phi_1 \wedge ... \wedge \phi_n \wedge \psi \in s$.

2.3 Let α, β be propositional formulas, let ϕ be formula contains K. Let α^p_ϕ and β^p_ϕ be results of replacing p by ϕ. For any formula set s, if $\alpha \in s$ implies $\beta \in s$, then $\alpha^p_\phi \in s$ implies $\beta^p_\phi \in s$.[11]

3.Relevant conditions:

3.1 $\neg(\phi|\psi) \in s$ *iff* $(\phi|\psi) \notin s$.

3.2 $\neg(\phi||\psi) \in s$ *iff* $(\phi||\psi) \notin s$.

3.3 $\neg(\phi \nmid \psi) \in s$ *iff* $(\phi \nmid \psi) \notin s$.

3.4 $(\phi|\psi) \in s$ *iff* $\phi \wedge \psi \in s, \neg\phi \wedge \psi \in s, \neg\phi \wedge \neg\psi \in s, \phi \wedge \neg\psi \notin s$.

3.5 $(\phi||\psi) \in s$ *iff* $\phi \wedge \psi \in s, \neg\phi \wedge \psi \notin s, \neg\phi \wedge \neg\psi \in s, \phi \wedge \neg\psi \notin s$.

3.6 $(\phi \nmid \psi) \in s$ *iff* $\phi \wedge \psi \in s, \neg\phi \wedge \psi \in s, \neg\phi \wedge \neg\psi \in s, \phi \wedge \neg\psi \in s$.

[9] Modus Ponens means form ϕ and $\phi \to \psi$, we can get ψ.

[10] Define $\phi \vee \psi := \neg(\neg\phi \wedge \neg\psi)$, and $\phi \to \psi := \neg(\phi \wedge \neg\psi)$.

[11] This condition can be seen as the preservation of monotonicity under substitution in higher-order knowledge.

3.7 Let α, β be propositional formulas, ϕ be formula contains $K, |, ||, \nmid$. Let α^p_ϕ and β^p_ϕ be results of replacing p by ϕ. For any formula set s, if $\alpha \in s$ implies $\beta \in s$, then $\alpha^p_\phi \in s$ implies $\beta^p_\phi \in s$.[12]

Definition 4. (semantics). *For each $\phi \in \mathcal{L}$, define ϕ is satisfied in $\mathcal{M}$ at state $u \in W$ as follows:*

- $\mathcal{M}, u \vDash \bot$ *never.*
- $\mathcal{M}, u \vDash p$ *iff* $u \in V(p)$.
- $\mathcal{M}, u \vDash \neg\phi$ *iff* $u \nvDash \phi$.
- $\mathcal{M}, u \vDash \phi \rightarrow \psi$ *iff* $u \vDash \phi$ *imples* $u \vDash \psi$.
- $\mathcal{M}, u \vDash K\phi$ *iff for every* $s \in F(u)$, $\neg\phi \notin s$.
- $\mathcal{M}, u \vDash (\phi|\psi)$ *never,* $\mathcal{M}, u \vDash (\phi||\psi)$ *never,* $\mathcal{M}, u \vDash (\phi \nmid \psi)$ *never.*[13]

Within this semantic framework, an agent's knowledge must always be evaluated against the set of possible knowledge bases available at the given state. Furthermore, since propositional relevance is restricted to estimate unknown propositions, any judgment regarding propositional relevance at a state point is inherently invalid.

Furthermore, strict irrelevance between propositions can be defined through strictly relevant sufficient conditions and strictly relevant equivalence:

Fact 1. *For every model $\mathcal{M} = (W, V, B, F)$, let $s \in B$, then $(\phi \nmid \psi) \in s$ if and only if $\neg(\phi|\psi) \wedge \neg(\neg\phi|\psi) \wedge \neg(\phi|\neg\psi) \wedge \neg(\neg\phi|\neg\psi) \wedge \neg(\phi||\psi) \wedge \neg(\neg\phi||\psi) \in s$ and $\phi \in s$, $\neg\phi \in s$, $\psi \in s$, $\neg\psi \in s$.*

Proof. From left to right: by ***Definition 3.3***, $(\phi \nmid \psi) \in s$ if and only if $\phi \wedge \psi \in s, \neg\phi \wedge \psi \in s, \neg\phi \wedge \neg\psi \in s, \phi \wedge \neg\psi \in s$. Since $\phi \wedge \psi \in s$, then $(\phi|\neg\psi) \notin s$ and $(\neg\phi||\psi) \notin s$; since $\neg\phi \wedge \psi \in s$, then $(\neg\phi|\neg\psi) \notin s$ and $(\phi||\psi) \notin s$; since $\neg\phi \wedge \neg\psi \in s$, then $(\neg\phi|\psi) \notin s$; since $\phi \wedge \neg\psi \in s$, then $(\phi|\psi) \notin s$. Therefore, $\neg(\phi|\psi) \wedge \neg(\neg\phi|\psi) \wedge \neg(\phi|\neg\psi) \wedge \neg(\neg\phi|\neg\psi) \wedge \neg(\phi||\psi) \wedge \neg(\neg\phi||\psi) \in s$. And $\phi \wedge \psi \in s$ implies $\phi \in s$ and $\psi \in s$, $\neg\phi \wedge \neg\psi \in s$ implies $\neg\phi \in s$ and $\neg\psi \in s$, then $(\phi \nmid \psi) \in s$ entails $\phi \in s$, $\neg\phi \in s$, $\psi \in s$, $\neg\psi \in s$.

From right to left: by ***Definition 3.3***, if $(\phi \nmid \psi) \notin s$:

Assume $\phi \wedge \psi \notin s$, as $\phi \in s$ and $\psi \in s$, then $\phi \wedge \neg\psi \in s$ and $\neg\phi \wedge \psi \in s$. Since $\neg(\phi|\psi) \in s$, then $\neg\phi \wedge \neg\psi \in s$. That implies $\phi|\neg\psi \in s$, a contradiction.

The other cases are same as above.

Fact 2. *For every model $\mathcal{M} = (W, V, B, F)$, let $u \in W$, then:*

(1) If $\mathcal{M}, u \vDash K(\phi \nmid \psi)$, then $\mathcal{M}, u \vDash K(\neg(\phi|\psi) \wedge \neg(\neg\phi|\psi) \wedge \neg(\phi|\neg\psi) \wedge \neg(\neg\phi|\neg\psi) \wedge \neg(\phi||\psi) \wedge \neg(\neg\phi||\psi))$.

(2) If $\mathcal{M}, u \vDash K(\neg(\phi|\psi) \wedge \neg(\neg\phi|\psi) \wedge \neg(\phi|\neg\psi) \wedge \neg(\neg\phi|\neg\psi) \wedge \neg(\phi||\psi) \wedge \neg(\neg\phi||\psi)) \wedge K\neg K\neg\phi \wedge K\neg K\phi \wedge K\neg K\neg\psi \wedge K\neg K\psi$, then $\mathcal{M}, u \vDash K(\phi \nmid \psi)$.

[12] This condition can be regard as the preservation of monotonicity under substitution in higher-order knowledge and relevant conditions.

[13] At a specific state, ϕ and ψ both have certain values, this situation contradicts our desired intuition, hence $\mathcal{M}, u \vDash (\phi|\psi)$ is always false.

Proof. (1): Suppose $\mathcal{M}, u \vDash K(\phi \nmid \psi)$, that is for every $s \in F(u)$: $\neg(\phi|\psi) \wedge \neg(\neg\phi|\psi) \wedge \neg(\phi|\neg\psi) \wedge \neg(\neg\phi|\neg\psi) \wedge \neg(\phi||\psi) \wedge \neg(\neg\phi||\psi) \in s$, then for every $s \in F(u)$: $(\phi|\psi) \notin s$, $(\neg\phi|\psi) \notin s$, $(\phi|\neg\psi) \notin s$, $(\neg\phi|\neg\psi) \notin s$, $(\phi||\psi) \notin s$, $(\neg\phi|\psi) \notin s$. That implies for every $s \in F(u)$: $(\phi|\psi) \vee (\neg\phi|\psi) \vee (\phi|\neg\psi) \vee (\neg\phi|\neg\psi) \vee (\phi||\psi) \vee (\neg\phi||\psi) \notin s$, then $\mathcal{M}, u \vDash K(\neg(\phi|\psi) \wedge \neg(\neg\phi|\psi) \wedge \neg(\phi|\neg\psi) \wedge \neg(\neg\phi|\neg\psi) \wedge \neg(\phi||\psi) \wedge \neg(\neg\phi||\psi))$.

(2): Suppose $\mathcal{M}, u \vDash K(\neg(\phi|\psi) \wedge \neg(\neg\phi|\psi) \wedge \neg(\phi|\neg\psi) \wedge \neg(\neg\phi|\neg\psi) \wedge \neg(\phi||\psi) \wedge \neg(\neg\phi||\psi)) \wedge K\neg K\neg\phi \wedge K\neg K\phi \wedge K\neg K\neg\psi \wedge K\neg K\psi$, that implies for every $s \in F(u)$: $\neg(\phi|\psi) \wedge \neg(\neg\phi|\psi) \wedge \neg(\phi|\neg\psi) \wedge \neg(\neg\phi|\neg\psi) \wedge \neg(\phi||\psi) \wedge \neg(\neg\phi||\psi) \in s$ and $\phi \in s$, $\neg\phi \in s$, $\psi \in s$, $\neg\psi \in s$. By **Fact** 1, for every $s \in F(u)$:$(\phi \nmid \psi) \in s$, that is $\mathcal{M}, u \vDash K(\phi \nmid \psi)$.

Bcak to the Barber Shop example, (α) $\neg c \rightarrow (\neg a \rightarrow b)$ can retain its original or be formalized as $\neg c|(\neg a \rightarrow b)$. However, it cannot be formalized as $\neg c \rightarrow (\neg a|b)$, because when $\neg c$ holds, the truth values only allow $a \wedge b$ and $a \wedge \neg b$, whereas $(\neg a|b)$ also requires $\neg a \wedge b$.

(β) only aims to negate $\neg a \wedge b$, but $(\neg a \rightarrow b)$ holds in multiple truth situations, so it cannot be negated. (β) can be formalized as $\neg(\neg a|b)$, because $(\neg a|b)$ requires every truth cases must exist. Once $\neg a \wedge b$ is negated, $(\neg a|b)$ is negated.

Thus, based on EL_{PKB} formalization of the example above, we find that it does not be Modus Tollens. Note that $a|(b|c)$ always fails to hold here, as the internal $(b|c)$ is always either true or false, while $a|\top$ and $a|\bot$ never hold.

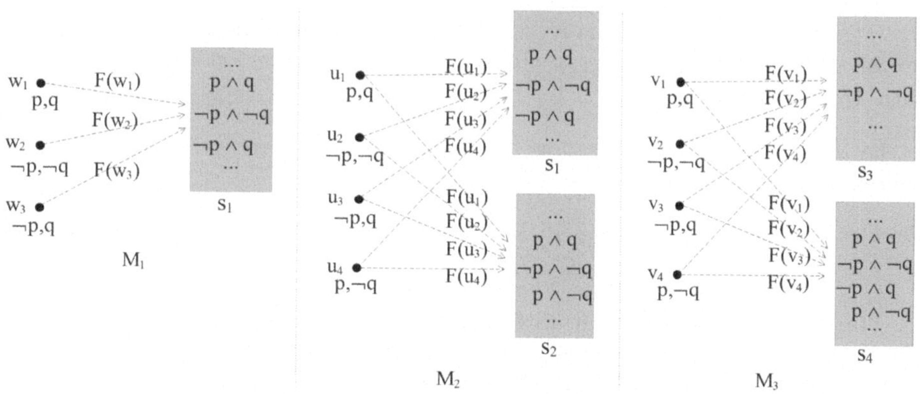

Fig. 2. The semantic model of the Candy House example.

Back to the Candy House example. In fig.2, models M_1, M_2 and M_3 respond to the characteristics of agents' cognitive states under the three scenarios in fig.1. States w_1, w_2, w_3, u_1, v_1 etc., represent actual-world situations. For instance, in world w_3, milk candy does not appear when the button is pressed, while fruit candy does. PKBs s_1, s_2, s_3, and s_4 represent the knowledge combinations an agent might possess in a given state, each corresponding to the properties of Candy Box 1, 2, 3, and 4, respectively. From fig.2, we obtain the following results:

In the case of the Box1, the relationship between the two cognitively uncertain propositions p and q is formalized as $(p|q)$. The situation in Box 2 should be $(q|p)$, the situation in Box 3 should be $(p||q)$, the situation in Box 4 should be $(p \nmid q)$. Meanwhile, the cognition of agent on the first day should be $K(p|q)$. The first case on the second day should be $\neg K\neg(p|q) \wedge \neg K\neg(q|p) \wedge K((p|q) \vee (q|p))$. The second case should be $\neg K\neg(p||q) \wedge \neg K\neg(p \nmid q) \wedge K((p||q) \wedge (p \nmid q))$.

For example, based on M_1 in Fig. 2, let us first examine possible world w_1: For every $s \in F(w_1)$, specifically s_1, the following holds: $p \wedge q \in s_1$, $\neg p \wedge \neg q \in s_1$, $\neg p \wedge q \in s_1$, $p \wedge \neg q \notin s_1$. By ***Definition 3.3.4***, this means $(p|q) \in s_1$. By ***Definition 3.3.1***, it follows that $\neg(p|q) \notin s_1$. Applying ***Definition*** 4, we derive $M_1, w_1 \models K(p|q)$. Similarly, we obtain $M_1, w_2 \models K(p|q)$ and $M_1, w_3 \models K(p|q)$. Thus, the agent's epistemic judgment in this scenario is $K(p|q)$.

3 Some Properties of Possible Knowledge Bases

Fact 3. *Let s be a set of formulas defined above, then:*

(1) $\neg(K(\phi \to \psi) \to (K\phi \to K\psi)) \notin s$.
(2) $\neg(K(\phi \wedge \psi) \leftrightarrow (K\phi \wedge K\psi)) \notin s$.
(3) $\neg(\neg K\neg(\phi \vee \psi) \leftrightarrow (\neg K\neg\phi \vee \neg K\neg\psi)) \notin s$.

Proof. We will prove (1), and (2)(3) are same.

If there is s such that $\neg(K(\phi \to \psi) \to (K\phi \to K\psi)) \in s$ holds, then $K(\phi \to \psi) \wedge \neg(K\phi \to K\psi) \in s$. That is $K(\phi \to \psi) \wedge K\phi \wedge \neg K\psi \in s$, by ***Definition3.2.2***, we can see $(\neg\phi \vee \psi) \wedge (\phi \wedge \neg\psi) \in s$, that is $(\phi \wedge \neg\psi) \wedge \neg(\phi \wedge \neg\psi) \in s$, a contradiction with ***Definition 3.1.7***.

By ***Definition 3.2.3***, fix β as $\top$, we can see s can preserve uniform substitution:

Fact 4. *Let α be formula and α^p_ϕ be result of replacing p by ϕ. For any formula set s defined above, if $\alpha \in s$, then $\alpha^p_\phi \in s$.*

This corollary ensures that all fundamental validities of normal modal logic persist in every possible knowledge base, with their existential integrity preserved under uniform substitution.Consequently, we get the following proposition:

Proposition 1. *For any $s \in B$, let s' be a maximal subset of s that contains no formulas in which $|$, $||$, $\nmid$ occur. Then s' is a normal modal logic.(define $\Box$ as K)*

Furthermore, we formally designate s' as the Basic Epistemic Modal Logic (BEML) fragment of s. This framework establishes deeper structural connections between arbitrary possible knowledge bases s and Kripke models: For every $s \in B$ there exists a unique s' and an corresponded Kripke model $\mathcal{N}$.

Corollary 1. *Each $s \in B$ is in bijective correspondence with its designated fragment s'.*

Prior to the construction of corresponding Kripke models, it is imperative to formally define the 'size' of formula set s:

Definition 5. *For every $s \in B$, let s' be the BEML-fragment of s. If there are at least n sets $a_1, ..., a_n$ s.t. $s' \subseteq \bigcup a_i$ and for each a_i: $\phi \in a_i$ if and only if $\neg\phi \notin a_i$.*[14] *Then we define $rank(s') = n$.*[15]

Example 1. Fix $s \in B$ and let $\{p, \neg p, q, \neg q, p \wedge q, \neg p \wedge q, p \wedge \neg q\} \subseteq s'$. Then s' needs to be divided into at least 3 subsets, which are: $\{p, q\}, \{\neg p, q\}, \{p, \neg q\}$.

Next, we can correspond s to a Kripke model.

Definition 6. *Let $s \in B$ and s' be the BEML-fragment of s. Let $rank(s') = n$, and the sets are $a_1, ..., a_n$. Let $\mathcal{N} = (W', R', V')$ be a Kripke model where:*

- *$|W'| = rank(s')$ and $W' = \{u_1, ..., u_n\}$;*
- *R' is the binary relation on W' defined by $R'u_iu_j$ if and only if for all formulas ϕ, $\phi \in a_j$ implies $\neg K \neg \phi \in a_i$;*
- *V' is the valuation defined by $u_i \in V'(p)$ if and only if $p \in a_i$.*

This definition is similar to the way that canonical models are defined in basic modal logic. In the same way, we can also prove the results we want by the corresponding existence lemma and truth lemma.

Lemma 1. *Fix a formula set s, let s' be the BEML-fragment of s. Then*

1. *if $\neg K \neg \phi \in a_i$, then there is $u_j \in W$ such that $R'u_iu_j$ and $\phi \in a_j$;*
2. *$\phi \in a_i$ if and only if $\mathcal{N}, u_i \vDash \phi$.*

Proof. Similar to the proof of existence lemma and truth lemma of basic modal logic.

Proposition 2. *(1) $\phi \in s$ if and only if there is $\phi \in a_i$ and $u_i \in W'$ s.t. $\mathcal{N}, u_i \vDash \phi$. (2) $\neg\phi \notin s$ if and only if $\mathcal{N} \vDash \phi$.*

Proof. By ***Lemma 1.2***, (1) is immediate,(2) can be obtained by (1) taking the inverse negative proposition.

Building upon the aforementioned propositions, each BEML fragment of knowledge base s bijectively corresponds to a Kripke model. Intuitively, possible knowledge bases can be viewed as epistemic state composites, over which propositional relevance operators act upon such composites.

To extend this framework to strictly relevant sufficient condition operators, we must employ global modal logic (alternatively termed universal modal logic). This enhanced system introduces dual global modalities E and U, Specifically:

[14] Avoid the notion of consistency since there are no syntactic definitions involved here.

[15] As the countability of the propositional variables set Φ, $rank(s') \leqslant \aleph_1$.

$$\mathcal{M}, w \models E\phi \text{ if and only if } \exists u \in W : \mathcal{M}, u \models \phi;$$

$$\mathcal{M}, w \models U\phi \text{ if and only if } \forall u \in W : \mathcal{M}, u \models \phi.$$

The axiom system, completeness and model definability of global modal logic can be referred to some references [22–24].

Proposition 3. *For every $s \in B$, let $\mathcal{N}$ be the Kripke model generated by s'. Then $(\phi|\psi) \in s$ if and only if $E(\phi \wedge \psi) \wedge E(\neg\phi \wedge \psi) \wedge E(\neg\phi \wedge \neg\psi) \wedge \neg E(\phi \wedge \neg\psi)$ is satisfied in $\mathcal{N}$. $(\phi||\psi) \in s$ if and only if $E(\phi \wedge \psi) \wedge E(\neg\phi \wedge \neg\psi) \wedge \neg E(\neg\phi \wedge \psi) \wedge \neg E(\phi \wedge \neg\psi)$ is satisfied in $\mathcal{N}$. $(\phi \nmid \psi) \in s$ if and only if $E(\phi \wedge \psi) \wedge E(\neg\phi \wedge \neg\psi) \wedge E(\neg\phi \wedge \psi) \wedge E(\phi \wedge \neg\psi)$ is satisfied in $\mathcal{N}$.*

Proposition 4. *Let $\mathcal{M} = (W, V, B, F)$ be a model, for every $s \in B$, there is a kripke model $\mathcal{N}_s$, translate $(a|b)$, $(a||b)$, $(a \nmid b)$as above. Then for all formulas ϕ, $\phi \in s$ if and only if ϕ is satisfied in $\mathcal{N}_s$.*

For any $s \in B$, $\mathcal{N}_s$ is defined as a Kripke model generated by s, and $\mathcal{N}_B = \{\mathcal{N}_s | s \in B\}$ is a class of Kripke models generated by M.

4 Model Properties and Corresponding Definitions

Proposition 5. *Here are some formulas that are valid in the model:*

(1) $K\phi \rightarrow KK\phi$.
(2) $K(\phi|\psi) \rightarrow K(\phi \rightarrow \psi)$.
(3) $K\phi \rightarrow \neg(K(\phi|\psi) \vee K(\phi||\psi) \vee K(\phi \nmid \psi))$.

Proof. The proof of (1):let $\mathcal{M} = (W, V, B, F)$ be a model, for any state $u \in W$, suppose $\mathcal{M}, u \models K\phi$. Then for every $s \in F(u)$, $\neg\phi \notin s$, by ***Definition 3.2.1***, we have $\neg K\phi \notin s$. Therefore, $\mathcal{M}, u \models KK\phi$.

Proposition 5(1) corresponds to the positive introspection property in epistemic logic. In basic epistemic logic, the realization of an agent's positive introspection requires the Kripke model to be defined over a transitive frame class. However, within the possible knowledge base model framework, positive introspection becomes an inherently valid property.

Note that: the necessitation rule (RN) from the Hilbert-style calculus of basic modal logic fails here. While $\mathcal{M} \models K\phi \rightarrow KK\phi$ holds universally across all EL_{PKB} models, one can construct the countermodel: $\mathcal{M}' \not\models K(K\phi \rightarrow KK\phi)$.

Intuitively, this implies that truths of the world do not necessarily constitute agent's knowledge. In basic modal logic, RN can be interpreted as a form of global semantic consequence: $\phi \models^g_{\mathbb{M}} \Box\phi$. Although RN does not hold in EL_{PKB}, we demonstrate that global semantic consequences remain locally preservable:

Proposition 6. *Let $s \in B$ and $\mathcal{N}$ be the generated model by s. For all formulas ϕ and ψ, if $\phi \Vdash^g_{\mathcal{N}} \psi$, then for every $\mathcal{M}$, $\mathcal{M} \models K\phi \rightarrow K\psi$.*

Proof. Suppose $\phi \Vdash^g_{\mathcal{N}} \psi$ and there is a model $\mathcal{M} = (W, V, B, F)$ such that $\mathcal{M} \vDash K\phi$. Then for any $s \in B$, $\neg\phi \notin s$, by ***Proposition*** 4 $\mathcal{N} \vDash \phi$. As $\phi \Vdash^g_{\mathcal{N}} \psi$, we have $\mathcal{N} \vDash \psi$, by ***Proposition*** 4, $\neg\psi \notin s$ and $\mathcal{M} \vDash K\psi$. Therefore $\mathcal{M} \vDash K\phi \to K\psi$.

When we introduce more definitions of possible knowledge bases sets B and functions F, we can bring some new properties to EL_{PKB} model:

Proposition 7. *Let $\mathcal{M} = (W, V, B, F)$ be a model, such that for every $s \in B$, if $\phi \wedge \psi \in s$ entails $\phi \wedge \neg K \neg \psi \in s$, then $\mathcal{M} \vDash K(K\phi \to \phi)$.*
Proof. Suppose $u \in W$ and $\mathcal{M}, u \vDash \neg K(K\phi \to \phi)$. Then there is $s \in F(u)$ s.t. $\neg(K\phi \to \phi) \in s$, that is $K\phi \wedge \neg\phi \in s$. Define $\psi_1 := K\phi$ and $\psi_2 := \neg\phi$, then we see $\psi_1 \wedge \psi_2 \in s$, hence $\psi_1 \wedge \neg K \neg \psi_2 \in s$. Therefore $K\phi \wedge \neg K \neg\neg\phi \in s$, by

Definition 3.2.2, $\phi \wedge \neg\phi \in s$, a contradiction.

We can also obtain the model properties of the model $\mathcal{N}$ generated by s.

Proposition 8. *Let $\mathcal{M} = (W, V, B, F)$ be a model, such that for every $s \in B$, if $\phi \wedge \psi \in s$ entails $\phi \wedge \neg K \neg \psi \in s$, then $\mathcal{N}_B$ is a class of reflexive models.*
Proof. As $\mathcal{M} \vDash K(K\phi \to \phi)$, then for every $s \in B$, $\neg(K\phi \to \phi) \notin s$. By ***Proposition*** 4, that is $\mathcal{N}_s \vDash K\phi \to \phi$. Then, for every state $a \in \mathcal{N}_s$ and every formula ϕ, $\mathcal{N}_B, a \vDash K\phi$ implies $\mathcal{N}_s, a \vDash \phi$, by ***Definition*** 6, $(a, a) \in R$. Therefore, $\mathcal{N}_s$ is a reflexive model and $\mathcal{N}_B$ is a class of reflexive models.

Since RN is absent, we can only attain the cognitive recognition of knowledge's facticity–that agents know their knowledge is correct–by corresponding possible knowledge bases with reflexive Kripke models.

Crucially, even with epistemic recognition of knowledge facticity, this does not guarantee the factual grounding of the agent's knowledge ($K\phi \to \phi$). Additional conditionals are required to enforce such factual correspondence.

Notably, while ***Proposition*** 5 demonstrates the universal validity of positive introspection within EL_{PKB}, $K(K\phi \to KK\phi)$ is not universal valid.

Next, we give the conditions for $K(K\phi \to KK\phi)$ to be valid and prove it:

Proposition 9. *Let $\mathcal{M} = (W, V, B, F)$ be a model, such that for every $s \in B$, if $\psi \wedge \neg KK\neg\phi \in s$ implies $\psi \wedge \neg K \neg \phi \in s$, then:*

- *$\mathcal{M} \vDash K(K\phi \to KK\phi)$;*
- *$\mathcal{N}_B$ is a class of transitive models.*

Proof. (1) Suppose $u \in W$ and $\mathcal{M}, u \vDash \neg K(K\phi \to KK\phi)$. Then there is $s \in F(u)$ s.t. $\neg(K\phi \to KK\phi) \in s$, that is $K\phi \wedge \neg KK\phi \in s$. Define $\psi_1 := K\phi$ and $\psi_2 := \neg\phi$, then $\psi_1 \wedge \neg KK\neg\psi_2 \in s$, hence $\psi_1 \wedge \neg K \neg \psi_2 \in s$. That is $K\phi \wedge \neg K \neg\neg\phi$, a contradiction.

(2) As $\mathcal{M} \vDash K(K\phi \to KK\phi)$, then for every $s \in B$, $\neg(K\phi \to KK\phi) \notin s$. By ***Proposition*** 4, that is $\mathcal{N}_s \vDash K\phi \to KK\phi$. Then, for every model $\mathcal{N}_s \in \mathcal{N}_B$ and state $a \in \mathcal{N}_s$ and every formula ϕ, we have $\mathcal{N}_s, a \vDash K\phi$ implies $\mathcal{N}_s, a \vDash KK\phi$. Therefore, $\mathcal{N}_s$ is a transitive model and $\mathcal{N}_B$ is a class of transitive models.

In fact, the model enables the expression of numerous different properties, which meaningfully distinguish the cognitive capacities of agents. The Table 1 below visually illustrates the relationships between these cognitive capabilities and the properties and definitions of the model.

Table 1. Cognitive properties and model conditions

Conditions	Rules and Formulas	$\mathcal{N}_B$	Cognitive capabilities
$p \in s$ implies $\exists u \in W$ s.t $u \in V(p)$	$\mathcal{M} \vDash p$ entails $\mathcal{M} \vDash Kp$.	/	Propositional generalization
$u \vDash p$ implies $\exists s \in B$ s.t $p \in s$	$\mathcal{M} \vDash Kp \rightarrow p$	/	Propositional facticity
$\phi \wedge \psi \in s$ implies $\phi \wedge \neg K \neg \psi \in s$	$\mathcal{M} \vDash K(K\phi \rightarrow \phi)$	Reflexive	Cognitive facticity
$\psi \wedge \neg KK \neg \phi \in s$ implies $\psi \wedge \neg K \neg \phi \in s$	$\mathcal{M} \vDash K(K\phi \rightarrow KK\phi)$	Transitive	Cognitive positive introspection
$\phi \wedge \psi \in s$ implies $\phi \wedge K \neg K \neg \psi \in s$	$\mathcal{M} \vDash K(\phi \rightarrow K \neg K \neg \phi)$	Symmetric	Knowing the negation of true propositions is not knowledge
$\phi \in s$ implies $\neg K \neg \phi \in s$	$\mathcal{M} \vDash KK\phi \rightarrow K\phi$	Left-unbounded	No unrecognized state
for every $s \in B$, $K \bot \notin s$	$\mathcal{M} \vDash K \neg K \neg \top$	Right-unbounded	No state without recognizing

5 Future Prospects

One open problem deserving further investigation is the axiomatization of EL_{PKB}. We have demonstrated that the RN principle fails to hold and established a weaker version (Proposition 6). It remains critical to explore how these findings will alter and challenge the axiomatization framework.

Another significant research direction lies in knowledge revision and update mechanisms within EL_{PKB}. The structural properties of possible knowledge bases give rise to two distinct operational modalities for epistemic updates in EL_{PKB}: (1) altering the mapping $F(u)$ at state u, and (2) modifying the constituent possible knowledge bases s. When combined with an agent's varying cognitive capacities, these operations may hold greater research significance or reveal novel theoretical insights into their interplay. In the future, we can also integrate "knowledge revision and update mechanisms within EL_{PKB}" to assist AI systems in enhancing the evaluation of logical relevance within a dynamic cognitive framework and improving reasoning under uncertainty.

Acknowledgments. This study was funded by the Major Project of the National Social Science Foundation (19ZDA041).

References

1. Chen, X.: Research on formalization and semantic interpretations of correlation degree prediction in large language models. CAAI Trans. Intell. Syst. **18**, 894–900 (2023)
2. Scholes, M.S.: Artificial intelligence and uncertainty. Risk Sci. **1**, 100004 (2025)
3. Bastounis, A., Campodonico, P., van der Schaar, M., Adcock, B., Hansen, A.C.: On the consistent reasoning paradox of intelligence and optimal trust in AI: the power of "I don't know". arXiv:abs/2408.02357 (2024)
4. Gibbins, P.: Material implication, the sufficiency condition, and conditional proof. Analysis **39**(1), 21–24 (1979)
5. Levin, Y.: Sufficient conditions, conditional logic, and transitivity. KRITERION – J. Philos. **17**(1), 15–22 (2003)
6. Lewis, C.I.: Strict implication–an emendation. J Philos. Psychol. Sci. Methods **17**(11), 300–302 (1920)
7. Gherardi, G., Orlandelli, E.: Non-normal super-strict implications. In: Non-Classical Logic. Theory and Applications (2022)

8. Anderson, A.R., et al.: Entailment: The Logic of Relevance and Neccessity, Vol. I. Princeton University Press, Princeton (1975)
9. Makinson, D.: Relevance Logic as a Conservative Extension of Classical Logic. In: Hansson, S. (ed.), David Makinson on Classical Methods for Non-Classical Problems, vol. 3 of Outstanding Contributions to Logic. Springer, Dordrecht (2014)
10. Sedlár, I., Vigiani, P.: Epistemic logics for relevant reasoners. J. Philos. Log. **53**, 1383–1411 (2024)
11. Väänänen, J.: Modal Dependence Logic. In: Apt, K.R., and van Rooij, R. (eds.) New Perspectives on Games and Interaction, vol. 4 of Texts in Logic and Games, pp. 237–254. Amsterdam University Press, Amsterdam (2008)
12. Väänänen, J.: Dependence Logic: A New Approach to Independence-Friendly Logic. Vol. 70 of London Mathematical Society Student Texts. Cambridge University Press, Cambridge (2007)
13. Hintikka, J.: The Principles of Mathematics Revisited. Cambridge University Press, Cambridge (1996)
14. Kontinen, J., Müller, J., Schnoor, H., and Vollmer, H.: Modal independence logic. J. Logic Comput. **27**(5), 1333–1352 (2017)
15. Lakemeyer, G.: Relevance from an epistemic perspective. Artif. Intell. **97**, 137–167 (1997)
16. Wen, X.: A modal logic for reasoning in contexts. In: AiML 2024, pp. 719–740 (2024)
17. Makinson, D.: Propositional relevance through letter-sharing. J. Appl. Log. **7**, 377–387 (2009)
18. Jarmużek, T.: Relating semantics as fine-grained semantics for intensional propositional logics. In: Giordani, A., Malinowski, J. (eds.) Logic in High Definition, pp. 13–30. Springer, Trends in Logical Semantics (2020)
19. Carroll, L.: A logical paradox. Mind **3**(11), 436–438 (1894)
20. Laplace, P.S.: Théorie analytique des probabilités. Courcier, Paris (1820)
21. Liu, F.: Diversity of agents and their interaction. J. Log Lang. Inf. **18**, 23–53 (2009)
22. Goranko, V., Passy, S.: Using the universal modality: gains and questions. J. Log. Comput. **2**, 5–30 (1992)
23. van Benthem, J.: The range of modal logic. J. Appl. Non Class. Logics **9** (1999)
24. Blackburn, P., de Rijke, M., Venema, Y.: Modal logic. In: Cambridge Tracts in Theoretical Computer Science (2001)

Formal Concept Analysis Applied in Knowledge Network: A Survey

Xv Zhang[1] and Weizhuo Li[1,2(✉)]

[1] School of Modern Posts, Nanjing University of Posts and Telecommunications, Nanjing, China
liweizhuo@amss.ac.cn

[2] State Key Laboratory for Novel Software Technology, Nanjing University, Nanjing, People's Republic of China

Abstract. With the rapid iterative development of artificial intelligence (AI) technologies, knowledge network is one of the core ways to express massive information, and the requirements of semantic analysis and knowledge mining of it are becoming more and more important. As a mathematical tool based on lattice theory, Formal Concept Analysis (FCA) has gradually attracted the attention of AI researchers in recent years because of its advantages of convenient modeling, strong interpretability and deep network node characteristics mining. As the summary of FCA's research works on knowledge network is lagging, we present a survey that first focuses on the research works of FCA for knowledge networks. We systematically summarize the existing methods from knowledge graph, social networks, semantic representations, machine learning and data mining. Finally, we give an outlook on the future directions of FCA applied in the knowledge network.

Keywords: Formal Concept Analysis · Knowledge Network · Knowledge Graph · Social Network · Semantic Representation

1 Introduction

With the rapid development of artificial intelligence (AI) technologies such as Large Language Models, Deep Learning and Knowledge Graph, Knowledge Network, as one of the core ways to express massive information and knowledge, its expression mode and analysis technology become more and more important. Nevertheless, how to represent the complex semantic relations of knowledge network efficiently and mine its deep knowledge association efficiently, has become the common concern of academia and industry. Formal Concept Analysis (FCA), as a mathematical tool based on lattice theory, has gradually attracted the attention of researchers of knowledge representation and reasoning in recent years because of its unique advantages in modeling convenience, strong interpretability and deep network node characteristics mining [1–3].

FCA constructs concept lattice (CL) through formal context (FC), and then presents the implicit relationship in data in an intuitive and structured way. For knowledge graph

M. Bonsangue and Y. Chen (Eds.): AILA 2025, CCIS 2668, pp. 64–78, 2026.
https://doi.org/10.1007/978-981-95-8262-4_5

completion, by analyzing the entities and their relationships in the knowledge graph, FCA can discover new semantic associations, supplement the lacking triples of the knowledge graph and improve its ability to reason [4, 5]. In the field of social network analysis, FCA has shown its unique value applied in community detection and relationship prediction. It regards users and their interactions in social networks as a formal context. Then, it identifies users with similar interests or behavior patterns. Finally, it could predict potential social relationships and provide strong support for personalized recommendation and information dissemination analysis [6, 7]. In the task of semantic representation, FCA transforms the complex semantic information into a structured concept lattice, which can enable the search engines to understand and process natural language texts more effectively, so that the performances of natural language processing tasks could be improved, such as information retrieval and text classification. In addition, it can help researchers and data analysts to discover hidden patterns and features in data [8–10]. Recently, the integration of FCA and Machine Learning technology provides a new idea that builds an intelligent system with strong interpretability and expressivity [11].

Combined with symbols reasoning and statistics reasoning has always become one of the most important research topics in AI. Although FCA has made several remarkable progresses in both theoretical research and practical application, the summary of research works about FCA applied in Knowledge Networks [12–14] is lagging. It is difficult to reflect on the latest developments and applications of FCA in knowledge networks. To fill this research gap, we try to collect the FCA's research works applied in the knowledge network in the past 20 years and conduct a comprehensive survey of them. Precisely, we systematically summarize the existing methods from knowledge graph, social networks, semantic representations, machine learning and data mining, and provide an outlook on future directions of FCA applied in knowledge network.

The rest of this paper is organized as follows. We present background knowledge in Sect. 2. We summarize existing works of FCA applied in knowledge network and give a comparison of them in Sect. 3. Section 4 shows the limitations of FCA and its Optimized works, followed by the conclusions and future direction in Sect. 5.

2 Preliminary

In this section, we first introduce basic notions of FCA, including formal context, formal concept and so on. Then, we display an example of FCA and related tool. Finally, we present Knowledge Network and its different representations.

2.1 Formal Concept Analysis

Formal Concept Analysis theory is mainly based on the groundbreaking work published by Ganter and Wille. FCA takes an input table, specifies a group of objects and their attributes, and finds the natural clusters of all attributes and all objects in the input data. Among them, the input table is called Formal Context, and the natural object cluster is a collection of all objects sharing a subset of common attributes, and also a collection of all attributes shared by one of the natural object clusters. At the same time, natural attribute clustering corresponds to natural object clustering one by one. Such a pair of natural object clusters and natural attribute clusters form a concept, which is considered the formal unit of human thinking [15]. It is based on a philosophical understanding that a concept consists of two parts: its extension belongs to all the objects of the concept, and its connotation consists of all the attributes shared by these objects. These concepts show an inductive hierarchy when organized into a lattice. A set of algorithms based on tools such as meaning and exploration are used to construct such a Formal Concept Lattice, which is helpful to further infer from the ideas clearly expressed as formal concepts.

The Formal Context [16] is given by a triple (G, M, I) and is denoted as K. This tuple consists of two sets G and M, as well as the relationship I between G and M. The elements of G are called the sets of objects, the elements of M are called the sets of attributes of the objects. I is defined as a binary relation $I \subseteq G \times M$, where (g, m) in I if and only if object g has attribute m. The tuples (A_i, B_i) are derived from the formal context (G, M, I), where A is the set of objects and B is the set of attributes. For each object in A that is not in A_i, there is an attribute in B_i that this object does not have. For each attribute in B that is not in B_i, there is an object in A_i that does not have this attribute.

For example, in the following text, we take four animals, Lion, Bee, Eagle, and Clownfish, as objects and take certain characteristics they possess as attributes. If the animal has the corresponding characteristics, then we associate the animal object with the attribute of that characteristic. The data in Table 1 is an example of a formal context, where the behavior objects are listed as attributes. Among them, the cell " ×" indicates that the object has this attribute. For example, the animal Lion has the characteristic of "Gregarious".

Table 1. An example of a formal context

	Terrestrial	Has the Tail	Gregarious	Eats nectar	Can fly	Has 6 legs
Lion	×	×	×			
Bee	×		×	×	×	×
Eagle	×	×			×	
Clownfish		×	×			

Formal concepts in FCA are defined as pairs (A, B), where $A \subseteq G, B \subseteq M$, and:

$$\begin{aligned} B &= \{m \in M \mid \forall g \in A : (g, m) \in I\} \\ A &= \{g \in G \mid \forall m \in B : (g, m) \in I\} \end{aligned} \tag{1}$$

According to Formula (1), the formal concept satisfies the following conditions: A is the set of all objects with the attribute set B; B is the set of all common attributes of the object set A [16, 17].

In the formal context, the relationship between objects and attributes is defined through the binary relation I. Specifically, for an object $g \in G$ and its property $m \in M$. If $(g, m) \in I$, it indicates that the object g has the property m. This kind of relationship can be deterministic (such as 1 and 0 in a binary matrix), or fuzzy (such as membership degree in a fuzzy relationship).

The Galois connection is a special correspondence between two partially ordered sets, that is, every connection of Galois languages will produce an isomorphic relationship. Galois duality is the Galois connection between two mutually dual partially ordered sets [18]. It is defined as follows:

Let $(A, \leq)$ and $(B, \leq)$ be two partially ordered sets, and the Galois connection between them is composed of two monotonic functions $F : A \rightarrow B$ and $G : B \rightarrow A$. Therefore, for all $a \in A$ and $b \in B$, we have:

$$F(a) \leq \mathit{bifa} \leq G(b), \tag{2}$$

When defining a concept as a pair (A, B), where A is the extension and B is the connotation, FCA considers a Galois duality. By minimizing one of A and B, we can always maximize the other, and vice versa.

The concept lattice is a lattice structure composed of all formal concepts according to the containment relationship, represented as $\mathcal{B}(G, M, I)$. In the concept lattice, there are two fundamental relationships between concepts [19]:

① Order Relation [16]: (A_1, B_1) and (A_2, B_2) are formal concepts in the Formal Concept Lattice $\mathcal{B}(G, M, I)$. The subconcept relationship represented by $\leq$ is as shown in Formula (3):

$$((A_1, B_1), \leq, (A_2, B_2)) \leftrightarrow A_1 \subseteq A_2, \leftrightarrow B_2 \subseteq B_1, \tag{3}$$

② Join and Meet: The Join of two concepts (A_1, B_1) and (A_2, B_2) is their least upper bound, denoted as $(A_1, B_1) \vee (A_2, B_2)$; Their Meet is their maximum lower bound, denoted as $(A_1, B_1) \wedge (A_2, B_2)$.

The Galois connections between concepts can be visualized in the form of concept lattices. The formal concept cells in Table 1 can be visualized using the Conexp-clj tool. Each individual node represents the formal concept in the concept cell, as shown in Fig. 1.

Conexp-clj is an FCA tool based on the Clojure language, aiming to provide efficient computing performance and flexible scalability. Its core algorithm is based on the construction and operation of concept lattices and utilizes the functional programming characteristics of Clojure to achieve efficient processing of large-scale datasets. Conexp-clj supports multiple FCA algorithms, including the Close-by-One(CbO) algorithm and its variants [20]. These algorithms can enumerate the closure set in a polynomial delay manner, ensuring the efficiency and accuracy of the calculation process. The development and application of Conexp-clj have been verified in multiple studies. For instance, Hanika [21] et al. described in detail the implementation and performance evaluation of Conexp-clj in their research, demonstrating its efficiency and reliability when dealing with large-scale datasets.

The process of using Conexp-clj is as follows: First, convert the input data into a formal context, that is, a triple (G, M, I), where $I \subseteq G \times M$ is the binary relation between the object and the property. Then, by using the CbO algorithm, the concept

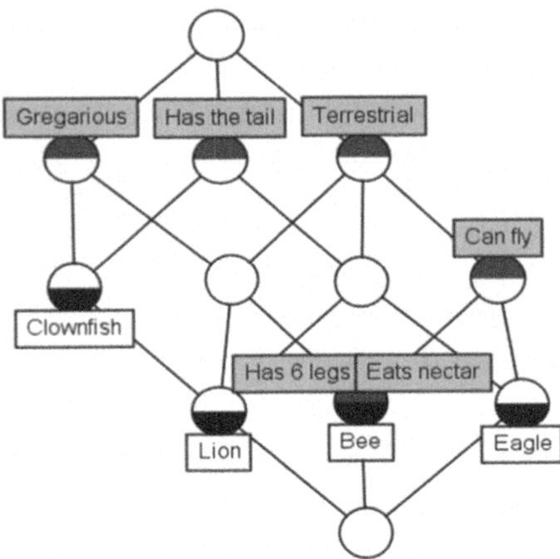

Fig. 1. The visualization of the formal concept grid in Table 1

lattice is gradually constructed from the formal context. The CbO algorithm gradually expands the closure set to ensure that the generation of each concept is based on the existing closures, thereby avoiding duplicate calculations. Conexp-clj supports various operations on concept lattices, including concept merging, splitting, filtering, etc., for further analysis and visualization.

Conexp-clj performs well when dealing with large-scale datasets, especially in the scenario of large-scale datasets, where it can efficiently handle datasets containing tens of thousands of objects and attributes. Meanwhile, it is applicable to processing data with multi-level structures and complex relationships, and supports incremental updates, capable of quickly updating the concept lattice when the data changes [20].

However, since this tool often processes by enumerating closure sets, in the worst case, the time complexity is $O(2^M)$ (where M is the attribute set), making it difficult to directly handle large-scale data. Moreover, recursive calls and intermediate closure storage may lead to memory bottlenecks, especially when there are a large number of attributes.

2.2 Knowledge Network

As one of the core ways to express massive information and knowledge, knowledge network has become more and more important in semantic analysis and knowledge mining. How to achieve above tasks has become the common concerns of academia and industry. In this section, we divide the knowledge network into three forms (i.e., directed graph, undirected graph and hypergraph), and exemplify them through knowledge graph, social network and complex events, respectively.

The directed graph is defined as $G = (V, E)$, where V is a set of nodes, which is a non-empty finite set, and E is an edge set, which is a directed edge. Each directed edge is composed of ordered the vertex pairs in vertex set V. The main representative of a directed graph is the knowledge graph (KG). As a semantic network based on graph structure, knowledge graph is used to represent entities and their semantic relationships, aiming at realizing the structural modeling of real-world knowledge. Among them, nodes represent objects in the real world, and have unique identities and attributes; The edge represents the semantic association between entities, which has directionality and types, such as attribute relationship and hierarchical relationship [22]. The basic unit of knowledge graph, is shaped like a triple of $(Entity1, Relationship, Entity2)$ or $(Entity, Attribute, Value)$, such as $(Einstein, Birthplace, Germany)$. Through the nodes and edges of the directed graph, the hierarchical structure and complex association of knowledge are expressed intuitively, which supports logical reasoning and semantic query.

The undirected graph is defined as $G = (V, E)$, where V is a node set and a non-empty finite set, and E is an edge set, in which each edge is composed of unordered vertex pairs in the vertex set V, and there is no direction. The main case of an undirected graph is the social network, whose graph structure is composed of nodes and edges, which is used to depict the relationship between social entities (such as people, organizations and groups) and emphasize the interaction between individuals, information dissemination and social structure. A Social network is usually represented by an undirected graph, which is suitable for the symmetrical relationship between entities and can be weighted or labeled. Nodes represent social entities, such as individuals, enterprises and communities. Social networks can analyze social behaviors, such as influence dissemination and community discovery, through node centrality and clustering. Common applications are reflected in social platform analysis, information dissemination, recommendation systems and public opinion monitoring [23]. It should be noted that the above Formal Concept Lattice is a special undirected graph, and the nodes of extent and intent have a partial order relationship in the lattice.

The Hypergraph is a triple $H = (V, E, L)$, where V is the node set, E is the edge set, and L is the label set of the edge. Each edge $e \in E$ is a subset of a node, representing a multivariate relationship [24]. Hypergraph can be expressed as a Formal Context, in which nodes are objects, edges are attributes, and labels are extensions of attributes. The application of hypergraph embodies the modeling of complex events: for example, in the "earthquake-rescue" event, there are many entity associations such as earthquake intensity, disaster-stricken area, rescue team, and material allocation, among which Vertex represents entities (such as concepts, objects, events, etc.) in the knowledge system and can carry attributes (such as name, type, description, etc.); Hyperedge: connecting multiple nodes, indicating the pluralistic relationship between nodes (such as "meeting" involving multiple participants and "teamwork" involving multi-person collaboration). Super edge can contain attributes (such as relationship type, timestamp, weight, etc.); Hierarchical structure: Hypergraphs can be nested with super edges to form a hierarchical knowledge structure (for example, a "project" consists of multiple "task" super edges, and each task contains subtask nodes). Generally speaking, the super edge can integrate the dynamic relationship of these event nodes, and can also be used to model the multivariate relationship. For the storage of this kind of hypergraph data information, NoSQL database is usually selected (such as a document database, key value database, graph database and column family database), and the specific selection should be based on the structural characteristics of the hypergraph.

3 The Works of FCA Applied in Knowledge Network

3.1 Systematic Literature Survey

We collected a large number of documents by using the academic literature website, and when we included them in the literature reference, we gave priority to the documents published in recent years, while excluding those from older years. We made an intensive reading analysis on the papers that put forward novel methods, integrated their methods, and summarized their applicability, advantages and disadvantages. Finally, we have collected 30 works related to FCA published in conferences and periodicals in the past ten years, subdivided them according to the research fields and task scenarios of FCA in the knowledge network, and summarized the maturity of each task with scenario solutions in different research fields, as shown in Table 2.

According to the evaluation results shown in the table, under the current research background, the application of FCA in Knowledge Graph, Social Networks, Semantic Representations, Combined with Machine Learning (ML) & Date Mining (DM) and other research fields has attracted attention. It also reflects the research enthusiasm in the task scenarios such as information retrieval and association, data classification and prediction, theoretical (complexity) analysis, community detection and Data fusion.

Among them, in the task scenario of information retrieval and association, Knowledge Base Representation, Knowledge Extraction, Knowledge Evolution, Association Rule Mining of Semantic Representations, Classification and Regression model of combined with ML& DM, Data Visualization, Granular concept analysis all show high maturity, but the research on Community Analysis, Social Internet of Things and Semantic Representations of Social Networks needs to be further explored.

In the data classification and prediction task, the association rule mining of Semantic Representations, the research on classification and regression model, Data Visualization combined with ML& DM is very mature. However, the research on Knowledge Representation of Knowledge Graph, Knowledge extraction, Social Internet of Things of Social Networks and Semantic Representations needs to be further explored.

Under the task scenario of theoretical (complexity) analysis, Knowledge Graph representation, Knowledge Evolution, Association Rule Mining of Semantic Representations, Classification and Regression model of Combined with ML& DM and Granular concept analysis are highly mature.

In the Community detection task, the research on Social Networks' Community Analysis, Social Internet of Things and Granular concept analysis is very mature. However, the Community Analysis of Social Networks, Association Rule Mining of Semantic Representations, classification and regression model Combined with ML& DM need to be further studied.

In the Data fusion task, the research on the base representation of the Knowledge Graph is very mature, while the research on Knowledge extraction of the Knowledge Graph, Knowledge Social Internet of Things of Social Networks needs to be further deepened. In other fields, there are many gaps in the corresponding task scenarios, which may be a new research trend in the near future and still need to be paid more attention in the future.

Table 2. Maturity of FCA's solution for each task scenario in different research fields: ● indicates that the research is relatively mature; ▲ indicates that there exist the room for improvement; ○ means that further research is needed to bridge the gap.

Research Field		Task scenario									
		Information retrieval and association		Data classification and prediction		Theoretical(complexity) analysis		Community detection		Data fusion	
		Maturity	References	Maturity	References	Maturity	References	Maturity	References	Maturity	References
Knowledge Graph	Knowledge Base Representation	●	[4][5][27][42][41]	▲	[4]	●	[24][41]	○		●	[24][27][42]
	Knowledge Extraction	●	[19][26]	▲	[19]	○		○		▲	[26]
	Knowledge Evolution	●	[29][43]	○		●	[29] [43]	○		○	
Social Networks	Community Analysis	▲	[6]	○		○		▲	[6]	○	
	Social Internet of Things	▲	[7]	▲	[28]	○		●	[7][28]	▲	[7]
Semantic Representations	Knowledge Representation	▲	[21]	▲	[21]	○		○		○	
	Association Rule Mining	●	[10][18][25][29][40]	●	[10][23][29]	●	[10][23][29]	▲	[23]	○	
Combined with ML& DM	Classification and Regression Model	●	[32][33]	●	[17][31][32][34]	●	[17][33]	▲	[32]	○	
	Data Visualization	●	[35][36]	●	[35][36]	○		○		○	
Granular concept analysis		●	[14][16][22]	●	[14][16][22]	●	[14][16]	●	[14]	○	

3.2 FCA Applied in Knowledge Graph

In the field of Knowledge Graph, with the open-source knowledge base of Wiki data, Hanika et al. [25] put forward an effective method to identify the comprehensible meaning implied in the data, and overcome the complexity problem that Wiki data cannot be directly modeled by extracting the context representation of Wiki data in a systematic way. Knowledge Graph describes entities through a large number of Resource Description Framework data (subject-predicate-object triplets), while scholars such as Yang et al. [26] have defined the concept lattice of RDF graphs. Since RDF data is essentially a triple graph, its connotation can be described by a graphic pattern. The graphic pattern closure is defined as the connected component of the graph through the simple form of graph realization. These graphic patterns correspond to join queries and can support the generalization of attributes, thus formalizing the concept map.

RDF data exists in independent and scattered resources, and needs to be centralized, navigated and searched to meet the application requirements of specific fields. Mehwis et al. [27] put forward a data integration method of FCA to create a navigation space on the semantic web data. This method extends FCA and provides centralized access to data generated by multiple resources by using RDF triples and RDF schemas from multiple independent sources. Then, SPARQL query can be put forward in this navigation space, so as to access these distributed resources from a platform and realize the purpose of information retrieval.

Ferré and Peggy Cellier [23] and others described the algorithm and performance evaluation of Graph-FCA in detail in their research, which proved its effectiveness in processing hypergraph data. A Pattern usually refers to a specific substructure or topological feature that appears repeatedly in a graph. Pattern basis is a set of basic patterns used to generate all concepts in a hypergraph. By using the generation algorithm, we extract the key patterns in the hypergraph and reduce the computational complexity [5]. After the concept lattice is generated by using the pattern base, the semantic analysis and Knowledge Representation in the data can be found by showing the conceptual relationship in the data through the hierarchical structure. Finally, the complexity of the concept lattice is reduced by the optimization algorithm, and the visualization and analysis efficiency are improved.

3.3 FCA Applied in Social Networks

The research progress of FCA technology in the identification and abstraction of core data structures in Social Networks has maintained a certain room for improvement. At present, scholars such as Hao et al. [6] have innovatively applied the FCA method to Social Network key structure detection, dynamic evolution management and entity abstract generation of Knowledge Graph in many papers, which fully demonstrated the powerful ability and unique advantages of FCA in dealing with complex network data.

In the identification of key structures of Social Networks, Hao et al. [28] put forward a unified framework method based on FCA. By constructing the Formal Context of Social Networks and generating concept lattices, the association between concepts and network structures is quantified by using concept interesting measures (such as stability and separability), and the joint detection of key structures such as maximum clique, bridge structure and structural hole is realized. This method effectively solves the problem of the high computational cost of traditional independent detection tasks, and verifies its efficiency and accuracy on several real network data sets. In the Social Internet of Things (SIoT) scenario, the research team further explored the problem of detecting diversified top-k maximum cliques. By proving the equivalence relationship between the concepts of maximum clique and equality, an intelligent greedy algorithm based on a stack data structure was designed, which significantly improved the maximum clique coverage under the premise of ensuring the diversity of results, showing the feasibility and superiority of the FCA method in dealing with large-scale complex networks.

Aiming at the challenge of dynamic changes in Social Networks, Yang et al. [7] proposed a dynamic maximum clique detection and evolution management method. By developing Add-FCA and Dec-FCA algorithms that are suitable for users to join and leave the scene, the efficient response to the dynamic changes of the Formal Context of Social Networks is realized, and by using the equivalence theorem between the concepts of equality and the maximum clique, the evolution modes of the maximum clique, such as invariance, change, addition and disappearance, are captured. The experimental results reveal that the maximum number of clusters decreases with the increase of parameter k, and verify the effectiveness of the algorithm in quantitative relationship analysis. Also, the increasing RDF description of entities leads to information overload.

In this context, automatic entity summarization has received extensive attention in recent years. Selecting the most concise and typical facts from the lengthy RDF data and briefly describing an entity has become the main goal. Yang et al. [26] and others proposed an incremental entity summarization method IES-FCA based on FCA. This method constructs concept lattice incrementally that considers the importance, redundancy and uniqueness of triples in combination with the improved ranking algorithm. Compared with the non-incremental methods, this method can reduce the time consumption, better than the existing algorithms in F1 measurement, MAP and NDCG.

3.4 FCA Applied in Semantic Representations

In order to break the limitations of data processing scale, Knowledge Representation and cross-domain applications, a new method is provided for knowledge discovery and semantic understanding of complex data. In addition to the current mature research fields, FCA has also carried out further research in the field of Representation Learning.

The FCA2VEC method proposed by Dürrschnabel et al. [21] aims to combine FCA with word embedding technology to solve the problem of efficient processing and interpretability of large-scale data sets. This method initializes semantic information by pre-training word vectors, and optimizes entity vectors by FCA embedding technology, thus preserving conceptual structure in a low-dimensional space. The core of the research is to realize the calculation of the covering relation and canonical basis of the concept lattice through the nonlinear embedding (Closure2Vec) and object/attribute vectorization (Object2Vec and Attribute2Vec) of the closure operator. Experiments show that this method is significantly superior to traditional methods in link prediction and attribute clustering tasks, especially in 3D embedding. For example, on Wiki44k data set, the average F1 score of FCA2VEC is nearly 30% higher than the random baseline, which proves its effectiveness in embedding the Knowledge Graph [29].

The DeepFCA framework proposed by Li et al. [30] focuses on the task of biomedical ontology matching. By combining FCA with pre-trained word vectors (such as word vectors on PubMed and Wikipedia), the entity vectors are optimized by synonyms and antonyms. By constructing a Formal Context based on tokens, this method extracts positive sample pairs from the concept lattice, and designs a loss function to narrow the vector distance of semantically similar entities. The experimental results show that it can obtain better performances than traditional FCA methods on OAEI data sets.

3.5 FCA Applied in Combined with ML and DM

Traditional FCA mainly deals with binary relational data, while Graph-FCA can deal with multivariate relational data by introducing the concept of n-ary, which has unique advantages in complex network analysis. The concept of n-ary is a binary group (X, Y), where x is a subset of nodes, y is a subset of edges, and it is satisfied that x is a closure of y and y is a closure of X. Closure operators are used to generate closures of nodes and edges, ensuring that every concept is generated based on existing closures.

Ferré et al. [5] described the algorithm and performance evaluation of Graph-FCA in their research. The core idea of Graph-FCA [4] is to expand the Formal Context into a hypergraph, and reveal the hierarchical structure and implicit relationship in the data through the generation of a schema base and the construction of a concept lattice.

Baixeries et al. [24] constructed a formal background, and associated an acyclic hypergraph with its symmetric dependency set, which proved that the formal background described the closure of acyclic hypergraphs accurately. This achievement not only supplements the FCA representation of AJD, but also shows the modular advantages of FCA in depicting RDBM dependency, which provides a new theoretical tool for database design, standardization and constraint reasoning.

Although FCA can generate a structured view of data and discover the implication relationship between data, it faces scalability problems when dealing with large-scale data, and it is difficult to integrate into neural network processes. Marquer et al. [31] and other scholars have studied the combination of deep learning and FCA, and put forward a framework called LatticeNN [32–34]. Through the deep generation model GraphRNN, the data-independent embedding model Bag of Attributes (BoA) has been developed, which opens up a new way for the realization of deep learning of FCA, is innovative in the embedding representation of formal concepts, and provides theoretical support and practical guidance for subsequent research [35, 36].

4 Optimization for FCA

4.1 Parallelization Improvement of the CbO Algorithm

To overcome the high complexity of FCA, Ganter et al. proposed the Close-by-One (CbO) algorithm [20]. It has become the core algorithm of FCA because of the completeness of its concept generation and it can enumerate closure sets by polynomial delay to ensure the efficiency and accuracy of the calculation process. CbO algorithm ensures that every concept is generated based on the existing closures by gradually expanding the closure set, thus avoiding repeated calculation.

In recent years, with the explosive growth of data scale, the traditional serial CbO algorithm faces a serious performance bottleneck when dealing with large-scale Formal Context because of the high reasoning complexity of FCA. To solve this problem, many scholars have proposed a variety of parallelization improvement schemes, mainly including GPU-based acceleration models and distributed memory architecture.

Distributed Close-by-One (DCbO) model is suitable for very large-scale Formal Context, which alleviates the performance bottleneck of the traditional serial CbO algorithm. It decomposes large-scale context into manageable chunks by horizontal and vertical partitions, which avoids the bottleneck of single-machine memory and enables the algorithm to handle larger data sets. By using the auxiliary structure of group ID and Cuckoo filter, the communication times and traffic between machines are significantly reduced, and the efficiency of distributed computing is improved [37]. Through MPI communication, the algorithm uses sparse matrix transmission to exchange only non-zero closure differences, which ensures correctness and non-repetition. However, its network communication cost accounts for 35% of the total time, which is a big challenge, and it is still necessary to further compress the transmitted data. Zou et al. [38] propose a new parallel algorithm for computing formal concepts, which is composed of two parallel phases. The new algorithm parallelizes both the computations of the top L recursion levels and the workload distribution, which decouples worker threads from the main thread so as to improve the efficiency of the algorithm. For DCbO, reducing communication overhead through advanced data compression techniques or optimizing the communication protocol could significantly enhance its scalability. In comparison, Zou et al.'s approach focuses more on parallelizing computations and workload distribution, which may offer better performance in scenarios with less communication-intensive tasks. However, in highly distributed environments where communication latency is significant, the trade-off between computation and communication needs to be carefully balanced to achieve optimal performance.

4.2 Incremental CbO Algorithm

The traditional serial CbO algorithm is suitable for static Formal Context, that is, the data will not change during the execution of the algorithm. When dealing with large-scale data, if the data changes dynamically, such as adding or deleting. The incremental Close-by-One (IncCbO) algorithm is an efficient concept lattice updating method for dynamic Formal Context, and its core goal is to calculate only the affected concept closures when the data increment arrives to avoid the overhead of total reconstruction.

In order to solve the problem of formal concept increment, Yang [26] et al. proposed the dynamic difference matrix model (IncCbO) algorithm. Only the concept of the changed part is recalculated, and the new concept is inserted into the original lattice structure, which greatly reduces the occupied memory, improves the FCA efficiency in a dynamic environment, and is suitable for the deployment of edge devices [39].

Marquer et al. [31] discussed how to combine these lattices through related concepts and concept alignment. It is emphasized that there are interactions between dimensions of related concepts, such as concept alignment and filtering, which may trigger more research on the application of FCA in neuroscience and concept learning, especially in different types of learning and concept structure modification.

Chen et al. [27] put forward the KG-CbO model algorithm, which maps the RDF triples in the Knowledge Graph to the Formal Context, and then uses the CbO algorithm to generate the ontology hierarchy, thus realizing the structural and hierarchical processing of the knowledge in the KG. It combines the rich Semantic Representation ability of Knowledge Graph and the deep mining ability of FCA to data structure [40].

Jens et al. [41] put forward the Neuro-CbO model, which uses graph neural network (GNN) to model the Formal Context, and predicts the priority of closure calculation by learning the embedded representation of nodes, thus optimizing the execution order of the CbO algorithm and improving the efficiency of concept lattice construction.

In order to improve the complexity of the algorithm, Zhu et al. [42] put forward knowledge state transfer methods based on attribute-oriented concept lattice for the conjunctive model and ability model respectively. This method has good performance when the skills cover a wide range, and the number of questions is large.

5 Conclusion and Future Direction

FCA plays an irreplaceable role in the research of knowledge representation and reasoning. This paper focused on the research works of FCA applied in knowledge network, which systematically summarized the existing methods in view of knowledge graph, social network, semantic representation, ML&DM. The value of FCA applied in knowledge networks has been indicated in the recent works of complex semantic representation and knowledge mining. Nevertheless, there still exist some problems to be solved which are listed as the future directions of FCA.

1. **FCA modeling based on Representation Learning**: As Deep Learning is good at feature extraction and representation of unstructured knowledge, FCA is good at finding structured tables and displaying them in the form of lattices. The combination of them could deeply mine domain knowledge. For example, the pre-training models of Deep Learning are utilized to provide the initial vectors with rich semantics for FCA. Then, with the help of FCA's concept lattice construction ability, knowledge can be further layered and systematized. It can improve the ability of domain knowledge reasoning and decision.
2. **Incremental FCA algorithm for Real-time Data**: With the dynamic data environment, the incremental FCA algorithm is still the key to enhancing the application value of FCA. Although the current algorithms can realize local updates, there still exist problems of cascade updates and data discarding. Therefore, it is necessary to develop an efficient incremental mechanism and reduce the computational complexity so that FCA can adapt to special scenarios with high real-time reasoning requirements.
3. **Visual and interpretable FCA for Analysis and Decision**: Due to the rise of large language models, it is important for the interpretability of AI. It is necessary to develop interactive visualization tools so that users can intuitively understand the hierarchical structure and semantic association of the concept lattice. Furthermore, the interpretation method of formal concept can be further explored, which can provide strong support for complex data analysis and decision-making.

To sum up, FCA has broad application prospects in theoretical research and actual data analysis of knowledge networks. The improvement and solution of the above problems can help FCA play an irreplaceable role in various tasks and help the innovation and development of AI.

References

1. Wenjie, C., Yufeng, W., Ruheng, L., et al.: An efficient location recommendation scheme based on clustering and data fusion. Comput. Electr. Eng. **77**, 289–299 (2019)
2. Yu, G., Yong, Y., Jiang, C., et al.: Formal concept analysis assisted large-scale global optimization and its application to cloud task scheduling. Complex Intell. Syst **11**(6), 245 (2025)
3. Huang, B., Li, J., Li, Q., et al.: Competence-based knowledge space theory from the perspective of formal concept analysis. Int. J. Mach. Learn. Cybern., 1–13 (2025)
4. Ferré, S.: Graph-FCA meets pattern structures. In: ICFCA, pp. 33–48 (2023)
5. Ferré, S.: A proposal for extending formal concept analysis to knowledge graphs. In: Lecture Notes in Computer Science, pp. 271–286 (2015)
6. Fei, H., Geyong, M., Zheng, P.: K-clique communities detection in social networks based on formal concept analysis. IEEE Syst. J. **11**(1), 250–259 (2015)
7. Yixuan, Y., Fei, H., Beibei, P., et al.: Dynamic maximal Cliques detection and evolution management in social internet of things: a formal concept analysis approach. IEEE Trans. Netw. Sci. Eng. **9**(3), 1020–1032 (2022)

8. Qiang, B., Guangqing, T.: Analysis of the progress and hotspots in applied research of FCA and concept lattice theory abroad. Data Anal. Knowl. Discov. **11**, 17–23 (2010)
9. Yunzhong, Z., Di, L., Yuanming, Z.: Research trend of knowledge discovery based on formal concept analysis. Inf. Sci. **36**(9), 153–158 (2018)
10. Chao, Z., Zhiyu, R., Wenchao, W.: Semantic roles mining algorithms based on formal concept analysis. Comput. Sci. **45**(12), 117–122+129 (2018)
11. Sarmah, A.K., Hazarika, S.M., Sinha, S.K.: Formal concept analysis: current trends and directions. Artif. Intell. Rev. **44**(1), 47–86 (2013). https://doi.org/10.1007/s10462-013-9404-0
12. Jonas, P., Dmitry, I.I., Sergei, O.K., et al.: Formal concept analysis in knowledge processing: a survey on applications. Expert Syst. Appl. **40**(16), 6538–6560 (2013)
13. Jonas, P., Sergei, O.K., Dmitry, I.I., et al.: Formal concept analysis in knowledge processing: a survey on models and techniques. Expert Syst. Appl. **40**(16), 6601–6623 (2013)
14. Li, J. H., Wei, L., Zhang, Z., et al.: Concept lattice theory and method and their research prospect. Pattern Recogn. Artif. Intell. **33**(07), 619–642 (2020)
15. László, K.: Conceptual clustering with application on FCA context. Expert Syst. Appl. **245**, 123013 (2024)
16. Jinhai, L., Yufei, L., Yunlong, M., et al.: Meso-granularity labeled method for multi-granularity formal concept analysis. J. Comput. Res. Dev. **57**(2), 447–458 (2020)
17. Lianbo, M., Fengrong, C., Huanxi, Z.: Formal concept analysis based grouping co-evolutionary optimization algorithms for arge-scale global optimization. Chin. J. Comput. **44**(7), 1310–1325 (2021)
18. Guanghua, G., Yuyao, C., Dong, C., et al.: Object image annotation based on formal concept analysis and semantic association rules. Acta Automatica Sinica **46**(4), 767–781 (2020)
19. Liwei, S., Zheng, Y., Hongping, L., et al.: Knowledge discovery and rule extraction based on heterogeneous network linguistic formal context. Pattern Recogn. Artif. Intell. **37**(5), 469–478 (2024)
20. Jan, K., Petr, K.: Systematic categorization and evaluation of CbO-based algorithms in FCA. Inf. Sci. **575**, 265–288 (2021)
21. Dominik, D., Tom, H., Maximilian, S.: FCA2VEC embedding techniques for formal concept analysis. In: Complex Data Analytics with Formal Concept Analysis, pp. 47–74 (2022)
22. Qian, H., Zhong, Y., Keyun, Q., et al.: A novel outlier detection approach based on formal concept analysis. Knowl. Based Syst **268**, 110486 (2023)
23. Jie, G., Fei, H., Zheng, P., et al.: Learning concept interestingness for identifying key structures from social networks. IEEE Trans. Netw. Sci. Eng. **8**(4), 3220–3232 (2021)
24. Jaume, B.: A formal context for closures of acyclic hypergraphs. In: ICFCA, pp. 259–273 (2019)
25. Hanika, T., Marx, M., Stumme, G.: Discovering implicational knowledge in Wiki data. In: ICFCA, pp. 315–323 (2019)
26. Erhe, Y., Fei, H., Yixuan, Y., et al.: Incremental entity summarization with formal concept analysis. IEEE Trans. Serv. Comput. **15**(6), 3289–3303 (2022)
27. Mehwish, A., Amedeo, N.: An approach towards classifying and navigating RDF data based on pattern structures. In: ICFCA, pp.33–48 (2015)
28. Fei, H., Zheng, P., Laurence, T.Y.: Diversified top-k maximal clique detection in social internet of things. Future Gener. Comput. Syst. **107**, 408–417 (2020)
29. Steffffen, S.: Concepts in application context. In: ICFCA, pp. 45–52 (2019)
30. Guoxuan, L.: DeepFCA: matching biomedical ontologies using formal concept analysis embedding techniques. In: ICMHI, pp. 259–265 (2020)
31. Esteban, M.: LatticeNN deep learning and formal concept analysis. Ph.D thesis (2020)
32. Egor, D., Sergei, O.K.: Decision concept lattice vs. decision trees and random forests. In: ICFCA, pp. 252–260 (2021)

33. Doudou, G., Weihua, X.: R-FCCL: an approach of fuzzy-based concept-cognitive learning with robustness for high-dimensional data. J. Comput. Res. Dev. **62**(2), 383–396 (2025)
34. Valverde-A, F.J., Pelaez-M, C.: Leveraging formal concept analysis to improve n-fold validation in multilabel classification. In: ICFCA, pp. 44–51 (2021)
35. Peter, E., Jean, V.: A survey of hybrid representations of concept lattices in conceptual knowledge processing. In: ICFCA, pp. 296–311 (2010)
36. Uta, P.: Representing concept lattices with Euler diagrams. In: ICFCA, pp. 183–197 (2023)
37. Jyoti, M.P., Sriram, K.: A hybrid partitioning strategy for distributed FCA. In: CLA, pp. 71–82 (2020)
38. Ligeng, Z., Tingting, H., Jianhua, D.: A new parallel algorithm for computing formal concepts based on two parallel stages. Inf. Sci. **586**, 514–524 (2022)
39. Uta, P.: Conceptual alignment with formal concept analysis. In: ICFCA, pp. 14–27 (2019)
40. Hua, M., Chang, L., Xiaolei, Y., et al.: Knowledge level extraction method based on concept lattice and its application. J. Huazhong Univ. Sci. Technol. **52**(11), 37–42 (2024)
41. Jens, K.: Concept lattices of RDF graphs. Comput. Sci., 81–91 (2015)
42. Yongfan, Z., Qingyuan, X., Yinfeng, Z., et al.: Knowledge-state transfer method based on attribute-oriented concept lattices. J. Chin. Comput. Syst. **45**(11), 2647–2655 (2024)

Norms and Metrics

Universal First-Order Theory of Relative Nearness for All Metric Spaces

Zhiguang Zhao(✉)

Taishan University, Taian, People's Republic of China
zhaozhiguang23@gmail.com

Abstract. In the present paper, we solve an open problem mentioned in [3], namely a complete description of the universal first-order theory of relative nearness relation, which is a ternary relation $N(w, v, u)$ which means that $d(w, v) < d(w, u)$, where $d(w, v)$ is the distance between w and v. Our axiomatization makes use of a variation of the Farkas' Lemma [6] on the solvability conditions of finite linear equation systems.

Keywords: Spatial logic · metric space · relative nearness

1 Introduction

Logics for reasoning about spatial features are growing more attentions (see [2] for a comprehensive reference). Spatial logics provide formal tools to express and reason about geometric structures such as topological spaces, metric spaces, etc. In the study of spatial logic, the ones about distance in a metric space are studied extensively [1,5,10–13,15,20]. Our focus in this paper is relative nearness, which has been studied in [4,9,16,17].

Relative nearness relation is a ternary relation $N(w, v, u)$ which means that $d(w, v) < d(w, u)$, where $d(w, v)$ is the distance between w and v. Typically, we require that d is a metric function on a metric space (W, d) satisfying certain conditions. In [3], the authors describe some properties that the relative nearness relation satisfies, but the complete description of the universal first-order theory of relative nearness relation is left as an open problem.

In our paper, we solve this open problem by using a variant of Farkas' Lemma [6] to characterize the metrizable finite models of the form $\mathcal{M} = (W, N)$ where W is a non-empty finite set and N is a ternary relation on W. Farkas' Lemma is a celebrated result in linear algebra and optimization theory, which is about the solvability conditions of finite linear equation (or inequation) systems. It has been used in the study of modal logic extended with the "most" modality M where $\mathsf{M}\varphi$ means that there are strictly more successors satisfying φ than successors satisfying $\neg\varphi$ [7] and monadic first-order logic without equality extended with the generalized unary quantifier $\mathsf{M}x$ where $\mathsf{M}x\varphi(x)$ means that there are more objects in the domain satisfying $\varphi(x)$ than objects satisfying $\neg\varphi(x)$ [8].

Our contributions are both technical and methodological: we not only provide a complete description of the universal first-order theory of relative nearness

M. Bonsangue and Y. Chen (Eds.): AILA 2025, CCIS 2668, pp. 81–94, 2026.
https://doi.org/10.1007/978-981-95-8262-4_6

relation by characterizing the metrizable finite models of the form $\mathcal{M} = (W, N)$ as described above, but also make use of tools from linear algebra and optimization theory, namely the Farkas' Lemma.

The structure of the paper is organized as follows: Sect. 2 gives all the necessary preliminaries on metric spaces and relative nearness relation. Section 3 gives the axiomatization of the universal first-order theory of relative nearness relation using a variant of Farkas' Lemma. Section 4 gives the conclusions of the paper.

2 Preliminaries

In the present section, we gives some preliminaries on metric space and relative nearness relation. For references, see [3,19].

Definition 1 (Metric Space). *A metric space is a pair (W, d) where W is a non-empty set and $d : W \times W \to \mathbb{R}$ is a metric (or distance function) on W such that for any $w, v, u \in W$:*

- $d(w, v) \geq 0$. *(Non-negativity)*
- $d(w, v) = 0$ *iff* $w = v$.
- $d(w, v) = d(v, w)$. *(Symmetry)*
- $d(w, v) + d(v, u) \geq d(w, u)$. *(Triangle inequality)*

Definition 2 (Relative Nearness Relation). *Given any metric space (W, d), the relative nearness relation N_d induced by d is a ternary relation on W such that $N_d(x, y, z)$ iff $d(x, y) < d(x, z)$.*

In what follows, we use $N_d(x, y, z)$ to indicate that $(x, y, z) \in N_d$ and $\sim N_d(x, y, z)$ to indicate that $(x, y, z) \in W^3 - N_d$. We use $\#(x, y, z)$ to indicate that x, y, z are all distinct.

We have the following properties of the relative nearness relation induced by a metric space:

Theorem 1. *For any metric space (W, d), the relative nearness relation N_d induced by d satisfies the following properties:*

1. *For any $x, y \in W$, $\sim N_d(x, y, y)$ holds.*
2. *For any $x, y \in W$ such that $x \neq y$, $N_d(x, x, y)$ holds.*
3. *For any $x, y \in W$, $\sim N_d(x, y, x)$ holds.*
4. *For any $x_1, \ldots, x_m, y_1, \ldots, y_m, z_1, \ldots, z_m, u_1, \ldots, u_n, v_1, \ldots, v_n, w_1, \ldots, w_n \in W$ such that $m \geq 1$, $n \geq 0$ and $(\{x_1, y_1\}, \ldots, \{x_m, y_m\}, \{u_1, w_1\}, \ldots, \{u_n, w_n\})$ and $(\{x_1, z_1\}, \ldots, \{x_m, z_m\}, \{u_1, v_1\}, \ldots, \{u_n, v_n\})$ are permutations of each other, if $\#(x_i, y_i, z_i)$ and $N_d(x_i, y_i, z_i)$ for all $1 \leq i \leq m$ and $\#(u_j, v_j, w_j)$ for all $1 \leq j \leq n$, then $N_d(u_j, v_j, w_j)$ holds for some $1 \leq j \leq n$.*

Proof. 1. For any $x, y \in W$, since $d(x, y) \geq d(x, y)$, we have $\sim N_d(x, y, y)$.

2. For any $x, y \in W$ such that $x \neq y$, since $d(x, x) = 0 < d(x, y)$, we have $N_d(x, x, y)$.
3. For any $x, y \in W$, since $d(x, y) \geq 0 = d(x, x)$, we have $\sim N_d(x, y, x)$.
4. For any $x_1, \ldots, x_m, y_1, \ldots, y_m, z_1, \ldots, z_m, u_1, \ldots, u_n, v_1, \ldots, v_n, w_1, \ldots, w_n \in W$ such that
   - $m \geq 1$,
   - $n \geq 0$,
   - and $(\{x_1, y_1\}, \ldots, \{x_m, y_m\}, \{u_1, w_1\}, \ldots, \{u_n, w_n\})$ and $(\{x_1, z_1\}, \ldots, \{x_m, z_m\}, \{u_1, v_1\}, \ldots, \{u_n, v_n\})$ are permutations of each other,
   - $\#(x_i, y_i, z_i)$ for all $1 \leq i \leq m$,
   - $N_d(x_i, y_i, z_i)$ for all $1 \leq i \leq m$,
   - $\#(u_j, v_j, w_j)$ for all $1 \leq j \leq n$,
   - $\sim N_d(u_j, v_j, w_j)$ holds for all $1 \leq j \leq n$,

   we have that $d(x_i, y_i) < d(x_i, z_i)$ for all $1 \leq i \leq m$ and $d(u_j, w_j) \leq d(u_j, v_j)$ for all $1 \leq j \leq n$. By adding them up, we have that the left-handside is the same as the right-handside, but the inequality is strict, a contradiction. Therefore the property holds.

Corollary 1. *1. For any $x, y, z, w \in W$, $N_d(x, y, z)$ and $N_d(x, z, w)$ imply $N_d(x, y, w)$.*
2. For any $x, y, z \in W$, $N_d(x, y, z)$ implies $\sim N_d(x, z, y)$.
3. For any $x, y, z, w \in W$, $N_d(x, y, z)$ implies $N_d(x, y, w)$ or $N_d(x, w, z)$.

Proof. 1. If some of x, y, z, w are equal, then it follows from Theorem 1(1)-(3). If $\#(x, y, z, w)$, then it follows from Theorem 1(4), by taking $(x_1, y_1, z_1) = (x, y, z)$, $(x_2, y_2, z_2) = (x, z, w)$, $(u_1, v_1, w_1) = (x, y, w)$. Indeed, $(\{x, y\}, \{x, z\}, \{x, w\})$ and $(\{x, z\}, \{x, w\}, \{x, y\})$ are permutations of each other.
2. If some of x, y, z are equal, then it follows from Theorem 1(1)-(3). If $\#(x, y, z)$, then it follows from Theorem 1(4), by taking $(x_1, y_1, z_1) = (x, y, z)$, $(x_2, y_2, z_2) = (x, z, y)$ and $n = 0$. Indeed, $(\{x, y\}, \{x, z\})$ and $(\{x, z\}, \{x, y\})$ are permutations of each other. Indeed, what we get is a contradiction from $N_d(x, y, z)$ and $N_d(x, z, y)$.
3. If some of x, y, z, w are equal, then it follows from Theorem 1(1)-(3). If $\#(x, y, z, w)$, then it follows from Theorem 1(4), by taking $(x_1, y_1, z_1) = (x, y, z)$, $(u_1, v_1, w_1) = (x, y, w)$, $(u_2, v_2, w_2) = (x, w, z)$. Indeed, $(\{x, y\}, \{x, w\}, \{x, z\})$ and $(\{x, z\}, \{x, y\}, \{x, w\})$ are permutations of each other.

3 The Axiomatization

In what follows, we will axiomatize the universal first-order theory of relative nearness relation using a variant of Farkas' Lemma.

3.1 The Axioms of Relative Nearness

The first-order language we consider only contains one non-logical symbol, which is a ternary predicate symbol N corresponding to the relative nearness relation. We define quantifier-free formulas as follows:

$$\varphi \ ::= x = y \mid Nxyz \mid \bot \mid \varphi \to \varphi$$

where x, y, z are individual variables. Then we define universal formulas as follows:

$$\theta \ ::= \varphi \mid \forall x\theta$$

where x is an individual variable. First-order formulas are defined as follows:

$$\psi \ ::= x = y \mid Nxyz \mid \bot \mid \psi \to \psi \mid \forall x\psi$$

$\neg, \wedge, \vee, \leftrightarrow, \exists x$ as well as all standard notions in first-order logic are defined as usual. We use $\forall\vec{x}$ to denote the quantifiers $\forall x_1 \ldots \forall x_n$, where $\vec{x}$ is the sequence $(x_1, \ldots, x_n)$.

For the semantics,

- A model $\mathcal{M} = (W, N^{\mathcal{M}})$ is such that W is a non-empty set and $N^{\mathcal{M}}$ is a ternary relation on W. We often omit the superscript of N when it is clear from the context.
- A model $\mathcal{M} = (W, N^{\mathcal{M}})$ is metrizable iff there is a metric $d : W \times W \to \mathbb{R}$ on W such that $N^{\mathcal{M}} = N_d$.
- Assignments, satisfaction relation, truth of sentences and validity are defined as usual.
- For any set Φ of formulas and any formula φ, we say that φ semantically follows from Φ (notation: $\Phi \vDash \varphi$), if for any model $\mathcal{M}$ and any assignment s on $\mathcal{M}$, if $\mathcal{M}, s \vDash \Phi$, then $\mathcal{M}, s \vDash \varphi$.

Definition 3 (Universal First-Order Theory). *We consider the universal first-order theory of a set Φ of sentences as $\mathsf{Th}_\forall(\Phi) := \{\varphi \mid \Phi \vDash \varphi$ and φ is a universal sentence$\}$. We say that Φ is the set of axioms of $\mathsf{Th}_\forall(\Phi)$ if Φ is also a set of universal sentences.*

Consider the set Φ_M of all universal sentences that are true on all metrizable models. We will prove that $\Phi_M = \mathsf{Th}_\forall(\Psi)$, where Ψ consists of the following universal sentences:

Definition 4 (Axioms of Relative Nearness). *Ψ consists of the following universal sentences:*

1. $\forall x \forall y \neg Nxyy$.
2. $\forall x \forall y (x \neq y \to Nxxy)$.
3. $\forall x \forall y \neg Nxyx$.
4. $\forall\vec{x}\forall\vec{y}\forall\vec{z}\forall\vec{u}\forall\vec{v}\forall\vec{w}(\bigwedge \#(x_i, y_i, z_i) \wedge \bigwedge \#(u_i, v_i, w_i) \wedge Nx_1y_1z_1 \wedge \ldots \wedge Nx_my_mz_m \wedge \neg Nu_1v_1w_1 \wedge \ldots \wedge \neg Nu_nv_nw_n \to \bot)$, *where the lists* $(\{x_1, y_1\}, \ldots, \{x_m, y_m\}, \{u_1, w_1\}, \ldots, \{u_n, w_n\})$ *and* $(\{x_1, z_1\}, \ldots, \{x_m, z_m\}, \{u_1, v_1\}, \ldots, \{u_n, v_n\})$ *are permutations of each other and* $m \geq 1, n \geq 0$.

3.2 Completeness

In this section, we will show that $\Phi_M = \mathsf{Th}_\forall(\Psi)$, i.e. Ψ axiomatizes the universal first-order theory of relative nearness.

Before proving the theorem, we first prove the following variations of Farkas' Lemma, which is about solvability of finite linear inequation systems. We use $\mathbb{N}$ and $\mathbb{Q}$ to denote the set of natural numbers and the set of rational numbers, respectively. We use $A^{n\times m}$ to denote an $n \times m$ matrix of elements in A and A^T to denote the transposition of the matrix A. We use $\mathbf{a} \leq \mathbf{b}$ to indicate that every coordinate of $\mathbf{a}$ is smaller than or equal to the corresponding coordinate in $\mathbf{b}$, $\mathbf{a} < \mathbf{b}$ to indicate that every coordinate of $\mathbf{a}$ is strictly smaller than the corresponding coordinate in $\mathbf{b}$, and $\mathbf{a} = \mathbf{b}$ to indicate that the two vectors are the same. We use $\mathbf{0}$ to denote a vector whose all coordinates are 0 and sometimes we use superscripts to indicate its dimension.

Lemma 1 (A Variation of Farkas' Lemma). *Consider a finite linear inequation system $\{\mathbf{AX} \geq \mathbf{0}, \mathbf{CX} > \mathbf{0}\}$, where $\mathbf{A} \in \mathbb{Q}^{n_1\times m}$, $\mathbf{C} \in \mathbb{Q}^{n_2\times m}$ and $\mathbf{X} = (x_1, \ldots, x_m)^T$ is a vector of variables, $n_1, n_2, m \geq 1$.*

The system has no non-negative real solution iff there are $\mathbf{b} \in \mathbb{N}^{n_1\times 1}$ and $\mathbf{0}^{n_2\times 1} \neq \mathbf{d} \in \mathbb{N}^{n_2\times 1}$ such that $\mathbf{b}^T\mathbf{A} + \mathbf{d}^T\mathbf{C} \leq \mathbf{0}^{1\times m}$, i.e. by adding up the rows of $\mathbf{A}$ and $\mathbf{C}$ (where each row can be used many times or not used at all), we can get a horizontal vector of non-positive numbers, such that the rows in $\mathbf{C}$ are used at least once.

Proof. We prove by induction on m.

- For the case $m = 1$, we essentially have a system $\{\mathbf{AX} \geq \mathbf{0}, \mathbf{CX} > \mathbf{0}\}$ of the form $\{a_1x \geq 0, \ldots, a_{n_1}x \geq 0, c_1x > 0, \ldots, c_{n_2}x > 0\}$.
  - If the system has a non-negative real solution $\mathbf{X} = x$ and there are $\mathbf{b} \in \mathbb{N}^{n_1\times 1}$ and $\mathbf{0}^{n_2\times 1} \neq \mathbf{d} \in \mathbb{N}^{n_2\times 1}$ such that $\mathbf{b}^T\mathbf{A} + \mathbf{d}^T\mathbf{C} \leq \mathbf{0}$, then $\{a_1x \geq 0, \ldots, a_{n_1}x \geq 0, c_1x > 0, \ldots, c_{n_2}x > 0\}$ has a non-negative real solution. Apparently $x \neq 0$, otherwise from $c_1x > 0$ we get $0 > 0$, a contradiction. Therefore $x > 0$, and thus $a_1, \ldots, a_{n_1} \geq 0, c_1, \ldots, c_{n_2} > 0$. Then since $\mathbf{b} \in \mathbb{N}^{n_1\times 1}$ and $\mathbf{0}^{n_2\times 1} \neq \mathbf{d} \in \mathbb{N}^{n_2\times 1}$, we have that $(\Sigma_{i=1}^{n_1} b_ia_i) + (\Sigma_{j=1}^{n_2} d_jc_j) > 0$, a contradiction to $\mathbf{b}^T\mathbf{A} + \mathbf{d}^T\mathbf{C} \leq \mathbf{0}$.
  - If the system has no non-negative real solution, then $\{a_1x \geq 0, \ldots, a_{n_1}x \geq 0, c_1x > 0, \ldots, c_{n_2}x > 0\}$ has no such solution.
    * If there is a $c_j \leq 0$, then consider $\mathbf{b} = (b_1, \ldots, b_{n_1})^T$ and $\mathbf{d} = (d_1, \ldots, d_{n_2})^T$ such that all b_i's and d_k's are 0 except that $d_j = 1$, then $(\Sigma_{i=1}^{n_1} b_ia_i) + (\Sigma_{j=1}^{n_2} d_jc_j) = c_jd_j \leq 0$, i.e. $\mathbf{b}^T\mathbf{A} + \mathbf{d}^T\mathbf{C} \leq \mathbf{0}$.
    * If $c_j > 0$ for all $j = 1, \ldots, n_2$, then the inequation system is equivalent to $\{a_1x \geq 0, \ldots, a_{n_1}x \geq 0, x > 0\}$. If $a_i \geq 0$ for all $i = 1, \ldots, n_1$, then the system has a solution $x = 1$, a contradiction. Therefore there is an a_i such that $a_i < 0$. Then for $a_i < 0$ and $c_j > 0$, since $a_i, c_j \in \mathbb{Q}$, there are $b_i, d_j \in \mathbb{N}$ such that $b_ia_i + d_jc_j = 0$ and $d_j > 0$. By taking all b_t's (where $t \neq i$) and d_k's (where $k \neq j$) to be 0, we get $\mathbf{b} \in \mathbb{N}^{n_1\times 1}$ and $\mathbf{0}^{n_2\times 1} \neq \mathbf{d} \in \mathbb{N}^{n_2\times 1}$ such that $\mathbf{b}^T\mathbf{A} + \mathbf{d}^T\mathbf{C} \leq \mathbf{0}$.

- Suppose we have proved the lemma for all $m \leq k$. For $m = k+1$, we essentially have a system $\{\mathbf{AX} \geq \mathbf{0}, \mathbf{CX} > \mathbf{0}\}$.
  - If the system has a non-negative real solution $\mathbf{X} = \mathbf{x}$ and there are $\mathbf{b} \in \mathbb{N}^{n_1 \times 1}$ and $\mathbf{0}^{n_2 \times 1} \neq \mathbf{d} \in \mathbb{N}^{n_2 \times 1}$ such that $\mathbf{b}^T\mathbf{A} + \mathbf{d}^T\mathbf{C} \leq \mathbf{0}^{1 \times m}$, then $\mathbf{b}^T\mathbf{Ax} + \mathbf{d}^T\mathbf{Cx} \leq 0$. However, from $\mathbf{Ax} \geq \mathbf{0}^{n_1 \times 1}$, $\mathbf{Cx} > \mathbf{0}^{n_2 \times 1}$, $\mathbf{b} \geq \mathbf{0}^{n_1 \times 1}$, $\mathbf{d} \geq \mathbf{0}^{n_2 \times 1}$ and $\mathbf{d} \neq \mathbf{0}^{n_2 \times 1}$ we get that $\mathbf{b}^T\mathbf{Ax} \geq 0$ and $\mathbf{d}^T\mathbf{Cx} > 0$, a contradiction to $\mathbf{b}^T\mathbf{Ax} + \mathbf{d}^T\mathbf{Cx} \leq 0$.
  - If the system has no non-negative real solution, denote
    * $\mathbf{X} = (x_1, \ldots, x_{k+1})^T$,
    * $\mathbf{A} = (a_{i,j})_{n_1 \times (k+1)}$,
    * $\mathbf{C} = (c_{i,j})_{n_1 \times (k+1)}$,
    * $(\mathbf{AX})_i = \Sigma_{j=1}^{k+1} a_{i,j} x_j$ as the i-th row of $\mathbf{AX}$,
    * $(\mathbf{CX})_\ell = \Sigma_{j=1}^{k+1} c_{\ell,j} x_j$ as the ℓ-th row of $\mathbf{CX}$,

    then the system $\{\Sigma_{j=1}^{k+1} a_{1,j} x_j \geq 0, \ldots, \Sigma_{j=1}^{k+1} a_{n_1,j} x_j \geq 0, \Sigma_{j=1}^{k+1} c_{1,j} x_j > 0, \ldots, \Sigma_{j=1}^{k+1} c_{n_2,j} x_j > 0\}$ has no non-negative real solution. Now we divide the lines into the following types:
    * $\Sigma_{j=1}^{k} a_{i,j} x_j + a_{i,k+1} x_{k+1} \geq 0$, where $a_{i,k+1} > 0$.
    * $\Sigma_{j=1}^{k} a_{i,j} x_j + a_{i,k+1} x_{k+1} \geq 0$, where $a_{i,k+1} = 0$.
    * $\Sigma_{j=1}^{k} a_{i,j} x_j + a_{i,k+1} x_{k+1} \geq 0$, where $a_{i,k+1} < 0$.
    * $\Sigma_{j=1}^{k} c_{\ell,j} x_j + c_{\ell,k+1} x_{k+1} > 0$, where $c_{\ell,k+1} > 0$.
    * $\Sigma_{j=1}^{k} c_{\ell,j} x_j + c_{\ell,k+1} x_{k+1} > 0$, where $c_{\ell,k+1} = 0$.
    * $\Sigma_{j=1}^{k} c_{\ell,j} x_j + c_{\ell,k+1} x_{k+1} > 0$, where $c_{\ell,k+1} < 0$.

    We denote the six sets of indices of i's and ℓ's as $I_1, I_2, I_3, L_1, L_2, L_3$ respectively, then we have that each type of inequation can be rewritten as follows:
    * $x_{k+1} \geq -\Sigma_{j=1}^{k} (a_{i,j}/a_{i,k+1}) x_j$, where $i \in I_1$.
    * $\Sigma_{j=1}^{k} a_{i,j} x_j \geq 0$, where $i \in I_2$.
    * $x_{k+1} \leq -\Sigma_{j=1}^{k} (a_{i,j}/a_{i,k+1}) x_j$, where $i \in I_3$.
    * $x_{k+1} > -\Sigma_{j=1}^{k} (c_{\ell,j}/c_{\ell,k+1}) x_j$, where $\ell \in L_1$.
    * $\Sigma_{j=1}^{k} c_{\ell,j} x_j > 0$, where $\ell \in L_2$.
    * $x_{k+1} < -\Sigma_{j=1}^{k} (c_{\ell,j}/c_{\ell,k+1}) x_j$, where $\ell \in L_3$.

    Now, the system has no non-negative real solution iff the following system has no non-negative real solutions:

$$\begin{cases} -\Sigma_{j=1}^{k} (a_{i,j}/a_{i,k+1}) x_j \leq -\Sigma_{j=1}^{k} (a_{i',j}/a_{i',k+1}) x_j \text{ where } i \in I_1 \text{ and } i' \in I_3 \\ -\Sigma_{j=1}^{k} (a_{i,j}/a_{i,k+1}) x_j < -\Sigma_{j=1}^{k} (c_{\ell,j}/c_{\ell,k+1}) x_j \text{ where } i \in I_1 \text{ and } \ell \in L_3 \\ -\Sigma_{j=1}^{k} (c_{\ell,j}/c_{\ell,k+1}) x_j < -\Sigma_{j=1}^{k} (a_{i,j}/a_{i,k+1}) x_j \text{ where } \ell \in L_1 \text{ and } i \in I_3 \\ -\Sigma_{j=1}^{k} (c_{\ell,j}/c_{\ell,k+1}) x_j < -\Sigma_{j=1}^{k} (c_{\ell',j}/c_{\ell',k+1}) x_j \text{ where } \ell \in L_1 \text{ and } \ell' \in L_3 \\ 0 \leq -\Sigma_{j=1}^{k} (a_{i,j}/a_{i,k+1}) x_j \text{ where } i \in I_3 \\ 0 < -\Sigma_{j=1}^{k} (c_{\ell,j}/c_{\ell,k+1}) x_j \text{ where } \ell \in L_3 \\ \Sigma_{j=1}^{k} a_{i,j} x_j \geq 0 \text{ where } i \in I_2 \\ \Sigma_{j=1}^{k} c_{\ell,j} x_j > 0 \text{ where } \ell \in L_2 \end{cases}$$

    The basic idea of this equivalence is as follows: each inequation determines the value of x_{k+1} as an interval. The system has non-negative real solutions iff the intersection of all intervals together with $[0, +\infty)$ is non-empty and the resulting system with one less variable has non-negative real solutions. Now we can re-organize the inequation system as follows:

$$\begin{cases} \Sigma_{j=1}^{k}(a_{i,k+1}a_{i',j} - a_{i',k+1}a_{i,j})x_j \geq 0 \text{ where } i \in I_1 \text{ and } i' \in I_3 \\ \Sigma_{j=1}^{k}(a_{i,k+1}c_{\ell,j} - c_{\ell,k+1}a_{i,j})x_j > 0 \text{ where } i \in I_1 \text{ and } \ell \in L_3 \\ \Sigma_{j=1}^{k}(c_{\ell,k+1}a_{i,j} - a_{i,k+1}c_{\ell,j})x_j > 0 \text{ where } \ell \in L_1 \text{ and } i \in I_3 \\ \Sigma_{j=1}^{k}(c_{\ell,k+1}c_{\ell',j} - c_{\ell',k+1}c_{\ell,j})x_j > 0 \text{ where } \ell \in L_1 \text{ and } \ell' \in L_3 \\ \Sigma_{j=1}^{k}a_{i,j}x_j \geq 0 \text{ where } i \in I_2 \cup I_3 \\ \Sigma_{j=1}^{k}c_{\ell,j}x_j > 0 \text{ where } \ell \in L_2 \cup L_3 \end{cases}$$

By induction hypothesis, this inequation system has no non-negative real solution iff we can use the left-handside of lines in the system above (where each line can also be used many times or not used at all) to add up to some linear combination of $x_1, \ldots, x_k$ such that all coefficients for $x_1, \ldots, x_k$ in this combination are non-positive and the strict inequations are used at least once. Then

$$\begin{aligned} &\Sigma_{j=1}^{k}(a_{i,k+1}a_{i',j} - a_{i',k+1}a_{i,j})x_j \\ &= a_{i,k+1}\Sigma_{j=1}^{k}a_{i',j}x_j - a_{i',k+1}\Sigma_{j=1}^{k}a_{i,j}x_j \\ &= a_{i,k+1}\Sigma_{j=1}^{k+1}a_{i',j}x_j - a_{i',k+1}\Sigma_{j=1}^{k+1}a_{i,j}x_j \\ &= a_{i,k+1}(\mathbf{AX})_{i'} - a_{i',k+1}(\mathbf{AX})_i, \end{aligned}$$

and similarly for other lines. Therefore, each type of inequations of the system can be rewritten as follows:

1. $a_{i,k+1}(\mathbf{AX})_{i'} - a_{i',k+1}(\mathbf{AX})_i \geq 0$, where $i \in I_1$ and $i' \in I_3$.
2. $a_{i,k+1}(\mathbf{CX})_\ell - c_{\ell,k+1}(\mathbf{AX})_i > 0$, where $i \in I_1$ and $\ell \in L_3$.
3. $c_{\ell,k+1}(\mathbf{AX})_i - a_{i,k+1}(\mathbf{CX})_\ell > 0$, where $\ell \in L_1$ and $i \in I_3$.
4. $c_{\ell,k+1}(\mathbf{CX})_{\ell'} - c_{\ell',k+1}(\mathbf{CX})_\ell > 0$, where $\ell \in L_1$ and $\ell' \in L_3$.
5. $(\mathbf{AX})_i - a_{i,k+1}x_{k+1} \geq 0$, where $i \in I_2 \cup I_3$.
6. $(\mathbf{CX})_\ell - c_{\ell,k+1}x_{k+1} > 0$, where $\ell \in L_2 \cup L_3$.

This inequation system has no non-negative real solution iff we can use the left-handside of lines in the system above (where each line can also be used many times or not used at all) to add up to some linear combination of $x_1, \ldots, x_k$ (notice that x_{k+1} always has coefficient 0) such that all coefficients for $x_1, \ldots, x_k$ in this combination are non-positive and the strict inequations are used at least once. This is essentially a linear combination of $(\mathbf{AX})_i$'s, $(\mathbf{CX})_\ell$'s and x_{k+1} such that the coefficients of $(\mathbf{AX})_i$'s, $(\mathbf{CX})_\ell$'s and x_{k+1} are all non-negative and the strict inequations are used at least once.

Apparently, all coefficients for $(\mathbf{AX})_i$'s, $(\mathbf{CX})_\ell$'s are positive in all inequations.

* If no inequations of the form $(\mathbf{AX})_i - a_{i,k+1}x_{k+1} \geq 0$ (for $i \in I_3$) or $(\mathbf{CX})_\ell - c_{\ell,k+1}x_{k+1} > 0$ (for $\ell \in L_3$) are used, then we have a linear combination of $(\mathbf{AX})_i$'s and $(\mathbf{CX})_\ell$'s such that the coefficients of $(\mathbf{AX})_i$'s and $(\mathbf{CX})_\ell$'s are all non-negative and the strict inequations are used at least once. Since strict inequations of type 2–4 have

positive coefficients of $(\mathbf{CX})_\ell$'s, we have non-negative $\mathbf{b} \in \mathbb{Q}^{n_1 \times 1}$ and $\mathbf{0}^{n_2 \times 1} \neq \mathbf{d} \in \mathbb{Q}^{n_2 \times 1}$ such that $\mathbf{b}^T\mathbf{A} + \mathbf{d}^T\mathbf{C} \leq \mathbf{0}^{1 \times m}$. By appropriate scaling, we can make sure that all coordinates of $\mathbf{b}$ and $\mathbf{d}$ are in $\mathbb{N}$.

* If some inequations of the form $(\mathbf{AX})_i - a_{i,k+1}x_{k+1} \geq 0$ (for $i \in I_3$) or $(\mathbf{CX})_\ell - c_{\ell,k+1}x_{k+1} > 0$ (for $\ell \in L_3$) are used, then we have a linear combination of $(\mathbf{AX})_i$'s, $(\mathbf{CX})_\ell$'s and x_{k+1} such that:
  · The coefficients of $(\mathbf{AX})_i$'s, $(\mathbf{CX})_\ell$'s and x_{k+1} (regarded as if they are variables) are all non-negative.
  · All coefficients of $x_1, \ldots, x_k$ in this combination are non-positive.
  · The strict inequations of types 2,3,4,6 (for $\ell \in L_3$) are used at least once.

  Then by erasing all $-a_{i,k+1}x_{k+1}$'s (for $i \in I_3$) and all $-c_{\ell,k+1}x_{k+1}$'s (for $\ell \in L_3$) in the system and use the same way to add them up, then we have a linear combination of $(\mathbf{AX})_i$'s and $(\mathbf{CX})_\ell$'s such that:
  · The coefficients of $(\mathbf{AX})_i$'s and $(\mathbf{CX})_\ell$'s are all non-negative.
  · All coefficients for $x_1, \ldots, x_k, x_{k+1}$ in this combination are non-positive.
  · The strict inequations of types 2,3,4,6 (for $\ell \in L_3$) are used at least once.

  Since strict inequations of type 2,3,4,6 have positive coefficients of $(\mathbf{CX})_\ell$'s, we have non-negative $\mathbf{b} \in \mathbb{Q}^{n_1 \times 1}$ and $\mathbf{0}^{n_2 \times 1} \neq \mathbf{d} \in \mathbb{Q}^{n_2 \times 1}$ such that $\mathbf{b}^T\mathbf{A} + \mathbf{d}^T\mathbf{C} \leq \mathbf{0}^{1 \times m}$. By appropriate scaling, we can make sure that all coordinates of $\mathbf{b}$ and $\mathbf{d}$ are in $\mathbb{N}$.

Therefore, in any case, we have that there are $\mathbf{b} \in \mathbb{N}^{n_1 \times 1}$ and $\mathbf{0}^{n_2 \times 1} \neq \mathbf{d} \in \mathbb{N}^{n_2 \times 1}$ such that $\mathbf{b}^T\mathbf{A} + \mathbf{d}^T\mathbf{C} \leq \mathbf{0}$.

Remark 1. Intuitively, Farkas' Lemma is a kind of soundness and completeness result in disguise. If we regard the rows of the finite linear inequation system as logical axioms, and the linear combination of the rows as a derivation rule, and the result of the linear combinations as theorems, then the lemma essentially states that the system is not satisfiable iff there is a linear combination of the "axioms" which can derive a contradiction, i.e. the system is not consistent.

We give a concrete example to illustrate how to determine whether a linear inequation system has non-negative real solutions:

Example 1. Let us consider the following linear inequation system:

$$\begin{cases} -x_1 + x_2 + x_3 > 0 \\ x_1 - x_2 + x_3 > 0 \\ x_1 + x_2 - x_3 > 0 \end{cases}$$

To check whether this system has non-negative real solutions, we first rewrite the inequation system as follows:

$$\begin{cases} x_2 > x_1 - x_3 \\ x_1 + x_3 > x_2 \\ x_2 > x_3 - x_1 \end{cases}$$

Then we transform the system above into the following system, which has non-negative real solutions iff the previous system has non-negative real solutions.

Basically, we eliminate all occurrences of x_2 by concatenating the inequalities where x_2 occurs on the left of $>$ and the inequalities where x_2 occurs on the right of $>$:

$$\begin{cases} x_1 + x_3 > x_1 - x_3 \\ x_1 + x_3 > x_3 - x_1 \end{cases}$$

Now we rewrite the system as follows:

$$\begin{cases} 2x_3 > 0 \\ 2x_1 > 0 \end{cases}$$

This system obviously has non-negative real solutions.

Now we have the following characterization result:

Theorem 2. *Given any finite model $\mathcal{M} = (W, N)$, $\mathcal{M}$ is metrizable iff $\mathcal{M}$ makes Ψ true in Definition 4.*

Proof. When $W = \{w\}$, $\mathcal{M}$ is metrizable by the metric function $d(w, w) = 0$. When $W = \{w, v\}$ has two elements, $\mathcal{M}$ is metrizable by the metric function d such that $d(w, w) = d(v, v) = 0$ and $d(w, v) = d(v, w) = 1$. In both cases the axioms in Ψ are true in $\mathcal{M}$. Therefore, it suffices to consider the situation where $|W| \geq 3$.

The left-to-right direction follows from Theorem 1. For the other direction, consider variables $x_{w,v}$ for all $w, v \in W$ which is intended to refer to the value of $d(w, v)$.

Then $\mathcal{M}$ is metrizable iff the following inequation system has non-negative real solutions:

$$\begin{cases} x_{w,v} > 0 \text{ (for all } w, v \in W \text{ such that } w \neq v) \\ x_{w,w} = 0 \text{ (for all } w \in W) \\ x_{w,v} = x_{v,w} \text{ (for all } w, v \in W) \\ x_{w,v} + x_{v,u} \geq x_{w,u} \text{ (for all } w, v, u \in W), \\ x_{w,v} < x_{w,u} \text{ (for all } (w, v, u) \in N) \\ x_{w,v} \geq x_{w,u} \text{ (for all } (w, v, u) \in W^3 - N) \end{cases}$$

Since Axioms 1–3 in Definition 4 describe all the conditions that should be met for tuples (x, y, z) that contain repeated elements, therefore once Axioms 1–3 are true, it suffices to consider all the tuples (x, y, z) such that $\#(x, y, z)$.

By taking $x_{w,w} := 0$ for all $w \in W$, this inequation system has non-negative real solutions iff the following system has non-negative real solutions (for the last three lines, we also eliminate all the inequations with repeated elements; for the last two lines, they are guaranteed by Axioms 1–3):

$$\begin{cases} x_{w,v} > 0 \text{ (for all } w, v \in W \text{ such that } w \neq v) \\ x_{w,v} = x_{v,w} \text{ (for all } w, v \in W \text{ such that } w \neq v) \\ x_{w,v} + x_{v,u} \geq x_{w,u} \text{ (for all } w, v, u \in W \text{ such that } \#(w, v, u)), \\ x_{w,v} < x_{w,u} \text{ (for all } (w, v, u) \in N \text{ such that } \#(w, v, u)) \\ x_{w,v} \geq x_{w,u} \text{ (for all } (w, v, u) \in W^3 - N \text{ such that } \#(w, v, u)) \end{cases}$$

Since $x_{w,v} = x_{v,w}$ for all $w, v \in W$ such that $w \neq v$, we can change the notation for variables such that the variable $x_{w,v}$ becomes $x_{\{w,v\}}$, then the previous inequation system has non-negative real solutions iff the following inequation system has non-negative real solutions:

$$\begin{cases} x_{\{w,v\}} > 0 \text{ (for all } w, v \in W \text{ such that } w \neq v) \\ x_{\{w,v\}} + x_{\{v,u\}} - x_{\{w,u\}} \geq 0 \text{ (for all } w, v, u \in W \text{ such that } \#(w, v, u)). \\ x_{\{w,v\}} < x_{\{w,u\}} \text{ (for all } (w, v, u) \in N \text{ such that } \#(w, v, u)) \\ x_{\{w,v\}} \geq x_{\{w,u\}} \text{ (for all } (w, v, u) \in W^3 - N \text{ such that } \#(w, v, u)) \end{cases}$$

Let us re-order the inequalities as follows:

$$\begin{cases} x_{\{w,v\}} + x_{\{v,u\}} - x_{\{w,u\}} \geq 0 \text{ (for all } w, v, u \in W \text{ such that } \#(w, v, u)). \\ x_{\{w,v\}} - x_{\{w,u\}} \geq 0 \text{ (for all } (w, v, u) \in W^3 - N \text{ such that } \#(w, v, u)) \\ x_{\{w,v\}} > 0 \text{ (for all } w, v \in W \text{ such that } w \neq v) \\ x_{\{w,u\}} - x_{\{w,v\}} > 0 \text{ (for all } (w, v, u) \in N \text{ such that } \#(w, v, u)) \end{cases}$$

Let us denote the inequation system as $\{\mathbf{BX} \geq \mathbf{0}, \mathbf{CX} \geq \mathbf{0}, \mathbf{DX} > \mathbf{0}, \mathbf{EX} > \mathbf{0}\}$, where $\mathbf{B}$, $\mathbf{C}$, $\mathbf{D}$, $\mathbf{E}$ correspond to the four types of inequations. By Lemma 1, this system has no non-negative real solutions iff there are non-negative natural number vertial vectors $\mathbf{b}, \mathbf{c}, \mathbf{d}, \mathbf{e}$ such that $\mathbf{b}^T\mathbf{B} + \mathbf{c}^T\mathbf{C} + \mathbf{d}^T\mathbf{D} + \mathbf{e}^T\mathbf{E} \leq \mathbf{0}$ and $(\mathbf{d}^T, \mathbf{e}^T)$ contains at least one positive number.

Now let us denote $\Sigma\mathbf{b}$, $\Sigma\mathbf{c}$, $\Sigma\mathbf{d}$, $\Sigma\mathbf{e}$ as the sums of all numbers occurring in the vectors $\mathbf{b}$, $\mathbf{c}$, $\mathbf{d}$, $\mathbf{e}$, respectively.

Suppose $\mathcal{M}$ makes Ψ true but is not metrizable. Then in the inequation system above, there are $\mathbf{b}, \mathbf{c}, \mathbf{d}, \mathbf{e}$ satisfying the conditions above.

Then summing up all numbers in $\mathbf{b}^T\mathbf{B}+\mathbf{c}^T\mathbf{C}+\mathbf{d}^T\mathbf{D}+\mathbf{e}^T\mathbf{E}$, we have $\Sigma\mathbf{b}+\Sigma\mathbf{d}$, which should be non-positive. Since $\mathbf{b}, \mathbf{d}$ only contain natural numbers, we have that $\mathbf{b}$ and $\mathbf{d}$ are both zero vectors, so $\mathbf{c}^T\mathbf{C} + \mathbf{e}^T\mathbf{E} \leq \mathbf{0}$.

Since $\mathbf{d}$ is a zero vector and $(\mathbf{d}^T, \mathbf{e}^T)$ contains at least one positive number, it must be in $\mathbf{e}$. Therefore, from $\mathbf{c}^T\mathbf{C} + \mathbf{e}^T\mathbf{E} \leq \mathbf{0}$ we have that there are $x_{\{x_i,z_i\}} - x_{\{x_i,y_i\}}$ with $(x_i, y_i, z_i) \in N$ and $i = 1, \ldots, m$ $(m \geq 1)$ and $x_{\{u_j,v_j\}} - x_{\{u_j,w_j\}}$ with $(u_j, v_j, w_j) \notin N$ and $j = 1, \ldots, n$ $(n \geq 0)$ such that in their sum, all variables have non-positive coefficients. Since the sum of all the coefficients are 0, we have that it is only possible that for each variable, the sum of its coefficients is 0.

Now consider a variable $x_{w,v}$. If its coefficient in the sum is 0, then among all the (x_i, y_i, z_i)'s and (u_j, v_j, w_j)'s, $x_{w,v}$ occurs as $x_{\{x_i,y_i\}}$ or $x_{\{u_j,w_j\}}$ for the same number of times as $x_{\{x_i,z_i\}}$ or $x_{\{u_j,v_j\}}$. Then the lists $(\{x_1, y_1\}, \ldots, \{x_m, y_m\}, \{u_1, w_1\}, \ldots, \{u_n, w_n\})$ and $(\{x_1, z_1\}, \ldots, \{x_m, z_m\}, \{u_1, v_1\}, \ldots, \{u_n, v_n\})$ are permutations of each other. Then by the definition of the inequation system, we have that $x_{\{u_j,v_j\}} - x_{\{u_j,w_j\}}$ with $(u_j, v_j, w_j) \notin N$ and $j = 1, \ldots, m$ $(m \geq 1)$, and $x_{\{u_j,v_j\}} - x_{\{u_j,w_j\}}$ with $(u_j, v_j, w_j) \notin N$ and $j = 1, \ldots, n$ $(n \geq 0)$. Then by Axiom 4 in Definition 4 we get a contradiction. Therefore $\mathcal{M}$ is metrizable.

Theorem 3. *The universal first-order theory Φ_M of relative nearness relation is* $\mathsf{Th}_\forall(\Psi)$.

Proof. It is easy to check $\mathsf{Th}_\forall(\Psi) \subseteq \Phi_M$ by Theorem 1. For the other direction, consider a universal sentence $\forall\vec{x}\varphi(\vec{x})$ where φ is quantifier-free. If $\forall\vec{x}\varphi(\vec{x}) \notin \mathsf{Th}_\forall(\Psi)$, then $\Psi \cup \{\exists\vec{x}\neg\varphi(\vec{x})\}$ is satisfiable, so for $\exists\vec{x}\neg\varphi(\vec{x})$, take a finite vector of constants $\vec{c}$ which has the same length of $\vec{x}$ and consider formula $\neg\varphi(\vec{c})$. Then

$\Psi \cup \{\neg\varphi(\vec{c})\}$ is satisfiable on a model $\mathcal{M} = (W, N)$. Take the submodel of $\mathcal{M}$ whose domain consists of the interpretations of all constants in $\vec{c}$, then we get a finite model $\mathcal{M}'$ such that $\neg\varphi(\vec{c})$ is still satisfiable, and therefore $\exists\vec{x}\neg\varphi(\vec{x})$ is also satisfiable on $\mathcal{M}'$. Since $\mathcal{M}'$ is a submodel of $\mathcal{M}$ and Ψ is a set of universal sentences, we have that $\mathcal{M}' \models \Psi$. By Theorem 2, $\mathcal{M}'$ is metrizable. So $\{\exists\vec{x}\neg\varphi(\vec{x})\}$ is satisfiable in a metrizable finite model and $\forall\vec{x}\varphi(\vec{x})$ is falsifiable there. So $\forall\vec{x}\varphi(\vec{x}) \notin \Phi_M$.

3.3 Further Simplifications of the Axioms

As we can see from Axiom 4 in 4, the presentation of this axiom schema is rather complicated. In what follows, we will simplify this axiom schema to make the axiomatization simpler, which is mainly for theoretic purposes, but they will also be useful in the intuitive understanding of the axioms.

Definition 5 (The First Simplification). *Θ consists of the following universal sentences:*

1. $\forall x\forall y\neg Nxyy$.
2. $\forall x\forall y(x \neq y \to Nxxy)$.
3. $\forall x\forall y\neg Nxyx$.
4. $\forall\vec{x}\forall\vec{y}\forall\vec{z}\forall\vec{u}\forall\vec{v}\forall\vec{w}(Nx_1y_1z_1 \wedge \ldots \wedge Nx_my_mz_m \wedge \neg Nu_1v_1w_1 \wedge \ldots \wedge \neg Nu_nv_nw_n \to \bot)$, *where the lists* $(\{x_1, y_1\}, \ldots, \{x_m, y_m\}, \{u_1, w_1\}, \ldots, \{u_n, w_n\})$ *and* $(\{x_1, z_1\}, \ldots, \{x_m, z_m\}, \{u_1, v_1\}, \ldots, \{u_n, v_n\})$ *are permutations of each other and* $m \geq 1, n \geq 0$.

The idea behind this simplification is that even if we do not have the requirements that x_i, y_i, z_i $(i = 1, \ldots, m)$ are pairwise different and similarly for u_j, v_j, w_j $(j = 1, \ldots, n)$, the axiomatization is equivalent to the version with the requirements.

We have the following theorem:

Theorem 4. *Given any finite model $\mathcal{M} = (W, N)$, the following are equivalent:*

1. *$\mathcal{M}$ is metrizable.*
2. *$\mathcal{M}$ makes Ψ true in Definition 4.*
3. *$\mathcal{M}$ makes Θ true in Definition 5.*

Proof.
- The equivalence between 1 and 2 is from Theorem 2.
- For 1⇒3, suppose that $\mathcal{M}$ is metrizable but $\mathcal{M}$ does not make all axioms in Θ true. Then from 1⇔2, $\mathcal{M}$ makes the first three axioms true, so $\mathcal{M}$ falsifies some instance of Axiom 4, so there are $x_i, y_i, z_i \in W$ $(i = 1, \ldots, m)$ and $u_j, v_j, w_j \in W$ $(j = 1, \ldots, n)$ such that
  - $m \geq 1, n \geq 0$.
  - $N(x_i, y_i, z_i)$ for $i = 1, \ldots, m$.
  - $\sim N(u_j, v_j, w_j)$ for $j = 1, \ldots, n$.
  - $(\{x_1, y_1\}, \ldots, \{x_m, y_m\}, \{u_1, w_1\}, \ldots, \{u_n, w_n\})$ and $(\{x_1, z_1\}, \ldots, \{x_m, z_m\}, \{u_1, v_1\}, \ldots, \{u_n, v_n\})$ are permutations of each other.

Then consider the metric d for $\mathcal{M}$, then
- $d(x_i, y_i) < d(x_i, z_i)$ for $i = 1, \ldots, m$.
- $d(u_j, w_j) \leq d(u_j, v_j)$ for $j = 1, \ldots, n$.

Adding all the inequalities up, we will have a sum of distances smaller than the same sum, a contradiction. So $\mathcal{M} \vDash \Theta$.

- For 3⇒2, suppose that $\mathcal{M} \vDash \Theta$, then since every instance of the Axiom 4 in Ψ is a semantic consequence of the corresponding instance (the one without the pairwise difference statements) of Axiom 4 in Θ, we have that $\mathcal{M} \vDash \Psi$.

We can further simplify Axiom 4 such that we do not need to use the permutation condition. In what follows, we use $N_{\leq}xyz$ to represent $\neg Nxzy$ and $Mxyz$ to represent either $Nxyz$ or $N_{\leq}xyz$.

Definition 6 (The Second Simplification). *Δ consists of the following universal sentences:*

1. $\forall x \forall y \neg Nxyy$.
2. $\forall x \forall y (x \neq y \rightarrow Nxxy)$.
3. $\forall x \forall y \neg Nxyx$.
4. $\forall x_1 \ldots \forall x_n (Nx_1y_1z_1 \wedge Mx_2y_2z_2 \wedge \ldots \wedge Mx_ny_nz_n \rightarrow \bot)$, *where* $n \geq 1$ *and* $\{x_2, y_2\} = \{x_1, z_1\}$, $\{x_3, y_3\} = \{x_2, z_2\}$, $\{x_n, y_n\} = \{x_{n-1}, z_{n-1}\}$, $\{x_1, y_1\} = \{x_n, z_n\}$.

Intuitively, in Axiom 4 of Δ, we have inequalities of the form $d(x_1, y_1) < d(x_1, z_1)$, $d(x_2, y_2) < (\leq) d(x_2, z_2)$, $\ldots$, $d(x_{n-1}, y_{n-1}) < (\leq) d(x_{n-1}, z_{n-1})$, $d(x_n, y_n) < (\leq) d(x_n, z_n)$, and by adding them up, we have a strict inequality between two identical sums, a contradiction.

Theorem 5. *Given any finite model $\mathcal{M} = (W, N)$, the following are equivalent:*

1. *$\mathcal{M}$ is metrizable.*
2. *$\mathcal{M}$ makes Ψ true in Definition 4.*
3. *$\mathcal{M}$ makes Θ true in Definition 5.*
4. *$\mathcal{M}$ makes Δ true in Definition 6.*

Proof.
- The equivalence between 1,2,3 is from Theorem 5.
- 3⇒4 follows from that Δ is a special case of Θ.
- For 4⇒3, suppose that the antecedent holds for some $\vec{x}$, $\vec{y}$, $\vec{z}$, $\vec{u}$, $\vec{v}$, $\vec{w}$ such that $(\{x_1, y_1\}, \ldots, \{x_m, y_m\}, \{u_1, w_1\}, \ldots, \{u_n, w_n\})$ and $(\{x_1, z_1\}, \ldots, \{x_m, z_m\}, \{u_1, v_1\}, \ldots, \{u_n, v_n\})$ are permutations of each other. By the property of permutation, we can decompose the permutation into one or more disjoint cycles. Take the cycle such that N occurs positively in the antecedent (i.e. some x_i, y_i, z_i occur in the cycle), then we have a cycle of the form as described in the antecedent of Axiom 4 in Δ, so we get a contradiction.

4 Conclusions and Future Works

In the present paper, we give an axiomatization of the universal theory of relative nearness relation, using a variant of Farkas' Lemma. This result shows the usefulness of methods for linear algebra and optimization theory in problems in logics where certain numerical informations are involved. In addition, the result of the present paper will be useful in the study of modal logic, hybrid logic and conditional logic involving semantics based on metric spaces.
For future work, we mention the following topics:

- The first one is about the finite axiomatizability of the universal first-order theory of relative nearness. In this direction, either we find a finite axiomatization of the theory, or we can use the Ehrenfeucht-Fraisse game method to show that the universal first-order theory of relative nearness is not finitely axiomatizable.
- The second one is to consider the axiomatization of the modal logic and hybrid logic of relative nearness (see [2,3]) where the following binary modality $\langle N \rangle$ is used:

$$\begin{aligned}(W, N, V), w \Vdash \langle N \rangle(\varphi, \psi) &\text{ iff there exists } v, u \in W \text{ such that} \\ &Nwvu \text{ and } (W, N, V), v \Vdash \varphi \text{ and } (W, N, V), u \Vdash \psi.\end{aligned}$$

- Another topic is about conditional logic. In Lewis' account of conditional logic (see [14]), a formula $\varphi > \psi$ is true at w if among all φ-worlds, all the ones nearest to w make ψ true. Here the concept of "nearest" can be understood in terms of a metric space (see [18] for more discussions on this). It would be interesting to see if we can axiomatize conditional logic with respect to semantics based on metric spaces.

Acknowledgement. The research of the author is supported by Shandong Provincial Natural Science Foundation, China (project number: ZR2023QF021) and Taishan Young Scholars Program of the Government of Shandong Province, China (No.tsqn201909151).

References

1. Agnew, G., Gutierrez-Hougardy, U., Harding, J., Shapirovsky, I., West, J.: On distance logics of Euclidean spaces. ArXiv preprint arXiv:2501.04884 (2025)
2. Aiello, M., Pratt-Hartmann, I., van Benthem, J.: Handbook of spatial logics. Springer, Netherlands (2007)
3. Aiello, M., van Benthem, J.: A modal walk through space. J. Appl. Non-Classical Logics **12**(3–4), 319–363 (2002)
4. Cunha, F.: Modal logics for reasoning about distance spaces. Master's thesis, Universidade de Lisboa

5. Du, H., Alechina, N., Stock, K., Jackson, M.: The Logic of NEAR and FAR. In: Tenbrink, T., Stell, J., Galton, A., Wood, Z. (eds.) COSIT 2013. LNCS, vol. 8116, pp. 475–494. Springer, Cham (2013). https://doi.org/10.1007/978-3-319-01790-7_26
6. Farkas, G.: Theorie der einfachen ungleichungen. Journal für die reine und angewandte Mathematik (Crelles Journal) **1902**(124), 1–27 (1902)
7. Fu, X., Zhao, Z.: Modal logic with "most". Studia Logica (2024)
8. Fu, X., Zhao, Z.: An axiomatization of $\mathrm{MFO}^{-}(\mathrm{M})$ in finite models. Submitted (2025)
9. Giritli, M.: Logics for reasoning with comparative distances (2007)
10. Kurucz, A., Wolter, F., Zakharyaschev, M.: Modal logics for metric spaces: open problems. In: Artemov, S., Barringer, S., d'Avila Garcez, A.S., Lamb, L.C., Woods, J. (eds.) We Will Show Them: Essays in Honour of Dov Gabbay, volume 2, pp. 193–108. College Publications (2005)
11. Kutz, O.: Notes on logics of metric spaces. Stud. Logica. **85**(1), 75–104 (2007)
12. Kutz, O., Sturm, H., Suzuki, N.-Y., Wolter, F., Zakharyaschev, M.: Axiomatizing distance logics. J. Appl. Non-Classical Logics **12**(3–4), 425–439 (2002)
13. Kutz, O., Wolter, F., Sturm, H., Suzuki, N.-Y., Zakharyaschev, M.: Logics of metric spaces. ACM Trans. Comput. Logic **4**(2), 260–294 (2003)
14. Lewis, D.: Counterfactuals. Blackwell, Oxford (1973)
15. Shehtman, V., Kudinov, A., Shapirovsky, I.: On modal logics of hamming spaces. Advances Modal Logic **9**, 395–410 (2012)
16. Sheremet, M., Tishkovsky, D., Wolter, F., Zakharyaschev M.: Comparative similarity, tree automata, and Diophantine equations. In: Sutcliffe, G., Voronkov, A. (eds.) Logic for Programming, Artificial Intelligence, and Reasoning, pp. 651–665, Berlin, Heidelberg (2005). Springer Berlin Heidelberg
17. Sheremet, M., Wolter, F., Zakharyaschev, M.: A modal logic framework for reasoning about comparative distances and topology. Ann. Pure Appl. Logic **161**(4), 534–559 (2010)
18. van Benthem, J.: The logic of conditionals on outback trails. Logic J. IGPL **31**(6), 1135–1152 (2023)
19. van Benthem, J., Bezhanishvili, G.: Modal logics of space. In: Aiello, M., Pratt-Hartmann, I., Van Benthem, J. (eds.) Handbook of Spatial Logics, pp. 217–298. Springer, Netherlands, Dordrecht (2007)
20. Wolter, F., Zakharyaschev, M.: A logic for metric and topology. J. Symb. Log. **70**(3), 795–828 (2005)

On Residual Co-implications Derived from q-Rung Orthopair Fuzzy t-Conorms

Wen Sheng Du(✉)

School of Business, Zhengzhou University, Zhengzhou 450001, People's Republic of China
wsdu@zzu.edu.cn

Abstract. In this paper, we consider q-rung orthopair fuzzy (q-ROF) residual co-implications induced by q-ROF t-conorms. The expression corresponding to representable q-ROF t-conorms is provided explicitly. Moreover, the q-ROF residual implications and co-implications are employed to construct inclusion measures between q-ROF sets.

Keywords: Inclusion measures · Residual implications · Residual co-implications · q-rung orthopair fuzzy t-conorms

1 Introduction

Fuzzy implications [1] serve as a fundamental mechanism for modeling IF-THEN rules under uncertainty and vagueness. They quantify the truth values of fuzzy propositions, which makes them essential for processing human-like and linguistic rules. Over the past several decades, fuzzy implications have been widely used in approximate reasoning, decision-making, control systems, etc.

There are many classes of fuzzy implications with different properties to meet different requirements. Residual implications [2] are an important type of fuzzy implications obtained by the residuation property. De Baets [6] proposed residual co-implications, the dual connectives of residual implications, on a bounded ordered set. Ruiz and Torrens [12] studied the residual co-implications defined from idempotent uninorms. Wang and Fang [15] introduced the residual co-implications of left and right uninorms on a complete lattice. Su et al. [13,14] investigated the residual co-implications generated from pseudo-uninorms. Dai et al. [5] presented fuzzy co-implications on the poset of closed intervals.

Cornelis et al. [3] introduced some intuitionistic fuzzy implications, residual implications included, in intuitionistic fuzzy set environments. Hu and Wong [10] presented the interval-valued fuzzy residual implications and co-implications. Recently, Xie et al. [16] defined two kinds of q-ROF residual implications derived from q-ROF t-norms and q-ROF overlap functions. Unfortunately, the q-ROF residual co-implications are once again neglected in the existing study. In this paper, we will fill this gap and propose residual co-implications within the q-ROF framework.

M. Bonsangue and Y. Chen (Eds.): AILA 2025, CCIS 2668, pp. 95–103, 2026.
https://doi.org/10.1007/978-981-95-8262-4_7

Fuzzy implications are suggested for building inclusion measures in the fuzzy set community. Grzegorzewski and Mrówka [9] proposed a subsethood measure of intuitionistic fuzzy sets based on the Hamming distance. The resulted subsethood is a real number in $[0,1]$, which may lead to anomalies in some cases. Cornelis and Kerre [4] presented intuitionistic fuzzy inclusion measures whose results are intuitionistic fuzzy values. Following this line of thought, by using q-ROF residual implications and co-implications, two types of q-ROF inclusion degrees are developed in this paper.

In Sect. 2, we review basic concepts of t-(co)norms, residual (co-)implications, q-ROF t-(co)norms and q-ROF residual implications. In Sect. 3, we introduce residual co-implications on q-ROF values (q-ROFVs) and provide the explicit expression for representable q-ROF t-conorms. In Sect. 4, we propose two inclusion measures between q-ROF sets (q-ROFSs) by the use of q-ROF residual implications and co-implications. In Sect. 5, we conclude this paper.

2 Preliminaries

In this section, we mainly recall some well-known fuzzy connectives and some operations on q-ROFVs.

An ordered pair $\langle\mu,\nu\rangle$ is called a q-ROFV [8,17] if

$$0 \le \mu,\nu \le 1 \text{ and } 0 \le \mu^q + \nu^q \le 1, \tag{1}$$

where $q \ge 1$. Throughout this paper, the set of all q-ROFVs is denoted by Δ. The order relation in Δ is defined as

$$\langle\mu_1,\nu_1\rangle \preceq \langle\mu_2,\nu_2\rangle \text{ iff } \mu_1 \le \mu_2, \nu_1 \ge \nu_2. \tag{2}$$

Obviously, the least element and the greatest element in Δ associated with relation $\preceq$ are $\langle 0,1\rangle$ and $\langle 1,0\rangle$, respectively.

Similar to t-(co)norms on $[0,1]$ [11], one can define t-(co)norms on q-ROFVs with respect to order $\preceq$. In this paper, we focus on representable [7] q-ROF t-norms $\mathcal{T}$ and t-conorms $\mathcal{S}$. Concretely, there exists a pair of t-norm T and t-conorm S such that for all $\mathbb{x} = \langle\mu_1,\nu_1\rangle, \mathbb{y} = \langle\mu_2,\nu_2\rangle \in \Delta$,

$$\mathcal{T}(\mathbb{x},\mathbb{y}) = \left\langle \sqrt[q]{T(\mu_1^q,\mu_2^q)}, \sqrt[q]{S(\nu_1^q,\nu_2^q)} \right\rangle, \tag{3}$$

$$\mathcal{S}(\mathbb{x},\mathbb{y}) = \left\langle \sqrt[q]{S(\mu_1^q,\mu_2^q)}, \sqrt[q]{T(\nu_1^q,\nu_2^q)} \right\rangle, \tag{4}$$

which are shortly denoted as $\mathcal{T} = (T,S)$ and $\mathcal{S} = (S,T)$, respectively. In what follows, we always assume that T is a left-continuous t-norm, and its dual t-conorm S is right-continuous. In addition, the standard q-ROF negation [17] is $\mathcal{N}(\langle\mu,\nu\rangle) = \langle\nu,\mu\rangle$ for all $\langle\mu,\nu\rangle \in \Delta$.

Example 1. The representable q-ROF t-(co)norms produced by some popular t-(co)norms are as follows: for $\mathbb{x} = \langle \mu_1, \nu_1 \rangle, \mathbb{y} = \langle \mu_2, \nu_2 \rangle \in \Delta$,

$$\mathcal{T}_{\mathcal{M}}(\mathbb{x}_1, \mathbb{x}_2) = \langle \mu_1 \wedge \mu_2, \nu_1 \vee \nu_2 \rangle,$$
$$\mathcal{S}_{\mathcal{M}}(\mathbb{x}_1, \mathbb{x}_2) = \langle \mu_1 \vee \mu_2, \nu_1 \wedge \nu_2 \rangle.$$
$$\mathcal{T}_{\mathcal{P}}(\mathbb{x}_1, \mathbb{x}_2) = \left\langle \mu_1 \mu_2, \sqrt[q]{\nu_1^q + \nu_2^q - \nu_1^q \nu_2^q} \right\rangle,$$
$$\mathcal{S}_{\mathcal{P}}(\mathbb{x}_1, \mathbb{x}_2) = \left\langle \sqrt[q]{\mu_1^q + \mu_2^q - \mu_2^q \mu_1^q}, \nu_1 \nu_2 \right\rangle.$$
$$\mathcal{T}_{\mathcal{L}}(\mathbb{x}_1, \mathbb{x}_2) = \left\langle \sqrt[q]{\max\left(\mu_1^q + \mu_2^q - 1, 0\right)}, \sqrt[q]{\min\left(\nu_1^q + \nu_2^q, 1\right)} \right\rangle,$$
$$\mathcal{S}_{\mathcal{L}}(\mathbb{x}_1, \mathbb{x}_2) = \left\langle \sqrt[q]{\min\left(\mu_1^q + \mu_2^q, 1\right)}, \sqrt[q]{\max\left(\nu_1^q + \nu_2^q - 1, 0\right)} \right\rangle.$$

Definition 1 [16]**.** *Let $\mathcal{T}$ be a q-ROF t-norm. The residual implication derived from $\mathcal{T}$ is as follows: for $\mathbb{x}, \mathbb{y} \in \Delta$,*

$$\Theta_{\mathcal{T}}(\mathbb{x}, \mathbb{y}) = \sup\{\mathbb{z} \in \Delta : \mathcal{T}(\mathbb{x}, \mathbb{z}) \preceq \mathbb{y}\}. \tag{5}$$

Theorem 1 [16]**.** *Let $\mathbb{x} = \langle \mu_1, \nu_1 \rangle$, $\mathbb{y} = \langle \mu_2, \nu_2 \rangle$ be two q-ROFVs and $\mathcal{T}$ be a representable q-ROF t-norm determined by (T, S). Then we have*

$$\Theta_{\mathcal{T}}(\mathbb{x}, \mathbb{y}) = \left\langle \sqrt[q]{\theta_T(\mu_1^q, \mu_2^q) \bigwedge \theta_T(1 - \nu_1^q, 1 - \nu_2^q)}, \sqrt[q]{\psi_S(\nu_1^q, \nu_2^q)} \right\rangle, \tag{6}$$

where θ_T and ψ_S are residual implication and residual co-implication derived respectively from T and S. These two operators are defined as: for $x, y \in [0, 1]$,

$$\theta_T(x, y) = \sup\{z \in [0, 1] : T(x, z) \leq y\},$$
$$\psi_S(x, y) = \inf\{z \in [0, 1] : S(x, z) \geq y\}.$$

3 Residual Co-implications on q-ROFVs

In this section, the q-ROF residual co-implications are generated by q-ROF t-conorms and the expression is given for the representable case.

Definition 2. *Let $\mathcal{S}$ be a q-ROF t-conorm. The mapping $\Psi_{\mathcal{S}} : \Delta^2 \to \Delta$ is defined by: $\mathbb{x}, \mathbb{y} \in \Delta$,*

$$\Psi_{\mathcal{S}}(\mathbb{x}, \mathbb{y}) = \inf\{\mathbb{z} \in \Delta : \mathcal{S}(\mathbb{x}, \mathbb{z}) \succeq \mathbb{y}\}. \tag{7}$$

By the monotonicity of $\mathcal{S}$, clearly, we have $\Psi_{\mathcal{S}}(\mathbb{x}, \mathbb{y})$ decreases as $\mathbb{x}$ increases, while increases as $\mathbb{y}$ increases. For some specific q-ROFVs, we have $\Psi_{\mathcal{S}}(\langle 0, 1 \rangle, \langle 0, 1 \rangle) = \langle 0, 1 \rangle$, $\Psi_{\mathcal{S}}(\langle 1, 0 \rangle, \langle 1, 0 \rangle) = \langle 0, 1 \rangle$ and $\Psi_{\mathcal{S}}(\langle 0, 1 \rangle, \langle 1, 0 \rangle) = \langle 1, 0 \rangle$. Therefore, operation $\Psi_{\mathcal{S}}$ is indeed a residual co-implication. Furthermore, we have $\Psi_{\mathcal{S}}(\langle 1, 0 \rangle, \mathbb{x}) = \Psi_{\mathcal{S}}(\mathbb{x}, \langle 0, 1 \rangle) = \langle 0, 1 \rangle$ for all $\mathbb{x} \in \Delta$.

Theorem 2. *Let* $\mathbb{x} = \langle \mu_1, \nu_1 \rangle$, $\mathbb{y} = \langle \mu_2, \nu_2 \rangle$ *be two* q-ROFVs *and* $\mathcal{S} = (S, T)$ *be a representable* q-ROF *t-conorm. Then, the* q-ROF *residual co-implication* $\Psi_{\mathcal{S}}(\mathbb{x}, \mathbb{y})$ *can be expressed as*

$$\Psi_{\mathcal{S}}(\mathbb{x}, \mathbb{y}) = \left\langle \sqrt[q]{\psi_S(\mu_1^q, \mu_2^q)}, \sqrt[q]{\theta_T(\nu_1^q, \nu_2^q) \bigwedge \theta_T(1-\mu_1^q, 1-\mu_2^q)} \right\rangle. \tag{8}$$

Proof. From Definition 2, it follows that

$$\begin{aligned} \Psi_{\mathcal{S}}(\mathbb{x}, \mathbb{y}) &= \inf\{\mathbb{z} \in \Delta : \mathcal{S}(\mathbb{x}, \mathbb{z}) \succeq \mathbb{y}\} \\ &= \inf\{\mathbb{z} = \langle \mu, \nu \rangle \in \Delta : S(\mu_1^q, \mu^q) \geq \mu_2^q, T(\nu_1^q, \nu^q) \leq \nu_2^q\} \\ &= \inf\{(\mu, \nu) \in [0,1]^2 : \mu^q \geq \psi_S(\mu_1^q, \mu_2^q), \nu^q \leq \theta_T(\nu_1^q, \nu_2^q), \mu^q + \nu^q \leq 1\} \\ &= \left\langle \sqrt[q]{\psi_S(\mu_1^q, \mu_2^q)}, \sqrt[q]{\theta_T(\nu_1^q, \nu_2^q) \bigwedge \theta_T(1-\mu_1^q, 1-\mu_2^q)} \right\rangle. \end{aligned}$$

For a better understanding of the proof, the feasible regions for two cases and their respective minimal element are displayed in Fig. 1. It can be seen that Eq. (8) cannot be written incorrectly as:

$$\Psi_{\mathcal{S}}(\mathbb{x}, \mathbb{y}) = \left\langle \sqrt[q]{\psi_S(\mu_1^q, \mu_2^q)}, \sqrt[q]{\theta_T(\nu_1^q, \nu_2^q)} \right\rangle.$$

The second component of non-membership in Eq. (8) can ensure the result is always a q-ROFV.

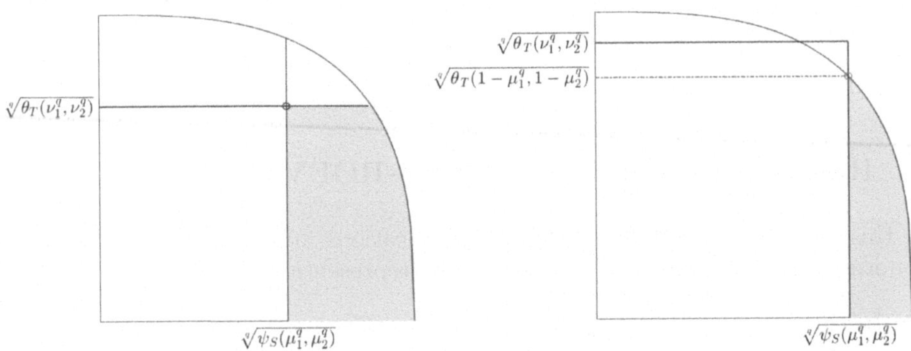

Fig. 1. Two cases of feasible regions and minimal elements in the proof of Theorem 2.

Example 2. For nilpotent minimum T_{nM} and nilpotent maximum S_{nM}: $T_{nM}(x,y) = \begin{cases} 0, & \text{if } x+y \leq 1, \\ x \wedge y, & \text{otherwise,} \end{cases}$ and $S_{nM}(x,y) = \begin{cases} 1, & \text{if } x+y \geq 1 \\ x \vee y, & \text{otherwise,} \end{cases}$ their residual implication and co-implication are

$$\theta_{T_{nM}}(x,y)=\begin{cases}1, & \text{if } x\le y\\ \max(1-x,y), & \text{if } x>y\end{cases}$$

$$\psi_{S_{nM}}(x,y)=\begin{cases}\min(1-x,y), & \text{if } x<y\\ 0, & \text{if } x\ge y\end{cases}$$

If one construct q-ROF t-conorm $\mathcal{S}_{n\mathcal{M}}$ by T_{nM} and S_{nM}, i.e., $\mathcal{S}_{n\mathcal{M}}=(S_{nM},T_{nM})$, its residual co-implication $\Psi_{\mathcal{S}_{n\mathcal{M}}}$ is computed as follows.

- If $\mu_1<\mu_2,\nu_1\le\max(\mu_2,\nu_2)$, then either $\mu_2\ge\max(\nu_1,\nu_2)$ or $\nu_2\ge\max(\mu_2,\nu_1)$ holds. By $\mu_1<\mu_2$, we always have $\psi^{1/q}_{S_{nM}}(\mu_1^q,\mu_2^q)=\min\big(\sqrt[q]{1-\mu_1^q},\mu_2\big)$ and $\theta^{1/q}_{T_{nM}}(1-\mu_1^q,1-\mu_2^q)=\max\big(\mu_1,\sqrt[q]{1-\mu_2^q}\big)$. Moreover, if $\mu_2\ge\max(\nu_1,\nu_2)$, it follows that $\theta^{1/q}_{T_{nM}}(\nu_1^q,\nu_2^q)=1$ if $\nu_1\le\nu_2$. Otherwise, $\theta^{1/q}_{T_{nM}}(\nu_1^q,\nu_2^q)=\max\big(\sqrt[q]{1-\nu_1^q},\nu_2\big)$. Clearly, we have $\mu_1\le\sqrt[q]{1-\nu_1^q}$ and $\sqrt[q]{1-\mu_2^q}\le\sqrt[q]{1-\nu_1^q}$, and hence $\max\big(\mu_1,\sqrt[q]{1-\mu_2^q}\big)\le\sqrt[q]{1-\nu_1^q}\le\max\big(\sqrt[q]{1-\nu_1^q},\nu_2\big)$. While if $\nu_2\ge\max(\mu_2,\nu_1)$, then $\theta^{1/q}_{T_{nM}}(\nu_1^q,\nu_2^q)=1$. Therefore, in all subcases, we have $\theta^{1/q}_{T_{nM}}(\nu_1^q,\nu_2^q)\ge\theta^{1/q}_{T_{nM}}(1-\mu_1^q,1-\mu_2^q)$. Thus, $\Psi_{\mathcal{S}_{n\mathcal{M}}}(\mathbb{x},\mathbb{y})=\big\langle\min\big(\sqrt[q]{1-\mu_1^q},\mu_2\big),\max\big(\mu_1,\sqrt[q]{1-\mu_2^q}\big)\big\rangle$.
- If $\mu_1<\mu_2,\nu_1>\max(\mu_2,\nu_2)$, then $\psi^{1/q}_{S_{nM}}(\mu_1^q,\mu_2^q)=\min\big(\sqrt[q]{1-\mu_1^q},\mu_2\big)$, $\theta^{1/q}_{T_{nM}}(\nu_1^q,\nu_2^q)=\max\big(\sqrt[q]{1-\nu_1^q},\nu_2\big)$, $\theta^{1/q}_{T_{nM}}(1-\mu_1^q,1-\mu_2^q)=\max\big(\mu_1,\sqrt[q]{1-\mu_2^q}\big)$. By the conditions $\nu_1>\mu_2$ and $\langle\mu_2,\nu_2\rangle\in\varDelta$, we have $\sqrt[q]{1-\nu_1^q}\le\sqrt[q]{1-\mu_2^q}$ and $\nu_2\le\sqrt[q]{1-\mu_2^q}$. Therefore, it follows that $\max\big(\sqrt[q]{1-\nu_1^q},\nu_2\big)\le\sqrt[q]{1-\mu_2^q}\le\max\big(\mu_1,\sqrt[q]{1-\mu_2^q}\big)$.
Thus, $\Psi_{\mathcal{S}_{n\mathcal{M}}}(\mathbb{x},\mathbb{y})=\big\langle\min\big(\sqrt[q]{1-\mu_1^q},\mu_2\big),\max\big(\sqrt[q]{1-\nu_1^q},\nu_2\big)\big\rangle$.
- If $\mu_1\ge\mu_2,\nu_1\le\nu_2$, then $\psi^{1/q}_{S_{nM}}(\mu_1^q,\mu_2^q)=0$, $\theta^{1/q}_{T_{nM}}(\nu_1^q,\nu_2^q)=\theta^{1/q}_{T_{nM}}(1-\mu_1^q,1-\mu_2^q)=1$. Thus, $\Psi_{\mathcal{S}_{n\mathcal{M}}}(\mathbb{x},\mathbb{y})=\langle0,1\rangle$.
- If $\mu_1\ge\mu_2,\nu_1>\nu_2$, then $\psi^{1/q}_{S_{nM}}(\mu_1^q,\mu_2^q)=0$, $\theta^{1/q}_{T_{nM}}(\nu_1^q,\nu_2^q)=\max\big(\sqrt[q]{1-\nu_1^q},\nu_2\big)$, $\theta^{1/q}_{T_{nM}}(1-\mu_1^q,1-\mu_2^q)=1$. Thus, $\Psi_{\mathcal{S}_{n\mathcal{M}}}(\mathbb{x},\mathbb{y})=\big\langle0,\max\big(\sqrt[q]{1-\nu_1^q},\nu_2\big)\big\rangle$.

Now we can summarize the above cases and conclude that

$$\Psi_{\mathcal{S}_{n\mathcal{M}}}(\mathbb{x}_1,\mathbb{x}_2)$$
$$=\begin{cases}\big\langle\min\big(\sqrt[q]{1-\mu_1^q},\mu_2\big),\max\big(\mu_1,\sqrt[q]{1-\mu_2^q}\big)\big\rangle, & \text{if } \mu_1<\mu_2,\nu_1\le\max(\mu_2,\nu_2),\\ \big\langle\min\big(\sqrt[q]{1-\mu_1^q},\mu_2\big),\max\big(\sqrt[q]{1-\nu_1^q},\nu_2\big)\big\rangle, & \text{if } \mu_1<\mu_2,\nu_1>\max(\mu_2,\nu_2),\\ \langle0,1\rangle, & \text{if } \mu_1\ge\mu_2,\nu_1\le\nu_2,\\ \big\langle0,\max\big(\sqrt[q]{1-\nu_1^q},\nu_2\big)\big\rangle, & \text{if } \mu_1\ge\mu_2,\nu_1>\nu_2.\end{cases}$$

Similarly, the residual co-implications derived from q-ROF t-conorms listed in Example 1 are as follows:

$$\Psi_{\mathcal{S_M}}(\mathbb{x}_1,\mathbb{x}_2)=\begin{cases}\langle \mu_2, \sqrt[q]{1-\mu_2^q}\rangle, & \text{if } \mu_1<\mu_2, \nu_1\le\nu_2,\\ \langle \mu_2,\nu_2\rangle, & \text{if } \mu_1<\mu_2, \nu_1>\nu_2,\\ \langle 0,1\rangle, & \text{if } \mu_1\ge\mu_2, \nu_1\le\nu_2,\\ \langle 0,\nu_2\rangle, & \text{if } \mu_1\ge\mu_2, \nu_1>\nu_2.\end{cases}$$

$$\Psi_{\mathcal{S_P}}(\mathbb{x}_1,\mathbb{x}_2)=\begin{cases}\left\langle \sqrt[q]{\frac{\mu_2^q-\mu_1^q}{1-\mu_1^q}}, \frac{\nu_2}{\nu_1}\right\rangle, & \text{if } \mu_1<\mu_2, \frac{1-\mu_1^q}{\nu_1^q}<\frac{1-\mu_2^q}{\nu_2^q},\\ \left\langle \sqrt[q]{\frac{\mu_2^q-\mu_1^q}{1-\mu_1^q}}, \sqrt[q]{\frac{1-\mu_2^q}{1-\mu_1^q}}\right\rangle, & \text{if } \mu_1<\mu_2, \frac{1-\mu_1^q}{\nu_1^q}\ge\frac{1-\mu_2^q}{\nu_2^q},\\ \langle 0,1\rangle, & \text{if } \mu_1\ge\mu_2, \nu_1\le\nu_2,\\ \left\langle 0,\frac{\nu_2}{\nu_1}\right\rangle, & \text{if } \mu_1\ge\mu_2, \nu_1>\nu_2.\end{cases}$$

$$\Psi_{\mathcal{S_L}}(\mathbb{x}_1,\mathbb{x}_2)=\begin{cases}\langle \sqrt[q]{\mu_2^q-\mu_1^q}, \sqrt[q]{1+\mu_1^q-\mu_2^q}\rangle, & \text{if } \mu_1<\mu_2, \mu_1^q+\nu_1^q\le\mu_2^q+\nu_2^q,\\ \langle \sqrt[q]{\mu_2^q-\mu_1^q}, \sqrt[q]{1-\nu_1^q+\nu_2^q}\rangle, & \text{if } \mu_1<\mu_2, \mu_1^q+\nu_1^q>\mu_2^q+\nu_2^q,\\ \langle 0,1\rangle, & \text{if } \mu_1\ge\mu_2, \nu_1\le\nu_2,\\ \langle 0, \sqrt[q]{1-\nu_1^q+\nu_2^q}\rangle, & \text{if } \mu_1\ge\mu_2, \nu_1>\nu_2.\end{cases}$$

4 Inclusion Degrees of q-ROFSs

In this section, based on the q-ROF residual (co-)implications, two graded inclusion degrees for q-ROFSs are developed.

The set of all q-ROFSs on X is denoted by q-ROFS(X), and a q-ROFS A is represented by $A=\sum_{x\in X}\langle\mu_A(x),\nu_A(x)\rangle/x$. For $A,B\in q$-ROFS(X), we say A is included in B [17], denoted by $A\subseteq B$, iff $A(x)\preceq B(x)$, $\forall x\in X$.

Definition 3. *Let $\Theta_{\mathcal{T}}$ and $\Psi_{\mathcal{S}}$ be q-ROF residual implication and co-implication and X be the universe of discourse. For two q-ROFSs A and B, the two types of degrees to which A is included in B are defined as*

$$\mathrm{Inc}^{(1)}(A,B)=\inf_{x\in X}\Theta_{\mathcal{T}}(A(x),B(x)), \tag{9}$$

$$\mathrm{Inc}^{(2)}(A,B)=\inf_{x\in X}\mathcal{N}(\Psi_{\mathcal{S}}(B(x),A(x))). \tag{10}$$

The following theorem shows that $\mathrm{Inc}^{(1)}(\cdot,\cdot)$ and $\mathrm{Inc}^{(2)}(\cdot,\cdot)$ both satisfy the axiomatic definition of inclusion measures [18].

Theorem 3. *Let $\mathrm{Inc}^{(i)}(\cdot,\cdot)$, $i=1,2$ be two measures of q-ROFSs. Then the following statements hold: for all $A,B,C\in q$-ROFS(X),*

(1) $\langle 0,1\rangle\preceq\mathrm{Inc}^{(i)}(A,B)\preceq\langle 1,0\rangle$.
(2) $\mathrm{Inc}^{(i)}(A,B)=\langle 1,0\rangle$ *iff* $A\subseteq B$.
(3) *If* $A\subseteq B$, *then* $\mathrm{Inc}^{(i)}(A,C)\succeq\mathrm{Inc}^{(i)}(B,C)$ *and* $\mathrm{Inc}^{(i)}(C,A)\preceq\mathrm{Inc}^{(i)}(C,B)$.

Example 3. Take $X = \{x_1, x_2, x_3, x_4\}$ and $A = \langle 0.6, 0.7\rangle/x_1 + \langle 0.2, 0.8\rangle/x_2 + \langle 0.1, 0.4\rangle/x_3 + \langle 0.5, 0.6\rangle/x_4$ and $B = \langle 0.4, 0.5\rangle/x_1 + \langle 0.3, 0.9\rangle/x_2 + \langle 0.7, 0.6\rangle/x_3 + \langle 0.4, 0.2\rangle/x_4$. They both can be regarded as q-ROFSs with $q = 2$. Then, based on different q-ROF residual (co-)implications, four possible inclusion measures between A and B are collected in Table 1.

Table 1. Inclusion degrees of A and B based on different q-ROF logical operations.

Inclusion Degrees	$\Theta_{\mathcal{T_M}}/\Psi_{\mathcal{S_M}}$	$\Theta_{\mathcal{T_P}}/\Psi_{\mathcal{S_P}}$	$\Theta_{\mathcal{T_L}}/\Psi_{\mathcal{S_L}}$	$\Theta_{\mathcal{S}_{\mathrm{n}\mathcal{M}}}/\Psi_{\mathcal{S}_{\mathrm{n}\mathcal{M}}}$
$\mathrm{Inc}^{(1)}(A,B)$	$\langle 0.4, 0.9\rangle$	$\langle 0.6667, 0.6872\rangle$	$\langle 0.8944, 0.4472\rangle$	$\langle 0.8, 0.6\rangle$
$\mathrm{Inc}^{(2)}(A,B)$	$\langle 0.4, 0.6\rangle$	$\langle 0.6667, 0.4880\rangle$	$\langle 0.8944, 0.4472\rangle$	$\langle 0.8, 0.6\rangle$
$\mathrm{Inc}^{(1)}(B,A)$	$\langle 0.1, 0.7\rangle$	$\langle 0.1429, 0.5774\rangle$	$\langle 0.7211, 0.5657\rangle$	$\langle 0.7141, 0.7\rangle$
$\mathrm{Inc}^{(2)}(B,A)$	$\langle 0.2, 0.7\rangle$	$\langle 0.3333, 0.6963\rangle$	$\langle 0.7211, 0.6928\rangle$	$\langle 0.7141, 0.7\rangle$

It can be seen from Table 1 that there is no static relation between $\mathrm{Inc}^{(1)}(\cdot,\cdot)$ and $\mathrm{Inc}^{(2)}(\cdot,\cdot)$. For example, $\mathrm{Inc}^{(1)}(A,B)$ is less than $\mathrm{Inc}^{(2)}(A,B)$ by $\Theta_{\mathcal{T_M}}/\Psi_{\mathcal{S_M}}$; $\mathrm{Inc}^{(1)}(B,A)$ is greater than $\mathrm{Inc}^{(2)}(B,A)$ by $\Theta_{\mathcal{T_L}}/\Psi_{\mathcal{S_L}}$; $\mathrm{Inc}^{(1)}(A,B)$ equals to $\mathrm{Inc}^{(2)}(A,B)$ by $\Theta_{\mathcal{S}_{\mathrm{n}\mathcal{M}}}/\Psi_{\mathcal{S}_{\mathrm{n}\mathcal{M}}}$; $\mathrm{Inc}^{(1)}(B,A)$ and $\mathrm{Inc}^{(2)}(B,A)$ are incomparable by $\Theta_{\mathcal{T_P}}/\Psi_{\mathcal{S_P}}$.

Example 4. Take $A = \sum_{x\in[0,\infty)} \langle \frac{1}{1+x^2}, \frac{x}{1+x^2}\rangle/x$ and $B = \sum_{x\in[0,\infty)} \langle \frac{1}{2}, \frac{1}{2}\rangle/x$. Obviously, they are both q-ROFSs on $[0,\infty)$ with $q = 2$. Then, for $\Psi_{\mathcal{S}} \in \{\Psi_{\mathcal{S_M}}, \Psi_{\mathcal{S_P}}, \Psi_{\mathcal{S_L}}, \Psi_{\mathcal{S}_{\mathrm{n}\mathcal{M}}}\}$, we have

$$
\begin{aligned}
\mathrm{Inc}^{(2)}(A,B) &= \inf_{x\in[0,1]\cup(1,\infty)} \mathcal{N}\big(\Psi_{\mathcal{S}}(\langle \tfrac{1}{2}, \tfrac{1}{2}\rangle, \langle \tfrac{1}{1+x^2}, \tfrac{x}{1+x^2}\rangle)\big)\\
&= \begin{cases}
\inf\limits_{x\in[0,1)} \langle \frac{x}{1+x^2}, \frac{1}{1+x^2}\rangle \bigwedge \inf\limits_{x\in[1,\infty)} \langle \frac{x}{1+x^2}, 0\rangle, & \text{if } \Psi_{\mathcal{S}} = \Psi_{\mathcal{S_M}},\\
\inf\limits_{x\in[0,1)} \Big\langle \sqrt{\frac{4((1+x^2)^2-1)}{3(1+x^2)^2}}, \sqrt{\frac{4-(1+x^2)^2}{3(1+x^2)^2}} \Big\rangle \bigwedge \inf\limits_{x\in[1,\infty)} \langle \frac{2x}{1+x^2}, 0\rangle, & \text{if } \Psi_{\mathcal{S}} = \Psi_{\mathcal{S_P}},\\
\inf\limits_{x\in[0,1)} \Big\langle \sqrt{\frac{5(1+x^2)^2-4}{4(1+x^2)^2}}, \sqrt{\frac{4-(1+x^2)^2}{4(1+x^2)^2}} \Big\rangle \bigwedge & \text{if } \Psi_{\mathcal{S}} = \Psi_{\mathcal{S_L}},\\
\quad \inf\limits_{x\in[1,\infty)} \Big\langle \sqrt{\frac{3(1+x^2)^2+4x^2}{4(1+x^2)^2}}, 0\Big\rangle, & \\
\inf\limits_{x\in[0,1)} \Big\langle \max\Big(\sqrt{\frac{(1+x^2)^2-1}{(1+x^2)^2}}, \frac{1}{2}\Big), \min\Big(\frac{1}{1+x^2}, \frac{\sqrt{3}}{2}\Big)\Big\rangle \bigwedge & \text{if } \Psi_{\mathcal{S}} = \Psi_{\mathcal{S}_{\mathrm{n}\mathcal{M}}},\\
\quad \inf\limits_{x\in[1,\infty)} \langle \frac{\sqrt{3}}{2}, 0\rangle, &
\end{cases}\\
&= \begin{cases}
\langle 0, 1\rangle \wedge \langle 0, 0\rangle, & \text{if } \Psi_{\mathcal{S}} = \Psi_{\mathcal{S_M}} \text{ or } \Psi_{\mathcal{S}} = \Psi_{\mathcal{S_P}},\\
\langle \frac{1}{2}, \frac{\sqrt{3}}{2}\rangle \bigwedge \langle \frac{\sqrt{3}}{2}, 0\rangle, & \text{if } \Psi_{\mathcal{S}} = \Psi_{\mathcal{S_L}} \text{ or } \Psi_{\mathcal{S}} = \Psi_{\mathcal{S}_{\mathrm{n}\mathcal{M}}},
\end{cases}\\
&= \begin{cases}
\langle 0, 1\rangle, & \text{if } \Psi_{\mathcal{S}} = \Psi_{\mathcal{S_M}} \text{ or } \Psi_{\mathcal{S}} = \Psi_{\mathcal{S_P}},\\
\langle \frac{1}{2}, \frac{\sqrt{3}}{2}\rangle, & \text{if } \Psi_{\mathcal{S}} = \Psi_{\mathcal{S_L}} \text{ or } \Psi_{\mathcal{S}} = \Psi_{\mathcal{S}_{\mathrm{n}\mathcal{M}}}.
\end{cases}
\end{aligned}
$$

Analogously, for $\Theta_{\mathcal{T}} \in \{\Theta_{\mathcal{T}_{\mathcal{M}}}, \Theta_{\mathcal{T}_{\mathcal{P}}}, \Theta_{\mathcal{T}_{\mathcal{L}}}, \Theta_{\mathcal{T}_{n\mathcal{M}}}\}$, we have

$$\mathrm{Inc}^{(1)}(A,B) = \inf_{x\in[0,1]\cup(1,\infty)} \Theta_{\mathcal{T}}\big(\langle \tfrac{1}{1+x^2}, \tfrac{x}{1+x^2}\rangle, \langle \tfrac{1}{2}, \tfrac{1}{2}\rangle\big) = \langle \tfrac{1}{2}, \tfrac{1}{2}\rangle.$$

5 Conclusions

In this paper, we have proposed the q-ROF residual co-implications and provided their applications. The main findings are: (1) the q-ROF residual co-implication $\Psi_{\mathcal{S}}$ derived from a representable q-ROF t-conorm $\mathcal{S} = (S, T)$ has been presented by using ψ_S and θ_T; (2) two inclusion measures of q-ROFSs have been developed based on q-ROF residual implications and co-implications, respectively.

In further analysis, comparisons with other inclusion degrees are required. And applications of q-ROF residual (co-)implications to approximate reasoning deserve a deeper study to explore their potential benefits.

Acknowledgements. This study was funded by the National Natural Science Foundation of China (Grant No. 12271493), the Natural Science Foundation of Henan (Grant No. 242300421154) and the Training Program for Young Backbone Teachers in Higher Education Institutions of Henan Province (Grant No. 2024GGJS001).

References

1. Baczyński, M., Jayaram, B.: Fuzzy Implications. Springer-Verlag, Berlin (2008)
2. Baczyński, M., Jayaram, B.: (S, N)-and R-implications: a state-of-the-art survey. Fuzzy Sets Syst. **159**(14), 1836–1859 (2008)
3. Cornelis, C., Deschrijver, G., Kerre, E.E.: Implication in intuitionistic fuzzy and interval-valued fuzzy set theory: construction, classification, application. Int. J. Approx. Reason. **35**(1), 55–95 (2004)
4. Cornelis, C., Kerre, E.: Inclusion measures in intuitionistic fuzzy set theory. In: the 7th European Conference on European Conference on Symbolic and Quantitative Approaches to Reasoning and Uncertainty, pp. 345–356. Springer (2003)
5. Dai, J., Dan, Y., Pan, X.: Fuzzy implications and coimplications on the poset of closed intervals. Comput. Appl. Math. **43**(7), 397 (2024)
6. De Baets, B.: Coimplicators, the forgotten connectives. Tatra Mt. Math. Publ. **12**, 229–240 (1997)
7. Deschrijver, G., Cornelis, C., Kerre, E.E.: On the representation of intuitionistic fuzzy t-norms and t-conorms. IEEE Trans. Fuzzy Syst. **12**(1), 45–61 (2004)
8. Du, W.S.: Yager's type weighted power means of q-rung Orthopair fuzzy information and their applications to multi-criteria decision making. Comput. Appl. Math. **44**(2), 161 (2025)
9. Grzegorzewski, P., Mrówka, E.: Subsethood measure for intuitionistic fuzzy sets. In: 2004 IEEE International Conference on Fuzzy Systems. vol. 1, pp. 139–142. IEEE (2004)
10. Hu, B.Q., Wong, H.: Generalized interval-valued fuzzy rough sets based on interval-valued fuzzy logical operators. Int. J. Fuzzy Syst. **15**(4), 381–391 (2013)

11. Klement, E.P., Mesiar, R., Pap, E.: Triangular Norms. Kluwer Academic Publishers, Dordrecht (2000)
12. Ruiz, D., Torrens, J.: Residual implications and co-implications from idempotent uninorms. Kybernetika **40**(1), 21–38 (2004)
13. Su, Y., Liu, H.W.: Characterizations of residual coimplications of pseudo-uninorms on a complete lattice. Fuzzy Sets Syst. **261**, 44–59 (2015)
14. Su, Y., Wang, Z.: Pseudo-uninorms and coimplications on a complete lattice. Fuzzy Sets Syst. **224**, 53–62 (2013)
15. Wang, Z., Fang, J.X.: Residual coimplicators of left and right uninorms on a complete lattice. Fuzzy Sets Syst. **160**(14), 2086–2096 (2009)
16. Xie, L., Li, W., Yang, B.: Neighborhood-related q-rung orthopair fuzzy covering-based rough set models and their applications for multi-attribute decision making. Comput. Appl. Math. **43**(6), 380 (2024)
17. Yager, R.R.: Generalized orthopair fuzzy sets. IEEE Trans. Fuzzy Syst. **25**(5), 1222–1230 (2017)
18. Zhang, W.X., Leung, Y.: Theory of including degrees and its applications to uncertainty inferences. In: 1996 Asian Fuzzy Systems Symposium: Soft Computing in Intelligent Systems and Information Processing, pp. 496–501. IEEE (1996)

Preservation of Superdistributivity Between Triangular Norms Under Transformations

Xiya Lu and Gang Li(✉)

School of Mathematics and Statistics, Qilu University of Technology (Shandong Academy of Sciences), Jinan 250353, China
gangli17@qlu.edu.cn

Abstract. The study of superdistributivity for triangular norms is of great significance in fuzzy logic and uncertain reasoning. By analyzing distributivity inequalities, it not only compensates for the limitations of traditional logical operations but also optimizes model construction in fields such as decision analysis and artificial intelligence. This paper investigates the preservation of superdistributivity between triangular norms under some transformations, such as functional transformations and additive generator transformations.

Keywords: triangular norm · superdistributivity · triangular subnorm · additive generator

1 Introduction

The origin of triangular norms(t-norms) can be traced back to 1942, when Karl Menger first introduced the concept of triangular functions while constructing statistical metric spaces [1]. After many years of development, they play an important role across various domains including fuzzy systems, fuzzy control and information aggregation [2–4]. In particular, the algebraic properties of triangular norms provide a rigorous mathematical framework for constructing fuzzy rules and integrating heterogeneous data sources. However, when t-norms undergo specific transformations to meet application requirements, some algebraic properties may be compromised. This paper discusses the preservation of superdistributivity in triangular norms transformations. Distributivity is a crucial property that governs the relationship between operators. In classical logic, for instance, the distributive law of multiplication over addition forms the cornerstone of algebraic systems. Similarly, in fuzzy logic, studying distributivity between t-norms facilitates the construction of more sophisticated logical systems. In recent years, the superdistributivity and subdistributivity were also discussed in [11,12]. This paper specifically investigates the preservation of superdistributivity for t-norm under some transformations. It is well known that the superdistributivity (subdistributivity) between two operators preserves

M. Bonsangue and Y. Chen (Eds.): AILA 2025, CCIS 2668, pp. 104–112, 2026.
https://doi.org/10.1007/978-981-95-8262-4_8

under the order isomorphism [11]. Hence, the investigation of superdistributivity preservation for t-norm (t-conorm) under some transformations carries significant theoretical importance.

The main theoretical advancement of this paper consists in a complete characterization of superdistributivity preservation for transformed t-norms. First, based on triangular subnorms, we prove that the superdistributivity property remains valid when they are transformed to triangular norms. Second, we analyze the superdistributivity of triangular norms under a transformation based on a monotonic function and t-norms. Furthermore, we investigate the superdistributivity of continuous Archimedean triangular norms under additive generator transformations base on Minkowski inequality and prove that superdistributivity is preserved under specific conditions for certain parametric families.

After this introduction, we give some fundamental preliminaries relevant to the content discussed in this paper in Sect. 2. We discusses the preservation of superdistributivity under transformations, supported by concrete examples in Sect. 3. Finally, we summarize the work with a brief summary of the main contributions.

2 Preliminaries

In this section, we provide foundational definitions and properties related to triangular norms.

Definition 1. *[5–9] The two variable function $T : [0,1]^2 \to [0,1]$ is t-norm, for all $l, m, n \in [0,1]$, which complies with the axioms $(T1) - (T4)$:*
$(T1)$ $T(l,m) = T(m,l)$.
$(T2)$ $T(T(l,m), n) = T(l, T(m,n))$.
$(T3)$ $T(l,m) \leq T(m,n)$ *whenever* $m \leq n$.
$(T4)$ $T(l,1) = l$.

Let T be a t-norm. As a direct consequence, $T(l,m) \leq \min(l,m)$ for all $(l,m) \in [0,1]^2$. T is strictly monotone if $T(l,m) < T(l,n)$ for all $l > 0$ and $m < n$; T is called Archimedean if there exists some natural number $a \in \mathbb{N}$, $l_T^{(a)} = T(\underbrace{l, ..., l}_{a}) < m$ whenever $(l,m) \in]0,1[^2$; It is called strict if T satisfies both the continuity property and strictly monotone; T is called nilpotent if it is continuous and there exists some positive integer a with $l_T^{(a)} = 0$ for each $l \in]0,1[$.

It is well established that every continuous Archimedean t-norm is classified as strict or nilpotent.For the corresponding concepts and properties of t-conorms, the readers are advised to refer to the monographs [5].

Below we introduce two basic t-norms, which are extensively discussed in the work.

$$\begin{aligned} Lukasiewicz \;\; t-norm \;\; T_L(l,m) &= \max(l+m-1, 0), \\ Product \;\; t-norm \;\; T_P(l,m) &= l \cdot m \end{aligned}$$

In the subsequent discussion, we present several construction methods of t-norms.

Definition 2. *[5] Let $\psi : [u,v] \to [w,z]$ with $[u,v],[w,z] \subseteq [-\infty,\infty]$ be non-increasing and non-constant. The pseudo-inverse $\psi^{(-1)} : [w,z] \to [u,v]$ is characterized by*

$$\psi^{(-1)}(\beta) = \sup\{\alpha \in [u,v] : \psi(\alpha) > \beta\}$$

Moreover, $\psi^{(-1)} = \psi^{-1}$ if and only if ψ is a bijection, ψ^{-1} is the inverse function of ψ. If ψ is strictly monotone, then $\psi^{(-1)} \circ f = \mathrm{id}_{[u,v]}$.

Definition 3. *[5, 10] The function $\Phi : [0,1]^2 \to [0,1]$ is called a t-subnorm if it fulfills the axioms $(T1)-(T3)$, and $\Phi(l,m) \leq \min(l,m)$ for all $l,m,n \in [0,1]$.*

Proposition 1. *[5, 10] If A is a t-subnorm, then the two variable function $T_{[A]} : [0,1]^2 \to [0,1]$ is characterized by*

$$T_{[A]}(l,m) = \begin{cases} A(l,m) & (l,m) \in [0,1[^2, \\ \min(l,m) & \textit{otherwise}, \end{cases}$$

is a triangular norm.

Theorem 1. *[5] Given a non-decreasing function $\eta : [0,1] \to [0,1]$ and a t-norm T satisfying:*

(i) *$T(\eta(l),\eta(m)) \in Ran(\eta) \cup [0, f(0^+)]$, for all $l,m \in [0,1[$;*
(ii) *$\eta \circ \eta^{(-1)}(T(\eta(l),\eta(m))) = T(\eta(l),\eta(m))$ whenever $(l,m) \in [0,1]^2$ with $T(\eta(l),\eta(m)) \in Ran(\eta)$.*

The function $T_{[\eta]} : [0,1]^2 \to [0,1]$ given by

$$T_{[\eta]}(l,m) = \begin{cases} \eta^{(-1)}(T(\eta(l),\eta(m))) & (l,m) \in [0,1[^2, \\ \min(l,m) & \textit{otherwise}. \end{cases} \tag{1}$$

is a t-norm.

Definition 4. *[5] Let the function $h : [0,1] \to [0,\infty]$ is called additive generator of a t-norm T if it is strictly decreasing, vanishes at 1 and $\lim_{l\to 0^+} h(l) = h(0)$, satisfying for any $(l,m) \in [0,1]^2$ we get*

$$h(l) + h(m) \in Ran(h) \cup [h(0),\infty],$$
$$T(l,m) = h^{(-1)}(h(l) + h(m)).$$

Example 1. [5] We give now some additive generators $h : [0,1] \to [0,\infty]$ that satisfy the conditions in Definition 4, and characterize the corresponding t-norms they induce.

(i) For the function $h(l) = 1 - l$, which yields T_L.

(ii) If we put for each $\mu \in]0, 1]$

$$h_\mu(l) = \begin{cases} -\log(\mu l) & l \in [0, 1[, \\ 0 & l = 1, \end{cases} \tag{2}$$

then the expression (2) induces

$$T_\mu(l, m) = \begin{cases} \mu l m & (l, m) \in [0, 1[^2, \\ \min(l, m) & \text{otherwise.} \end{cases} \tag{3}$$

Lemma 1. *With $h : [0, 1] \to [0, \infty]$ as additive generator of t-norm T.*

(i) *If T be a continuous Archimedean, then for every $\mu \in]0, \infty[$, the function $t^\mu : [0, 1] \to [0, \infty]$ given by*

$$h^\mu(l) = (h(l))^\mu \tag{4}$$

acts as an additive generator for a continuous Archimedean t-norm $T^{(\mu)}$.

(ii) *If T be a strict t-norm, then for every $\mu \in]0, \infty[$, the function $h_\mu : [0, 1] \to [0, \infty]$ given by*

$$h_\mu(l) = h((h)^{-1}(\mu h(l))) \tag{5}$$

acts as an additive generator for a continuous Archimedean t-norm $T_{(\mu)}$.

Lemma 1 introduces an approach to constructing new t-norms by applying different transformations to a given additive generator.

Definition 5. *[11] Let $F, G : [0, 1]^2 \to [0, 1]$ be two operations.*

(i) *F is left subdistributive with respect to G if*

$$F(l, G(m, n)) \leq G(F(l, m), F(l, n)) \quad \textit{for any} \;\; l, m, n \in [0, 1].$$

(ii) *F is left superdistributive with respect to G if*

$$F(l, G(m, n)) \geq G(F(l, m), F(l, n)) \quad \textit{for any} \;\; l, m, n \in [0, 1].$$

Similarly, the right subdistributivity and superdistributivity can be defined. It is obvious that the left subdistributivity (superdistributivity) is equivalent to right subdistributivity (superdistributivity) if the two operations F, G are commutative.It is easy to see that the order isomorphism preserves both left and right subdistributivity and superdistributivity between t-norms (or t-subnorms) (see Theorem 4.8 in [11]).

3 Superdistributivity Under Transformation of t-Norm Operators

This section deals with the preservation of superdistributivity between t-norms under the transformations.

Proposition 2. *Let $J, K : [0,1]^2 \to [0,1]$ be two t-subnorms and $T_{[J]}, T_{[K]}$ be the corresponding t-norms. If J is superdistributive over K, then $T_{[J]}$ is superdistributive over $T_{[K]}$.*

Proof. Suppose J is superdistributive over K. By Proposition 1, $T_{[J]}$ and $T_{[K]}$ are given by

$$T_{[J]}(l,m) = \begin{cases} J(l,m) & (l,m) \in [0,1[^2, \\ \min(l,m) & \text{otherwise,} \end{cases}$$

$$T_{[K]}(l,m) = \begin{cases} K(l,m) & (l,m) \in [0,1[^2, \\ \min(l,m) & \text{otherwise.} \end{cases}$$

Clearly, $T_{[J]}$ is superdistributive over $T_{[K]}$ for all $l, m, n \in [0,1[$. In the following, we prove that the superdistributivity holds for at lest one of l, m, n equals 1.

(i) If $l = 1$, then $T_{[J]}(l, T_{[K]}(m,n)) = T_{[K]}(m,n) = T_{[K]}(T_{[J]}(l,m), T_{[K]}(l,n))$.
(ii) If $m = 1$, then

$$T_{[J]}(l, T_{[K]}(m,n)) = T_{[J]}(l,n),$$
$$T_{[K]}(T_{[J]}(l,m), T_{[J]}(l,n)) = T_{[K]}(l, T_{[J]}(l,n)).$$

By Definition 1, we have $T_{[J]}(l,n) \geq T_{[K]}(l, T_{[J]}(l,n))$ and $T_{[J]}(l, T_{[K]}(m, n)) \geq T_{[K]}(T_{[J]}(l,m), T_{[J]}(l,n))$.
(iii) If $n = 1$, the proof follows the analogous approach to case (ii).

These imply, $T_{[J]}$ is superdistributive over $T_{[K]}$.

Example 2. Assume t-subnorms J, K defined by $J(l,m) = 0$, $K(l,n) = \frac{1}{2}xy$ for all $(l,m) \in [0,1]^2$. Clearly, J is superdistributive over K due to $J(l, K(m,n)) = K(J(l,m), J(l,n)) = 0$ for all $(l,m,n) \in [0,1]^3$. Their corresponding t-norms are defined by, respectively:

$$T_{[J]}(l,m) = \begin{cases} 0 & (l,m) \in [0,1[^2, \\ \min(l,m) & \text{otherwise,} \end{cases}$$

$$T_{[B]}(l,m) = \begin{cases} \frac{1}{2}lm & (l,m) \in [0,1[^2, \\ \min(l,m) & \text{otherwise.} \end{cases}$$

It is obvious that $T_{[J]}$ is superdistributive over $T_{[K]}$.

Proposition 3. *Let $\eta : [0,1] \to [0,1]$ be a non-decreasing function, T_1 and T_2 be t-norms for which the requirements of Theorem 1. If T_1 is superdistributive over T_2, then $T_{1[\eta]}$ is superdistributive over $T_{2[\eta]}$, where $T_{1[\eta]}$, $T_{2[\eta]}$ are the t-norms from the expression (1).*

Proof. By Eq. (1), $T_{1[\eta]}$ and $T_{2[\eta]}$ are given by

$$T_{1[\eta]}(l,m) = \begin{cases} \eta^{(-1)}(T_1(\eta(l),\eta(m))) & (l,m) \in [0,1[^2, \\ \min(l,m) & \text{otherwise}, \end{cases}$$

$$T_{2[\eta]}(l,m) = \begin{cases} \eta^{(-1)}(T_2(\eta(l),\eta(m))) & (l,m) \in [0,1[^2, \\ \min(l,m) & \text{otherwise}. \end{cases}$$

Clearly, when one of l, m, or n equals 1, $T_{1[\eta]}$ is superdistributive over $T_{2[\eta]}$. Consider $l,m,n \in [0,1[$. If $T_2(\eta(m),\eta(n)) \in Ran(\eta)$ then

$$\begin{aligned} T_{1[\eta]}(l, T_{2[\eta]}(m,n)) &= \eta^{(-1)}(T_1(\eta(l), \eta(\eta^{(-1)}(T_2(\eta(m),\eta(n)))))) \\ &= \eta^{(-1)}(T_1(\eta(l), T_2(\eta(m),\eta(n)))) \\ T_{2[\eta]}(T_{1[\eta]}(l,m), T_{1[\eta]}(l,n)) &= \eta^{(-1)}(T_2(\eta(\eta^{(-1)}(T_1(\eta(l),\eta(m)))), \eta(\eta^{(-1)}(T_1(\eta(l),\eta(n)))))) \\ &= \eta^{(-1)}(T_2(T_1(\eta(l),\eta(m)), T_1(\eta(l),\eta(n)))) \end{aligned}$$

T_1 is superdistributive over T_2, and function $\eta^{(-1)}$ is non-decreasing, this implies

$$F(f(x), G(f(y), f(z))) \geq G(F(f(x), f(y)), F(f(x), f(z))).$$

$$T_{1[\eta]}(l, T_{2[\eta]}(m,n)) \geq T_{2[\eta]}(T_{1[\eta]}(l,m), T_{1[\eta]}(l,n)).$$

Besides, if $T_2(\eta(m),\eta(n)) \leq \eta(0^+)$ then

$$T_{1[\eta]}(l, T_{2[\eta]}(m,n)) = 0 = T_{2[\eta]}(T_{1[\eta]}(l,m), T_{1[\eta]}(l,n)).$$

Therefore, $T_{1[\eta]}$ is superdistributive over $T_{2[\eta]}$.

Example 3. Consider T_P and T_L. Obviously, T_P is superdistributive over T_L (see Table 3 in [11]). Given an unary function $\eta : [0,1] \to [0,1], \eta(l) = cl$, where parameter $c \in]0,1[$. It is obvious that η is a bijection from $[0,1] \to [0,c]$, and it is strictly increasing. Thus, the construction approach presented in Theorem 1 holds for arbitrary t-norms.

$$T_{P[\eta]}(l,m) = \begin{cases} \frac{1}{c} \cdot lm & (l,m) \in [0,1[^2, \\ \min(l,m) & \text{otherwise}, \end{cases}$$

$$T_{L[\eta]}(l,m) = \begin{cases} \frac{1}{c} \cdot \max(l+m-1,0) & (l,m) \in [0,1[^2, \\ \min(l,m) & \text{otherwise}. \end{cases}$$

Trivially, $T_{P[\eta]}$ is superdistributive over $T_{L[\eta]}$, which one of l,m,n equals 1. When $l,m,n \in [0,1[$, we get $T_{P[\eta]}(l, T_{L[\eta]}(m,n)) = \frac{1}{c^2}\max(lm+ln-l,0)$ and $T_{L[\eta]}(T_{P[\eta]}(l,m), T_{P[\eta]}(l,n)) = \frac{1}{c^2}\max(lm+ln-1,0)$. Therefore, $T_{P[\eta]}$ is superdistributive over $T_{L[\eta]}$.

Proposition 4. *For some t-norm T, its additive generator is $h : [0,1] \to [0,\infty]$, let $r, s \in [0,\infty]$. If $r \geq s$, then $T^{(r)}$ is superdistributive over $T^{(s)}$.*

Proof. By Definition 4 we obtain

$$T^{(\mu)}(l,m) = h^{(-1)}(h^{\mu}(l) + h^{\mu}(m))^{\frac{1}{\mu}}.$$

Therefore,

$$\begin{aligned} T^{(r)}(l, T^{(s)}(m,n)) &= h^{(-1)}\left[h^{r}(l) + h^{r}(T^{(s)}(m,n))\right]^{\frac{1}{r}} \\ &= h^{(-1)}\left[h^{r}(l) + (h^{s}(m) + h^{s}(n))^{\frac{r}{s}}\right]^{\frac{1}{r}} \end{aligned} \tag{6}$$

$$\begin{aligned} &T^{(s)}(T^{(r)}(l,m), T^{(a)}(l,n)) \\ &= h^{(-1)}\left[h^{s}(T^{(r)}(l,m)) + h^{s}(T^{(r)}(l,n))\right]^{\frac{1}{s}} \\ &= h^{(-1)}\left[(h^{r}(l) + h^{r}(m))^{\frac{s}{r}} + (h^{r}(l) + h^{r}(n))^{\frac{s}{r}}\right]^{\frac{1}{s}} \end{aligned} \tag{7}$$

By the Minkowski's inequality in [13], we have

$$\begin{aligned} (h^{r}(l) + h^{r}(m))^{\frac{s}{r}} + (h^{r}(l) + h^{r}(n))^{\frac{s}{r}} &\geq ((h^{s}(l) + h^{s}(l))^{\frac{r}{s}} + (h^{s}(m) + h^{s}(n))^{\frac{r}{s}})^{\frac{s}{r}} \\ &\geq (h^{r}(l) + (h^{s}(m) + h^{s}(n))^{\frac{r}{s}})^{\frac{s}{r}} \end{aligned} \tag{8}$$

Hence,

$$\left((h^{r}(l) + h^{r}(m))^{\frac{s}{r}} + (h^{r}(l) + h^{r}(n))^{\frac{s}{r}}\right)^{\frac{1}{s}} \geq (h^{r}(l) + (h^{s}(m) + h^{s}(n))^{\frac{r}{s}})^{\frac{1}{r}} \tag{9}$$

As $h^{(-1)}$ is strictly decreasing, we conclude,

$$T^{(r)}(l, T^{(s)}(m,n)) \geq T^{(s)}(T^{(r)}(l,m), T^{(r)}(l,n)).$$

That is, $T^{(r)}$ is superdistributive over $T^{(s)}$.

Example 4. By Example 1, we know that $h(l) = 1 - l$ acts as an additive generator for T_L. Now let's consider the t-norms family $T_L^{(\mu)}$, which is obtained through additive generator of T_L from Lemma 1. By Eq. (4), we have $h^{\mu}(l) = (1-l)^{\mu}$ and $T_L^{(\mu)}(l,m) = \max(1 - ((1-l)^{\mu} + (1-m)^{\mu})^{\frac{1}{\mu}}, 0)$, $\mu \in]0, +\infty[$. By simple computation, we can see that $T_L^{(r)}$ is superdistributive over $T_L^{(s)}$ for $r \geq s$.

Example 5. Now we consider the superdistributivity of the t-norms family $T_P^{(\mu)}$, which is obtained by applying the method from Lemma 1 to the additive generator of T_P. For T_P, its additive generator is $h(l) = -\log l$, then $h^{\mu}(l) = (-\log l)^{\mu}$ is additive generator of $T_P^{(\mu)}$. By Definition 4,

$$T_P^{(\mu)}(l,m) = \exp(-\left[(-\log l)^{\mu} + (-\log m)^{\mu}\right]^{\frac{1}{\mu}}).$$

By the computation, $T_P^{(r)}$ is superdistibutive over $T_P^{(s)}$ for $r \geq s$.

Remark 1. Note that $h_\mu(l) = 1 - l^\mu$ is the additive generator of t-norm $T_{L(\mu)}$ by Eq. (5). $T_{L(\mu)}(l,m) = \max((l^\mu + m^\mu - 1)^{\frac{1}{\mu}}, 0)$ by Definition 4. If $T_{L(\mu)}(l,m)$, $T_{L(\mu)}(l,n)$, $T_{L(\mu)}(m,n) \geq 0$, then for $r, s \in]0, +\infty[$ with $r \geq s$,

$$T_{L(r)}(l, T_{L(s)}(m,n)) = (l^r + (m^s + n^s - 1)^{\frac{r}{s}})^{\frac{1}{r}},$$

$$T_{L(s)}(T_{L(r)}(l,m), T_{L(r)}(l,n)) = ((l^r + m^r - 1)^{\frac{s}{r}} + (l^r + n^r - 1)^{\frac{s}{r}} - 1)^{\frac{1}{s}}.$$

It is impossible to obtain the superdistributivity of $T_{L(r)}$ and $T_{L(s)}$. In fact, if $r \geq s, T_{L(s)}$ is superdistributive over $T_{L(r)}$ (see Theorem 5.14 in [11]).

4 Conclusion

In the paper, we analyze the preservation of superdistributivity of t-norms under some transformations which include the transformation between t-norms and t-subnorms, T and T_η through the general function η, and those related to the additive generators. Due to the duality of t-conorms and t-norms, these conclusions can be easily generalized to t-conorms. For example, assume that $J, K : [0,1]^2 \to [0,1]$ are two t-supernorms [5] and $S_{[J]}, S_{[K]}$ are the corresponding t-conorms. If J is subdistributive over K, then $S_{[J]}$ is subdistributive over $S_{[K]}$.

Acknowledgements. This work is supported by National Nature Science Foundation of China under Grant 61977040 and Natural Science Foundation of Shandong Province under Grant ZR2019MF055.

References

1. Menger, K.: Statistical metrics. Proc. Nat. Acad. U. S. A. **28**, 535–537 (1942)
2. Li, Y.M.: Fuzzy Systems Analysis. Science Press, Beijing (2005)
3. Wang, L.X.: A Course in Fuzzy Systems and Control. Prentice-Hall PTR, Englewood Cliffs, NJ (1997)
4. Qin, F.: Research on Mathematical Models based on Information Aggregation. Shaanxi Normal University, Xi'an (2007)
5. Klement, E.P., Mesiar, R., Pap, E.: Triangular norms. Springer Science & Business Media (2013)
6. Schweizer, B., Sklar, A.: Statistical metric spaces. Pacific J. Math **10**, 313–334 (1960)
7. Schweizer, B., Sklar, A.: Associative functions and statistical triangle inequalities. Publ. Math. Debrecen **8**, 169–186 (1961)
8. Perry, P., Roy, B.: The use of fuzzy outranking relations in preference modelling. Fuzzy Sets Syst. **49**(1), 33–53 (1992)
9. Fodor, J.C.: Contrapositive symmetry of fuzzy implications. Fuzzy Sets Syst. **69**(2), 141–156 (1995)
10. Palmeira, E.S., Bedregal, B.R.C.: Extension of t-subnorms on complete lattices via retractions. U. S. A., 1-6 (2011)

11. Drewniak, J., Rak, E.: Subdistributivity and superdistributivity of binary operations. Fuzzy Sets Syst. **161**(2), 189–201 (2010)
12. Drewniak, J., Rak, E.: Distributivity inequalities of monotonic operations. Fuzzy Sets Syst. **191**, 62–71 (2012)
13. Saminger-Platz, S.: The dominance relation in some families of continuous Archimedean t-norms and copulas. Fuzzy Sets Syst. **160**(14), 2017–2031 (2008)

The Modularity Condition of T-Uninorms over Semi-t-Operators

Keyi Xiao[1], Yong Su[2], and Wenwen Zong[1](✉)

[1] School of Mathematical Sciences, University of Jinan, Jinan 250022, Shandong, People's Republic of China
zongwen198811@163.com

[2] School of Mathematical Sciences, Suzhou University of Science and Technology, Suzhou 215009, Jiangsu, People's Republic of China

Abstract. The modularity equation involving aggregation functions holds significant value in fuzzy sets theory. This paper investigates the modularity condition of T-uninorms over semi-t-operators under no additional assumptions. Moreover, when the underlying pseudo-t-norm of the semi-t-operator is commutative, a universal framework for the structures of modular T-uninorm and semi-t-operator pairs is presented.

Keywords: aggregation functions · modularity · T-uninorms · semi-t-operators

1 Introduction

Aggregation functions serve as essential tools across multiple disciplines such as fuzzy logic, decision theory, approximate reasoning and image processing [2, 3, 5, 10]. Aggregation functions possessing annihilator elements play a pivotal role in modeling rational decision-making processes. These functions are most notably connected to Arrow's impossibility theorem (see [5] for details), while also playing a significant role in the analysis of aggregation functions operating on a bipolar scale (see [2, 3] for details).

T-uninorm is a prominent class of aggregation functions with annihilator. And the function is built upon nullnorms and conjunctive uninorms. At the same time, by relaxing the commutativity constraint of t-operators, semi-t-operators generalize both t-operators and nullnorms.

In the research of aggregation functions, in addition to characterizing internal structure and exploring their algebraic properties, equations about aggregation functions are always helpful in the domain of fuzzy set theory and fuzzy logic [1]. In particular, the modularity condition has become one of the core issues of research in recent years. Not only is modularity strongly correlated to the distributivity condition, but it also can be regarded as a restricted general associative equation. As is widely known, the former is in most cases necessary in fuzzy connectives, and the later is also important in fuzzy set theory. Based on this, many scholars have conducted lots of research on this new topic.

M. Bonsangue and Y. Chen (Eds.): AILA 2025, CCIS 2668, pp. 113–120, 2026.
https://doi.org/10.1007/978-981-95-8262-4_9

Mas et al. [8] characterized the modularity condition involving t-operators and uninorms belonging to the $U_{\max}$ and $U_{\min}$. Zhang et al. [13] established the solution of modularity equation involving uni-nullnorm(null-uninorm) and overlap (grouping) function. The modularity condition between uninorm pairs has been studied by Su et al. [9], in which no fewer than one uninorm belongs to the generic classes.

In the previous study, the modularity of semi-t-operators and semi-uninorms under the assumption that both of them have continuous underlying functions has been studied by Zhan et al. [11,12]. Then, Zhao and Liu [14] investigates the modulairity condition between T-uninorms and semi-t-operators with continuous underlying functions, besides, the structures of modular T-uninorms and semi-t-operators pairs are obtained through the assumption that T-uninorms own the underlying uninorm that is locally internal on the boundary. This paper investigates the more general case that the functions are without any further assumptions. And on this basis, we make further characterization of their structure when the underlying pseudo-t-norm of semi-t-operator is commutative. The new perspective offers a fresh look at the modularity equation, presenting several solutions that were previously overlooked. Consequently, we believe that this research supplements existing studies of the modularity equation.

This paper is structured into four sections. Section 2 briefly reviews basic definitions and existing results used in this paper. The modular T-uninorms and semi-t-operators pairs is characterized in Sect. 3, while Sect. 4 outlines concluding remarks.

2 Preliminaries

Some fundamental concepts and well-known results required later are reviewed in this section.

Definition 1. *[6] Let A be a binary function on $[0,1]$. Then A is called an aggregation function if it is non-decreasing in each variable, and 0 and 1 is the idempotent element of A, respectively.*

Definition 2. *[9] Let $e_G \in [0,1]$, and let G be a binary aggregation function on $[0,1]$. Then G is called a uninorm if it fulfills associativity, commutativity, and has a neutral element e_G.*

When $e_G = 1$, a uninorm becomes a *t-norm* and when $e_G = 0$, it is a *t-conorm*. For any uninorm G it holds that $G(1,0) \in \{0,1\}$. And we say G is *conjuctive* when $G(1,0) = 0$. Otherwise, G is *disjunctive*. We define $\mathcal{G}_{e_G}$ as the class of uninorms with neutral element e_G, $\mathcal{G}^c$ and $\mathcal{G}^d$ as the class of conjunctive uninorms and disjunctive uninorms, respectively.

Definition 3. *[7] Let $h \in]0,1]$, and P be a binary aggregation function on $[0,1]$. Then P is called a T-uninorm if it fulfills associativity, commutativity, has an annihilator element h, and*

- *$P(1,\cdot)$ exhibits continuity, $P(0,\cdot)$ is discontinuous.*
- *$P(e_P,\cdot)$ is continuous and $P(e_P,0)=0$, whereas $e_P\in]0,1[$ is the idempotent element of P.*

The structural properties of T-uninorms can be characterized as follows.

Theorem 1. *[7] Let $h\in]0,1]$, and P be a binary aggregation function on $[0,1]$. Then P is a T-uninorm with an annihilator element h if and only if*

$$P(\beta,\gamma)=\begin{cases} hU_P(\frac{\beta}{h},\frac{\gamma}{h}) & \text{if } 0\le\beta,\gamma\le h,\\ h+(1-h)T_P(\frac{\beta-h}{1-h},\frac{\gamma-h}{1-h}) & \text{if } h\le\beta,\gamma\le 1,\\ h & \text{otherwise,}\end{cases} \tag{1}$$

where $T_P\in\mathcal{G}_1$, and $U_P\in\mathcal{G}^d_{e_G}$ with $e_G=\frac{e_P}{h}$.

Denote by $\mathcal{P}^T_{e_P,h}$ the class of all T-uninorms with $0<e_P<h\le 1$, which have annihilator element h, the underlying functions $U_P\in\mathcal{G}^d_{e_G}$ and $T_P\in\mathcal{G}_1$, respectively. In particular, if $h=1$, a T-uninorm becomes a disjunctive uninorm.

Definition 4. *[4] A function $T:[0,1]^2\to[0,1]$ is called a* pseudo-t-norm *if it is associative, increasing in each variable and has a neutral element* 1.

A function $S:[0,1]^2\to[0,1]$ is called a pseudo-t-conorm *if it is associative, increasing in each variable and has a neutral element* 0.

Definition 5. *[4] An aggregation function $Q:[0,1]^2\to[0,1]$ is classified as a* semi-t-operator *if it is associative, increasing in each variable, and Q_0,Q_1,Q^0,Q^1 are continuous, where $Q_0=Q(0,\beta),Q_1=Q(1,\beta),Q^0=Q(\beta,0)$ and $Q^1=Q(\beta,1)$ for any $\beta\in[0,1]$.*

Let $\mathcal{Q}_{s,t}$ denote the set of semi-t-operators Q such that $Q(0,1)=s$ and $Q(1,0)=t$.

Theorem 2. *[4] The function $Q\in\mathcal{Q}_{s,t}$ if and only if*

- *when $s\le t$,*

$$Q(\beta,\gamma)=\begin{cases} sS_Q\left(\frac{\beta}{s},\frac{\gamma}{s}\right) & \text{if } 0\le\beta,\gamma\le s,\\ t+(1-t)T_Q\left(\frac{\beta-t}{1-t},\frac{\gamma-t}{1-t}\right) & \text{if } t\le\beta,\gamma\le 1,\\ s & \text{if } 0\le\beta\le s\le\gamma\le 1,\\ t & \text{if } 0\le\gamma\le t\le\beta\le 1,\\ \beta & \text{otherwise,}\end{cases} \tag{2}$$

- *when $s\ge t$,*

$$Q(\beta,\gamma)=\begin{cases} tS_Q\left(\frac{\beta}{t},\frac{\gamma}{t}\right) & \text{if } 0\le\beta,\gamma\le t,\\ s+(1-s)T_Q\left(\frac{\beta-s}{1-s},\frac{\gamma-s}{1-s}\right) & \text{if } s\le\beta,\gamma\le 1,\\ s & \text{if } 0\le\beta\le s\le\gamma\le 1,\\ t & \text{if } 0\le\gamma\le t\le\beta\le 1,\\ \gamma & \text{otherwise,}\end{cases} \tag{3}$$

where T_Q *is a pseudo-t-norm, and* S_Q *is a pseudo-t-conorm.*

Definition 6. *[8] Let* $P, Q : [0,1]^2 \to [0,1]$ *be two functions. Define that* P *is modular over* Q *if for any* $0 \le \beta, \gamma, \theta \le 1$ *with* $\theta \le \beta$*, the following equation holds,*

$$P(\beta,\, Q(\gamma,\, \theta)) = Q(P(\beta,\, \gamma),\, \theta)\,. \tag{4}$$

Lemma 1. *[14] If* $P \in \mathcal{P}^T_{e_P,h}$ *is modular over* $Q \in \mathcal{Q}_{s,t}$*, then* $h \le t$*.*

3 Modularity Condition of T-Uninorms over Semi-t-Operators

Commutativity simplifies the analysis, allowing consideration of only the modularity Eq. (4). We extend the investigation for the modularity of $P \in \mathcal{P}^T_{e_P,h}$ over $Q \in \mathcal{Q}_{s,t}$.

Lemma 2. *If* $h \le t$*,* $P \in \mathcal{P}^T_{e_P,h}$ *is modular over* $Q \in \mathcal{Q}_{s,t}$*, then:*

(i) $P(\beta,\gamma) = \min(\beta,\gamma)$ *for any* $h \le \min(\beta,\gamma) \le t \le \max(\beta,\gamma) \le 1$*.*
(ii) $P(\beta,\gamma) = P(\gamma,\beta) = Q(\beta,\gamma)$ *for any* $t \le \beta,\gamma \le 1$ *with* $\gamma \le \beta$*.*

Proof. Suppose that P and Q satisfy Eq. (4).

(i) Setting $\beta \in [h,t]$, $\theta = 0$ and $\gamma = 1$ into Eq. (4), then $h \le P(\beta,\gamma) \le t$, we obtain $P(\beta, Q(1,0)) = P(\beta,t)$, and $Q(P(\beta,1),0) = Q(\beta,0) = \beta$, implying that item (i) holds, for the reason that P is monotonous and commutative, 1 is the neutral element of T_P.

(ii) Substituting $\beta,\theta \in [t,1]$ and $\gamma = 1$ with $\theta \le \beta$ into Eq. (4). We then obtain $P(\beta, Q(1,\theta)) = P(\beta,\theta)$ and $Q(P(\beta,1),\theta) = Q(\beta,\theta)$, implying that item (ii) holds, for the reason that P is commutative. □

Depending on Lemma 2 and the relationship between h, e_P, s and t, we divide our work into the following four subcases: 1. $s < e_P < h \le t$; 2. $e_P \le s \le h \le t$; 3. $h < s \le t$; 4. $h \le t < s$.

3.1 $s < e_P < h \le t$

Lemma 3. *If* $s < e_P < h \le t$*,* $P \in \mathcal{P}^T_{e_P,h}$ *is modular over* $Q \in \mathcal{Q}_{s,t}$*, then*

(i) $P(\beta,\gamma) = \min(\beta,\gamma)$ *for any* $(\beta,\gamma) \in [0,e_P] \times [0,s] \cup [0,s] \times [0,e_P]$*.*
(ii) $S_Q = \max$*.*
(iii) for any $\beta \in [e_P,h]$*, we have either* $P(\beta,\gamma) = \gamma$ *for all* $0 \le \gamma \le s$ *or* $P(\beta,\gamma) = P(\beta,0)$ *for all* $0 \le \gamma \le s$*.*

Proof. Suppose that P and Q satisfy Eq. (4).

(i) Setting $\beta \in [0, e_P]$, $\theta \in [0, s]$ with $\theta \leq \beta$ and setting $\gamma = 0$ into Eq. (4), we obtain

$$P(\beta, \theta) = P(\beta, Q(0, \theta)) = Q(P(\beta, 0), \theta) = Q(0, \theta) = \theta .$$

implying that for any $(\beta, \gamma) \in [0, e_P] \times [0, s] \cup [0, s] \times [0, e_P]$, $P(\beta, \gamma) = \min(\beta, \gamma)$ by the commutativity of P.

(ii) Substituting $\beta = \theta \in [0, s]$ and setting $\gamma = e_P$ into Eq. (4), we then obtain

$$\beta = P(\beta, e_P) = P(\beta, Q(e_P, \beta)) = Q(P(\beta, e_P), \beta) = Q(\beta, \beta) ,$$

implying that for any $0 \leq \beta, \gamma \leq s$, $Q(\beta, \gamma) = \max(\beta, \gamma)$.

(iii) Substituting $\beta \in [e_P, h]$, $\theta \in [0, s]$ and setting $\gamma = 0$ into Eq. (4). Then we obtain

$$P(\beta, \theta) = P(\beta, Q(0, \theta)) = Q(P(\beta, 0), \theta) = \max\{P(\beta, 0), \theta\} . \tag{5}$$

If $P(\beta, \theta) > P(\beta, 0)$, then Eq. (5) yields $P(\beta, \theta) = \theta$. Thus, either $P(\beta, \theta) = P(\beta, 0)$ or $P(\beta, \theta) = \theta$ holds. Let $x_P \in [e_P, h]$ and

$$\alpha = \sup\{m \in [0, s] \mid P(\beta_P, m) = P(\beta_P, 0)\}.$$

Below, we show that $\alpha = 0$ or $\alpha = s$. Otherwise, suppose that $\alpha \in]0, s[$. Then $P(\beta_P, \theta) = P(\beta_P, 0)$ if $0 \leq \theta < \alpha$, and $P(\beta_P, \theta) = \theta$ if $\alpha < \theta \leq s$. The associativity of P implies that for $y \in]\alpha, s[$ and $z \in]0, \alpha[$, we have

$$P(\beta_P, 0) = P(\beta_P, \theta) = P(\beta_P, P(\gamma, \theta)) = P(P(\beta_P, \gamma), \theta) = P(\gamma, \theta) = \theta ,$$

contradicting the fact that $P(\beta_P, 0)$ is a constant. Bringing all finding above together, we deduce that for any given $\beta \in [e_P, h]$, we have either $P(\beta, \gamma) = \gamma$ for all $0 \leq \gamma \leq s$ or $P(\beta, \gamma) = P(\beta, 0)$ for all $0 \leq \gamma \leq s$. □

Under the additional assumption that the underlying function T_Q of Q is commutative, the subsequent theorem holds.

Theorem 3. *Let $s < e_P < h \leq t$, $Q \in \mathcal{Q}_{s,t}$ with T_Q is commutative and $P \in \mathcal{P}^T_{e_P,h}$. Then P and Q satisfy Eq. (4) if and only if:*

(i) $P(\beta, \gamma) = \min(\beta, \gamma)$ *for any* $(\beta, \gamma) \in [h, t] \times [t, 1] \cup [t, 1] \times [h, t]$.
(ii) $P(\beta, \gamma) = \min(\beta, \gamma)$ *for any* $(\beta, \gamma) \in [0, e_P] \times [0, s] \cup [0, s] \times [0, e_P]$.
(iii) $S_Q = \max$.
(iv) for any $\beta \in [e_P, h]$, *either* $P(\beta, \gamma) = \gamma$ *for all* $0 \leq \gamma \leq s$ *or* $P(\beta, \gamma) = P(\beta, 0)$ *for all* $0 \leq \gamma \leq s$.
(v) $P(\beta, \gamma) = Q(\beta, \gamma)$ *for any* $(\beta, \gamma) \in [t, 1]^2$.

Proof. Suppose that P and Q satisfy Eq. (4). Items (i)-(v) can be obviously obtained by Lemma 2, Lemma 3 together with the commutativity of T_Q.

Reciprocally, a direct computation shows that P is modular over Q. □

Example 1. Let $s < e_P < h \leq t$ and U'_P be any uninorm. Considering P_1, Q_1 be binary aggregation functions on $[0,1]$ defined by

$$P_1(\beta,\gamma) = \begin{cases} s + (h-s)U'_P(\frac{\beta-s}{h-s}, \frac{\gamma-s}{h-s}) & \text{if } s \leq \beta, \gamma \leq h, \\ h & \text{if } 0 \leq \min(\beta,\gamma) \leq h \leq \max(\beta,\gamma) \leq 1, \\ \min(\beta,\gamma) & \text{otherwise,} \end{cases}$$

$$Q_1(\beta,\gamma) = \begin{cases} \max(\beta,\gamma) & \text{if } 0 \leq \beta, \gamma \leq s, \\ \min(\beta,\gamma) & \text{if } t \leq \beta, \gamma \leq 1, \\ s & \text{if } 0 \leq \beta \leq s \leq \gamma \leq 1, \\ t & \text{if } 0 \leq \gamma \leq t \leq \beta \leq 1, \\ \beta & \text{otherwise.} \end{cases}$$

Theorem 3 indicates that P_1 is modular over Q_1.

3.2 $e_P \leq s \leq h \leq t$

Lemma 4. *If $e_P \leq s \leq h \leq t$, $P \in \mathcal{P}^T_{e_P,h}$ is modular over $Q \in \mathcal{Q}_{s,t}$, then $P(\beta,\gamma) = \max(\beta,\gamma)$ for any $0 \leq \min(\beta,\gamma) \leq s < \max(\beta,\gamma) \leq h$.*

Theorem 4. *Let $e_P \leq s \leq h \leq t$, $Q \in \mathcal{Q}_{s,t}$ with T_Q is commutative and $P \in \mathcal{P}^T_{e_P,h}$. Then P is modular over Q if and only if:*

(i)

$$P(\beta,\gamma) = \begin{cases} sU'_P(\frac{\beta}{s}, \frac{\gamma}{s}) & \text{if } 0 \leq \beta, \gamma \leq s, \\ \max(\beta,\gamma) & \text{if } 0 \leq \min(\beta,\gamma) \leq s < \max(\beta,\gamma) \leq h, \\ s + (h-s)S'_P(\frac{\beta-s}{h-s}, \frac{\gamma-s}{h-s}) & \text{if } s \leq \beta, \gamma \leq h, \\ h + (t-h)T'_P(\frac{\beta-h}{t-h}, \frac{\gamma-h}{t-h}) & \text{if } h \leq \beta, \gamma \leq t, \\ \min(\beta,\gamma) & \text{if } h \leq \min(\beta,\gamma) \leq t \leq \max(\beta,\gamma) \leq 1, \\ t + (1-t)T_Q(\frac{\beta-t}{1-t}, \frac{\gamma-t}{1-t}) & \text{if } t \leq \beta, \gamma \leq 1, \\ h & \text{otherwise,} \end{cases}$$

$$Q(\beta,\gamma) = \begin{cases} sS_Q(\frac{\beta}{s}, \frac{\gamma}{s}) & \text{if } 0 \leq \beta, \gamma \leq s, \\ t + (1-t)T_Q(\frac{\beta-t}{1-t}, \frac{\gamma-t}{1-t}) & \text{if } t \leq \beta, \gamma \leq 1, \\ s & \text{if } 0 \leq \beta \leq s \leq \gamma \leq 1, \\ t & \text{if } 0 \leq \gamma \leq t \leq \beta \leq 1, \\ \beta & \text{otherwise,} \end{cases}$$

where $T'_P, T_Q \in \mathcal{G}_1$, S_Q is a pseudo-t-conorm, $S'_P \in \mathcal{G}_0$ and $U'_P \in \mathcal{G}_{e_G}$ with $e_G = \frac{e_P}{s}$.

(ii) U'_P is modular over S_Q.

3.3 $h < s \leq t$

Lemma 5. *If $h < s \leq t$, $P \in \mathcal{P}^T_{e_P,h}$ is modular over $Q \in \mathcal{Q}_{s,t}$, then*

(i) $P(\beta,\gamma)=\min(\beta,\gamma)$ *for any* $(\beta,\gamma)\in[h,1]\times[h,s]\cup[h,s]\times[h,1]$.
(ii) $Q(\beta,\gamma)=\max(\beta,\gamma)$ *for any* $(\beta,\gamma)\in[h,s]\times[0,s]\cup[0,s]\times[h,s]$.

Theorem 5. *Let* $h<s\le t$, $Q\in\mathcal{Q}_{s,t}$ *with* T_Q *is commutative and* $P\in\mathcal{P}^T_{e_P,h}$. *Then* P *is modular over* Q *if and only if:*

(i)

$$P(\beta,\gamma)=\begin{cases} hU_P(\frac{\beta}{h},\frac{\gamma}{h}) & \text{if } 0\le\beta,\gamma\le h,\\ s+(t-s)T'_P(\frac{\beta-s}{t-s},\frac{\gamma-s}{t-s}) & \text{if } s\le\beta,\gamma\le t,\\ t+(1-t)T_Q(\frac{\beta-t}{1-t},\frac{\gamma-t}{1-t}) & \text{if } t\le\beta,\gamma\le 1,\\ h & \text{if } 0\le\min(\beta,\gamma)\le h\le\max(\beta,\gamma)\le 1,\\ \min(\beta,\gamma) & \text{otherwise,}\end{cases}$$

$$Q(\beta,\gamma)=\begin{cases} hS'_Q(\frac{\beta}{h},\frac{\gamma}{h}) & \text{if } 0\le\beta,\gamma\le h,\\ s & \text{if } 0\le\beta\le s\le\gamma\le 1,\\ \beta & \text{if } s\le\beta\le t,\ 0\le\gamma\le 1,\\ t+(1-t)T_Q(\frac{\beta-t}{1-t},\frac{\gamma-t}{1-t}) & \text{if } t\le\beta,\gamma\le 1,\\ t & \text{if } 0\le\gamma\le t\le\beta\le 1,\\ \max(\beta,\gamma) & \text{otherwise,}\end{cases}$$

where $T'_P, T_Q\in\mathcal{G}_1$, S'_Q *is a pseudo-t-conorm, and* $U_P\in\mathcal{G}^d_{e_G}$ *with* $e_G=\frac{e_P}{h}$.
(ii) U_P *is modular over* S'_Q.

3.4 $h\le t<s$

Lemma 6. *If* $h\le t<s$, $P\in\mathcal{P}^T_{e_P,h}$ *is modular over* $Q\in\mathcal{Q}_{s,t}$, *then*

(i) $P(\beta,\gamma)=\min(\beta,\gamma)$ *for any* $(\beta,\gamma)\in[h,1]\times[h,s]\cup[h,s]\times[h,1]$.
(ii) $Q(\beta,\gamma)=\max(\beta,\gamma)$ *for any* $(\beta,\gamma)\in[h,t]\times[0,t]\cup[0,t]\times[h,t]$.

Theorem 6. *Let* $h\le t<s$, $Q\in\mathcal{Q}_{s,t}$ *with* T_M *is commutative and* $P\in\mathcal{P}^T_{e_P,h}$. *Then* P *is modular over* Q *if and only if:*

(i)

$$P(\beta,\gamma)=\begin{cases} hU_P(\frac{\beta}{h},\frac{\gamma}{h}) & \text{if } 0\le\beta,\gamma\le h,\\ h & \text{if } 0\le\min(\beta,\gamma)\le h\le\max(\beta,\gamma)\le 1,\\ s+(1-s)T_Q(\frac{\beta-s}{1-s},\frac{\gamma-s}{1-s}) & \text{if } s\le\beta,\gamma\le 1,\\ \min(\beta,\gamma) & \text{otherwise,}\end{cases}$$

$$Q(\beta,\gamma)=\begin{cases} hS'_Q(\frac{\beta}{h},\frac{\gamma}{h}) & \text{if } 0\le\beta,\gamma\le h,\\ s & \text{if } 0\le\beta\le s\le\gamma\le 1,\\ \gamma & \text{if } 0\le\beta\le 1,\ t\le\gamma\le s,\\ s+(1-s)T_Q(\frac{\beta-s}{1-s},\frac{\gamma-s}{1-s}) & \text{if } s\le\beta,\gamma\le 1,\\ t & \text{if } 0\le\gamma\le t\le\beta\le 1,\\ \max(\beta,\gamma) & \text{otherwise,}\end{cases}$$

where $T_Q\in\mathcal{G}_1$, S'_Q *is a pseudo-t-conorm, and* $U_P\in\mathcal{G}^d_{e_G}$ *with* $e_G=\frac{e_P}{h}$.
(ii) U_P *is modular over* S'_Q.

4 Conclusions

This work studied the modularity condition of T-uninorms over semi-t-operators in most general settings. We establish complete necessary and sufficient conditions that modularity equation holds with an additional assumption that the underlying pseudo-t-norm of semi-t-operators satisfies commutativity. Some new solutions to the modularity equation, which had not been included in earlier studies, were obtained by removing the continuity assumptions.

References

1. Aczél, J.: Lectures on Munctional Equations and Their Applications. Acad. Press, New York (1966)
2. Da Silva, R., Raufaste, E.: A psychological study of bipolarity in the possibilistic framework. In: Proceedings of IPMU-04, Perugia, Italy, pp. 975–981 (2004). https://doi.org/10.1007/978-3-642-17280-9_5
3. Dubois. D., kaci, S., Prade, H.: Bipolarity in reasoning and decision-an introduction. The Case of the Possibility Theory Framework, Proceedings of IPMU-04, Perugia, Italy, pp. 959–966 (2004). https://doi.org/10.1002/int.20297
4. Drygás, P.: Distributivity between semi-t-operators and semi-nullnorms. Muzzy Sets Syst. **264**, 100–109 (2015). https://doi.org/10.1016/j.fss.2015.01.015
5. Mung, L.W., Mu K.S.: An axiomatical approach to rational decision making in a fuzzy environment. In: L.A. Zadeh, Ed., Muzzy Sets and their Applications to Cognitive and Decision Processes. New York: Academic Press, pp. 227–256 (1975). https://doi.org/10.1007/978-1-4613-1365-6_11
6. Nrabisch, M.: Aggregation Munctions. Cambridge University Press, New York (2009)
7. Mas, M., Mesiar, R., Monserrat, M., et al.: Aggregation operators with annihilator. Int. J. Neneral Syst. **34**(1), 17–38 (2005). https://doi.org/10.1080/03081070512331318347
8. Mas, M., Mayor, N., Torrens, J.: The modularity condition for uninorms and t-operators. Muzzy Sets Syst. **126**(2), 207–218 (2002). https://doi.org/10.1016/S0165-0114(01)00055-0
9. Su, Y., Liu, H., Riera, J.V., Aguilera, D.R., Torrens, J.: The modularity condition for uninorms revisited. Muzzy Sets Syst. **357**, 27–46 (2019). https://doi.org/10.1016/j.fss.2018.02.008
10. Torra, V., Narukawa, Y.: Modeling Decisions: Information Musion and Aggregation Operators. Springer-Verlag, Berlin Heidelberg (2007)
11. Zhan, H., Wang, Y., Liu, H.: The modularity condition for semi-t-operators and semi-uninorms. Muzzy Sets Syst. **334**, 36–59 (2018). https://doi.org/10.1016/j.fss.2017.05.025
12. Zhan, H., Wang, Y., Liu, H.: The modularity condition for semi-t-operators. Muzzy Sets Syst. **346**, 108–126 (2018). https://doi.org/10.1016/j.fss.2017.10.015
13. Zhang, T.H., Qin, M., Liu, H.W., Wang, Y.M.: Modularity conditions between overlap (grouping) function and uni-nullnorm or null-uninorm. Muzzy Sets Syst. **414**, 94–114 (2021). https://doi.org/10.1016/j.fss.2020.08.018
14. Zhao, Y., Liu, H.: The modularity equation for semi-t-operators and T-uninorms. Int. J. Approximate Reasoning **146**, 106–118 (2022). https://doi.org/10.1016/j.ijar.2022.04.005

Probabilistic and Fuzzy Systems

Multi-view Discriminant Analysis with Posterior Probability Graph Weighting

Pei Jihong[1,2], Lin Xiaoan[2], Li Meihua[2], Zhao Yang[3(✉)], and Yang Xuan[3]

[1] Guangdong Key Laboratory of Intelligent Information Processing, Shenzhen University, Shenzhen, China
jhpei@szu.edu.cn

[2] College of Electronics and Information Engineering, Shenzhen University, Shenzhen, China

[3] College of Computer Science and Software Engineering, Shenzhen University, Shenzhen, China
zhaoyang1990@szu.edu.cn

Abstract. Multi-view Discriminant Analysis is a supervised multi-view learning method widely used in pattern recognition fields. When one view's data gets affected, the labels may contain errors, making the label reliability of that view's dataset questionable. To address the above issue, the Multi-view Discriminant Analysis with Posterior Probability Graph Weighting (MvDA-PPG) method is proposed for reliable multi-view learning tasks in unreliable labeling environments. This method optimizes the posterior probability matrix by introducing the sample posterior probability graph. Moreover, it reduces the impact of data from unreliably labeled views on the performance of multi-view learning by adjusting the weights of some views. Experimental results demonstrate that the KMvDA-PPG method helps reduce the influence of unreliable labels by applying posterior probability weighting to samples containing unreliable labeled views. This improves classification accuracy and robustness. The paper conducted experiments on three widely used datasets. Theoretical analysis and experimental results indicate that the improved KMvDA-PPG algorithm exhibits excellent classification recognition performance.

Keywords: Multi-view discriminant analysis · Unreliable labeling environments · Consistency constraints · Posterior probability Graph

1 Introduction

In the era of big data, we often encounter datasets with multiple views. These views may originate from different data sources, measurement methods, or involve information from different domains. Typically, these views possess certain structure and features. However, using a single view for classification recognition

M. Bonsangue and Y. Chen (Eds.): AILA 2025, CCIS 2668, pp. 123–136, 2026.
https://doi.org/10.1007/978-981-95-8262-4_10

can lead to overfitting and underfitting problems. Therefore, utilizing multi-view learning methods to extract information from each view and combine them effectively has become an active research area.

In single-view learning, Linear Discriminant Analysis (LDA) [1] [2] is a widely used supervised learning method. Uncorrelated Linear Discriminant Analysis (ULDA) [3] is an extension of LDA, and Sun et al. proposed obtaining the optimal projection matrix with minimal redundant information by applying ULDA. The Multi-view Uncorrelated Linear Discriminant Analysis (MULDA) [4] combines the advantages of ULDA and CCA by extracting uncorrelated features within each view and projecting them onto a shared subspace. Later, the Generalized Multiview Analysis (GMA) [5] was proposed to incorporate supervised information, resulting in a discriminative common subspace. However, GMA focuses only on intra-view discriminant information while ignoring inter-view discriminant information. To address this issue, the Multi-view Discriminant Analysis (MvDA) [6] was introduced with the objective of maximizing class-wise distances across all views and minimizing class-wise within-distances to find optimal projection directions that map data onto a shared subspace. However, MvDA is limited to linear spaces, prompting the development of Kernel Multi-view Discriminant Analysis (KMvDA) [7]. Yang et al. proposed a Robust Multi-view Discriminant Analysis with Viewpoint Consistency (RMvDA-VC) [8] to tackle noisy data problems. Peng et al. proposed "Deep Supervised Multi-View Learning With Graph Priors" [11], which constructs a discriminative similarity graph based on multi-view input labels and pairwise relationships as prior knowledge. Nevertheless, in multi-resolution image classification tasks, low-resolution images can be difficult to differentiate due to label noise, which may degrade classification performance. Li et al. introduced Weighted Multi-view Discriminant Analysis (WMvDA) [9], assigning different weights to each view to enhance MvDA's accuracy under unreliable label environments.

In this paper, Multi-view Discriminant Analysis with Posterior Probability Graph Optimization (MvDA-PPG) is proposed. The algorithm constructs and optimizes a sample posterior probability graph to more finely describe the categorical properties of samples, thereby reducing the impact of potentially unreliable labels on performance. It also decreases the weights of views with unreliable labels to minimize their impact on overall learning performance. This method is extended to the kernel space to find more optimal linear relationships in high-dimensional feature spaces, effectively handling non-linear data distributions in original spaces and further improving classification performance.

In summary, our contributions are as follows:

(1) We propose a Multi-view Discriminant Analysis with Posterior Probability Graph Weighting (MvDA-PPG). This method leverages sample posterior probability information to build a graph model that optimizes the posterior probability matrix, making it closer to the true label distribution. Based on view-wise data reliability and consistency assessments, we adjust each view's weight to ensure reliable views play a more significant role in model training.

(2) On the basis of the unified framework proposed in Contribution (1), a new multi-view learning algorithm is further designed. The algorithm not only inherits the core idea of the framework, but also optimizes the processing of nonlinear data. We introduce Kernel Multi-view Discriminant Analysis with Posterior Probability Graph Weighting for unreliable label environments (KMvDA-PPG). This method effectively addresses non-linear data distribution issues in original spaces by finding optimal linear relationships in high-dimensional feature spaces, further enhancing classification performance.

2 Related Work

Multi-view Discriminant Analysis [6] extends traditional Linear Discriminant Analysis (LDA) [2] to multi-view data. Its core idea is to project multiple views of data into a shared latent subspace while maximizing class-wise distances and minimizing class-wise within-distances within that subspace.

Given c classes, there are v views of datasets $X_j \in \mathbf{R}^{\mathbf{d_j}} (j = 1, 2, ..., j, ..., v)$, where d_j represents the feature dimension size of the j-th view. The projection results can be represented as $y_{ijk} = W_j^T x_{ijk}$ $(i = 1, \cdots, c; j = 1, \cdots, v; k = 1, \cdots, n_{ij})$, where x_{ijk} denotes the k-th training sample in the i-th class of the j-th view, and W_j represents the projection matrix for the j-th view. The optimization target function of the MvDA algorithm can be represented as follows:

$$\max_{W_1, W_2, \cdots, W_v} \frac{Tr(S_B^y)}{Tr(S_W^y)}, \tag{1}$$

where S_W^y represents the within-class scatter matrix, and S_B^y represents the between-class scatter matrix.

In MvDA [6], view consistency constraints were introduced to obtain the optimization objective function of Multi-view Discriminant Analysis with view consistency:

$$\max_{W_1, W_2, \cdots, W_v} \frac{Tr(S_B^y)}{Tr(S_W^y) + \lambda \sum_{j,l=1}^{v} ||\beta_j - \beta_l||_2^2}, \tag{2}$$

where λ is the balance parameter. In view consistency constraints $\sum_{j,l=1}^{v} ||\beta_j - \beta_l||_2^2$, β_j is the feature matrix extracted from the projection matrix W_j.

The between-class scatter matrix mainly measures the differences between centers of different categories, while the within-class scatter matrix reflects the differences between samples within the same category. By optimizing the ratio of within-class and between-class scatter matrices, MvDA can find a projection direction that best distinguishes different categories, significantly improving classification and recognition accuracy. However, in environments with unreliable labels, views containing unreliable labels will affect the projection matrix. Moreover, within the same view, the importance of information contained in each sample varies. Unlike MvDA which does not consider the different importance degrees of samples to their respective categories while calculating between-class and within-class scatter matrices, this paper proposes a method that introduces posterior probability matrix as sample weights, thereby reducing the impact of unreliable labels on model training and enhancing model robustness.

3 Multi-view Discriminant Analysis with Posterior Probability Graph Weighting

This section introduces the general framework, target function construction, and optimization process of Multi-view Discriminant Analysis with Posterior Probability Graph Weighting in unreliable label environments, as well as its extension to kernel methods.

3.1 Overview

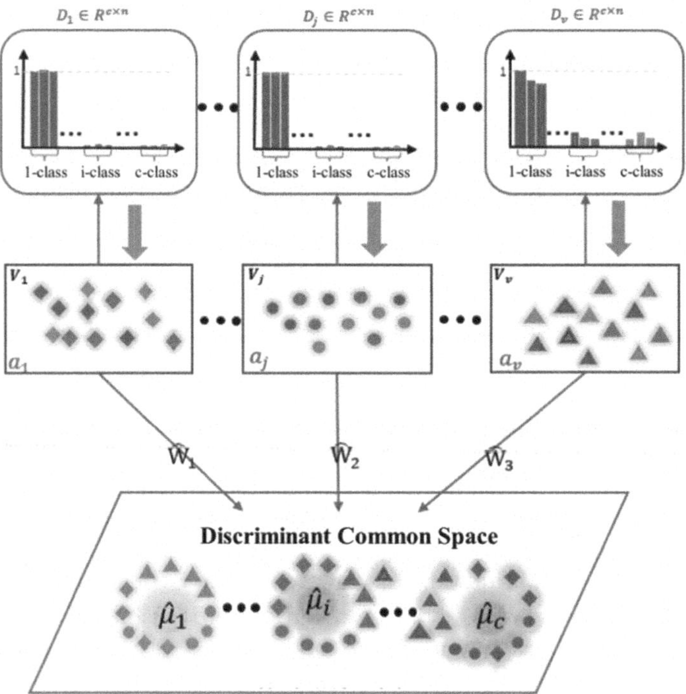

Fig. 1. Algorithm Diagram of Multi-view Discriminant Analysis with Posterior Probability Graph Weighting.

As shown in Fig. 1, MvDA-PPG utilizes the similarity between different samples to construct a posterior probability graph matrix for views with unreliable labels. It uses the distributional information provided by the posterior probability matrix as sample weights to correct for unreliable labels. Then, it assigns different weights to each view based on the importance of information in different views. Based on the weights of different views, it constructs weighted multi-view between-class and within-class scatter matrices and projects samples from v different views into the same latent subspace using v linear transformations. After projection, samples of the same class are grouped as closely together as possible, while samples of different classes are moved as far apart from each other as possible.

MvDA-PPG projects samples from different views into a common discriminant subspace by applying a set of linear transformations. Each view corresponds to one transformation. Here, D_j is the posterior probability matrix for the j-th view. Different colors represent different classes, and different shapes represent different views.

3.2 Model of MvDA-PPG

Define a set $X_j = \{x_{ijk} | i = 1, \cdots, c; k = 1, \cdots, n_{ij}; j = 1, \cdots, v\}$, where the projection result is denoted as $Y_j = \{W_j^T x_{ijk} | i = 1, \cdots, c; k = 1, \cdots, n_{ij}; j = 1, \cdots, v\}$. Here, x_{ijk} represents the k-th sample of the i-th class in the j-th view. Let c be the number of classes, v the number of views, and n_{ij} the number of samples in the i-th class for the j-th view. Then, the optimization objective function of the MvDA-PPG algorithm can be represented as follows:

$$\max_{\widehat{W}_1, \widehat{W}_2, \cdots, \widehat{W}_v} \frac{Tr(\hat{S}_B^y)}{Tr(\hat{S}_W^y) + \lambda \sum_{j,l=1}^{v} ||\beta_j - \beta_l||_2^2}, \tag{3}$$

where $\hat{S}_W^y$ and $\hat{S}_B^y$ denote the weighted within-class and between-class scatter matrices obtained using multiple views' data, respectively. β_j is the feature matrix extracted from the projection matrix $W_j = X_j \beta_j$. Weighted within-class scatter matrix $\hat{S}_W^y$ and weighted between-class scatter matrix $\hat{S}_B^y$ are defined as follows:

$$\hat{S}_W^y = \sum_{i=1}^{c} \sum_{j=1}^{v} a_j \sum_{k=1}^{n_{ij}} (y_{ijk} - \hat{\mu}_i)(y_{ijk} - \hat{\mu}_i)^T, \tag{4}$$

$$\hat{S}_B^y = \sum_{i=1}^{c} n_i (\hat{\mu}_i - \hat{\mu})(\hat{\mu}_i - \hat{\mu})^T. \tag{5}$$

In Eq. 4, a_j is the weight of the j-th view, and $\hat{\mu}$ and $\hat{\mu}_i$ represent the weighted mean of all samples and the weighted mean of the i-th class after projection, which can be calculated as follows:

$$\hat{\mu}_i = \sum_{j=1}^{v} a_j \frac{1}{n_{ij}} \sum_{t=1}^{n} d_j^{it} y_{ijt}, \tag{6}$$

$$\hat{\mu} = \frac{1}{c} \sum_{i=1}^{c} \sum_{j=1}^{v} a_j \frac{1}{n_{ij}} \sum_{t=1}^{n} d_j^{it} y_{ijt}. \tag{7}$$

MvDA-PPG finds a projection direction by solving the optimization Eq. 3, maximizing between-class scatter and minimizing within-class scatter, while ensuring that the main projection vector passes through the densest reliable data points. To suppress the influence of unreliable labeled samples, we introduce sample posterior probability graphs and adjust the weights of unreliable labeled views to penalize the sample space.

The posterior probability matrix $D_j \in \mathbf{R^{c \times n}}$ provides the probability of each sample belonging to different classes. It is used as the weighted value for samples to obtain the weighted class centers $\hat{\mu}_i$ and overall sample center $\hat{\mu}$. For views containing unreliable labels, the posterior probability matrix D_j can be obtained through the following optimization problem:

$$\min_{D_j} ||X_j - X_j G_j||_F^2 + \alpha ||L_j - D_j||_F^2, \quad s.t.\ D_j \geq 0\,, \tag{8}$$

where $G_j = D_j^T D_j B_j$ is the posterior probability graph matrix, $D_j = (D_j^1, D_j^2, ..., D_j^n)$ is the posterior probability matrix, and Matrix B_j is the normalized matrix of correlation matrix $R = D_j^T D_j$. D_j^k indicates the probability distribution of the k-th sample belonging to different categories. α is a balancing parameter. $L_j \in \mathbf{R^{c \times n}}$ is the label matrix after one-hot encoding of the original labels.

Let $Y_j = X_j D_j^T D_j B_j$, then Y is represented as:

$$[y_j^1, y_j^2, ..., y_j^n] = \left[\sum_{k=1}^{n} x_j^k G_{k1}, \sum_{k=1}^{n} x_j^k G_{k2}, ..., \sum_{k=1}^{n} x_j^k G_{kn}\right], \tag{9}$$

where y_j is the j-th element in Y. y_j represents the weighted sum of the relevance between the k-th sample and its posterior probability with other samples, and G_{ki} denotes the relevance between the k-th sample and its posterior probability with other samples. Specifically, for sample x_j^m, if there exists another sample x_j^n that belongs to the same category as x_j^m, then their relevance $[R]_{mn}$ will be relatively large. This larger relevance makes a greater contribution in the weighted sum process, making the smoothed result more similar to the original sample x_j^m. Therefore, this method reduces the error caused by considering only sample a and improves overall accuracy and robustness.

Using the update formula with multiplication to optimize the objective Eq 8, we obtain the following update formula:

$$N = 2D_j^{(t)} B_j X_j^T X_j + D_j^{(t)} X_j^T X_j B_j^T + \alpha L_j, \tag{10}$$

$$D = D_j^{(t)} X_j^T X_j D_j^{(t)^T} D_j^{(t)} B_j B_j^T + D_j^{(t)} B_j B_j^T D_j^{(t)^T} D_j^{(t)} X_j^T X_j + \alpha D_j^{(t)}, \tag{11}$$

$$D_j^{(t+1)} = D_j^{(t)} \odot (N/D), \tag{12}$$

$$D_j^{(t+1)} = D_j^{(t+1)} \cdot diag\left[\left[\left[D_j^{(t+1)}\right]^T \mathbf{1}_n\right]^T\right]^{-1}, \tag{13}$$

where $\odot$ denotes element-wise multiplication. Equation 13 is for normalizing D_j obtained in each iteration. The posterior probability matrix D_j provides the probability of each sample belonging to different classes, which can be used as reliability weights for sample categories.

Upon simplifying Eq. 4, the view-weighted within-class scatter matrix $\hat{S}_W^y$ can be expressed in matrix form:

$$\hat{S}_W^y = \left[\widehat{W}_1^T, ..., \widehat{W}_v^T\right] \begin{bmatrix} \widehat{\Psi}_{11} & \cdots & \widehat{\Psi}_{1v} \\ \vdots & \ddots & \vdots \\ \widehat{\Psi}_{1v} & \cdots & \widehat{\Psi}_{vv} \end{bmatrix} \begin{bmatrix} \widehat{W}_1 \\ \vdots \\ \widehat{W}_v \end{bmatrix} = \widehat{W}^T \widehat{\Psi} \widehat{W}, \tag{14}$$

where matrix $\hat{\Psi}$ is the weighted within-class scatter coefficient matrix, with each block $\widehat{\Psi}_{jl}$ having the following form:

$$\hat{\Psi}_{jl} = \begin{cases} \sum_{i=1}^{c}(a_j \sum_{k=1}^{n_{ij}} x_{ijk} x_{ijk}^T - a_j a_j n_{ij} \mu_{ij}^{x1} \mu_{ij}^{x2^T} \\ -a_j a_j n_{ij} \mu_{ij}^{x2} \mu_{ij}^{x1^T} + a_j a_j n_{ij} \mu_{ij}^{x2} \mu_{ij}^{x2^T}), & j = l \\ \\ \sum_{i=1}^{c} \left(a_j a_l n_{ij} \mu_{ij}^{x2} \mu_{ii}^{x2^T} - a_j a_l n_{ij} \mu_{ij}^{x1} \mu_{ii}^{x2^T} - a_j a_l n_{ij} \mu_{ij}^{x2} \mu_{ii}^{x1^T} \right). & j \neq l \end{cases} \tag{15}$$

Similarly, the view-weighted between-class scatter matrix $\hat{S}_B^y$ can be expressed as follows:

$$\hat{S}_B^y = \left[\widehat{W}_1^T, ..., \widehat{W}_v^T\right] \begin{bmatrix} \widehat{B}_{11} & \cdots & \widehat{B}_{1v} \\ \vdots & \ddots & \vdots \\ \widehat{B}_{1v} & \cdots & \widehat{B}_{vv} \end{bmatrix} \begin{bmatrix} \widehat{W}_1 \\ \vdots \\ \widehat{W}_v \end{bmatrix} = \widehat{W}^T \widehat{B} \widehat{W}, \tag{16}$$

where matrix $\hat{B}$ is the weighted within-class scatter coefficient matrix, with each block $\hat{B}_{jl}$ having the following form:

$$\hat{B}_{jl} = \sum_{i=1}^{c} n_i a_j a_l \mu_{il}^{x2} \mu_{il}^{x2^T} - \frac{n_i}{c} \sum_{i=1}^{c} a_j \mu_{ij}^{x2} \sum_{i=1}^{c} a_l \mu_{il}^{x2^T}. \tag{17}$$

In Eq. 3, consistency constraints across views $\sum_{j,l=1}^{v} ||\beta_j - \beta_l||_2^2 = Tr\left(\widehat{W}^T M \widehat{W}\right)$, where matrix M is:

$$M = \begin{bmatrix} M_{11} & \cdots & M_{1v} \\ \vdots & \ddots & \vdots \\ M_{v1} & \cdots & M_{vv} \end{bmatrix}. \tag{18}$$

The elements in matrix M are:

$$M_{jl} = \begin{cases} 2(v-1)P_j^T P_j, & j = l \\ -2P_j^T P_l, & j \neq l \end{cases}, \tag{19}$$

where $P_j = \left(X_j^T X_j\right)^{-1} X_j^T$. Therefore, its optimization problem can be rewritten as follows:

$$\max_{\widehat{W}_1, \widehat{W}_2, \cdots, \widehat{W}_v} \frac{Tr(\widehat{W}^T \widehat{B} \widehat{W})}{Tr(\widehat{W}^T (\widehat{\Psi} + \lambda M) \widehat{W})}. \tag{20}$$

Thus, Eq. 20 can be solved using generalized eigenvalue decomposition:

$$\hat{B}\widehat{W} = \gamma(\widehat{\Psi} + \lambda M)\widehat{W}. \tag{21}$$

Solving Eq. 21 yields n eigenvalues and their corresponding eigenvectors. The top d largest eigenvalues' eigenvectors are selected as projection directions, and the samples are projected into a shared d-dimensional subspace.

3.3 Kernel MvDA-PPG

To extend MvDA-PPG to non-linear spaces, we map the original image data X using $\varphi \colon \mathbf{R^d} \to \mathcal{F}$. In the kernel feature space, samples are represented as $\varphi(X_j)$, and the projection matrix is given by $W_j^T = \xi_j^T \varphi(X_j)^T$. Therefore, when the model in Eq. 3 is extended to the kernel space, we obtain a kernel Multi-view Discriminant Analysis with Posterior Probability Graph Weighting, which can be formulated as follows:

$$\max_{\hat{\xi}_1, \hat{\xi}_2, \cdots, \hat{\xi}_v} \frac{Tr(\hat{\xi}^T \hat{B} \hat{\xi})}{Tr(\hat{\xi}^T (\hat{\Psi} + \lambda M) \hat{\xi})}. \tag{22}$$

In the kernel space, the mean of original data and weighted class mean are represented as:

$$\mu_{ij}^{x1} = \frac{1}{n_{ij}} \sum_{k=1}^{n_{ij}} \varphi(x_{ijk}), \tag{23}$$

$$\mu_{ij}^{x2} = \frac{1}{n_{ij}} \sum_{t=1}^{n} d_j^{it} \varphi(x_{ijt}). \tag{24}$$

$\hat{\Psi}$ and $\hat{B}_{jl}$ are block matrices, and the blocks $\hat{\Psi}_{jl}$ and $\hat{B}_{jl}$ can be simplified as follows:

$$\widehat{\Psi}_{jl} = \begin{cases} \sum_{i=1}^{c} (a_j \sum_{k=1}^{n_{ij}} \varphi(x_{ijk}) \varphi(x_{ijk})^T - a_j a_j n_{ij} \mu_{ij}^{x1} \mu_{ij}^{x2^T} \\ -a_j a_j n_i \mu_{ij}^{x2} \mu_{ij}^{xT} + a_j a_j n_{ij} \mu_{ij}^{x2} \mu_{ij}^{x2^T}), & j = l \\ \\ \sum_{i=1}^{c} \left(a_j a_l n_{ij} \mu_{ij}^{x2} \mu_{il}^{x2^T} - a_j a_l n_{ij} \mu_{ij}^{x1} \mu_{il}^{x2^T} - a_j a_l n_{ij} \mu_{ij}^{x2} \mu_{il}^{x1^T} \right), & j \neq l \end{cases} \tag{25}$$

$$\hat{B}_{jl} = \sum_{i=1}^{c} n_i a_j a_l \mu_{il}^{x2} \mu_{il}^{x2^T} - \frac{n_i}{c} \sum_{i=1}^{c} a_j \mu_{ij}^{x2} \sum_{i=1}^{c} a_l \mu_{il}^{x2^T}. \tag{26}$$

Equation 22 can be solved using generalized eigenvalue decomposition:

$$\hat{B}\hat{\hat{\xi}} = \gamma(\hat{\Psi} + \lambda M)\hat{\hat{\xi}}. \tag{27}$$

Solving Eq. 27 yields n eigenvalues and their corresponding eigenvectors. The first d largest eigenvalues' eigenvectors are then chosen as the projection directions, and samples are projected into a shared d-dimensional subspace.

Table 1 outlines the steps for kernel Multi-view Discriminant Analysis with Posterior Probability Graph Weighting in unreliable label environments.

Table 1. kernel Multi-view Discriminant Analysis with Posterior Probability Graph Weighting (KMvDA-PPG)

Algorithm 1: KMvDA-PPG.

Input: Datasets X and corresponding labels;
Parameters a_j with $\sum_{j=1}^{v} a_j = 1$;
Gaussian kernel parameter σ balancing parameter α.

Output: Projection matrices $\xi = \xi_1, \xi_j, \cdots, \xi_v$ and Classification accuracy of test samples.

Step 1: Preprocess data, randomly divide into training and testing sets, initialize models.

Step 2: Construct posterior probability relevance graph using Eq 12.

Step 3: Optimize using Eq 13 to obtain posterior probability matrix D_j.

Step 4: Calculate sample numbers n_{ij} and kernel function mappings K_j.

Step 5: Compute nonlinear mapped within-class scatter matrix $\hat{\psi}$ using Eq 25.

Step 6: Compute nonlinear mapped between-class scatter matrix $\hat{B}$ using Eq 26.

Step 7: Solve for projection matrices ξ using Eq 27.

Step 8: Project training and test samples onto a common space using projection matrices.

Step 9: Classify test samples using k-nearest neighbor(KNN) classifier.

Step 10: Calculate classification accuracy of test samples.

4 Experiments

In this section, we demonstrate the classification performance of the proposed Kernel Multi-view Discriminant Analysis with Posterior Probability Graph Weighting in unreliable label environments (KMvDA-PPG). First, we introduce the datasets and parameter settings. Then, we compare this algorithm with other multi-view classification algorithms and analyze the classification results. Next, we conduct experiments using different kernel functions to validate the advantage of the chosen Gaussian kernel function. Finally, we perform ablation studies to verify the necessity of each module in the algorithm.

4.1 Datasets and Experimental Settings

This paper utilizes publicly available datasets: Coil-20, MNIST and MFD. Coil-20 dataset contains 20 objects with 1440 grayscale images taken at various angles, resized to 32×32, 16×16, and 8×8 pixels for three different views. MNIST dataset comprises 70,000 handwritten digits, resized to 28×28, 14×14, and 7×7 pixels for three views. MFD dataset mainly consists of handwritten digits totaling 2000 samples. In the experiment, the first view uses a 216-dimensional contour-related feature, the second view uses a 64-dimensional KL transformation coefficient feature, and the third view uses pixel features, with each image downsized to 7×8 pixels.

In the experiment, the datasets were first processed to obtain the required three views for the experiments. Then, all views of the dataset were preprocessed into standardized data format. Next, the dataset was randomly divided into training and testing sets, with randomly selected 80% of total samples used for training and the rest for testing.

For the balancing parameter α, Gaussian kernel parameter σ, and each view's weight a_j, they are set as follows: The label constraint balancing parameter α is suggested to be traversed within the (0,1) range. The Gaussian kernel function parameter σ is suggested to be traversed within the [2,4] range, with optimal values found through multiple experiments. Each view's weight parameter a_j is traversed within the (0,1) range, with $\sum_{j=1}^{v} a_j = 1$. By considering the importance of different views and assigning weights accordingly, optimal values were found to better control the weight size of each view participating in training. The bold font is used to denote the optimal performance, while the values enclosed in parentheses represent the standard deviation of the replicated experiments.

4.2 Image Classification Results in Unreliable Labeling Environment

To validate the performance of our algorithm, we compared the proposed MvDA-PPG and KMvDA-PPG with previous methods WMvDA [9], KWMvDA [9], MvDA [6], RMvDA [8], DMVTSVM [10], and GMLDA [5] on MNIST, Coil-20, MFD datasets in terms of classification accuracy and standard deviation. All methods were used with optimal parameter settings. The experiments mainly investigate the relationship between the number of unreliable labels for a specific class in a view and recognition rate. During training, we randomly select some data from the low-resolution view of one class and set them as unreliable labels. The results are shown in Table 2, Table 3 and Table 4, where PUL represents the proportion of unreliable labels in the low-resolution view.

The experimental results indicate that our proposed KMvDA-PPG method demonstrates high classification accuracy across different datasets and varying

Table 2. Different PUL in Unreliable Labels Environment on MNIST Dataset

PUL	0.1	0.2	0.4
MvDA [6]	77.85(3.77)	76.55(3.97)	71.80(5.24)
GMLDA [5]	77.30(7.06)	76.37(5.70)	70.88(2.56)
RMvDA [8]	81.37(6.70)	77.75(5.35)	72.12(3.56)
DMVTSVM [10]	83.50(2.69)	82.95(2.97)	79.00(2.64)
WMvDA [9]	79.20(4.15)	76.88(5.50)	73.83(6.26)
KWMvDA [9]	84.93(3.15)	83.03(2.50)	79.38(3.06)
MvDA-PPG	79.58(2.36)	78.00(2.56)	74.78(1.83)
KMvDA-PPG	**85.03(2.52)**	**83.25(2.76)**	**79.88(2.01)**

Table 3. Different PUL in Unreliable Labels Environment on Coil-20 Dataset

PUL	0.1	0.2	0.4
MvDA [6]	87.53(5.50)	87.30(5.51)	85.73(6.09)
GMLDA [5]	77.37(5.73)	74.70(7.25)	70.00(8.54)
RMvDA [8]	91.53(4.50)	90.38(5.15)	88.73(2.94)
DMVTSVM [10]	92.98(3.20)	92.85(3.24)	92.12(3.40)
WMvDA [9]	91.20(4.20)	91.23(3.87)	89.43(5.30)
KWMvDA [9]	98.62(1.60)	97.63(3.15)	95.87(2.32)
MvDA-PPG	98.57(0.72)	97.56(0.82)	95.80(1.24)
KMvDA-PPG	**98.76(1.32)**	**97.80(0.72)**	**95.95(1.26)**

numbers of unreliable labels. This highlights the ability of KMvDA-PPG to extract more feature information, performing well in environments with unreliable labels.

As the number of unreliable labels increases, classification accuracy gradually decreases, demonstrating a significant impact on classification recognition. However, our proposed KMvDA-PPG method maintains high classification precision compared to other methods, especially when compared to MvDA. Moreover, it has a relatively low standard deviation, indicating more stable performance across multiple experiments.

In the KMvDA-PPG method, we primarily employ the RBF kernel function to map original images into a high-dimensional RKHS space, enabling samples to exhibit linearity in this high-dimensional space. We evaluated the impact of linear kernel functions, RBF kernel functions, and polynomial kernel functions on image classification performance using MNIST, Coil-20, MFD datasets, as shown in Table 5.

The experimental results show that the classification performance of KMvDA-PPG using RBF kernel function outperforms those using linear and polynomial kernels. This indicates that there exists non-linearity in images, making it difficult for linear methods to extract certain features. Nonlinear mapping

Table 4. Different PUL in Unreliable Labels Environment on MFD Dataset

PUL	0.1	0.2	0.4
MvDA [6]	90.30(1.62)	88.48(2.37)	80.25(3.07)
GMLDA [5]	90.60(1.78)	87.58(1.63)	79.28(2.42)
RMvDA [8]	90.35(1.28)	87.52(1.70)	88.20(2.56)
DMVTSVM [10]	92.57(1.35)	90.95(0.83)	89.12(0.97)
WMvDA [9]	92.48(1.34)	91.53(1.11)	88.20(1.26)
KWMvDA [9]	95.15(1.24)	93.48(1.43)	89.70(1.24)
MvDA-PPG	93.10(1.50)	91.75(1.82)	**89.92(1.35)**
KMvDA-PPG	**95.38(1.59)**	**93.63(1.84)**	89.83(1.46)

Table 5. Classification Accuracy of Different Kernel Functions in the KMvDA-PPG Method on Three Datasets

	MNIST	Coil-20	MFD
Linear kernel	54.75(3.60)	61.33(3.24)	89.40(2.20)
Polynomial kernel	80.25(3.76)	97.40(2.55)	92.27(1.48)
RBF kernel	**85.03(2.52)**	**97.80(0.72)**	**93.63(1.84)**

enables samples to exhibit linearity in high-dimensional space, allowing more information extraction for superior recognition. To validate the effectiveness of KMvDA-PPG for classification tasks proposed in this paper, experiments were conducted comparing KNN classifiers, SVM, and DNN classifiers. The results using MFD dataset for WMvDA, MvDA-PPG, KWMvDA, and KMvDA-PPG methods are shown in Table 6, the PUL parameter is set to 0.2.

Table 6. Classification Accuracy of Different Classifiers on MFD Dataset

	WMvDA	MvDA-PPG	KWMvDA	KMvDA-PPG
SVM classifier	88.95(2.80)	89.00(3.06)	90.25(2.65)	90.40(2.80)
DNN classifier	90.98(1.50)	81.27(2.06)	93.40(2.34)	93.27(1.78)
KNN classifier	**91.53(1.11)**	**91.75(1.82)**	**93.48(1.43)**	**93.63(1.84)**

Upon comparison of the classification results of KNN classifier, SVM classifier, and DNN classifier on MFD dataset, it was observed that KMvDA-PPG method outperformed other classifiers when using KNN classifier for classification. Additionally, both KNN classifier and DNN classifier are easy to implement and require no training, thus verifying the suitability of choosing KNN classifier.

5 Conclusion

This paper proposes two novel methods: Multi-view Discriminant Analysis with Posterior Probability Graph Weighting (MvDA-PPG) and Kernel Multi-view Discriminant Analysis with Posterior Probability Graph Weighting (KMvDA-PPG). Initially, for views with unreliable labels, a sample posterior probability graph matrix is constructed by leveraging the similarity among different samples, aiming to optimize the posterior probability matrix. In contrast, for the remaining views, the one-hot encoding of sample labels is utilized as their posterior probability matrix. Subsequently, weights are allocated to different views in accordance with the significance of view information. Furthermore, reconstructed Reproducing Kernel Hilbert Space (RKHS) multi-view within-class and between-class scatter matrices are established. The optimal projection direction is then determined based on these scatter matrices. Eventually, classification tasks are executed within the common subspace. Experimental results on the MNIST, Coil-20, and MFD datasets demonstrate that the proposed KMvDA-PPG effectively tackles the problem of unreliable labels in multi-view learning. By integrating posterior probability graph optimization, view weight adjustment, and the kernel method, it enhances the classification performance and robustness of the model in comparison to other existing methods.

Acknowledgments. This work was supported in part by the National Natural Science Foundation of China (62201355, 62071303), Guangdong Basic and Applied Basic Research Foundation (2024A1515010977), Shenzhen Science and Technology Projection (JCYJ20220531102407018), Guangdong Provincial Key Laboratory (2023B1212060076), Guangdong Province Key Laboratory of Popular High Performance Computers (2017B030314073).

References

1. Friedman, M., Kandel, A.: Introduction to Pattern Recognition: Statistical, Structural, Neural, and Fuzzy Logic Approaches. World Scientific, Singapore (1999)
2. Wang, H., Lu, X., Hu, Z., et al.: Fisher discriminant analysis with L1-norm. IEEE Trans. Cybern. **44**(6), 828–842 (2013)
3. Zhang, X., Chu, D.: Sparse uncorrelated linear discriminant analysis. In: International Conference on Machine Learning, pp. 45–52. PMLR (2013)
4. Yang, M., Sun, S.: Multi-view uncorrelated linear discriminant analysis with applications to handwritten digit recognition. In: 2014 International Joint Conference on Neural Networks (IJCNN), pp. 4175–4181. IEEE (2014)
5. Sharma, A., Kumar, A., Daume, H. et al.: Generalized multiview analysis: a discriminative latent space. In: 2012 IEEE Conference on Computer Vision and Pattern Recognition, pp. 2160–2167. IEEE (2012)
6. Kan, M., Shan, S., Zhang, H., et al.: Multi-view discriminant analysis. IEEE Trans. Pattern Anal. Mach. Intell. **38**(1), 188–194 (2015)
7. Li, X., Gui, J., Li, P.: Randomized kernel multi-view discriminant analysis. arXiv preprint arXiv:2004.01143 (2020)

8. Yang, X.F., Li, C.N., Shao, Y.H.: Robust multi-view discriminant analysis with view-consistency. Inf. Sci. **596**, 153–168 (2022)
9. Li, M., Zhao, Y., Pei, J. et al.: Weighted consistent multi-view discriminant analysis in unreliable labeling environment. In: International Conference on AI Logic and Applications, pp. 271–280. Springer Nature Singapore, Singapore (2023). https://doi.org/10.1007/978-981-99-7869-4_22
10. Xie, X.J., Li, Y., Sun, S.: Deep multi-view multiclass twin support vector machines. Inf. Fus. **91**, 80–92 (2023)
11. Hu, P., et al.: Deep supervised multi-view learning with graph priors. IEEE Trans. Image Process. **33**, 123–133 (2024)

MFGB-S3W Denoiser: Multi-scale Fuzzy Granular-Ball and Sequential Three-Way Decision for Remote Sensing Image Denoising

Jingjing Qian and Shuhua Su(✉)

School of Mathematics, Physics and Statistics, Shanghai University of Engineering Science, Songjiang, Shanghai 201620, People's Republic of China
Sushuhua913@163.com

Abstract. Existing denoising algorithms for remote sensing images (RSIs) often suffer from high noise sensitivity, insufficient retention of local details, and loss of information due to non-discriminatory denoising. Therefore, this paper proposes a denoising algorithm based on multi-scale fuzzy granular ball (MFGB) and sequential three-way decision (S3WD), denoted as the MFGB-S3W denoiser. First, a noise outlier assessment method is designed based on fuzzy rough set theory to quantify the sample noise outlier score to distinguish the noisy image from the normal image; second, the MFGB space is constructed to capture the global structural correlation and the local detail differences of the image through the multi-granularity feature fusion. Finally, combined with the S3WD mechanism, the image is segmented layer by layer to realize the precise localization of the noisy image. Experimental results demonstrate that the proposed model yields superior performance in terms of mAP_{50}, PSNR, SSIM, and ERGAS on the NWPU VHR-10 and RSOD remote sensing datasets, outperforming the Blind2Unblind method without MFGB and S3WD fusion, as well as the DnCNN and BM3D approaches. The proposed method effectively suppresses noise while preserving noise-free images, offering a promising solution for denoising complex RSIs.

Keywords: Fuzzy rough set · Sequential three-way decision · Granular ball · Image denoising

1 Introduction

As remote sensing technology rapidly advances, high-resolution RSIs play an Irreplaceable role in various fields such as environmental monitoring, land-use planning, and disaster assessment [1]. However, due to the combined effects of sensor noise, atmospheric interference, and transmission errors during the imaging process, the original RSIs are often severely affected by noise pollution. These noises lead to issues such as blurring of fine feature details and loss of edge information, which directly undermine subsequent recognition tasks and reduce the practical value of the data [2]. Therefore, effectively removing noise while preserving key image features has become one of the core challenges within remote sensing informatics.

M. Bonsangue and Y. Chen (Eds.): AILA 2025, CCIS 2668, pp. 137–150, 2026.
https://doi.org/10.1007/978-981-95-8262-4_11

In recent years, deep learning (DL) has made significant progress, becoming a crucial methodology for RSI processing and recognition [3]. Research scholars are committed to employing DL techniques to enhance the performance of RSI recognition, and an array of enhanced algorithmic frameworks has been introduced to address the noise issue in RSIs. Many scholars improve the classical denoising algorithm BM3D [4]. For example, Chen et al. [5] introduce a localized patch correspondence framework leveraging edge-guided exploration and residual refinement mechanisms, improving BM3D to better handle the high similarity at the edges of RSIs. In addition, subsequent algorithms such as DGDN [6] and DLRP [7] also achieve excellent performance in the field of denoising. These algorithms typically denoise all images indiscriminately, which may result in over-denoising of clean images, resulting in degradation of primary data integrity and compromised accuracy in downstream recognition tasks.

Rough set theory, as an effective soft computing method, demonstrates superior performance in handling classification problems under uncertainty. Since the introduction of the 3WD method by Yao [8], which is grounded in rough set theory, it has been widely adopted by researchers in the domains of classification and anomaly detection. Yuan et al. [9] develop an incremental learning paradigm grounded in progressively fuzzified three-way principles. Luo et al. [10] propose a 3WD model basis integrated learning. Ying et al. [11] develop the NCDM denoising module by integrating the S3WD framework. However, these traditional methods often struggle to capture multi-scale information when processing complex data. To address this issue, many researchers have incorporated granular computing to enhance data processing efficiency. Xia et al. [12] propose the theory of granular balls based on granular computing, which specifies both granular ball labeling and inter-ball distance metrics, and further derives the foundational models of GBSVM and GBkNN. Building upon these developments, Gao et al. [13] designed an outlier detection methodology operating across scales via fuzzy rough approximations to accurately identify various types of outliers. Zhang et al. [14] investigate three-way neighborhood feature regions and corresponding fusion measures to enhance outlier detection. However, the aforementioned methods rely solely on a single application of 3WD for detection, overlooking dynamic decision-making scenarios characterized by uncertainty and incomplete information.

Therefore, to overcome inherent constraints in current denoising methodologies and simultaneously enhance the performance of RSI recognition, this paper proposes a novel denoising framework by integrating MFGB and S3WD. The resulting MFGB-S3W denoiser is capable of accurately identifying noisy images, thereby improving the overall denoising effect. The main contributions of this work are summarized as follows:

(1) To evaluate the noise level of samples, a fuzzy rough set-based method is developed to accurately identify noise outliers.
(2) To better capture both local details and global structures of RSIs, a MFGB space is constructed.
(3) By integrating MFGB and S3WD, and incorporating a self-supervised learning strategy, an efficient denoising algorithm is proposed that not only accurately identifies noisy images but also avoids over-denoising in noise-free images.

The subsequent sections develop as follows. Section 2 introduces the theoretical background. Section 3 elaborates on the proposed MFGB-S3W denoiser. Section 4 demonstrates the effectiveness of the MFGB-S3W denoiser through comprehensive experiments. Section 5 provides the conclusion of the study and outlines potential directions for future research.

2 Preliminaries

2.1 Fuzzy Rough Set

If there are no decision attributes in *A*, then the data is called a fuzzy information system and is defined as $FIS = (U, A, V, f)$, where $V = \cup_{a \in A} V_a$. On each attribute $a \in A$, the mapping function *f* relates each sample $x \in U$ to the value of attribute *a*, which can be expressed as $f(x, a) \in V_a$.

Definition 1. [15] The definition of fuzzy relation *R* on *U* is as $R : U \times U \mapsto [0, 1]$, and it satisfies the following properties:

$$\begin{aligned} &R(x, x) = 1; \\ &R(x, y) = R(y, x); \\ &R(x, z) \geq \vee_{y \in U} (R(x, y) \wedge R(y, z)), \end{aligned} \tag{1}$$

where *R*(*x*, *y*) represents the fuzzy similarity between samples *x* and *y* under *R*.

Definition 2. [13] Let attribute subset $B \subseteq A$ generate fuzzy relation R_B through induction. It can be calculated by $R_B(x_i, x_j) = \wedge_{a \in B} R_a(x_i, x_j)$, where $R_a(x_i, x_j)$ is defined as follows:

$$R_a(x_i, x_j) = \begin{cases} 1 - \left|f_a(x_i) - f_a(x_j)\right|, & \left|f_a(x_i) - f_a(x_j)\right| \leq \varepsilon_a, \\ 0, & \left|f_a(x_i) - f_a(x_j)\right| > \varepsilon_a, \end{cases} \tag{2}$$

where ε_a is a parameter threshold, computed from $\varepsilon_a = \frac{std(a)}{\delta}$, while $std(a)$ signifies the standard deviation of attribute *a*, and δ represents an adjustable parameter.

Definition 3. [13] As for all sets of attribute $B \subseteq A$, its fuzzy relation with density can be defined as:

$$U/\tilde{R}_B = \{[\tilde{x}_1]_B, [\tilde{x}_2]_B, ..., [\tilde{x}_n]_B\}, \tag{3}$$

where $[\tilde{x}_i]_B = (\tilde{R}_B(x_i, x_1), \tilde{R}_B(x_i, x_2), ..., \tilde{R}_B(x_i, x_n))$ is denoted as the fuzzy granule with density of sample x_i,and $\tilde{R}_B(x_i, x_j) = \wedge_{a \in B} \tilde{R}_a(x_i, x_j)$.

The cardinality of $[\tilde{x}_i]_B$ is calculated as $|[\tilde{x}_i]_B| = \sum_{j=1}^{n} \tilde{R}_B(x_i, x_j)$, $1 \leq |[\tilde{x}_i]_B| \leq n$.

Definition 4. [13] For any sample $x \in U$, with respect to attribute $a \in A$, the fuzzy granule density is given by:

$$Den_a(x) = \frac{|[x]_a|}{|U|}, \tag{4}$$

where $|[x]_a|$ represents the cardinality of the fuzzy granule $[x]_a$.

Definition 5. [13] To any two samples x_i and x_j, the relative fuzzy granular density of them with respect to attribute $a \in A$ is defined as:

$$Rel\_Den_a(x_i, x_j) = \exp\{-\lambda \left\| Den_a(x_i) - Den_a(x_j) \right\|_2^2\}, \quad (5)$$

where λ is a weighted parameter, and $\|\cdot\|_2$ is 2-norm.

2.2 S3WD

S3WD integrates multi-granularity structures to enable dynamic decision-making. Its core idea is to construct a hierarchical granularity framework that iteratively makes decisions regarding objects inside the boundary region, progressing from coarse to fine levels.

Definition 6. [16] Let $FIS = (U, A, V, f)$ be a fuzzy information system and $A = \{A_1, A_2, ..., A_m\}$ be an attribute subset family with $A_1 \subseteq A_2 \subseteq ... \subseteq A_m \subseteq A$. Then STWD can be expressed as:

$$GS_i = (U_i, A_i \cup D, V_i, f_i), \quad (6)$$

$$GS = (GS_1, GS_2, ..., GS_q), \quad (7)$$

where $i = 1, 2, ..., m$, GS_i represents the i-th granularity space of GS,and GS expresses the multi-granularity space.

Let $X_i \subseteq U_i$ and the threshold of i-th layer be (α_i, β_i), the three regions of the i-th layer can be expressed as:

$$\begin{aligned} POS_{(\alpha_i,\beta_i)}(X_i) &= \{x \in U_i | v_i(x) > \alpha_i\}; \\ BND_{(\alpha_i,\beta_i)}(X_i) &= \{x \in U_i | \beta_i \leq v_i(x) \leq \alpha_i\}; \\ NEG_{(\alpha_i,\beta_i)}(X_i) &= \{x \in U_i | v_i(x) < \beta_i\}, \end{aligned} \quad (8)$$

where U_i indicates the i-th layer domain, and $v_i(x)$ is the i-th evaluation function.

3 The Proposed Method

In real-world RSI recognition tasks, noise degrades image clarity and negatively impacts recognition performance. To enhance model performance, it is common practice to apply denoising to input images based on their noise levels before performing the recognition task. Such unmediated processing may excessively alter noise-free images, reducing downstream detection efficacy. In order to solve this problem, this paper proposes the MFGB-S3W Denoiser, which identifies and selectively denoises noisy images to obtain high-quality RSIs, thereby enhancing the training effectiveness of subsequent object detection tasks.

Specifically, a noise outlier score is first designed based on fuzzy rough set theory to quantify image noise. Then, MFGB space is constructed to comprehensively detect noise at different scale. Finally, the S3WD framework is constructed based on the previous two parts to distinguish the noisy images, and the Blind2Unblind self-supervised denoising algorithm is utilized to achieve efficient denoising.

The working procedure of the MFGB-S3W denoiser model proposed in this paper and the subsequent object detection task completion process are shown in Fig. 1. The pseudocode for the MFGB-S3W algorithm is shown in Fig. 2.

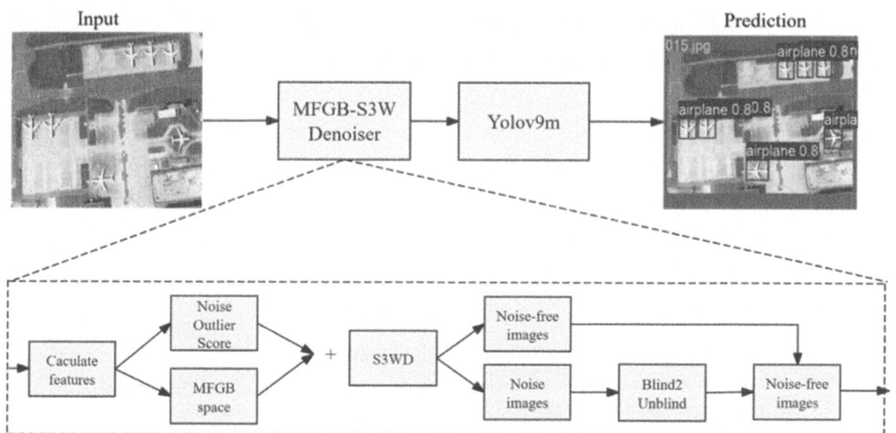

Fig. 1. Complete workflow diagram of the model in this paper

3.1 Noise Outlier Score

In the subsection, we proposes a method for calculating the noise outlier score. This score is constructed based on both the fuzzy granularity density of the attributes and their significance. A larger score indicates a higher likelihood that the sample is a noisy image. The whole calculation process is described as follows.

First, all images $U = (x_1, x_2, ..., x_n)$ are input, and their attribute values including means (MEA), standard deviation (STD), Sobel (SOB), Laplacian (LAP), angular second moment (ASM), entropy (ENT), homogeneous (HOM), and dissimilarity (DIS), are computed [18].

Second, for all attributes $a \in A$, the fuzzy granule density $Den_a(x_i)$, relative fuzzy granule density $Rel\_Den_a(x_i, x_j)$, and fuzzy similarity degree with density $\tilde{R}_a(x_i, x_j)$ are calculated according to Eqs. (2)–(5). In addition, for an attribute set $B \subseteq A$, the cardinality of the fuzzy granule with density $|[\tilde{x}_i]_B|$ is calculated according to Eq. (3), and thereby calculate the significance of B as follows [13]:

$$Sig(B) = -\log \sum_{x \in U} \frac{|[\tilde{x}]_B|}{|U|}. \tag{9}$$

```
Algorithm MFGB-S3W Denoiser
Input: All images U = (x_1, x_2, ..., x_n), similarity threshold δ, weighted parameter λ,
and the noise ratio estimation r_i.
Output: Noise-free images
Initialization: GBS = {GB_1, GB_2, ..., GB_n}
Calculate: MEA, STD, SOB, LAP, ASM, ENT, HOM, DIS for all images to
constitute a fuzzy information system FIS = (U, A, V, f).
Calculate: The fuzzy granule density Den_a(x_i), relative fuzzy granule
density Rel_Den_a(x_i, x_j) and fuzzy similarity degree with density R̃_a(x_i, x_j) by
Eqs. (3)-(8).
for i = 1 → m do
  calculate NS_{A_i}(x) by Eqs. (9)-(15).
end for
for i = 1 → m do
    for each pair (GB_o, GB_j) in GBS
      if dis_{A_i}(GB_o, GB_j) ≤ ε_{A_i}
        merge GB_o and GB_j
      else continue
    end for
end for
return MFGB space
while BND_{(α_i, β_i)}(X_i) = ϕ
for i = 1 → m do
    for e = 1 → E
      calculate P_i^e(x), v_i^e, H_i^e by Eqs. (19)-(20)
    end for
    calculate μ_i(x), P_i(x) by Eqs. (21)-(22)
return α_i and β_i
determine the three-way regions by Eq. (24)
end for
end while
return POS(X) = POS_{(α_1, β_1)}(X_1) ∪ ... ∪ POS_{(α_z, β_z)}(X_z)
Input the noisy images POS(X) into Blind2Unblind algorithm
The denoised images POS(X̃) are obtained
Return Noise-free images X̃ = POS(X̃) ∪ NEG(X)
Output Noise-free images
```

Fig. 2. Pseudocode for MFGB-S3W Denoiser.

Third, all attributes $a \in A$ and subsets of attributes $A_i \subseteq A$ are ranked for significance. The specific sorting rules are as follows [13]:

$$AQ = \langle a'_1, a'_2, \ldots, a'_m \rangle, \tag{10}$$

where $Sig(\{a'_i\}) \geq Sig(\{a'_{i+1}\})$. From this, it can be obtained.

$$ASQ = \langle A_1, A_2, \ldots, A_m \rangle, \tag{11}$$

where A_i is an attribute subset form of the top i attributes in AQ.

Finally, the noise outlier score (NS) for each image under all attribute subsets can be calculated as described in the following definition.

Definition 7. The NS of sample $x \in U$ with respect to each attribute subset $A_i \subseteq A$ are obtained as follows:

$$NS_{A_i}(x) = 1 - Sig(A_i)\frac{\left|[\tilde{x}]_{A_i}\right|}{|U|}. \tag{12}$$

In this subsection, the calculation of significance for all attribute subsets $O(|A||U|^2)$ is an upper bound on time complexity. For each sample, the time to compute its noise outlier score is $O(|A|)$. As a result, the time complexity for this part can be expressed as $O(|A||U|^2)$.

3.2 MFGB Space

Granular ball computing, built upon information granularity, uses granular balls to model data samples for clustering and classification purposes.

Definition 8. [17] Let GB be a granular ball containing similar samples from U and $GBS = \{GB_1, GB_2, ..., GB_n\}$ be the set of granular balls. For any granular ball $GB_i \in GBS$, the center and radius of GB_i are defined as:

$$\begin{aligned} c_i &= \frac{1}{|GB_i|}\sum_{x \in GB_i} x, \\ r_i &= \max_{x \in GB_i} \|x - c_i\|_2. \end{aligned} \tag{13}$$

Meanwhile, multi-scale learning serves as an effective strategy to enhance model performance. To more accurately identify noisy images, we construct granular-ball clustering structures at different scales based on granular ball computing theory, thereby forming a MFGB space. The detailed construction process is described as follows.

To begin with, initialize the set of granular-balls $GBS = \{GB_1, GB_2, ..., GB_n\}$ by considering each sample as an independent granular-ball.

Then, calculate the fuzzy similar degree between all granular balls two by two with respect to attribute $a \in A$. The specific formula is as follows:

$$R_a(GB_o, GB_j) = \begin{cases} 1 - dis_a(GB_o, GB_j), & dis_a(GB_o, GB_j) \le \varepsilon_a, \\ 0, & otherwise, \end{cases} \tag{14}$$

where

$$GB_o, GB_j \in GBS,\ \ dis_a(GB_o, GB_j) = \max(\left|f_a(c_o) - f_a(c_j)\right| - \left|r_o^{\frac{1}{|A|}} + r_j^{\frac{1}{|A|}}\right|, 0)$$

According to Eq. (14), the fuzzy similarity relations of granular-balls under individual attributes can be aggregated into the fuzzy similarity relation under an attribute subset, as detailed below.

Definition 9. Let $A_i \subseteq A$ and $a_q \in A_i$, the fuzzy similarity relation under A_i is defined as:

$$R_{A_i}(GB_o, GB_j) = \frac{\sum_{q=1}^{k} R_{a_q}(GB_o, GB_j)}{k}, \quad (15)$$

where k is the number of attributes in A_i.

When $dis_{A_i}(GB_o, GB_j) \leq \varepsilon_{A_i}$ where $o \neq j$, these two granular balls aggregate into a single granular ball. Thus we can get the granular ball at the i-th scale.

Ultimately, we iterate through all the subsets of the attributes $A_i \in A$ to obtain a collection of E scales granular balls, which ultimately forms a MFGB space.

In this subsection, the computational cost for granular ball initialization is $O(n)$, which in turn computes the fuzzy similarity of a single attribute, at which point the number of granular ball pairs is about n^2, and the total time complexity amounts to $O(|A|n^2)$. Next, the subset similarity of the attributes is aggregated, at which point the time complexity is $O(|A|n^2)$. The process of merging the granular ball is at most $O(n^2)$ times and at least $O(n)$ times, so the time complexity is at most $O(n^2)$. In summary, the total computational complexity associated with this subsection is $O(|A|n^2)$.

3.3 MFGB-S3W Denoiser

The multi-scale space provides more comprehensive information about the data, enabling more effective detection of both global and local noise. Therefore, based on the previous two subsections, we propose a denoising method that fuses S3WD with MFGB. The denoising module operates according to the following detailed procedure.

First, the noise outlier scores of the samples at different scales are computed and converted to noise outlier probabilities, the conversion process is defined as follows.

Definition 10. For any sample $x \in U_i$, the possibility of noise outlier $P_i^e(x)$ in the e-th scale is defined as follows:

$$P_i^e(x) = \begin{cases} \frac{NS_i^e(x) - NS_i^{e_{ti}}}{2(\max(NS_i^e) - NS_i^{e_{ti}})} + \frac{1}{2}, & NS_i^e(x) > NS_i^{e_{ti}}, \\ \frac{NS_i^e(x) - \min(NS_i^e)}{2(NS_i^{e_{ti}+1} - \min(NS_i^e))}, & otherwise, \end{cases} \quad (16)$$

where $NS_i^e(x)$ denotes the noise outlier score of sample x under attribute subset A_i at the e-th level scale,$NS_i^{e_{t_i}}$ denotes the t_i-th largest value in the outlier score vector $NS_{A_i}^e$, and t_i is the number of noisy images obtained from the noise ratio estimation r_i,which is computed by the product of the ratio r_i and the sample size $|U_i|$.

Second, in order to better integrate the effects of the different scales, the weights of each sample at each scale will be calculated. Under the attribute subset A_i, the weight of the e-th scale and the weight of the sample x are calculated as follows [13]:

$$v_i^e = 1 - \frac{\sum_{x \in U} H_i^e(x)}{U_i}, \quad (17)$$

$$H_i^e(x) = -P_i^e(x) \log P_i^e(x) - (1 - P_i^e(x)) \log(1 - P_i^e(x)), \tag{18}$$

where $H_i^e(x)$ is the average information entropy of x.

$$\mu_i(x) = 1 - \frac{\sum_{e=1}^{E} v_i^e \cdot H_i^e(x)}{E}, \tag{19}$$

where E is the number of scales.

When the noisy image is not clearly distinguishable from the normal image, the probability of noise anomaly of the sample is often unstable close to 0.5. Under these circumstances, the average information entropy of the sample is close to 1, and the weight is close to 0.

Third, compute the threshold pairs (α_i, β_i) and the weighted noise outlier probability $P_i(x)$ for all samples within attribute subset A_i, as follows [13]:

$$P_i(x) = \frac{\sum_{e=1}^{E} v_i^e \cdot P_i^e(x)}{\sum_{e=1}^{E} v_i^e}, \tag{20}$$

$$\begin{aligned} \alpha_i &= OP(\lceil |U|(1 - r + \Delta r) \rceil), \\ \beta_i &= OP(\lceil |U|(1 - r - \Delta(1 - r)) \rceil), \end{aligned} \tag{21}$$

where $OP(s)$ is the s-th probability of the noise outlier, and Δ is a parameter responsible for specifying the field size.

Fourth, according to the Eq. (8), all images will be divided into three regions $POS_{(\alpha_i,\beta_i)}(X)$, $BND_{(\alpha_i,\beta_i)}(X)$ and $NEG_{(\alpha_i,\beta_i)}(X)$ to get the decision result of the i-th layer. The positive region is the noisy outlier probability greater than α_i is regarded as noise images, and the probability lower than β_i is the noise-free images. Samples with noise outlier probability between α_i and β_i are considered uncertain samples and are put into the boundary region, requiring further identification.

Thus the samples in $BND_{(\alpha_i,\beta_i)}(X_i)$ are used as the sample set U_{i+1} in the $i+1$ level, where $U_{i+1} \subseteq U_i$. The final iteration ends when the bounding region is empty.

Fifth, aggregate the positive region samples obtained from each layer to obtain the set of all noisy images, which is defined as follows:

Definition 11. The set of all noisy images $POS\ (X)$ is obtained based on the decision making results of each layer.

$$POS(X) = POS_{(\alpha_1,\beta_1)}(X_1) \cup \ldots \cup POS_{(\alpha_z,\beta_z)}(X_z), \tag{22}$$

where z is the number of layers on which the iteration stops.

Ultimately, all images classified as noise are denoised using Blind2Unblind [19]. Noise-free images are not processed to avoid excessive denoising.

In here we consider the maximum time complexity of the S3WD process, i.e., the subset of attributes all iterated through, which in reality will be less than this computed time complexity. In the computation of Eqs. (16)–(20), the time complexity is $O(|U_i||A_i|E)$ for all of them. The time complexity in determining the confidence threshold is $O(|A||U_i|\log|U_i|)$. Finally, when performing sequential three-way decision iterations, the maximum time complexity is $O(|A||U|\log|U|)$.

Combining the previous two subsections, the cumulative time cost of the algorithm in this paper is $O(|A||U|^2)$.

4 Experiment

4.1 Datasets

This paper selects the NWPU VHR-10 [20] and RSOD [21] high-resolution RSI benchmark datasets for validation. Comprising 650 target-containing images and 150 without targets, the NWPU VHR-10 dataset provides both positive and negative samples for evaluation. Each positive image includes at least one target instance, with a total of 3,651 annotated instances spanning 10 categories, such as aircraft, ships, and baseball fields. Additionally, the RSOD dataset consists of 976 aerial and satellite images focusing on four types of infrastructure targets. It provides pixel-level annotations, offering a valuable benchmark for object detection research.

Examples cover 10 different object classes, such as airplanes, ships, and baseball-diamond. We randomly divide the data into 80% for training and 20% for testing, and further extract 20% of the training set as the validation set. To simulate a noisy environment, the noise ratio is set to 30%, i.e., for each category of image 30% to add random Gaussian noise ($\delta = 25$). The effect of adding noise to the image is shown in Fig. 3.

Fig. 3. Comparison of noisy images and noise-free images.

4.2 Experimental Setup

Experimental Details. This experiment was conducted on an Ubuntu 18.04 LTS system using version name CUDA11.1, PyTorch 1.8.1 and four NVIDIA RTX 3090 GPUs with

24G of graphics memory on a single card. Before denoising the test image using the Blind2Unblind algorithm, pre-training was performed using the ImageNet validation set into noise, with the batch size set to 8, and an initial learning rate of 0.001. During the training of the YOLOv9m [22] object detection algorithm, the initial learning rate was also set to 0.001. A learning rate decay strategy was applied, where the learning rate was reduced by a factor of 10 after 100 epochs. The training lasted for a total of 150 epochs with a batch size of 16.

Evaluation Metrics. In this paper, we mainly use the following metrics to measure the experimental effects, including mAP_{50}, Peak Signal-to-Noise Ratio (PSNR), Structural Similarity Index Measure (SSIM) and Erreur Relative Globale Adimensionnelle de Synthèse (ERGAS). The corresponding formula is as follows.

mAP_{50} is the average precision AP for all categories at an IOU threshold of 0.5.

$$AP = \int_0^1 P(R)dR, \tag{23}$$

where $P = \frac{TP}{TP+FP}$, $R = \frac{TP}{TP+FN}$.

$$PSNR = 10 \cdot \log_{10} \frac{(s_{l_{\max}})^2}{MSE(s_l, \hat{s}_l)}, \tag{24}$$

where s_l is noise-free image, $\hat{s}_l$ is denoised image, and $s_{l_{\max}}$ is the maximum value of s_l.

$$SSIM = \frac{(2\mu_{\hat{s}_l}\mu_{s_l} + c_1)(2\sigma_{\hat{s}_l s_l} + c_2)}{(\mu_{\hat{s}_l}^2 + \mu_{s_l}^2 + c_1)(\sigma_{\hat{s}_l}^2 + \sigma_{s_l}^2 + c_2)}, \tag{25}$$

where μ_{s_l} and $\mu_{\hat{s}_l}$ are the mean of s_l and $\hat{s}_l$ respectively. σ_{s_l} and $\sigma_{\hat{s}_l}$ is the standard deviation of s_l and $\hat{s}_l$. c_1 and c_2 are constants.

$$ERGAS = 100 \times \frac{h}{l} \sqrt{\frac{1}{N} \sum_{i=1}^{N} (\frac{RMSE_i}{\mu_i})^2}, \tag{26}$$

where N is the number of bands, $RMSE_i$ is the RMSE of the i-th band, μ_i is the mean value of the i-th band, and $\frac{h}{l} = 1$.

4.3 Comparative Analysis

In the experimental evaluation, a comparison is carried out among BM3D [4], DnCNN [23], Blind2Unblind [19], and the proposed approach using the NWPU VHR-10 and RSOD datasets. The detailed results are presented in Table 1. As summarized in Table 1, our model demonstrates superior performance over other denoising algorithms on both the NWPU VHR-10 and RSOD datasets. On the NWPU VHR-10 dataset, our model achieved an mAP_{50} of 86.4%, representing a 0.6% improvement over Blind2Unblind, which does not incorporate the MFGB-S3W framework. In addition, it attained a PSNR of 32.2 dB, a SSIM of 87.7%, and an ERGAS value of 10.6. On the RSOD dataset, our model further demonstrated its robustness by achieving an mAP_{50} of 93.6%, a PSNR of 33.5 dB, and an SSIM of 89.8%. Meanwhile, the ERGAS value decreased to 6.6, indicating improved radiometric fidelity. Overall, the proposed denoising method not only enhanced image quality but also significantly improved the performance of object detection tasks.

Table 1. Performance comparison of various denoising algorithms on different datasets

Denoising algorithm	NWPU VHR-10 Dataset				RSOD Dataset			
	mAP_{50}	PSNR	SSIM (%)	ERGAS	mAP_{50}	PSNR	SSIM (%)	ERGAS
BM3D	83.4	29.9	80.7	11.6	86.3	30.6	83.4	7.5
DnCNN	81.1	30.1	79.3	11.4	89.6	31.3	83.9	6.9
Blind2Unblind	85.8	31.4	87.5	10.7	92.9	33.4	87.1	6.7
Our model	**86.4**	**32.2**	**87.7**	**10.6**	**93.6**	**33.5**	**89.8**	**6.6**

Figure 4 shows the before and after comparisons of the noiseless image processed by excessive denoising, and it can be found that the image after excessive denoising loses a lot of original details. Meanwhile in Fig. 5, the four states of an image with noise-free, noisy, denoising by DnCNN, BM3D and our model are shown from left to right, which visually demonstrates the degradation caused by noise and highlights the varying effectiveness of different denoising algorithms.

Fig. 4. Noise-free image after over denoising.

Fig. 5. Visual comparison of noise-free images, noisy images, and denoised images.

5 Conclusion

In this paper, the proposed MFGB-S3W denoiser is a denoising method integrating MFGB and S3WD, which can accurately identify noisy regions and realize adaptive denoising. Experimental results show that MFGB-S3W outperforms existing algorithms in mAP_{50}, PSNR SSIM and ERGAS metrics on RSI datasets. The proposed method effectively avoids excessive smoothing in noisy regions. In addition, the model can be combined with other denoising algorithms to further explore its practical value and application potential.

References

1. Mena, F., Arenas, D., Nuske, M., Dengel, A.: Common practices and taxonomy in deep multiview fusion for remote sensing applications. IEEE J. Sel. Top. Appl. Earth Observations Remote Sens. **17**, 4797–4818 (2024). https://doi.org/10.1109/JSTARS.2024.3361556
2. Feng, W., Long, Y., Wang, S., Quan, Y.: A review of addressing class noise problems of remote sensing classification. J. Syst. Eng. Electron. **34**(1), 36–46 (2023). https://doi.org/10.23919/JSEE.2023.000034
3. Cheng, X., Sun, Y., Zhang, W., Wang, Y., Cao, X., Wang, Y.: Application of deep learning in multitemporal remote sensing image classification. Remote Sens. **1**(15), 385 (2023). https://doi.org/10.3390/rs15153859
4. Danielyan, A., Katkovnik, V., Egiazarian, K.: BM3D frames and variational image deblurring. IEEE Trans. Image Process. **21**(4), 1715–1728 (2011). https://doi.org/10.1109/TIP.2011.2176954
5. Chen, J., Li, H., Chen, T., Hu, B., Liu, S.: A denoising method of remote sensing images based on improved BM3D. In: 4th International Conference on Computer Science and Application Engineering on Proceedings, pp.1–6. ACM, Zhuhai (2020). https://doi.org/10.1145/3424978.3425125
6. Huang, Z., Zhu, Z., Wang, Z., Shi, Y., Fang, H., Zhang, Y.: DGDNet: deep gradient descent network for remotely sensed image denoising. IEEE Geosci. Remote Sens. Lett. **20**, 1–5 (2023). https://doi.org/10.1109/LGRS.2023.3241642
7. Huang, Z., Wang, Z., Zhu, Z., Zhang, Y., Fang, H., Shi, Y., et al.: DLRP: learning deep low-rank prior for remotely sensed image denoising. IEEE Geosci. Remote Sens. Lett. **19**, 1–5 (2022). https://doi.org/10.1109/LGRS.2022.3167401
8. Yao, Y.: Three-way decisions with probabilistic rough sets. Inf. Sci. **180**(3), 341–353 (2010). https://doi.org/10.1016/j.ins.2009.09.021
9. Yuan, K., Xu, W., Li, W., Ding, W.: An incremental learning mechanism for object classification based on progressive fuzzy three-way concept. Inf. Sci. **584**, 127–147 (2022). https://doi.org/10.1016/j.ins.2021.10.058
10. Luo, J., Hu, M.: A bipolar three-way decision model and its application in analyzing incomplete data. Int. J. Approximate Reasoning **152**, 94–123 (2023). https://doi.org/10.1016/j.ijar.2022.10.011
11. Ying, L., Miao, D., Zhang, Z.: A robust one-stage detector for SAR ship detection with sequential three-way decisions and multi-granularity. Inf. Sci. **667**, 120436 (2024). https://doi.org/10.1016/j.ins.2024.120436
12. Xia, S., Liu, Y., Ding, X., Luo, Y.: Granular ball computing classifiers for efficient, scalable and robust learning. Inf. Sci. **483**, 136–152 (2019). https://doi.org/10.1016/j.ins.2019.01.010

13. Gao, C., Tan, X., Zhou, J., Ding, W., Pedrycz, W.: Fuzzy granule density-based outlier detection with multi-scale granular balls. IEEE Trans. Knowl. Data Eng. **37**(5), 1182–1197 (2025). https://doi.org/10.1109/TKDE.2024.3525003
14. Zhang, X., Yuan, Z., Miao, D.: Outlier detection using three-way neigh-borhood characteristic regions and corresponding fusion measurement. Knowl. Data Eng. **36**(5), 2082–2095 (2024). https://doi.org/10.1109/TKDE.2023.3312108
15. Dubois, D., Prade, H.: Rough fuzzy sets and fuzzy rough sets. Int. J. Gen. Syst. **17**(2–3), 191–209 (1990). https://doi.org/10.1080/03081079008935107
16. Tu, J., Su, S., Xu, J.: A novel grey relational clustering model under sequential three-way decision framework. Inf. Sci. **663**, 120248 (2024). https://doi.org/10.1016/j.ins.2024.120248
17. Xia, S., Peng, D., Meng, D., Zhang, C., Chen, Z.: Ball k-Means: Fast adaptive clustering with no bounds. IEEE Trans. Pattern Anal. Mach. Intell. **44**(1), 87–99 (2022). https://doi.org/10.1109/TPAMI.2020.3008694
18. Haralick, R., Shanmugam, K., Dinstein, H.: Textural features for image classification. IEEE Trans. Syst. Man Cybern. **6**, 610–621 (1973). https://doi.org/10.1109/TSMC.1973.4309314
19. Wang, Z., Liu, J., Li, G., Han, H.: Blind2Unblind: self-supervised image denoising with visible blind spots. In: 40th the Conference on Computer Vision and Pattern Recognition on Proceedings, pp. 2027–2036. IEEE, New Orleans (2022). https://doi.org/10.1109/CVPR52688.2022.00207
20. Cheng, G., Zhou, P., Han, J.: Learning rotation-invariant convolutional neural networks for object detection in VHR optical remote sensing images. IEEE Trans. Geosci. Remote Sens. **54**(12), 7405–7415 (2016). https://doi.org/10.1109/TGRS.2016.2601622
21. Long, Y., Gong, Y., Xiao, Z., Liu, Q.: Accurate object localization in remote sensing images based on convolutional neural networks. IEEE Trans. Geosci. Remote Sens. **55**(5), 2486–2498 (2017). https://doi.org/10.1109/TGRS.2016.2645610
22. Wang, C., Yeh, I., Liao, H.: YOLOv9: learning what you want to learn using programmable gradient information. In: 18th European Conference on Computer Vision, pp.1–21. Springer, Milan (2024). https://doi.org/10.1007/978-3-031-72751-1_1
23. Zhang, K., Zuo, W., Chen, Y., Meng, D., Lei, Z.: Beyond a Gaussian denoiser: residual learning of deep CNN for image denoising. IEEE Trans. Image Process. **26**(7), 3142–3155 (2017). https://doi.org/10.1109/TIP.2017.2662206

Response Performance of Fuzzy Systems Derived from the Symmetric Quintuple Implicational Method

Yiming Tang(✉), Dongqing Li, Yifan Huang, Jianwei Gao, Liu Liu, and Jingyuan Xu

Anhui Province Key Laboratory of Affective Computing and Advanced Intelligent Machine, School of Computer and Information, Hefei University of Technology, Hefei 230601, China
tym608@163.com

Abstract. Based on the symmetric quintuple implicational (SQI) method proposed by us, in this study, we propose a new fuzzy system based on the SQI method (SQI fuzzy system for short) and conduct strict theoretical and practical research on its response performance. To begin with, in order to address the limitations of traditional fuzzy reasoning methods, we innovatively introduce the SQI method into the fuzzy system. This advancement optimizes the similarity calculation between the rule base and the input, and generalizes the fuzzy implication operator at the same time. In addition, the SQI fuzzy system is systematically constructed. For multi-rule scenarios, we formalize its implementation framework by adopting a singleton fuzzifier and a centroid defuzzifier to ensure compatibility with the actual operating environment. Finally, the response performance of the system under the multi-rule configuration of R-implication operators and other classical operators is analyzed.

Keywords: The CRI method · the Triple I method · symmetric quintuple implicational method · fuzzy system

1 Introduction

Since Zadeh introduced the concepts of fuzzy sets and fuzzy logic [1–4], the research on fuzzy reasoning algorithms has been very extensive. The performance of fuzzy control system [5–8] fundamentally depends on these reasoning mechanisms. However, the traditional combinatorial reasoning rule (CRI) shows significant limitations, because it only depends on a single fuzzy implication operator and combination operation, thus deviating from the semantic core of logical implication. In order to solve these shortcomings and support the logical basis of CRI, Wang [7] proposed the triple I algorithm, which extends the reasoning process to include triple meanings. Subsequently, Wang [9] established the optimal solution of general fuzzy reasoning within this framework. Zhang and Yang [10] further promoted the field by introducing the triple I algorithm based on generalized roots into the normative fuzzy logic system, while Pei [11] developed the logic framework of the triple I algorithm based on monotone norms.For the

M. Bonsangue and Y. Chen (Eds.): AILA 2025, CCIS 2668, pp. 151–158, 2026.
https://doi.org/10.1007/978-981-95-8262-4_12

Fuzzy Modus Ponens (FMP) problem, the triple I algorithm yields the minimal solution B^* such that

$$(A(x) \to B(y)) \to \big(A^*(x) \to B^*(y)\big) \quad (1)$$

gets the maximum value for any $x \in X, y \in Y$. In addition, the solution A^* of the FMT problem is the maximum fuzzy set such that (1) obtains the maximum value.

Despite its improved logical rigor, the triple I method does not account for the similarity between inputs and rule antecedents (e.g., A^* and A), which can result in ineffective approximations in certain cases. To overcome this limitation, Zhou et al. [12] introduced the quintuple implication principle (QIP) algorithm. For the FMP problem, QIP identifies the minimal B^* such that

$$(A(x) \to B(y)) \to \big(\big(A^*(x) \to A(x)\big) \to \big(A^*(x) \to B^*(y)\big)\big) \quad (2)$$

Attains the maximum value for any $x \in X, y \in Y$. The solution A^* of the FMT problem is the one making

$$(A(x) \to B(y)) \to \big(\big(B(y) \to B^*(y)\big) \to \big(A(x) \to A^*(x)\big)\big). \quad (3)$$

Get the minimum fuzzy set that makes what achieve the maximum value.

Building on these developments, we [13] proposed the symmetric triple I method, which generalizes both the triple I and CRI approaches. This method revises expression (1) to

$$(A(x) {\to_1} B(y)) {\to_2} \big(A^*(x) {\to_1} B^*(y)\big), \quad (4)$$

where $\to_1$ and $\to_2$ denote distinct implication operators. In [13], we provided its definition, a unified solution, and an analysis of its reductivity. As a generalized approach, this method facilitates the development of more optimized fuzzy systems.

Subsequently, we [14] extended the sustainment measure and introduced a novel symmetric implication method that encompasses both symmetric implication algorithms and the triple I method as special cases. Further advancing this work, we [15] proposed the symmetric quintuple implicational (SQI) method, which generalizes expression (4) to

$$(A(x) {\to_1} B(y)) {\to_2} \big(\big(A^*(x) {\to_1} A(x)\big) {\to_2} \big(A^*(x) {\to_1} B^*(y)\big)\big). \quad (5)$$

Building upon these foundations, this study proposes a new fuzzy system based on the SQI method, termed the SQI fuzzy system. We conduct a comprehensive analysis of its establishment and response performance, employing R-implication and other classical operators.

2 Preliminaries

Definition 1. [16] let a binary operation T $[0,1]^2 \to [0,1]$ satisfy the following conditions ($a, b, c \in [0,1]$): (i) $T(a, b) = T(b, a)$; (ii) $T(a, T(b, c)) = T(T(a, b), c)$; (iii) $T(1, a) = a$; (iv) if $a < b$, that $T(a, c) < T(b, c)$. Then T is called an $t-$ norm on [0,1]. If t additionally satisfies $T(a, \vee\{x_i|i \in P\}) = \vee\{T(a \otimes x_i)\}(a, x_i \in [0,1], P \neq \phi)$, then T is termed a left-continuous $t-$ norm.

Definition 2. [17] let I be a mapping satisfying $[0,1]^2 \rightarrow [0,1]$:

$$I(0,0) = I(0,1) = I(1,1) = 1, I(1,0) = 0. \tag{6}$$

Then I is defined as an implication operator on [0,1].

Definition 3. [16] let T and I be two mappings $[0,1]^2 \rightarrow [0,1]$. The pair (T,I) is defined as an adjoint pair if the following adjoint condition holds ($a, b, c \in [0,1]$):

$$T(a, b) \leq c \textit{ if and only if } a \leq I(b, c). \tag{7}$$

Definition 4. [18] the double residual operator is defined as ($a, b \in [0,1]$).

$$a \leftrightarrow b = I(a, b) \wedge I(b, a). \tag{8}$$

Definition 5. [17] a function I: $[0,1]^2 \rightarrow [0,1]$ is called an R-implication operator if there exists a left-continuous $t-$ norm T satisfying:

$$I(a, b) = \vee\{y \in [0,1] | T(a, y) \leq b\}, a, b \in [0,1]. \tag{9}$$

and

$$T(a, b) = \wedge\{x \in [0,1] | b \leq I(a, x)\}, a, b \in [0,1]. \tag{10}$$

Lemma 1. [16] let T be a left-continuous $t-$ norm on [0,1], and I be derived from Eq. (9). If (T,I) forms an adjoint pair, then for all $a, b, c, x_i \in [0,1]$ and any non-empty index set P, I satisfies: (C1) Non-decreasing in b: $b_1 \leq b_2 \Rightarrow I(a, b_1) \leq I(a, b_2)$; (C2) Right-continuous in b; (C3) Non-increasing in a: $a_1 \leq a_2 \Rightarrow I(a_2, b) \leq I(a_1, b)$; (C4) $a \leq b \Rightarrow I(a, b) = 1$; (C5) $I(1, a) = a$; (C6) $a \leq I(b, c) \iff b \leq I(a, c)$; (C7) $I(a, I(b, c)) = I(b, I(a, c))$; (C8) $inf\{I(a, x_i) | i \in P\} = I(a, inf\{x_i | i \in P\})$; (C9) $inf\{I(x_i, b) | i \in P\} = I(sup\{x_i | i \in P\}, b)$.

Where $a, b, c, x_i \in [0,1]$ and P is non-empty.

Lemma 2. [16] let I be an R-implication operator and (T, I) form an adjoint pair. If the biimplication operator $\leftrightarrow$ is related to I and derived from Eq. (8), then $\leftrightarrow$ satisfies the following properties: (C10) $a \leftrightarrow a = 1$; (C11) $a \leftrightarrow b \leq a \leftrightarrow T(b, I(b, a))$; (C12) $T((a \leftrightarrow b), (b \leftrightarrow c)) \leq a \leftrightarrow c$; (C13) $(a \leftrightarrow b) \wedge (c \leftrightarrow d) \leq (a \wedge c) \leftrightarrow (b \wedge d)$; (C14) $(a \leftrightarrow b) \vee (c \leftrightarrow d) \leq (a \vee c) \leftrightarrow (b \vee d)$; (C15) $T((a \leftrightarrow b), (c \leftrightarrow d)) \leq T(a, c) \leftrightarrow T(b, d)$.

Definition 6. Let Z be a non-empty family of sets. A function C: $Z \rightarrow [0,1]$ is called a fuzzy set on Z. The collection of all such fuzzy subsets over ZZZ is denoted by $F(Z)$.

Definition 7. Let $F(Z)$ denote the family of all fuzzy subsets on Z. We define the fuzzy partial order $\leq_F$ as follows: $A \leq_F B \iff A(z_0) \leq_F B(z_0)$ for all $\forall A, B \in F(Z)$.

Lemma 3. The pair $< F(Z), \leq_F >$ forms a complete lattice.

3 The Proposed SQI Fuzzy Systems

3.1 Fuzzy Rules

In practical applications, multi-rule fuzzy systems are commonly utilized. In this section, we will explore how to incorporate the newly proposed algorithm into multi-rule systems for handling multiple fuzzy rules. Specifically, the Fuzzy Modus Ponens (FMP) is reformulated into a more complex form:

$$\text{FMP : Given n rules } A_i \to B_i \text{ and input } A^*\text{, compute the output } B^*. \tag{11}$$

Here $A_i, A^* \in F(x), B_i, B^* \in F(y)$ $(i = 1,2, \ldots, n)$.

Let NS be a system with n fuzzy rules $A_i \to B_i$, where each rule $A_i \to B_i$ is represented by the following fuzzy relation:

$$R_i(x, y) = I(A_i(x), B_i(y)). \tag{12}$$

For multi-rule NS systems, there are generally two strategies.

The first is FITA (First Infer Then Aggregate). That is, we initially convert the fuzzy relation R_i into a fuzzy inference rule $I(A_i(x), B_i(y))$, then perform compositional inference between A^* and R_i to obtain corresponding results B_i', and finally aggregate B_i' to acquire the ultimate result B^*.

The second method is FATI (First Aggregate Then Infer). That is, we first transform the multiple fuzzy rules of NS into a single fuzzy relation R_i, then directly perform compositional inference between A^* and R_i to derive the final result B^*.

3.2 Construction of Fuzzy Systems

A complete fuzzy system additionally includes a fuzzifier and a defuzzifier. The conventional approach typically employs a singleton fuzzifier and centroid defuzzifier method. Specifically, the process is as follows [19]:

(i) Map x^* is mapped to a singleton fuzzy set:

$$A^*(x) = \begin{cases} 1, & x = x^* \\ 0, & x \neq x^* \end{cases} \text{ (denoted as } A^*_{x^*}\text{);}$$

(ii) We perform fuzzy inference using the SQI method to obtain the fuzzy set $B^*(y)$;

(iii) We apply the centroid defuzzification method: $y^* = \frac{\int_y yB^*(y)dy}{\int_y B^*(y)dy}$.

Thus, for each input x^*, a unique $y^* = f(x^*)$ can be obtained. This constructs a Single-Input Single-Output (SISO) fuzzy system based on the SQI method (abbreviated as the SQI fuzzy system). Here, y $= f(x)$ is called the response function of this fuzzy system, and the performance of the response function is referred to as response performance.

Definition 8. Let Z be an arbitrary non-empty set, and $C = \{C_i\}_{(1 \le i \le n)}$ be a family of normal fuzzy sets on Z, where each C_i has exactly one peak point Z_i (i.e., $C_i(Z_i) = 1$).

If the following condition holds that $(\forall z \in Z)(\sum_{i=1}^{n} C_i(z) = 1)$ then C is defined as a fuzzy partition on Z. Here, C_i are called primitives of C, and C is termed a primitive family of Z.

Remark 1. From Definition 8, it directly follows that $(\forall i, j)(i \neq j \Rightarrow z_i \neq z_j)$ and the Kronecker property holds for $C_i(z_j) = \delta_{ij}$, where: $\delta_{ij} = \begin{cases} 1, & i = j \\ 0, & i \neq j \end{cases}$.

The following assumptions are given: Let A $= \{A_i\}_{(1 \leq i \leq n)}$ and B $= \{B_i\}_{(1 \leq i \leq n)}$ be fuzzy partitions on X and Y respectively, where X and Y are real-number intervals that $X = [a, b]$, $Y = [c, d]$, with peak points ordered as $a < x_1 < x_2 < \cdots < x_n < b, c < y_1 < y_2 < \cdots < y_n < d$, where x_i, y_i are the peak points of A_i, B_i respectively. Additionally, A_i, B_i are assumed to be integrable. These assumptions are readily satisfiable in practical applications.

Let $h_1 = y_1 - c$, $h_i = y_i - y_{i-1}\hat{q} = 2,3, \cdots, n)$, and $h = \max_{1 \leq i \leq n} \{h_i\}$. Considering that A and B are fuzzy partitions, they satisfy the Kronecker property:

$$A_i(x_j) = \delta_{ij} = B_i(y_j).$$

By the definition of definite integrals, for the centroid defuzzifier, we have:

$$y^* = \frac{\int_I yB^*(y)dy}{\int_I B^*(y)dy} \approx \frac{\sum_{i=1}^{n} y_i B^*(y_i)h_i}{\sum_{i=1}^{n} B^*(y_i)h_i}. \tag{13}$$

4 Response Performance of the Proposed SQI Fuzzy Systems

Proposition 2. ([15]) let $\rightarrow_1$ be an R-implication operator and $\otimes_1$ its adjoint left-continuous t-norm. In fuzzy systems employing the SQI method, the FITA solution of MinP-SQI is given by:

$$B^*(y) = \vee_{i=1}^{n} \bigvee_{x \in X} \{A^*(x) \otimes_1 ((A^*(x) \rightarrow_1 A_i(x)) \otimes_2 (A_i(x) \rightarrow_1 B_i(y)))\}, y \in Y.$$

Proposition 3. ([15]) let $\rightarrow_1$ be an R-implication operator and $\otimes_1$ its adjoint left-continuous t-norm. In fuzzy systems employing the SQI method, the FATI solution of MinP-SQI is given by:

$$B^*(y) = \vee_{i=1}^{n} \bigvee_{x \in X} \{A^*(x) \otimes_1 ((A^*(x) \rightarrow_1 A_i(x)) \otimes_2 R(x, y))\}, y \in Y.$$

where R is obtained using the SQI method in the fuzzy system from (12).

Theorem 1. Let $\rightarrow_1$ be an R-implication operator. There exists $A^* = \{A_i^*\}(1 \leq i \leq n)$ such that the FITA solution of the SQI method for the SQI fuzzy system approximates a univariate piecewise interpolation function, where: $\psi(x) = \sum_{i=1}^{n} A_i^*(x) y_i$, where A^* forms a fuzzy partition on X. Furthermore, when $\{y_i\}(1 \leq i \leq n)$ are equidistant, A^* degenerates to $\psi(x) = \sum_{i=1}^{n} A_i^*(x) y_i$.

Proof: According to Proposition 2, in fuzzy systems employing the SQI method, the FITA solution of MinP-SQI is:

$$B^*(y) = \vee_{i=1}^{n} \vee_{x \in X} \{A^*(x) \otimes_1 ((A^*(x) \to_1 A_i(x)) \otimes_2 (A_i(x) \to_1 B_i(y)))\}, y \in Y.$$

where $\otimes_1$ is the adjoint left-continuous t-norm of $\to_1$.

Given that $B_k(y_i) = \vartheta_{ki}$ and the implication $\to_2$ satisfies (6), the following can be derived from (13):

$$y^* \approx \frac{\sum_{i=1}^{n} h_i [\vee_{k=1}^{n} (A_k{}^*(x) \otimes_1 ((A_k{}^*(x) \to_1 A_k(x)) \otimes_2 (A_k(x) \to_1 B_k(y_i)))] y_i}{\sum_{i=1}^{n} h_i [\vee_{k=1}^{n} (A_k{}^*(x) \otimes_1 ((A_k{}^*(x) \to_1 A_k(x)) \otimes_2 (A_k(x) \to_1 B_k(y_i)))]} = \frac{\sum_{i=1}^{n} h_i A_i(x^*) y_i}{\sum_{i=1}^{n} h_i A_i(x^*)}. \tag{14}$$

Noticing that $A = \{A_i\}_{(1 \le i \le n)}$ is a fuzzy partition on X, there exists an $i \in (1 \le i \le n)$ such that $A^*(x^*) > 0$. Consequently, $\sum_{i=1}^{n} h_i A_i(x^*) > 0$ and Eq. (14) is well-defined.

Let $A_i^*(x^*) = h_i A_i(x^*) / \sum_{i=1}^{n} h_i A_i(x^*)$, then we have $y^* \approx \sum_{i=1}^{n} h_i A_i^*(x^*)$, and define: $A^* = \{A^*\}_{1 \le i \le n}$, $\psi(x) = \sum_{i=1}^{n} A_i^*(x) y_i$. Noting that $A_k(x_i) = \vartheta_{ki}$, we have:

$$\psi(x_i) = \sum_{k=1}^{n} A_k^*(x_i) y_k = \frac{\sum_{k=1}^{n} h_k A_k(x_i) y_k}{\sum_{k=1}^{n} h_k A_k(x_i)} = y_i.$$

Therefore, $\psi(x)$ is a piecewise univariate interpolation function.

Moreover, the equality

$$\sum_{i=1}^{n} A_i^*(x) = h_i A_i(x^*) / \sum_{i=1}^{n} h_i A_i(x) = 1$$

is valid ($x \in X$), Therefore, A^* forms a fuzzy partition on X.

Finally, when $\{y_i\}(1 \le i \le n)$ are equidistant (i.e., $(\forall i)(h_i = h)$), it clearly follows that $A_i^* = A_i$, $A^* = A$ and consequently one has: $\psi(x) = \sum_{i=1}^{n} A_i(x) y_i$.

Q. E.D.

According to Proposition 3, we can prove Theorem 2 using a similar method.

Theorem 2. Let $\to_1$ be an R-implication operator. There exists $A^* = \{A_i^*\}(1 \le i \le n)$ such that the FATI solution of the SQI method for the SQI fuzzy system approximates a univariate piecewise interpolation function, where: $\psi(x) = \sum_{i=1}^{n} A_i^*(x) y_i$, where A^* forms a fuzzy partition on X. Furthermore, when $\{y_i\}(1 \le i \le n)$ are equidistant, A^* degenerates to A (i.e., $\psi(x) = \sum_{i=1}^{n} A_i^*(x) y_i$).

Similarly, when we assume that $\to_1$ is the I_R-implication ($I_R(x, y) = 1 - \mathrm{x} + \mathrm{xy}$) and I_{KD}-implication ($I_{KD}(x, y) = (1 - x) \vee y$) respectively, we can use this method to prove that their FITA and FATI solutions approximate a univariate piecewise fitting function for SQI fuzzy systems.

Remark 2. Here we elucidate the meaning of "approximation" in the aforementioned theorem. For centroidal fuzzy cases, it is evident that the core idea of "approximation" lies in (13). Based on the definition of definite integrals, the following interpretation can be derived (considering the uniform distribution of $\{q_1, y_1, y_2, \cdots, y_n, q_2\}$). First, if n is large, then $\sum_{i=1}^{n} y_i B^*(y_i)h_i / \sum_{i=1}^{n} B^*(y_i)h_i$ becomes a better approximation of $\int_Y yB^*(y)dy / \int_Y B^*(y)dy$.

Furthermore, for any ε > 0, there exists N such that for all n > N:

$$\left| \int_Y yB^*(y)dy \Big/ \int_Y B^*(y)dy - \sum_{i=1}^{n} y_i B^*(y_i)h_i \Big/ \sum_{i=1}^{n} B^*(y_i)h_i \right| < \varepsilon.$$

By the aforementioned theorem, the fuzzy system constructed using the SQI method is a universal approximator, and thus should be prioritized in practical applications.

5 Conclusions

This paper proposes a novel fuzzy system based on the SQI method, with rigorous theoretical and practical investigations into its response characteristics.

To address the limitations of conventional fuzzy inference methods, we introduce the SQI method into fuzzy systems, optimizing similarity computation between rule bases and inputs while generalizing fuzzy implication operators. Subsequently, we systematically construct the SQI fuzzy system using a singleton fuzzifier and centroid defuzzifier, formalizing a multi-rule implementation framework compatible with real-world applications. Finally, we analyze the system's response performance under R-implication operators and other classical operators in multi-rule configurations.

In the future, we will attempt to combine fuzzy clustering [20–22] with the SQI fuzzy system to establish a new clustering-reasoning mode.

Acknowledgment. It was subsidized from National Natural Science Foundation of China (62576130, 62176083, 62176084) and Fundamental Research Funds for Central Universities of China (PA2023GDSK0061).

References

1. Deshpande, S.B., Mangalwede, S.R.: Artificial nero fuzzy inference model for location and time aware M-Learning system-an empirical investigation. Int. J. Intell. Sustain. Comput. **1**(2), 115–127 (2021)
2. Evstifeev, A.A., Zaeva, M.A.: The method of planning the process of refueling vehicles using artificial intelligence and fuzzy logic methods. Procedia Comput. Sci. **190**, 252–255 (2021)
3. Oliveira, L., Argou, A., Dilli, R., et al.: Exploring fuzzy set consensus analysis in IoT resource ranking. Eng. Appl. Artif. Intell. **109**, 104617 (2022)
4. Vivek, K., Subbarao, K.V., Routray, W., et al.: Application of fuzzy logic in sensory evaluation of food products: a comprehensive study. Food Bioprocess Technol. **13**, 1–29 (2020)
5. Xiao, F.: A distance measure for intuitionistic fuzzy sets and its application to pattern classification problems. IEEE Trans. Syst., Man, Cybern.: Syst. **51**(6), 3980–3992 (2019)

6. Chen, C.L., Chen, P.C.: Analysis and design of fuzzy control system. Fuzzy Sets Syst. **57**(2), 125–140 (1993)
7. Wang, G.J.: The full-implication triple I algorithm for fuzzy reasoning. Sci. China Ser. E: Technol. Sci. **29**(1), 43–53 (1999). (in Chinese)
8. Zeng, W., Guo, Z., Zhang, H., et al.: Fuzzy inference-based control and decision system for precise aeration of sewage treatment process. Electron. Lett. **57**(3), 112–115 (2021)
9. Wang, G.J.: Formalized theory of general fuzzy reasoning. Inf. Sci. **160**(1–4), 251–266 (2004)
10. Zhang, J., Yang, X.: Some properties of fuzzy reasoning in propositional fuzzy logic systems. Inf. Sci. **180**(23), 4661–4671 (2010)
11. Pei, D.: Formalization of implication based fuzzy reasoning method. Int. J. Approximate Reasoning **53**(5), 837–846 (2012)
12. Zhou, B., Xu, G., Li, S.: The quintuple implication principle of fuzzy reasoning. Inf. Sci. **297**(2), 202–215 (2015)
13. Tang, Y.M., Yang, X.Z.: Symmetric implicational method of fuzzy reasoning. Int. J. Approximate Reasoning **54**(8), 1034–1048 (2013)
14. Tang, Y.M., Pedrycz, W.: On the α(u, v)-symmetric implicational method for R- and (S, N)-implications. Int. J. Approximate Reasoning **92**, 212–231 (2018)
15. Tang, Y.M., Bao, G.Q.: On the symmetric quintuple implicational method of fuzzy reasoning. Iran. J. Fuzzy Syst. **18**(4), 113–129 (2021)
16. Wang, G.J., Fu, L.: Unified forms of triple I method. Comput. Math. Appl. **49**(5–6), 923–932 (2005)
17. Mas, M., Monserrat, M., Torrens, J., et al.: A survey on fuzzy implication functions. IEEE Trans. Fuzzy Syst. **15**(6), 1107–1121 (2007)
18. Wang, G., Duan, J.: On robustness of the full implication triple I inference method with respect to finer measurements. Int. J. Approximate Reasoning **55**(3), 787–796 (2014)
19. Tang, Y.M., Ren, F.J.: Fuzzy systems based on universal triple I method and their response functions. Int. J. Inf. Technol. Decis. Mak. **16**(2), 443–471 (2017)
20. Tang, Y.M., Pan, Z.F., Hu, X.H., Pedrycz, W., Chen, R.H.: Knowledge-induced multiple kernel fuzzy clustering. IEEE Trans. Pattern Anal. Mach. Intell. **45**(12), 14838–14855 (2023)
21. Tang, Y.M., Gao, J.W., Pedrycz, W., Xi, L., Ren, F.J.: An overall framework of modeling, clustering and evaluation for trapezoidal information granules. IEEE Trans. Fuzzy Syst. **32**(6), 3484–3496 (2024)
22. Tang, Y.M., Wu, W.B., Pedrycz, W., et al.: Clustering interval and triangular granular data: modeling, execution, and assessment. IEEE Trans. Neural Netw. Learn. Syst. **36**(6), 10000–10014 (2025)

Optimization and Efficiency

Optimization Scheme for Flexible Job Shop Scheduling Considering Parallel Operations and Sequence Constraints of Jobs

Zhaohuan Zhuang[1,2] and Yong Zhang[1,2](✉)

[1] College of Electronics and Information Engineering, Shenzhen University, Shenzhen 518060, China
yzhang@szu.edu.cn
[2] Guangdong Provincial Key Laboratory of Intelligent Information Processing, Shenzhen 518060, China

Abstract. This paper investigates the Flexible Job Shop Scheduling Problem with Parallel Operations and Job Priority Constraints (JSPCPOJP). To address the limitations of existing job shop scheduling models that fail to accurately describe this type of problem, a mixed-integer programming-based optimization model is constructed. An improved genetic algorithm (RPEGA) is proposed to effectively solve the problem. The algorithm employs a Mixed Sequence and Operation Selection (MSOS) encoding method, a deep recursive population initialization mechanism, and POXIC crossover and EIB mutation operators that satisfy the problem constraints. It also combines elitism and roulette wheel selection strategies. The algorithm is validated through a simulation environment. The results show that the RPEGA algorithm can generate feasible solutions that meet the constraints of parallel operations and job priorities, significantly reducing the solution time. It demonstrates high solution efficiency and practicality, providing an effective method for solving similar scheduling problems in actual production.

Keywords: Flexible Job Shop Scheduling · Parallel Operations · Job Priority Constraints · Genetic Algorithm · Deep Recursive Population Initialization

1 Introduction

In the process of production in an engineering workshop, the following two situations may sometimes occur. First, some operations of different jobs need to be combined and processed in parallel. For example, a single cutting machine allows the simultaneous cutting of two jobs in one cutting task. Compared with the serial execution of tasks, this method can significantly reduce the total execution time of the cutting operations. Second, there are precedence constraints between different jobs. For example, in the production of an engineering sign, the processing of the sign base and the bending plate is required. The processing of the bending plate needs the base as a raw material. Therefore, the base must be processed before the bending plate begins processing. From a priority perspective, the priority of the base job is higher than that of the bending

M. Bonsangue and Y. Chen (Eds.): AILA 2025, CCIS 2668, pp. 161–175, 2026.
https://doi.org/10.1007/978-981-95-8262-4_13

plate job. The parallel cutting operations and the priority order between the base and the bending plate break the constraints of the job shop scheduling problem that a machine cannot process multiple different jobs at the same time and that jobs have the same priority. The introduction of this constraint significantly increases the complexity of intelligent workshop scheduling optimization. Among them, how to effectively deal with the collaborative optimization problem of parallel operations while satisfying the technological sequence constraints of jobs has become a technical challenge that urgently needs to be solved in the field of engineering workshop production scheduling. Therefore, this study defines it as Flexible Job Shop Scheduling Considering Parallel Operations and Job Priorities (JSPCPOJP).

2 Related Work

Domestic and international scholars have formed a relatively complete theoretical system in the research of job shop scheduling problems. From the perspective of model constraints, researchers have mainly considered machine availability, transportation time, transportation resources, and operation waiting time [1]. Although the above constraints increase the complexity of the construction and optimization of the Job Shop Scheduling (JSP) model, they significantly improve the model's fit to real production scenarios. With the deepening of research, scholars have expanded the Flexible Job Shop Scheduling Problem (FJSP) by introducing technological flexibility (such as alternative machines, variable process routes, and non-fixed operation sequences). However, it should be pointed out that whether it is the classical JSP or the FJSP, their core assumptions are still limited to the constraints of "a single job monopolizing machine resources" and "jobs having no correlation with each other [2]," and they do not cover the new constraint combination of parallel operation collaboration and job priority coupling that this study focuses on. Therefore, the consideration of parallel operations and job precedence constraints in this study is an important supplement to the existing JSP and FJSP research.

The research journey of optimization algorithms for the Flexible Job Shop Scheduling Problem (FJSP) can be primarily divided into the following two stages. Early Exploration Stage (1970s to 1990s): FJSP was first explicitly proposed by Brucker and Schlie in 1990 [3]. Prior to that, in 1977, Panwalkar and Lskander [4] introduced 113 allocation rules, which laid the foundation for subsequent research on scheduling problems. At that time, traditional exact algorithms such as branch and bound, cutting plane methods, and integer linear programming were widely used to solve FJSP. However, as the problem size increased, the computational complexity rose sharply, and the solution time failed to meet practical requirements. Heuristic and Metaheuristic Algorithm Emergence Stage (1990s to Early 21st Century): Metaheuristic algorithms such as Genetic Algorithm (GA), Particle Swarm Optimization (PSO), and Ant Colony Optimization (ACO) were gradually introduced [5]. These algorithms, with their wide search range, strong parallelism, and low dependence on problem models, were able to effectively address the challenges of solving large-scale FJSP.

Genetic algorithms possess a number of significant advantages, such as parallelism, flexibility, adaptability, and scalability. When solving the FJSP or the JSP, they can demonstrate relatively excellent performance. Therefore, many scholars currently tend to improve and optimize genetic algorithms as a basis for their research on the (F)JSP [6]. The solution mechanism of genetic algorithms is based on the genetic encoding of individuals. This encoding method can achieve flexible modeling and expression of the problem. Based on this, researchers can design and define appropriate encoding schemes and corresponding operational procedures according to the specific requirements of the actual problem, thereby more accurately characterizing the problem's constraints and objective functions. Moreover, the scalability of genetic algorithms allows them to be combined with various other optimization methods to form hybrid optimization algorithms, which can further enhance the efficiency and effectiveness of solving problems. Considering the complexity of the JSPCPOJP and the potential demonstrated by genetic algorithms in solving similar problems, this paper proposes to conduct an in-depth study on the JSPCPOJP based on genetic algorithms, with the aim of achieving efficient solutions to this problem.

3 JSPCPOJP Model

3.1 Problem Description

The JSPCPOJP problem can be described as follows: Given N jobs to be processed on M machines, each job has a fixed processing route. However, multiple operations from different jobs can be combined into parallel operations and processed simultaneously on the same machine. Additionally, there are precedence constraints across jobs. To better reflect the actual production requirements, the problem also considers machine flexibility, meaning that each operation can be processed on multiple alternative machines, and the processing time depends on the selected machine. The scheduling objective is to assign appropriate machines to each operation and determine the optimal processing sequence, while satisfying machine availability, operation sequence constraints, parallel operation coordination constraints, and precedence constraints across jobs, in order to optimize the system performance metrics (such as the makespan). Table 1 provides a specific example with 4 jobs and 4 machines, where the numbers below the machines indicate the processing times of the corresponding operations on those machines.

J1 represents job 1, O12 represents the second process of J1, and others are similar; J2 and J3 indicate that there are parallel execution processes in job 2 and job 3, and the corresponding processes are O22 and O33. The others are similar.

3.2 Mathematical Model

Based on the mixed-integer programming method [7], an optimization model is constructed with the objective of minimizing the maximum completion time, and its formal definition refers to the notation system shown in Table 2.

Objective Function:

$$C_{max} = min(max(C_m)) \quad 1 \leq m \leq M \tag{1}$$

Table 1. Example of JSPCPOJP

Workpiece	Pre Workpiece	Working Procedure	Optional Working Machine			
			M1	M2	M3	M4
J1	J2	O11	3	—	—	5
		O12	—	2	4	—
J2	—	O21	—	—	4	2
		O23	2	—	1	—
J3	—	O31	—	5	—	7
		O32	6	—	—	9
		O34	—	—	5	6
J4	—	O41	6	5	7	—
		O43	—	2	—	4
J5	—	O51	3	—	5	—
		O52	—	5	8	—
J6	—	O61	2	4	—	—
		O62	—	1	—	3
J2、J3	—	O22、O33	8	—	12	—
J2、J4	—	O24、O42	—	15	—	12

Constraints:

$$S_{IJ} + X_{IJm}P_{IJm} \leq C_{IJ} \quad \forall I, J, m \tag{2}$$

$$\sum_{m=1}^{M} X_{IJm} = 1 \quad \forall I,\ J \tag{3}$$

$$C_{IJ} \leq C_{max} \quad \forall I, J \tag{4}$$

$$C_{IJ} + Q(Y_{IJPKm} - 1) \leq S_{PK} \quad \forall I, J, P, K, m \tag{5}$$

$$C_{i(j-1)} \leq S_{U} \quad \forall I, J, O_{ij} \in O_{IJ} \tag{6}$$

$$S_{IJ} \geq 0, P_{IJm} > 0, C_{IJ} > 0 \quad \forall I, J, m \tag{7}$$

$$S_{ij} \times X_{IJm} = S_{pq} \times X_{IJm} \quad \forall O_{ij}, O_{pq} \in O_{IJ} \tag{8}$$

$$C_{ij} \times X_{IJm} = C_{pq} \times X_{IJm} \quad \forall O_{ij}, O_{pq} \in O_{IJ} \tag{9}$$

$$S_{ij} \geq C_{i'j}, \quad \forall i, j \tag{10}$$

The mathematical model established in this study takes the parallel operation OIJ as the basic modeling unit, where the specific composition element Oij corresponds to the actual job operation. The model aims to minimize the maximum completion time

(Eq. 1) and includes the following key constraints: First, it ensures that each operation is processed on only one machine (Eq. 3) and meets the rationality requirements of operation sequence, limiting the start time $\leq$ completion time (Eq. 2); The maximum completion time is defined as the maximum value among the completion times of all operations (Eq. 4); Second, it ensures that a machine can only process one operation at the same time (Eq. 5). In response to the characteristics of the problem, the model innovatively designs the process coupling constraint (Eq. 6), requiring that an operation must start after its predecessor operation in the same job is completed, and the parallel operation must wait for all related predecessor operations of its composition elements to be completed before it can start; It also strictly stipulates that the elements within the parallel operation must start and end synchronously (Eqs. 8–9). In addition, the model also considers the cross-job priority relationship constraint (Eq. 10), requiring that the start time of an operation cannot be earlier than the completion time of its predecessor operation in another job, and through the non-negative constraint (Eq. 7) to ensure the physical meaning of all time parameters.

Table 2. Explanation of Symbols

symbol	explain	symbol	explain
N	Number of pieces	$C_{IJ}(C_{ij})$	Completion time of $O_{IJ}(O_{ij})$
M	Number of machines	E_{IJm}	Completion time of O_{IJ} in machine m
I,P	Job number	P_{IJm}	Operation time of O_{IJ} in machine m
J,K	Operation set number	M_{IJ}	O_{IJ} optional machine set
m	Machine number	C_m	Completion time of the last process on machine m
O_{IJ}	Parallel operation $O_{IJ} = \{O_{ij}, O_{pq}, \ldots, O_{yz}\}$	Q	An Infinite Real Number
N_i	Number of operations of job i	X_{IJm}	Whether O_{IJ} works on machine m is 1, otherwise it is 0
O_{ij}	Process j of job i,j $\in [1, N_i]$	Y_{IJPKm}	Whether O_{IJ} precedes O_{PK} on machine m is 1, otherwise it is 0
$S_{IJ}(S_{ij})$	Start time of $O_{IJ}(O_{ij})$	$C_{i'j}$	The maximum completion time of the preceding job i' of job i

4 Algorithm Design

To effectively address the scheduling optimization problem with parallel operations and cross-job precedence constraints, this study innovatively proposes the RPEGA algorithm model.

4.1 Encoding and Decoding Design

This study employs the MSOS (Mixed Sequence and Operation Selection) [8] encoding method to encode the JSPCPOJP problem. Given that the JSPCPOJP problem mainly consists of two subproblems, namely Operation Sequencing (OS) and Machine Assignment (MS), the chromosome is divided into two parts using the MSOS encoding. The first part is the Operation Sequencing (OS) section, as shown in Fig. 1, which represents the processing order of the operations. The second part is the Machine Assignment (MS) section, which specifies the machines allocated to each operation.

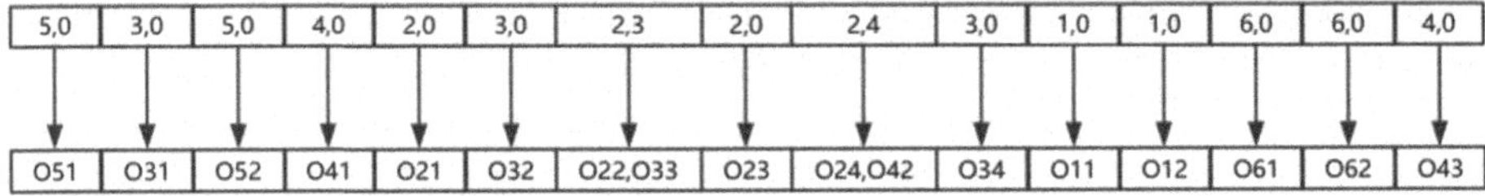

Fig. 1. Operation Encoding Sequence

When encoding the JSPCPOJP problem, each gene in the operation sequencing part is encoded using the index of the job set. The single operation and parallel operations are both represented by O_{ij}. To ensure consistency in the length of all genes, the number of elements in each gene is set to the maximum number of parallel operations, that is, $l = \max\{|O_{ij}|\}$, where i and j represent the indices of the job and operation, respectively. For cases where $|O_{ij}| < l$, the gene is padded with zeros to maintain uniform length, as shown in the first row of Fig. 1. In each gene, the frequency of a nonzero element i(with i ranging from [1, N]) appearing j times (with j ranging from [1, N_i]) represents the operation O_{ij} corresponding to job i, as shown in the second row of Fig. 1. In Fig. 1, the first "2,0" represents the single operation of Job 2, where "0" merely serves as a placeholder and has no practical significance. The notation "2,3" indicates a parallel operation between Job 2 and Job 3. Since "2" appears for the second time and "3" appears for the third time, "2,3" represents the parallel operation of the second operation of Job 2 and the third operation of Job 3.

Each gene in the machine code of the machine selection section is arranged from small to large according to the job and process, and its value x represents the xth machine among the available machines.

In the process of chromosome decoding, the encoded chromosome is first inputted, and the latest processing time (mp and jp) for each machine and each job is initialized to 0. Subsequently, each gene in the chromosome is traversed to explain the process represented by each gene. For example, gene "4,0" represents process 1 of job 4, while "2,5" indicates that process 2 of job 2 and process 1 of job 5 are parallel operations. Next, obtain the machine selection and execution time corresponding to each process, for example, the machine selection for "4,0" may be 1, and the execution time may be 1. Then, take the larger of the latest machining time (mp) of the current machine and the latest machining time (jp) of the current job as the starting time (startTime) of the process, and calculate the finishing time of the process as startTime plus execution time (time). Finally, update the latest processing time of the current machine and job to the completion time of the process. After the completion of gene traversal, the latest completion time among all processes is the total completion time of the entire production plan.

4.2 Deep Recursive Population Initialization Method

In the process of initializing process encoding for FJSP, it is only necessary to create a sequence that includes all job processes and randomly shuffle their order. If this method is directly applied to the JSPCPOJP problem, the generated chromosomes cannot meet the constraints of job priority and parallel operations. For this purpose, this study designed a deep recursive population initialization method. During the initialization of the chromosome operation encoding, an empty chromosome is first created, and the initial queue of jobs that can be selected is determined based on the job priority constraints. For example, given the job priority constraints ["1;2,3", "3;4,5", "5;6,8", "7;5,9"], job 1 can only start processing after jobs 2 and 3 are completed. Therefore, initially, only jobs 2, 4, 6, 8, and 9 can be selected to be added to the chromosome. Next, a job is randomly selected from the queue_choose queue, and it is determined whether its current operation is a parallel operation. If the current operation is not a parallel operation, the operation is directly added to the chromosome. For example, adding operation 1 of job 2 results in adding "2,0" to the chromosome. If the current operation is a parallel operation, the other jobs in the parallel combination need to be iterated. If any of the other jobs in the combination are not in the queue_choose queue (i.e., their higher-priority jobs are not completed), no operation is added this time. If all other jobs in the combination are in the queue_choose queue, the status of each job is further checked. If the job has not yet reached the parallel operation stage, its non-parallel operation is directly added; if the job has reached the parallel operation stage but it is not the parallel operation to be executed currently, the job is used as input to jump to the "insert parallel operation into chromosome" procedure. If all jobs have reached the parallel operation stage, the parallel operation is added to the chromosome. Once an operation is added to the chromosome, whether it is a parallel or non-parallel operation, if all operations of the job are completed, the job is removed from the queue_choose queue. At the same time, it is checked whether other jobs belonging to the same priority constraint condition have also been completed. If they have all been completed, the subsequent jobs of this job are added to the queue_choose queue. The initialization process is shown in Fig. 2.

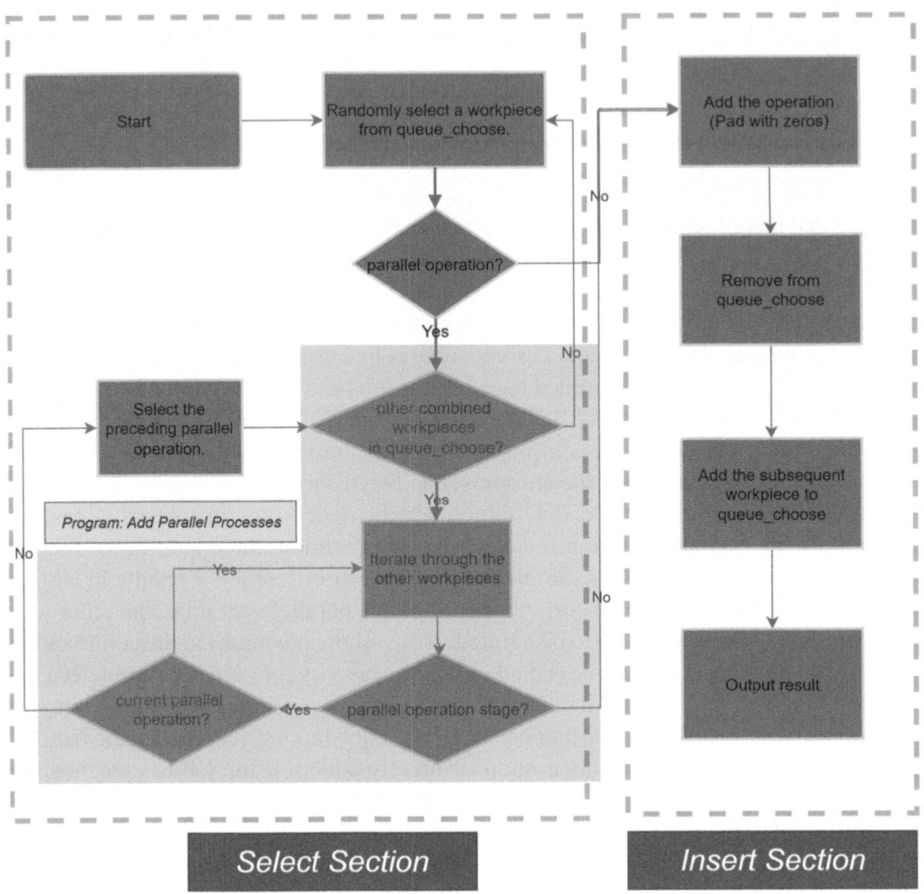

Fig. 2. Flowchart of Depth-First Recursive Initialization

4.3 Population Iteration Strategy

During the iterative process of the genetic algorithm, the key genetic operations involved include crossover, mutation, selection, and elitism [9]. For each generation of chromosomes, the mutation rate and crossover rate of the population are set in a segmented manner. The population is divided into three segments based on the fitness values: the top 20%, the middle 60% (20%–80%), and the bottom 20%. Segments with higher fitness values are assigned lower crossover and mutation rates to ensure the retention of high-quality individuals, while segments with lower fitness values are assigned higher crossover and mutation rates to ensure population diversity.

POXIC Crossover Operator

In genetic algorithms, crossover operations are a core component for generating offspring with superior genetic combinations. Common crossover methods include single-point crossover, multi-point crossover, uniform crossover, partially mapped crossover, operation sequence crossover, and extended sequence crossover [10]. However, these traditional crossover methods have limitations when dealing with parallel operations on the same machine, as they cannot effectively handle the coupling effects that arise, potentially leading to infeasible solutions in the offspring. To address this issue, a new crossover mechanism needs to be designed that satisfies the constraints of JSPCPOJP, ensuring the effectiveness and feasibility of the crossover operation. Based on the POX [11], this study proposes an improved crossover operator called POXIC (Precedence Operation Crossover Initiative Choose). The crossover principle is as follows: 1.Select one parent chromosome and identify the jobs that participate in the parallel constraints and job priority constraints. 2. Ensure that these jobs maintain the same processing order in the offspring chromosome as in the parent. 3. Select the remaining jobs from the other parent chromosome and fill them into the available positions in the offspring chromosome according to their processing order in the parent, thereby generating a new offspring chromosome. The advantage of this approach is that it ensures that subsequent jobs are not moved ahead of their predecessors and that parallel operations are executed within the specified number of operations. As shown in Fig. 3, jobs 1 and 2 have priority constraints, and jobs 2, 3, and 4 have parallel operation constraints. Therefore, jobs 1, 2, 3, and 4 are retained in their original positions from Parent 1 (P1) and added to the offspring chromosome (CP). Jobs 5 and 6 are then added to CP in the order they appear in Parent 2 (P2).

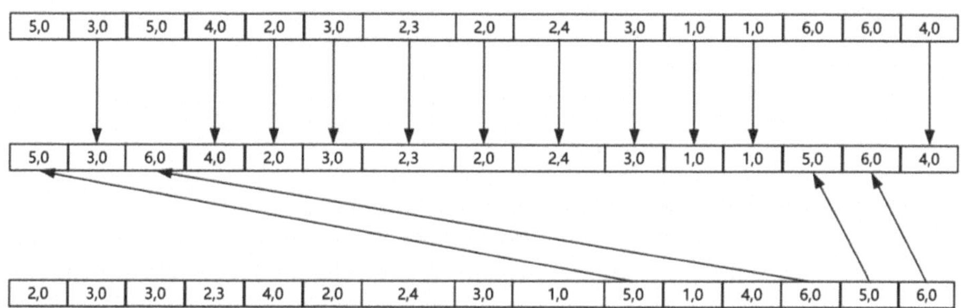

Fig. 3. POXIC Crossover Operator

The crossover operation for the machine encoding sequence is performed using a two-point crossover method [12].

EIB Mutation Operator

Mutation plays a crucial role in genetic algorithms by introducing new genetic diversity to prevent premature convergence and enhance the algorithm's local search capability. When solving the (F)JSP problem, common mutation operations include swap mutation, inversion mutation, insertion mutation, and single-point mutation [13]. However, when these mutation operations are applied to the problem in this study, that is, the mutation of operation sequences, their inherent randomness may disrupt the job priority constraints and parallel operation constraints. To ensure that the mutated operations still meet the constraints, this study proposes a boundary-based swap mutation operator, EIB (Exchange within the boundary). The implementation steps are as follows: a) Determine the swap boundary: Traverse the operation genes and set the gene positions of parallel operation x and the last operation y of the last job in the job priority constraint as the swap boundary. For operation x, both sides of its gene are set as boundaries, while for operation y, only the right side of its gene is set as a boundary. b) Divide the chromosome into n sub-chromosomes based on the boundaries. c) Randomly select a sub-chromosome with more than 2 genes from the n sub-chromosomes and randomly choose two gene positions within this sub-chromosome for swapping. As shown in Fig. 4, the genes (2,3) and (2,4) are parallel operations, and their left and right boundaries are set as swap boundaries. The gene (2,4) is the last operation of Job 2 and is the last operation in the job priority constraint 1 > 2, so its right boundary is set as a swap boundary. After determining the boundaries, the genes (4,0) and (3,0) in the first sub-chromosome are randomly selected for swapping, completing the mutation.

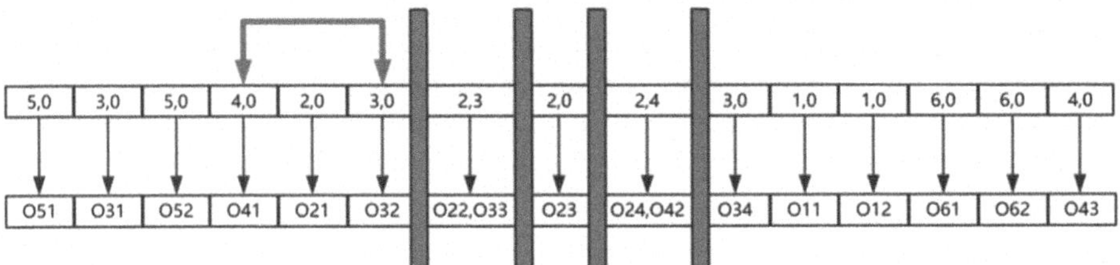

Fig. 4. EIB Mutation Operator

When implementing mutation operations on the machine encoding sequence, this study adopts a single-point mutation strategy.

The Selection and Retention Strategy of the Population

The selection of the population during the iterative process employs a combination of elitism and roulette wheel selection strategies [14]. The specific procedure is as follows: a) The new chromosomes generated by crossover and mutation in each generation are added to the population of the previous generation. b) The population, now including the new chromosomes, is sorted in descending order based on the fitness values of each chromosome, and the fitness values of all individuals are summed. c) The cumulative fitness value of each individual is divided by the total fitness value to obtain the probability interval for each individual. d) The top 20% of chromosomes with the highest fitness values are directly retained as elites for the next generation. e) For the remaining 80% of chromosomes, a random number between (0,1) is generated each time. The individual whose probability interval the random number falls into is selected and added to the new population.

5 Experiment

5.1 Simulation Environment

To verify the effectiveness of the improved genetic algorithm proposed in this study, a simulation environment needs to be established to solve the JSPCPOJP problem under the corresponding parameters using the improved genetic algorithm designed in this study.

The scheduling program was constructed using Java in this study, and all experiments were completed on a personal computer with the Windows 10 operating system, an Intel Core i7-8550U CPU, and 8GB of memory.

5.2 Effectiveness Validation

The scheduling was performed for the case in Table 1, with the population size set to 100 and the maximum number of iterations set to 50. The crossover rates for the top 20%, middle 40% (20%–60%), and bottom 20% of the population were set to 0.5, 0.7, and 0.9, respectively. The mutation rates for the top 20%, middle 40% (20%–60%), and bottom 20% of the population were set to 0.1, 0.3, and 0.5, respectively. TheGantt chart output is shown in Fig. 5:

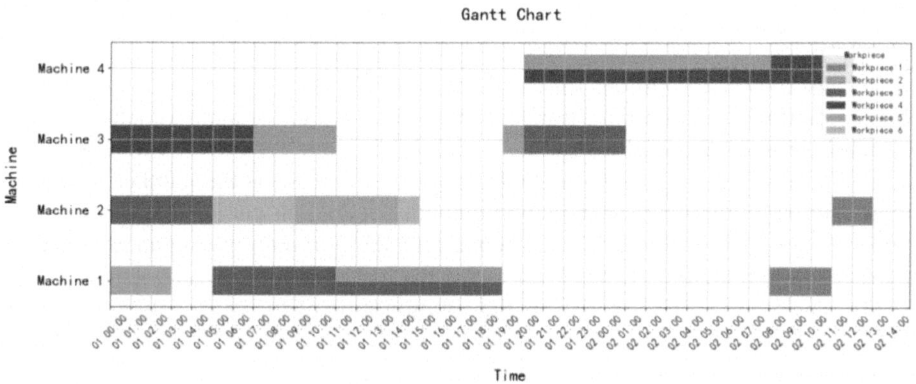

Fig. 5. Gantt Chart for Scheduling of Case 1

The inspection of the scheduling results shows that: Job 1 starts processing after Job 2 is completed. Before the parallel operations O22_O33 are processed, their preceding operations O21, O31, and O32 have been completed. Before the parallel operations O24_O42 are processed, their preceding operations O21, O22_O33, O23, and O41 have been completed. The scheduling results satisfy the job priority constraints and the parallel operation constraints.

5.3 Comparison with Exact Solution Methods

Based on the international benchmark instances of SFJS10 and MFJS1-4 [15], test instances POJPM1-10 were generated by randomly introducing one or two parallel operations and one or two priority constraints. The specifications of these instances are shown in Table 3:

Table 3. POJPM Instances

Test Case	Basic Case	Workpiece Priority	Parallel Operations	Available Machines	Operation Time
POJPM1	SFJS10	1>2	022,033	M1/M2/M4	22/21/24
POJPM2	SFJS10	1>2	021,031	M1/M2/M4	22/21/24
		1>3	022,033	M1/M2/M4	22/21/24
POJPM3	MFJS1	1>2	022,033	M1/M3	14/13
POJPM4	MFJS1	1>2	021,031	M2/M3/M4	21/20/22
		1>3	022,033	M1/M3	14/13
POJPM5	MFJS2	1>2	022,033	M1/M3	14/13
POJPM6	MFJS2	1>2	021,031	M2/M3/M4	21/20/22
		1>3	022,033	M1/M3	14/13
POJPM7	MFJS3	1>2	022,033	M1/M3	14/13
POJPM8	MFJS3	1>2	021,031	M4	22
		1>3	022,033	M1/M3	14/13
POJPM9	MFJS4	1>2	022,033	M1/M3	14/13
POJPM10	MFJS4	1>2	021,031	M4	22
		1>3	022,033	M1/M3	14/13

The exact optimal solutions for each case were obtained by traversing all possible solutions, and the solution time was recorded. Meanwhile, the approximate solutions for each case were obtained using RPEGA algorithm, and the solution time was also recorded. The results are shown in Table 4: where J represents the number of jobs in the instance, O represents the maximum number of operations per job, M represents the number of optional machines, Cmax1 represents the minimum makespan obtained by the exact solution method, Cmax2 represents the minimum makespan obtained by the RPEGA algorithm, CPUs1 represents the solution time of the exact solution method, and CPUs2 represents the solution time of the RPEGA algorithm. The unit of CPUs is milliseconds, and the unit of Cmax is hours.

Table 4. Comparison Results between Exact Solution Method and RPEGA Algorithm

Test Case	J x O x M	Cmax1	CPUs1	Cmax2	CPUs2
POJPM1	4 x 3 x 5	67	14064	67	4408
POJPM2	4 x 3 x 5	75	6018	75	3617
POJPM3	5 x 3 x 6	43	19189	43	4492
POJPM4	5 x 3 x 6	46	6140	46	3974
POJPM5	5 x 3 x 7	43	30451	43	4767
POJPM6	5 x 3 x 7	46	9193	46	4079
POJPM7	6 x 3 x 7	48	42659	48	5036
POJPM8	6 x 3 x 7	48	10390	48	3675
POJPM9	7 x 3 x 7	48	343193	48	5282
POJPM10	7 x 3 x 7	48	93655	48	4233

It can be seen that our algorithm is able to obtain feasible solutions for these small-scale JSPCPOJP instances while significantly reducing the solution time, thereby demonstrating the feasibility of the model. Below is an analysis of the time complexity of our algorithm: Let N be the population size, L represent the number of bits in a chromosome, P denote the number of parallel operations in a chromosome, b be the average number of jobs in parallel operations, S represent the number of job priority constraints in a chromosome, and c be the average number of jobs in each job priority constraint. In the worst case, the time complexities for the operations of initialization, crossover, mutation, and elitism are $O(N \times ((L\text{-}P\text{-}S) + Pb + Sc)$, $O(N \times L)$, $O(N \times L)$, and $O(\log(N) + O(N))$, respectively. Considering that in most cases, P, S, b, and c are smaller than L, the time complexities can be simplified to $O(N \times L)$, $O(N \times 2L)$, $O(N \times L)$, and $O(N)$, respectively. The overall time complexity is $O(N \times L)$.From this analysis, it can be inferred that the time complexity of our algorithm is not high, which accounts for its faster execution speed.

5.4 Algorithm Comparison

In order to compare the solution performance of RPEGA in large-scale instances, a case with dimensions of 20 × 14 × 10 was designed in this section. The maximum number of selectable machines for each operation was set to 2, and three job priority constraints as well as two parallel operation constraints were added. Subsequently, the instance was solved using the initial GA model (without the crossover and mutation segmentation probability operators), the genetic annealing model (SA), and the proposed RPEGA model, respectively. The solution iteration process is illustrated in Fig. 6:

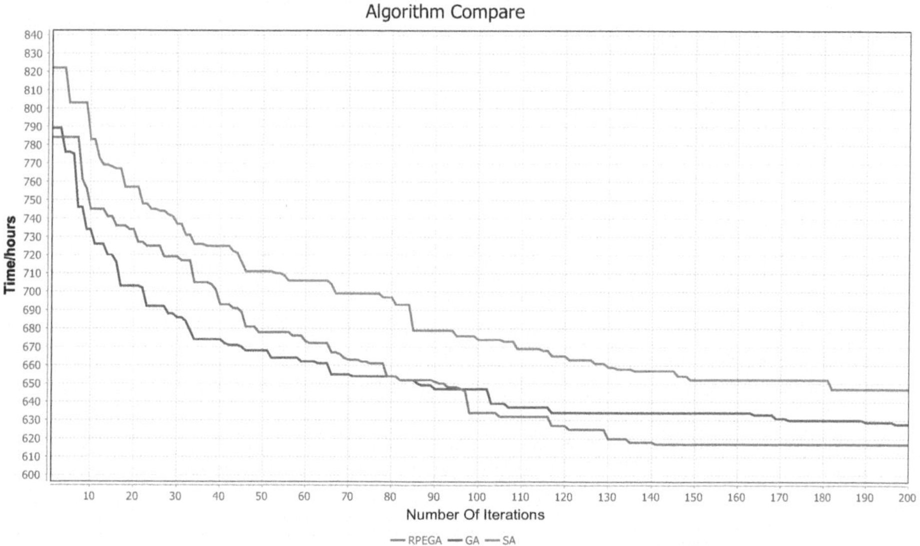

Fig. 6. Algorithm Comparison

It can be seen that in large-scale use cases, the RPEGA model can obtain better solutions within a limited number of iterations.

6 Conclusion

This paper addresses the Flexible Job Shop Scheduling Problem with Parallel Operations and Job Priority Constraints (JSPCPOJP) by constructing a corresponding optimization model and proposing an improved genetic algorithm (RPEGA). By introducing the Mixed Sequence and Operation Selection (MSOS) encoding method, a deep recursive population initialization mechanism, and improved crossover and mutation operators, the algorithm can effectively handle parallel operations and job priority constraints, generating feasible scheduling solutions that meet the constraints. Experimental results show that the RPEGA algorithm can quickly obtain approximate solutions close to the exact optimal solutions when solving small-scale JSPCPOJP problems, with significantly less solution time compared to exact solution methods. In the comparative tests on large-scale instances, the RPEGA algorithm obtained better solutions than the initial genetic algorithm and the genetic annealing algorithm within limited a number of iterations. This indicates that the RPEGA algorithm possesses superior global search capabilities and convergence speed when dealing with large-scale problems, and is capable of effectively addressing complex scheduling constraints. Future research can further explore the optimization potential of the algorithm to address more complex scheduling scenarios and larger-scale problem instances.

Acknowledgments. This work was supported by Guangdong Provincial Key Laboratory (Grant 2023B1212060076) and Shenzhen Science & Technology Plan (No. ZDCYKCX20250901093304006).

Disclosure of Interests. The authors have no competing interests to declare that are relevant to the content of this article.

References

1. Dauzère-Pérès, S., Ding, J., Shen, L., et al.: The flexible job shop scheduling problem: a review. Eur. J. Oper. Res. **314**(2), 409–432 (2024)
2. Xie, J., Gao, L., Peng, K., Li, X., Li, H.: Review on flexible job shop scheduling. IET Collaborative Intell. Manuf. **1**(3), 67–77 (2019)
3. Brucker, P., Schlie, R.: Job-shop scheduling with multi-purpose machines. Computing **45**(4), 369–375 (1990)
4. Panwalker, S., Wafik, L.: A survey of scheduling rules. Ops. Res. **25**(1), 45–61 (1977)
5. Chaudhry, I.A., Khan, A.A.: A research survey: review of flexible job shop scheduling techniques. Int. Trans. Oper. Res. **23**(3), 551–591 (2016)
6. Amjad, M.K., Butt, S.I., Kousar, R., et al.: Recent research trends in genetic algorithm based flexible job shop scheduling problems. Math. Probl. Eng. **2018**(1), 9270802 (2018)
7. Fattahi, P., Saidi Mehrabad, M., Jolai, F.: Mathematical modeling and heuristic approaches to flexible job shop scheduling problems. J. Intell. Manuf. **18**, 331–342 (2007)
8. Ho, N.B., Tay, J.C.: GENACE: an efficient cultural algorithm for solving the flexible job-shop problem. In: Proceedings of the 2004 Congress on Evolutionary Computation (IEEE Cat. No. 04TH8753), vol. 2, pp. 1759–1766. IEEE (2004)
9. Cheng, R., Gen, M., Tsujimura, Y.: A tutorial survey of job-shop scheduling problems using genetic algorithms, part II: hybrid genetic search strategies. Comput. Ind. Eng. **36**(2), 343–364 (1999)

10. Davis, L.: Job shop scheduling with genetic algorithms. In: Proceedings of the First International Conference on Genetic Algorithms and their Applications, pp. 136–140. Psychology Press (2014)
11. Zhang, C., Rao, Y., Li, P.: An effective hybrid genetic algorithm for the job shop scheduling problem. Int. J. Adv. Manuf. Technol. **39**, 965–974 (2008)
12. Watanabe, M., Ida, K., Gen, M.: A genetic algorithm with modified crossover operator and search area adaptation for the job-shop scheduling problem. Comput. Ind. Eng. **48**(4), 743–752 (2005)
13. Li, X., Guo, X., Tang, H., et al.: Survey of integrated flexible job shop scheduling problems. Comput. Ind. Eng. **174**, 108786 (2022)
14. Yu, F., Fu, X., Li, H., et al.: Improved roulette wheel selection-based genetic algorithm for TSP. In: 2016 International Conference on Network and Information Systems for Computers (ICNISC), pp. 151–154. IEEE (2016)
15. Bagheri, A., Zandieh, M., Mahdavi, I., et al.: An artificial immune algorithm for the flexible job-shop scheduling problem. Future Gener. Comput. Syst. **26**(4), 533–541 (2010)

Density-Aware Pairwise Constraint Propagation via Bidirectional Trees

Zixuan Liu[1], Chuan Qin[2(✉)], Zhiguo Long[2], and Hua Meng[1]

[1] School of Mathematics, Southwest Jiaotong University, Chengdu 611756, China
[2] School of Computing and Artificial Intelligence, Southwest Jiaotong University, Chengdu 611756, China
2023212479@my.swjtu.edu.cn

Abstract. Pairwise Constraints are widely used in semi-supervised learning. However, their limited quantity often restricts performance. To address this issue, pairwise constraint propagation (PCP) algorithms have been proposed to extend initial must-link and cannot-link constraints to more samples. In this paper, we propose an algorithm for density-aware pairwise constraint propagation via bidirectional trees to overcome the limitations of existing methods on complex manifold data. The approach constructs a hierarchical topology driven by local density, where each sample is associated with leader and follower points, forming bidirectional propagation trees. A sparse similarity matrix is built using both density differences and Euclidean distances, and a multi-path weighted mechanism computes propagation scores. Finally, an empirically selected optimal threshold is used to binarize the results and produce refined pairwise constraints. Experimental results demonstrate that the proposed method outperforms state-of-the-art PCP algorithms in terms of constraint accuracy and clustering performance.

Keywords: pairwise constraint propagation · constrained spectral clustering · semi-supervised learning

1 Introduction

Among various types of supervised information, class labels are commonly used and very informative. However, due to their high acquisition costs, it is often impractical to obtain large-scale labeled samples in many real-world scenarios. Consequently, researchers have increasingly focused on exploring more practical forms of weak supervision. This paper focuses on a widely used form of weak supervision, i.e., Pairwise Constraints [1] (PCs), which provide auxiliary supervised information by specifying the relationship between two samples and are generally easier and less costly to obtain. Currently, PCs have been widely applied in various machine learning tasks, including classification [2,3], clustering [4,5], feature selection [6], metric learning [7], image retrieval [8,9], and semi-supervised dimensionality reduction [10].

M. Bonsangue and Y. Chen (Eds.): AILA 2025, CCIS 2668, pp. 176–190, 2026.
https://doi.org/10.1007/978-981-95-8262-4_14

However, in practical applications, these PCs are still limited in quantity, and the performance of using only a few PCs is usually not satisfactory. To address this issue, researchers have proposed Pairwise Constraint Propagation (PCP) algorithms, which aim to extend limited initial constraints to a larger set of samples, thereby generating richer supervised information. For example, Wu et al. [11] incorporated non-negative matrix factorization into constraint propagation but considered only PCs (must-link constraints; MLs) that specifies which pairs of samples belong to the same class, neglecting PCs (cannot-link constraints; CLs) for samples that are not in the same class. Lu et al. [12] constructed separate propagation structures for ML and CL constraints. Given that CL constraints typically outnumber ML constraints significantly, Liu et al. [13] proposed a well-posed constrained optimization model to address this imbalance. Furthermore, Fu et al. [14] introduced low-rank matrix recovery and noise removal techniques into PCP, enhancing the robustness of the propagated constraints.

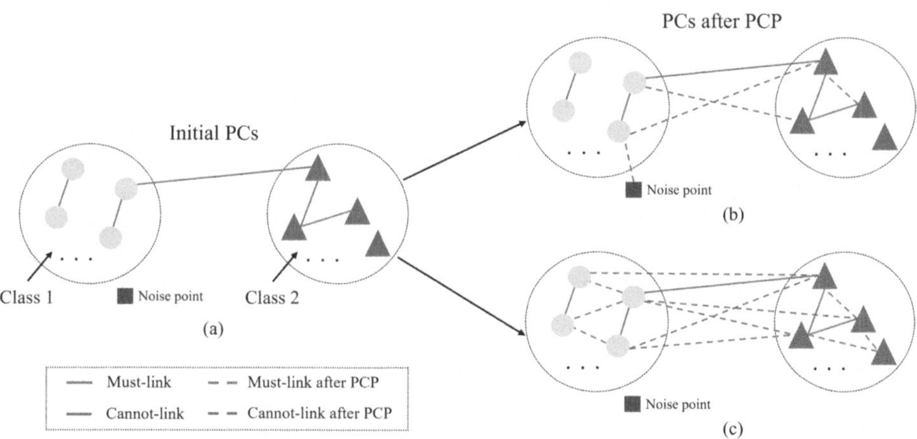

Fig. 1. Illustration of the advantage of the proposed method over existing ones. (a) Initial Pairwise Constraints Graph; (b) Pairwise Constraints Graph after Traditional PCP Method; (c) Pairwise Constraints Graph after Proposed PCP Method.

Although existing PCP methods have shown some success, they still struggle with data that exhibit complex manifold structures, such as face images, handwritten digits, and biomedical signals. Traditional global propagation approaches often propagate constraint information to irrelevant regions, causing error propagation and performance degradation. Meanwhile, local structures may be poorly modeled due to insufficient initial constraints, especially in sparsely labeled or noisy areas, as demonstrated in Fig. 1.

To tackle these challenges, this paper proposes an algorithm for density-aware pairwise constraint propagation via bidirectional trees (DABT-PCP). The algorithm improves modeling of complex manifold structures by building a hierarchical propagation framework based on local density distribution. The key contributions are summarized as follows:

1. A constraint propagation algorithm that exploits local density distribution and leader-follower hierarchical relationships to better model manifold geometry and capture nonlinear structures;
2. A new propagation mechanism via leader/follower bidirectional trees, reducing global error spread while improving coverage in sparsely constrained regions.

The rest of the paper is organized as follows: Sect. 2 reviews related PCP work; Sect. 3 presents the DABT-PCP algorithm and its use in constrained spectral clustering; Sect. 4 reports experimental results; and Sect. 5 concludes the paper with future research directions.

2 Related Work

2.1 Pairwise Constraint Propagation

Pairwise Constraints (PCs) provide weak supervision by indicating whether two samples belong to the same class. However, in practice, the number of available PCs is often limited, which constrains the performance of semi-supervised learning methods. To overcome this, PCP methods have been proposed to automatically infer additional constraints, expanding the initial set to cover the entire dataset and improve model performance. This section briefly reviews and discusses several representative PCP approaches.

Firstly, we introduce three typical PCP algorithms: E2CP [15], MC-PCP [16], and SPCP [17]. E2CP, proposed by Lu et al. [15], treats ML/CL as "soft labels" and propagates them using graph Laplacian regularization. It is efficient and suitable for large datasets, iteratively optimizing the similarity matrix to meet constraints. MC-PCP, introduced by Yang et al. [16], models constraint propagation as a low-rank matrix completion problem, optimizing the similarity matrix via nuclear norm minimization. This method is robust to noise and missing data, making it ideal for high-dimensional datasets. SPCP, developed by Fu et al. [17], uses symmetric graph regularization to decompose constraint propagation into binary label propagation subproblems. This approach can be directly applied to multi-class tasks, enhancing its applicability. These methods effectively extend limited PCs to improve semi-supervised learning performance.

Among various PCP methods, some use optimization frameworks. Li et al. [18] modeled the problem as a semidefinite programming (SDP) task, creating a smooth mapping function that places ML-constrained samples close together and CL-constrained samples farther apart. Yang et al. [19] and Fu et al. [14] converted PCP into a matrix completion problem, treating the propagated PCs as partially observed matrices and using matrix analysis for effective algorithms. Jia et al. [20] proposes a novel PCP model via dual adversarial manifold regularization to fully explore the potential of the limited initial, considering the adversarial relationship between ML and CL. With advances in machine learning, deep learning approaches have also been introduced into PCP research [21,22], aiming to improve constraint propagation by leveraging the powerful feature learning capabilities of deep neural networks.

2.2 Constrained Spectral Clustering

Spectral clustering (SC) [23] is widely used in machine learning tasks due to its excellent clustering performance and straightforward implementation. Traditional SC is an unsupervised method that relies solely on the data's similarity matrix for clustering. To overcome the limitations of traditional SC in unsupervised learning, researchers have proposed constrained spectral clustering, which incorporates PCs to adjust the similarity or Laplacian matrix, ensuring that clustering results align with supervisory information. Existing constrained spectral clustering methods can be broadly categorized into two types [24]: low-dimensional embedding learning methods and affinity matrix modification methods.

The first type adjusts the structure of the low-dimensional embedding space (i.e., the eigenvectors of the laplacian matrix) to comply with given PCs. These methods typically integrate constraint information into the optimization objective function to directly learn a low-dimensional representation that satisfies the constraints. For example, Li et al.'s CCSP [25] obtains initial low-dimensional embeddings via spectral decomposition of the Laplacian matrix and then optimizes these embeddings to align with initial PCs. Cucuringu et al. [26] and Jiang et al. [27] reformulate the constrained clustering problem as a generalized spectral method (GSM), solving it mathematically to derive low-dimensional embeddings that satisfy PCs. This approach leads to semi-supervised SC (S3C) [28].

The second type of method modifies the similarity (affinity) matrix W directly, either by adjusting its elements or learning a new matrix that incorporates PCs, before applying standard spectral clustering. For example, graph/kernel learning methods [29] [30] construct graphs or kernel matrices to represent data relationships, which are then used as affinity matrices in SC. To better utilize constraint information in guiding the clustering process, researchers have introduced constraint propagation mechanisms to refine the affinity matrix. For example. Fu et al. [14] introduced a PCP model with symmetric constraints, which was later extended using a joint low-rank mode [17] for improved constraint propagation. Jia et al. [31] introduced a unified PCP framework for constrained spectral clustering by simultaneously learning the propagation and affinity matrices. Specifically, the method is formulated as a bounded symmetric graph-regularized low-rank matrix completion problem, enabling more effective integration of PCs into the clustering process.

3 Method

The proposed method in this paper consists of three core stages: construction of density-aware topological structure, generation of bidirectional propagation trees, and the corresponding constraint propagation mechanism. The following sections provide detailed descriptions of these stages. The overall process of the algorithm is shown in Figure 2.

Let the input data matrix be $X = (x_1, x_2, \ldots, x_n) \in \mathbb{R}^{d \times n}$, where each sample $x_i \in \mathbb{R}^{d \times 1}$ is a d-dimensional vector. The (sparse) similarity matrix is represented as $S \in \mathbb{R}^{n \times n}$,where the element S_{ij} denotes the similarity between samples x_i and x_j. The initial pairwise constraint score matrix is denoted by F, in which F_{ij} represents the initial constraint score between x_i and x_j. The propagated pairwise constraint score matrix is denoted by F' (Fig. 2).

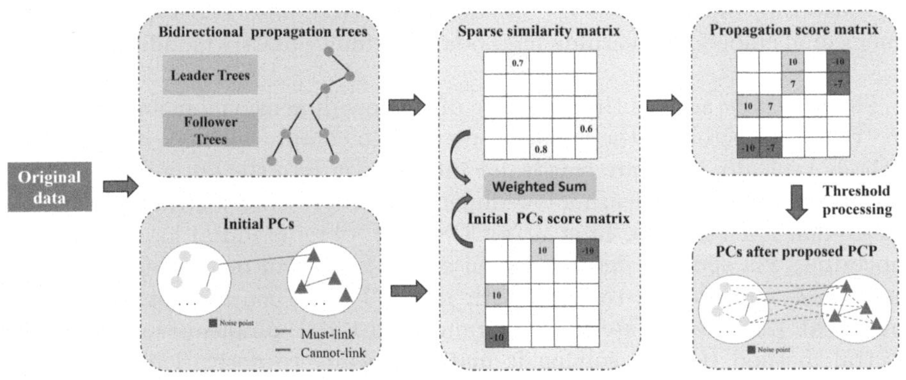

Fig. 2. The overall process of the proposed algorithm.

3.1 Construction of Density-Aware Topological Structure

The core task of this stage is to determine the “Leader Point” and “Follower Point” for each sample point. Specifically, for any sample point x_i, its leader point is defined as the nearest point with a higher density. The local density of each data point is calculated based on the average distance to its neighbors; a larger average distance indicates a more dispersed neighborhood, implying a lower local density.

Definition 1 (Local Density). *For a sample $x_i \in \mathbb{R}^d$, its* local density ρ_i *is defined as:*

$$\rho_i = exp(-(\frac{1}{k} \sum_{x_j \in \mathcal{N}_k(x_i)} d(x_i, x_j)^2)) \tag{1}$$

where $N_k(x_i)$ denotes the set of k-nearest neighbors of x_i,and $d(x_i, x_j)^2$ represents the squared Euclidean distance between x_i and x_j.

Algorithm 1. Generate Leader Trees

Input: Data set $X = \{x_1, x_2, ..., x_n\}$
Output: Leader tree set $L = \{L_1, L_2, ..., L_n\}$
Initialization: For each data point x_i, create empty sets $L_i = \emptyset$.
for each data point x_i **do**
  $x_{\text{current}} \leftarrow \text{leader}(x_i)$
  if $x_{\text{current}} \in N_k(x_i)$ **then**
    $L_i \leftarrow L_i \cup \{x_{\text{current}}\}$
    $x_{\text{current}} \leftarrow \text{leader}(x_{\text{current}})$
return L

Algorithm 2. Generate Follower Trees

Input: Data set $X = \{x_1, x_2, ..., x_n\}$
Output: Follower tree set $U = \{U_1, U_2, ..., U_n\}$
for each $x_i \in X$ **do**
  Initialize empty queue Q and create empty sets $U_i = \emptyset$.
  for each x_j where $\text{leader}(x_j) = x_i$ and $x_j \in X$ **do**
    if $x_j \in N_k(x_i)$ **then**
      $U_i \leftarrow U_i \cup \{x_j\}$, Q.Enqueue(x_j)
  while Q is not empty **do**
    $x_k \leftarrow Q$.Dequeue()
    for each x_m where $\text{leader}(x_m) = x_k$ and $x_m \in X$ **do**
      if $x_m \in N_k(x_i)$ and $x_m \notin U_i$ **then**
        $U_i \leftarrow U_i \cup \{x_m\}$, Q.Enqueue(x_m)
return U

Definition 2 (Leader Point and Follower Point). *Let x_j be the data point that satisfies $\rho_j > \rho_i$ and is closest to x_i, Then x_j is referred to as the* leader point *of x_i, and x_i is the* follower point *of x_j, This relationship is formally defined as:*

$$leader(x_i) = \{x_j | arg \min_{x_j : \rho_j > \rho_i} (d(x_i, x_j))\} \tag{2}$$

3.2 Generation of Bidirectional Trees

Unlike existing works, we construct bidirectional trees for constraint propagation, instead of just one directional of propagation. Bidirectional trees consist of two types of propagation paths for each sample point based on the density structure constructed in the previous section, i.e., *Leader Trees* and *Follower Trees*.

For each sample point x_i, its leader tree L_i is built by iteratively adding leader points of the added points in L_i that are among the k nearest neighbors, until no more such points can be found. Algorithm 1 outlines the detailed steps.

The follower tree of each sample point x_i is constructed similarly but in the reverse direction. That is, for each sample point x_i, its follower tree U_i is built by iteratively adding followers of the added points in U_i that are among the k-nearest neighbors of x_i, until no more such points can be found. This approach ensures constraint propagation in both directions and avoids erroneous diffusion associated with global propagation. Algorithm 2 gives the steps for the construction of follower trees.

Next, we construct a sparse similarity matrix S. For each data point x_i, we calculate its similarity to every point in its leader tree set L_i and follower tree set U_i. The similarity calculation formula is:

$$S_{ij} = \exp\left(-\frac{|\rho_i - \rho_j|}{\max(\rho)}\right) \cdot \exp\left(-\frac{d_{ij}^2}{\sigma_1^2}\right), x_j \in L_i \cup U_i \tag{3}$$

where ρ_i and ρ_j are the local densities of points x_i and x_j, respectively, and d_{ij} is the distance between points x_i and x_j. This similarity measure not only considers the distance between data points but also incorporates the factor of local density difference. This comprehensive consideration allows for a more accurate reflection of the actual similarity between data points.

3.3 Constraint Propagation Mechanism

With the bidirectional trees constructed, we can now proceed to the constraint propagation mechanism. We firstly define an initial pairwise constraint score matrix F based on the initial must-link $\mathcal{M}$ and cannot-link $\mathcal{C}$ constraints:

$$F_{ij} = \begin{cases} 10, & \text{if } (x_i, x_j) \in \mathcal{M}, \\ -10, & \text{if } (x_i, x_j) \in \mathcal{C}, \\ 0, & \text{otherwise.} \end{cases} \tag{4}$$

For each data point x_i, all points that have an initial constraint relationship with x_i form a set $P(x_i) = \{x_{i,i_1}, x_{i,i_2}, \ldots, x_{i,i_p}\}$. That is, if $x_j \in P(x_i)$ then $F_{ij} \neq 0$, where p is the number of points satisfying this condition.

Subsequently, we calculate the constraint propagation scores with the help of the previously obtained similarity matrix S_{ij} in Eq (3). For a given data point x_j, take any point x_i from $P(x_j)$, and traverse all points x_k in its leader tree set L_i and follower tree set U_i. We use the sparse similarity as a weight value to compute the propagated information F'_{kj}. The calculation formula is:

$$F'_{kj} = S_{ik} \cdot F_{ij} \cdot \exp(-\frac{d_{kj}^2}{\sigma_2^2}), x_k \in L_i \cup U_i \tag{5}$$

where S_{ik} represents the similarity between points x_i and x_k, which measures the strength of constraint propagation between two points. The constraint information F_{ij} between x_i and x_j is propagated through x_i as a relay point to x_k; S_{ik} acts as the weight value during the propagation process, resulting in the constraint propagation score F'_{kj} between x_k and x_j. The term $\exp(-\frac{d_{kj}^2}{\sigma_2^2})$ further

Algorithm 3. DABT-PCP

Input: Data set $X = \{x_1, x_2, ..., x_n\}$
Output: Constraint matrices M, C
Procedure:
Construct leader-follower relationships via Eq (1) & Eq (2)
Generate leader trees and follower trees using Algorithm 1 & Algorithm 2
Build similarity matrix S according to Eq (3)
Initialize constraint score matrix F via Eq (4)
Compute propagated score matrix F' via Eq (6)
Obtain propagated constraints M, C through Eq (7) & Eq (8)
return M, C

adjusts the propagation score based on the distance between x_k and x_j, ensuring that the propagation is appropriately attenuated with increasing distance.

Given that the constraint propagation path between x_k and x_j may involve multiple intermediate points, we comprehensively consider the contributions of multiple propagation paths to determine the final score. The formula is as follows:

$$F'_{kj} = (\frac{1}{p}\sum_{i=j_1}^{jp} S_{ik} \cdot F_{ij}) \cdot \exp(-\frac{d_{kj}^2}{\sigma_2^2})(x_k \in L_i \cup U_i) \tag{6}$$

We further requires that $F'_{kj} = F_{kj}$ if $(x_k, x_j) \in \mathcal{M} \cup \mathcal{C}$.

Depending on the positive or negative values of the elements, F' is divided into a must-link constraint score matrix F'^{+} and a cannot-link constraint score matrix F'^{-}. Subsequently, by setting a threshold τ for binarization of the scores, we obtain the propagated pairwise constraint information. The must-link constraint matrix M and cannot-link constraint matrix C are constructed by the following expressions respectively:

$$M_{ij} = \mathbb{I}\left(F_{ij}'^{+} > \tau\right) \tag{7}$$

$$C_{ij} = \mathbb{I}\left(F_{ij}'^{-} < \tau\right) \tag{8}$$

where $\mathbb{I}$ denotes the indicator function. Algorithm 3 gives the steps for the whole process.

3.4 Application in Constrained Spectral Clustering

This paper applies the proposed pairwise constraint propagation method to constrained spectral clustering [32]. Compared to normal spectral clustering, constrained spectral clustering further considers pairwise constraints to adjust the similarity or Laplacian matrix and requires that the clustering results align with supervised information.

Given an initial similarity matrix W, to improve constrained spectral clustering with pairwise constraints, inspired by literature [12], we update the initial similarity matrix W used in spectral clustering by incorporating the constraint information:

$$W_{ij}^{*} = \begin{cases} 1 - (1 - s_{ij} + d_{ij})(1 - w_{ij}) & s_{ij} - d_{ij} \geq 0 \\ (1 + s_{ij} - d_{ij})w_{ij} & s_{ij} - d_{ij} < 0 \end{cases} \tag{9}$$

where W_{ij}^{*} represents the $(i,j) - th$ element of the improved weight matrix $W^{*} \in \mathbb{R}^{n \times n}$. From the above formula, we can draw the following conclusions:

When $s_{ij} - d_{ij} > 0$, it suggests a must-link constraint between x_i and x_j, increasing w_{ij} so they are more likely to be clustered together. If $s_{ij} - d_{ij} < 0$, it indicates a cannot-link constraint, decreasing w_{ij} so they are likely to be in

Table 1. Details of the datasets.

Dataset	Samples(n)	Dimensions(d)	Classes(c)
Libras	360	90	15
UMIST	575	1024	20
MNIST	500	784	10
USPS	400	256	10
Yale	165	1024	15
ORL	400	5600	40

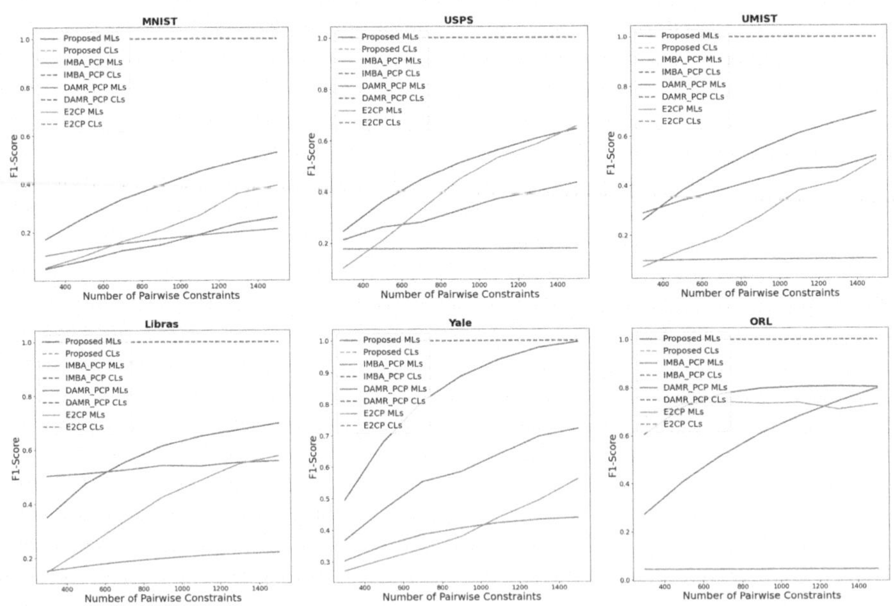

Fig. 3. Comparisons of the propagation capabilities of different PCP methods. Here, MLs and CLs refer to the must-link and cannot-link constraints, respectively.

different clusters. If $s_{ij} - d_{ij} = 0$, there is no clear constraint, and w_{ij} remains unchanged (Table 1).

4 Experiments

In this section, we first evaluate the propagation performance of the proposed PCP model and then apply it to constrained spectral clustering. Experiments are conducted on six benchmark datasets of varying scales, as summarized in Table 1.

4.1 Experimental Setup

To comprehensively evaluate the performance of the model, we randomly select initial PCs from real data based on label information. The number of constraint pairs ranges from 300 to 1500. To reduce the bias introduced by random sampling, each experimental scenario is repeated 20 times, with different initial PCs randomly selected each time, and the final results are averaged.

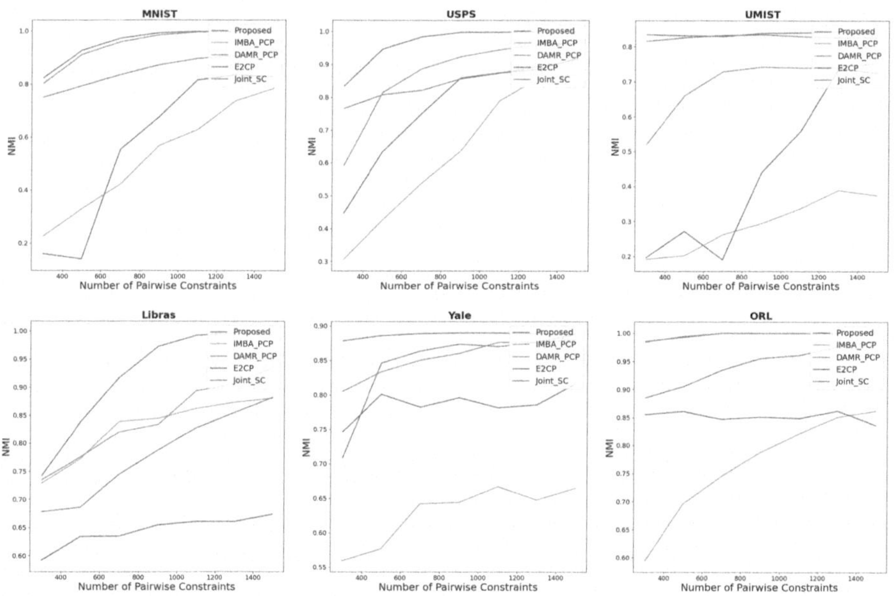

Fig. 4. Comparisons of the clustering performance by different semi-supervised clustering methods in terms of NMI.

Besides that, we construct the Laplacian matrix L using the k-nearest neighbor graph method, where the value of k is set to $\lfloor \log_2 n \rfloor + 1$ [33]. Additionally, we use the RBF kernel, with its variance σ set as the average distance from each sample to its k nearest neighbors. For fair comparison, all methods involving graph matrices are configured using the aforementioned approach. The parameters for all comparative methods are determined through exhaustive search to ensure optimal settings.

4.2 Evaluation of Constraint Propagation Performance

To validate the advantages of the proposed model in constraint propagation capabilities, we compared it with several state-of-the-art PCP algorithms, including E2CP [15], IMBA-PCP [13], and DAMR-PCP [20].

The adjusted similarity matrix is converted into binary constraints by applying a threshold, and these constraints are compared with the ground-truth constraints, the optimal threshold is determined through exhaustive search.

The commonly used F1 score is selected as the performance metric here, and we separate the F1 scores for must-link constraints and cannot-link constraints to avoid the imbalance between the two types of constraints. Figure 3 shows the performance of different PCP methods. Across all datasets, all methods achieve the highest F1 score on cannot-link constraints. This is because cannot-link constraints dominate the constraint set and are easier to identify during propagation. In contrast, must-link propagation is more challenging.

In terms of F1 scores on must-link constraints, the proposed method consistently outperforms existing methods, demonstrating not only stronger propagation capability but also a better ability to handle the imbalance between must-link and cannot-link constraints, leading to more accurate must-link propagation. Moreover, as the number of initial constraints increases, the F1 scores of most methods improve. This upward trend occurs because additional supervision provides more reliable anchor points for propagation, thereby reducing uncertainty and improving the precision of inferred constraints.

In conclusion, while preserving strong performance on cannot-link constraints, the proposed method significantly improves must-link propagation, highlighting its effectiveness in leveraging limited supervision under weakly supervised settings.

4.3 Evaluation of Constrained Clustering Performance

To comprehensively evaluate the performance in constrained clustering, we compare it not only with the three PCP methods mentioned earlier but also with another state-of-the-art constrained clustering algorithms, i.e., Joint-SC [31]. All PCP algorithms are integrated into the spectral clustering as described in Sect. 3.4, and the commonly used Normalized Mutual Information (NMI) is employed as the performance metric.

Figure 4 presents the clustering performance across six datasets. Table 2 records the NMI values of various constraint spectral clustering methods when the number of constraints is 300 and 900. The results show that our method achieves the highest NMI scores on nearly all datasets. Notably, on the Libras

Table 2. NMI values of different constrained clustering models.

Dataset	Number of PCs	IMBA-PCP	DAMR-PCP	E2CP	Joint-SC	Proposed
MNIST	300	0.22	**0.83**	0.7	0.75	0.82
	900	0.57	0.98	0.97	0.87	**0.99**
USPS	300	0.36	0.59	0.45	0.77	**0.84**
	900	0.59	0.9	0.84	0.84	**0.94**
UMIST	300	0.28	0.38	0.66	0.87	**0.96**
	900	0.38	0.86	0.89	0.91	**0.99**
Libras	300	0.73	0.14	0.59	0.68	**0.74**
	900	0.84	0.16	0.65	0.79	**0.97**
Yale	300	0.74	0.78	0.59	0.73	**0.99**
	900	0.89	0.99	0.70	**1**	**1**
ORL	300	0.59	**0.98**	0.70	0.88	**0.98**
	900	0.79	**1**	0.73	0.95	**1**

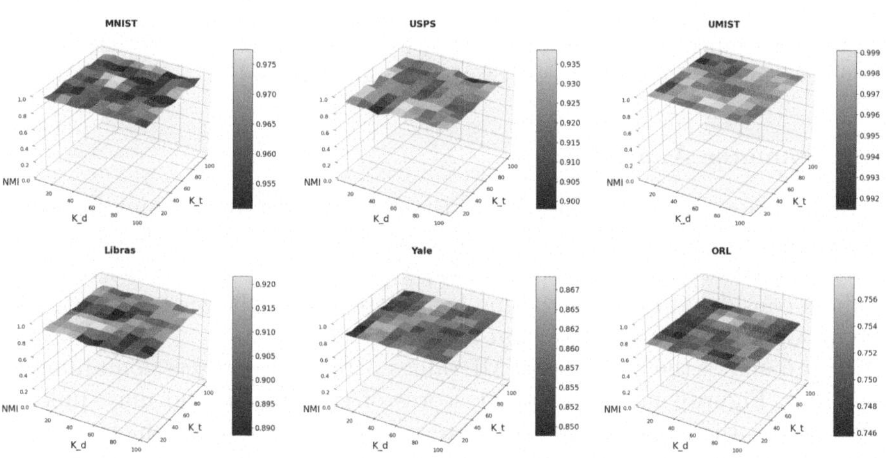

Fig. 5. Influence of neighborhood number on NMI value of constrained spectrum clustering.

dataset, our model demonstrates a significant advantage over competing methods. This indicates that the bidirectional constraint propagation tree indeed improves the quality of constraint propagation, enabling more effective utilization of initial constraints to guide the clustering process.

It is worth noting that both the quality and quantity of initial PCs have a substantial impact on performance. Therefore, as shown in the figure, the NMI scores of all methods tend to increase with more initial constraints. Particularly on the UMIST, ORL, and Yale datasets, our model achieves high NMI even with limited initial supervision. Moreover, our method generally yields the

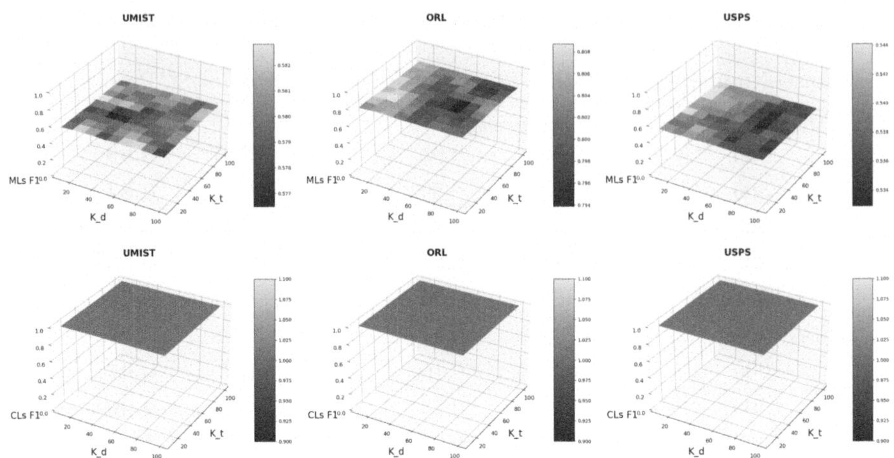

Fig. 6. Influence of neighborhood number on F1 value of propagation performance.

largest performance gain in terms of NMI, further confirming the reliability and effectiveness of the PCs generated by the proposed model.

4.4 Parameter Analysis

We conducted a sensitivity analysis of the key parameters, K_d and K_t. In our proposed model, K_d is the number of nearest neighbors considered for local density calculation (i.e., the k value in Eq. 1), while K_t is the number of nearest neighbors considered for constructing leader trees and follower trees (i.e., the k value in Algorithm 1 and Algorithm 2).

Figure 5 shows the results of NMI values across all datasets containing 600 initial PCs. Figure 6 presents the F1 scores of cannot-link and must-link constraints under the same conditions. It reveals that our model achieves optimal or near-optimal F1 and NMI values over a broad range of K_d and K_t settings. This indicates high robustness and adaptability of our model in both constraint propagation performance and clustering effectiveness.

5 Conclusion

This paper proposes a Density-Aware Pairwise Constraints Propagation via Bidirectional Trees (DABT-PCP) algorithm to better utilize limited initial pairwise constraints. The algorithm includes three main components: building a density-aware topology, generating bidirectional propagation trees, and applying an adaptive propagation mechanism. These components together improve performance on complex data compared to traditional methods. The key contribution is the integration of density-aware structures into constraint propagation, offering a new solution for semi-supervised learning on high-dimensional data.

This approach effectively captures data structure and improves constraint utilization. Experiments show that DABT-PCP outperforms existing PCP methods in both constraint propagation and clustering accuracy. Future work will explore its use in tasks such as metric learning and constraint-based deep learning to further evaluate its potential.

References

1. González-Almagro, G., et al.: Semi-supervised constrained clustering: an in-depth overview, ranked taxonomy and future research directions. Artif. Intell. Rev. **58**, 157 (2025)
2. Cai, W., et al.: Hierarchical domain adaptation projective dictionary pair learning model for EEG classification in IoMT systems. IEEE Trans. Comput. Soc. Syst. **10**(4), 1559–1567 (2022)
3. Wu, Z., et al.: UC-OWOD: Unknown-classified open world object detection. In: European Conference on Computer Vision LNCS, vol. 13657, pp. 193–210. Springer, Cham (2022)
4. Chen, R., et al.: Deep multi-view semi-supervised clustering with sample pairwise constraints. Neurocomputing **500**, 832–845 (2022)
5. Cai, J., et al.: A review on semi-supervised clustering. Inf. Sci. **632**, 164–200 (2023)
6. Lai, J., et al.: Adaptive graph learning for semi-supervised feature selection with redundancy minimization. Inf. Sci. **609**, 465–488 (2022)
7. Yang, Z., et al.: Simple stochastic and online gradient descent algorithms for pairwise learning. Adv. Neural. Inf. Process. Syst. **34**, 20160–20171 (2021)
8. Xie, Y., et al.: D3still: Decoupled differential distillation for asymmetric image retrieval. Proc. IEEE/CVF Conf. Comput. Vis. Pattern Recognit. 17181–17190 (2024)
9. Ge, C., Wang, J., Qi, Q., et al.: Scene-level sketch-based image retrieval with minimal pairwise supervision. In: Proceedings of the AAAI Conference on Artificial Intelligence, vol. 37, no. 1, pp. 650–657 (2023)
10. Zhou, M.C.: Evolutionary optimization methods for high-dimensional expensive problems: a survey. IEEE/CAA J. Autom. Sinica **11**(5), 1092–1105 (2024)
11. Wu, W., et al.: Pairwise constraint propagation-induced symmetric nonnegative matrix factorization. IEEE Trans. Neural Netw. Learn. Syst. **29**(12), 6348–6361 (2018)
12. Lu, Z., Ip, H.H.S.: Constrained spectral clustering via exhaustive and efficient constraint propagation. In: Daniilidis, K., Maragos, P., Paragios, N. (eds.) ECCV 2010. LNCS, vol. 6316, pp. 1–14. Springer, Heidelberg (2010). https://doi.org/10.1007/978-3-642-15567-3_1
13. Liu, H., Jia, Y., Hou, J., et al.: Imbalance-aware pairwise constraint propagation. In: Proceedings of the ACM International Conference on Multimedia, pp. 1605–1613 (2019)
14. Fu, Z.: Pairwise constraint propagation via low-rank matrix recovery. Comput. Vis. Media **1**, 211–220 (2015)
15. Lu, Z., Peng, Y.: Exhaustive and efficient constraint propagation: a graph-based learning approach and its applications. Int. J. Comput. Vis. **103**(3), 306–325 (2013)
16. Yang, Z., et al.: Matrix completion for cross-view pairwise constraint propagation. In: Proceedings of the International Conference on Multimedia, pp. 897–900 (2014)

17. Fu, Z., et al.: Symmetric graph regularized constraint propagation. In: Proceedings of the AAAI Conference on Artificial Intelligence, vol. 25, no. 1, pp. 350–355 (2011)
18. Li, Z., Liu, J., Tang, X.: Pairwise constraint propagation by semidefinite programming for semi-supervised classification. In: Proceedings of the 25th International Conference on Machine Learning, pp. 576–583 (2008)
19. Yang, Z., Hu, Y., Liu, H., et al.: Matrix completion for cross-view pairwise constraint propagation. In: Proceedings of the 22nd ACM International Conference on Multimedia, pp. 897–900 (2014)
20. Jia, Y., et al.: Pairwise constraint propagation with dual adversarial manifold regularization. IEEE Trans. Neural Netw. Learn. Syst. **31**(12), 5575–5587 (2020)
21. Tiezzi, M., et al.: Deep constraint-based propagation in graph neural networks. IEEE Trans. Pattern Anal. Mach. Intell. **44**(2), 727–739 (2021)
22. Marra, G., et al.: Local propagation in constraint-based neural networks. In: 2020 International Joint Conference on Neural Networks (IJCNN), pp. 1–8. IEEE (2020)
23. Von Luxburg, U.: A tutorial on spectral clustering. Stat. Comput. **17**, 395–416 (2007)
24. Wang, X., Qian, B., Davidson, I.: On constrained spectral clustering and its applications. Data Min. Knowl. Discov. **28**, 1–30 (2014)
25. Li, Z., Liu, J.: Constrained clustering by spectral kernel learning. In: 2009 IEEE 12th International Conference on Computer Vision, pp. 421–427. IEEE (2009)
26. Cucuringu, M., et al.: Simple and scalable constrained clustering: a generalized spectral method. In: Artificial Intelligence and Statistics. PMLR, Proc. Mach. Learn. Res., vol. 51, pp. 445–454 (2016)
27. Jiang, C., Xie, H., Bai, Z.: Robust and efficient computation of eigenvectors in a generalized spectral method for constrained clustering. In: Artificial Intelligence and Statistics PMLR, Proc. Mach. Learn. Res., vol. 54, pp. 757–766 (2017)
28. Jia, Y., Kwong, S., Hou, J.: Semi-supervised spectral clustering with structured sparsity regularization. IEEE Signal Process. Lett. **25**(3), 403–407 (2018)
29. Li, C.G., You, C., Vidal, R.: Structured sparse subspace clustering: a joint affinity learning and subspace clustering framework. IEEE Trans. Image Process. **26**(6), 2988–3001 (2017)
30. Jia, Y., Liu, H., Hou, J., et al.: Clustering-aware graph construction: a joint learning perspective. IEEE Trans. Signal Inf. Process. Netw. **6**, 357–370 (2020)
31. Jia, Y., et al.: Joint optimization for pairwise constraint propagation. Trans. Neural Netw. Learn. Syst. **32**(7), 3168–3180 (2020)
32. Wang, X., Qian, B., Davidson, I.: On constrained spectral clustering and its applications. Data Min. Knowl. Discov. **28**, 1–30 (2014)
33. Von Luxburg, U.: A tutorial on spectral clustering. Stat. Comput. **17**, 395–416 (2007)

Efficient Algorithm and Implementation for Boole Reduction of Large Logic Expressions

Kailin Xuan(✉)

The Bishop's School, San Diego, CA 92037, USA
kailinx20@gmail.com

Abstract. Boolean algebra, introduced in the 19th century by the mathematician, philosopher, and logician George Boole, has been foundational in mathematics, logic, computer science, machine proofs, and digital electronics. Recently, a new framework, the "Algebra of Boole," proposed by Professor Norman J. Wildberger, offers a more natural and powerful alternative. To apply this new framework to important areas, such as artificial intelligence, complex machine proofs, and large-scale circuit designs, it is essential to develop a method for automatically reducing complicated logic expressions into a simple standard form. This paper is on developing an efficient algorithm and implementation for Boole Reduction, a process that simplifies large logic and Boole expressions into compact, canonical forms. By utilizing Key Boole Properties from the Algebra of Boole, the algorithm processes arbitrarily complex logic expressions, reducing them iteratively to a canonical form through sophisticated reduction techniques until no further simplifications are possible. Expressions with varying complexity, from simple binary operations to large multi-variable expressions, are used to test the algorithm. Results show a significant improvement in reduction speed and computational efficiency compared to brute-force methods, demonstrating the algorithm's feasibility in handling complex logic expressions. One of the aims of this work is also to stimulate research in the framework of the Algebra of Boole as well as its applications in areas such as propositional logic, AI reasoning, and the optimization of digital circuit designs.

Keywords: Algebra of Boole · Artificial Intelligence · Logic Reduction Algorithm

1 Introduction

The primary objective of this research is to develop a fast, efficient, and scalable algorithm for Boole reduction. By focusing on simplifying expressions using Key Boole Properties, the proposed algorithm is designed to handle arbitrarily large logic or Boole expressions, simplifying them into their canonical form. Central to this approach is the Algebra of Boole, which serves as a structured framework

M. Bonsangue and Y. Chen (Eds.): AILA 2025, CCIS 2668, pp. 191–199, 2026.
https://doi.org/10.1007/978-981-95-8262-4_15

for logical reasoning, artificial intelligence, and circuit analysis. Unlike traditional Boolean algebra, this redefinition involves XOR-based addition, leading to more algebraic calculations and a more powerful treatment of logical relationships, particularly in applications such as AI reasoning and machine proof. This research contributes to advancing computational logic within the framework of the Algebra of Boole.

1.1 Boolean Algebra and Algebra of Boole

Boolean algebra, or logical algebra, is a field of mathematics introduced and developed by George Boole in the 19th century. Boole took the logic that had been established over the past 2000 years, building on Aristotle's work, and created a mathematical framework to model it [2]. Professor Norman Wildberger, in his series of YouTube public lectures, proposed a new Algebra of Boole system that behaves differently from classical Boolean algebra [12]. In the Algebra of Boole, addition is defined as XOR, where only one element can be true at a time for the statement to be true.

In this paper, we use term "logic expression" to refer to expressions written with logic symbols such as &(AND), |(OR), →(Implication). A "`Boolean expression`" denotes the expression written with Boolean algebra where the addition operator "+" represents logic OR (sometimes expressed as $\oplus$ to avoid confusion with the plus sign in Algebra of Boole). A "`Boole expression`" refers to an expression with the Algebra of Boole where the addition "+" means logic XOR. All these kinds of expressions try to model any Boolean function $f : B_2^n \rightarrow B_2$, where $B_2 = \{0, 1\}$ is a set of binary values, and n represents the dimension, or arity, of the function.

Table 1 displays the operations for two variables in the Algebra of Boole, compared to Boolean algebra. In the table, the top row contains the Algebra of Boole representation, while the bottom row is the Boolean algebra representation. The upper part and the lower part together present a complete table, the lower part being the horizontal continuation of the upper part due to space constraints.

For example, the logic OR expression A|B would be expressed as A+B (in Boolean algebra, Boolean expression) and A+B+AB (Algebra of Boole, Boole expression). Variables are written either in capital or lower case.

Professor Norman J. Wildberger, in his 31-part YouTube lecture series, demonstrates the better mathematical and algebraic properties of the Algebra of Boole than Boolean algebra and various techniques to simplify expressions using the Algebra of Boole. Drawing from a close reading of George Boole's original writings, he argues that the Algebra of Boole is more natural and powerful than Boolean algebra, and Boole's intended system was more aligned with this algebraic framework, rather than what we now call Boolean algebra. In particular, Wildberger proved that every Boole expression can be reduced to a canonical form. For instance, the canonical form for three variables is _ + _a + _b + _c + _ab + _ac + _bc + _abc, where each underscore represents a coefficient (either 0 or 1). This structure generalizes to any number of variables. He then called for a computer program to perform the reduction of any large logic expressions to canonical form by using Algebra of Boole, which is vital for applications in propositional logic, AI reasoning and circuit designs.

Table 1. Comparison of Algebra of Boole and Boolean Algebra

Algebra of Boole	A	B	A+B	AB	A+AB	B+AB	A+B+AB
	0	0	0	0	0	0	0
	0	1	1	0	0	1	1
	1	0	1	0	1	0	1
	1	1	0	1	0	0	1
Logic Connector			XOR	&(AND)			| (OR)
Boolean Algebra	A	B	$A\bar{B}+\bar{A}B$	AB	$A\bar{B}$	$\bar{A}B$	A+B

Algebra of Boole	1+A	1+B	1+A+B	1+AB	1+A+AB	1+B+AB	1+A+B+AB
	1	1	1	1	1	1	1
	1	0	0	1	1	0	0
	0	1	0	1	0	1	0
	0	0	1	0	1	1	0
Logic Connector	~				→	→	
Boolean Algebra	$\bar{A}$	$\bar{B}$	$AB+\bar{A}\bar{B}$	$\bar{A}+\bar{B}$	$\bar{A}+B$	$A+\bar{B}$	$\bar{A}\bar{B}$

1.2 Circuit Analysis, Computer Science, and AI Applications

There has been extensive research, program implementation, and application areas using Boolean algebra. Here, we mention a few potential application areas of the Algebra of Boole and Boole Reduction.

In circuit analysis, the goal is often to determine the output based on the given inputs and gate configurations or to simplify the logic for efficient design and implementation [3,7]. Logic gates, which are devices that lay the basis for digital circuits, implement Boolean functions [11]. There are seven basic logic gates: AND, OR, XOR, NOT, NAND, NOR, and XNOR. Each Boolean operation corresponds to a physical logic gate in a circuit. Simplifying Boole expressions means fewer gates, which saves power, space, and cost in circuit design.

Computer Science deals with computer hardware, computer programming, and efficiency [1,6]. Boolean algebra has played a fundamental role in this field. The new framework, Algebra of Boole, and logic reduction could find applications in hardware and software verifications, machine proofs, and Boolean satisfiability (SAT) problems [4]. In AI-driven reasoning systems and applications, many inferences are made based on hypotheses and knowledge bases [5,8,10]. The ability to reduce complex logic expressions allows AI systems to make faster and more efficient inferences and reason through the possibilities more quickly. AI models also use logic in decision trees and logic-based AI, as it allows for the navigation of complex scenarios. As AI continues to evolve and tackle increasingly complex problems, the role of Boole Reduction in optimizing logic-based systems will continue to grow in importance, facilitating more effective AI solutions.

2 Reduction and Algorithm in the Algebra of Boole

Though the Algebra of Boole is a better framework than Boolean algebra, an efficient algorithm and implementation for Boole Reduction are necessary to apply the Algebra of Boole in practical application areas. In the first such implementation [9], the logic expression is converted to the Boole expression first. The program then employs expand() function from SymPy, a symbolic mathematics library, to transform the expression to be a sum of monomials(terms) and perform reduction for each monomial. This approach is computationally intensive and is thus referred to as the "Brute-force" method.

While the Brute-force method is useful in Boole Reduction for logic expression reduction, it can face problems when there are many inference steps in the area such as long AI reasoning and machine proof. For example, with the following type of logic expression:

$$(a \rightarrow b)\&(b \rightarrow c)(c \rightarrow d)(d \rightarrow e)(e \rightarrow f)\cdots$$

Its corresponding Boole expression would be:

$$(1 + a + ab)(1 + b + bc)(1 + c + cd)(1 + d + de)(1 + e + ef)\cdots$$

Let size n indicate the number of implication ($\rightarrow$) symbols or number of steps of inference. The number of terms generated after expansion grows at a rate close to 3^n. In other words, when $n = 18$, there would be around 3^{18}, or 387420489, expanded monomials before reduction. The computation time increases exponentially as $O(3^n)$. Such exponential factor causes the computation time to process large logic expressions to grow rapidly as n increases.

To overcome this rapid increase in computational time, a New Algorithm (**BRP**) is proposed in this paper and implemented in Python. The core idea is to partition the Boole expression into groups of sub-expressions. For example, the Boole expression $(1+a+ab)(1+b+bc)(1+c+cd)(1+d+de)(1+e+ef)(1+f+fg)$ could be partitioned into two groups $(1 + a + ab)(1 + b + bc)(1 + c + cd)$ and $(1+d+de)(1+e+ef)(1+f+fg)$, which are then reduced incrementally. In this way, the number of expanded monomials can usually be kept in a relatively small size. The following outlines the Key Boole Properties used in the algorithm:

Key Boole Properties:

1. Idempotence (Any Boolean variable multiplied by itself is equal to the variable, removing redundancy): $A^2 = A$
2. Complementarity: $A(1 + A) = 0$ or $A + A = 0$

By using Key Boole Properties, any Boole expressions can be reduced to the canonical form. For example, Modus Ponens, which states $(p\&(p \rightarrow q)) \rightarrow q$, the correspondent Boole expression and reduction is as follows:

$$
\begin{aligned}
&(1 + (p((1 + p + pq))) + (p((1 + p + pq)))q) \quad \texttt{(Boole conversion)}\\
=&1 + p + pp + ppq + (p + pp + ppq)q \quad \texttt{(Algera)}\\
=&1 + p + p + pq + pq + ppq + ppqq \quad \texttt{(Using Idempotence property)}\\
=&1 + p + p + pq + pq + pq + pq \quad \texttt{(Using Complementarity)}\\
=&1
\end{aligned}
$$

Algorithm 1 shows the Boole Reduction with Partition (BRP), the new algorithm for reducing Logic expressions.

Algorithm 1: Boole Reduction with Partition (BRP)

Input: Logic expression E, minimum partition size n_{Minimum}
Output: Canonical Boole expression E_c

Parse the logic expression E and convert it to a Boole expression E_b using Table 1 (Comparison of Algebra of Boole and Boolean Algebra).
Partition E_b into groups of sub-expressions $E_1, E_2, \ldots, E_n$ such that each E_i has a string length $\geq n_{\text{Minimum}}$ for $i \in [1, n-1]$, ensuring balanced parentheses.
Initialize $E_c \leftarrow \emptyset$.
for $i \leftarrow 1$ **to** n **do**
    Append E_i to E_c, expanding E_c to a sum of monomials.
    Apply Boole reduction on the monomials in E_c using Key Boole Properties.
Reorder the monomials in E_c to obtain the canonical form.

Remark 1: The algorithm could easily be adapted to perform parallel and recursive reduction of neighboring groups after partition of Boole expressions, potentially bringing more performance gains, especially for very large expressions in AI, SAT solving, and symbolic computation.

Remark 2: All propositional formulas can be converted to Conjunctive Normal Form (CNF), which is a standard format for logic simplification, SAT solving, and digital design. Using De Morgan's laws, implications and negations can be transformed into conjunctions and disjunctions. For instance, $(A \rightarrow B)$ becomes $(\sim A|B)$. These rules allow even complex formulas to be rewritten as a conjunction (&) of disjunctions (|). For satisfiability problems, any formula can be further transformed into 3-CNF (clauses with exactly three literals) by introducing auxiliary variables through techniques such as Tseitin Encoding.

3 Results and Discussion

The Boole reduction algorithm, with the computer program, successfully simplifies large and complex input logic expressions to their minimal forms by applying the New Algorithm. The following example demonstrates how the program processes and reduces Boole expressions:

One of the most important logical principles in mathematical proof and scientific reasoning is Modus Ponens, which states $(p\&(p \to q)) \to q$. Using the program, this expression simplifies to 1, confirming that the logical inference holds. The following is the Python program's prompt, input, and output.

- Entered logic expression: $(p\&(p \to q)) \to q$
- Boole expression:$(1 + (p((1 + p + pq))) + (p((1 + p + pq)))q)$
- Reduced Boole expression: 1

Logical inference is also a critical part of AI reasoning and knowledge representation. Consider Lewis Carroll's logical puzzle [12]:

i: `it is interesting`	m: `it is modern`	y: `it is your poem`
p: `it is popular`	a: `it is affected`	s: `it is about bubbles`

Given the hypotheses:

$$i \to p, m \to a, y \to s, a \to\sim p, \sim m \to\sim s,$$

can one conclude that "your poem is not interesting" $(y \to\sim i)$? After this inference is inputted into the program, the output is 1, which affirms that "your poem is not interesting," confirming the validity of the conclusion.

- Entered logic expression: $((i \to p)\&(m \to a)\&(y \to s)\&(a \to (\sim p))\&((\sim m) \to (\sim s))) \to (y \to (\sim i))$
- Boole expression: $(1+(((1+i+ip))((1+m+ma))((1+y+ys))((1+a+a((1+p))))((1+((1+m))+((1+m))((1+s)))))+(((1+i+ip))((1+m+ma))((1+y+ys))((1+a+a((1+p))))((1+((1+m))+((1+m))((1+s)))))((1+y+y((1+i)))))$
- Reduced Boole expression: 1

In real-world applications, knowledge bases can consist of hundreds of logical hypotheses,making inference an exceedingly complex task beyond human capability. Traditional methods of reasoning struggle with this scale, but by utilizing the Algebra of Boole and Boole Reduction program, logical inference is transformed into a purely algebraic and computational process. AI systems can perform logic reduction to provide the inference answer within seconds, highlighting how it is a powerful tool for applications in automated reasoning, expert systems, and complex decision-making processes.

Calculation time is incorporated in a complex test case, which contains a large number of terms and reductions throughout the process. Table 2 shows the Brute-Force and new algorithm **BRP** calculation times for Boole reduction, where the size n indicates the number of implication $(\to)$ symbols or number

Table 2. Comparison of Brute-Force and Optimized Algorithm Calculation Times for Boolean Reduction as Size n Increases

Size n	Brute-force Time (sec)	New Algorithm Time (sec)
6	0.11	0.068
7	0.25	0.24
8	0.62	0.64
9	1.72	1.11
10	4.81	1.45
11	13.86	2.37
12	39.68	5.10
13	108.74	13.12
18	1803.64	114.19

Table 3. Comparison of Brute-Force and Optimized Algorithm Calculation Times for Boolean Reduction as Number of Clauses Increases

<table>
<tr><th>Number of Clauses</th><th>Expression Used</th><th>Brute-force Time (sec)</th><th>New Algorithm Time (sec)</th></tr>
<tr><td>6</td><td>(~a) & (b | (~c)) & (d | e | (~f)) & ((~g) | h | i) & (j | (~b)) & (c | d | (~e))</td><td>1.00</td><td>0.57</td></tr>
<tr><td>7</td><td>((~a) | b | c) & (d | (~e)) & ((~f) | g) & (h | i | (~j)) & ((~b) | a) & (c | d | (~f)) & ((~g) | h)</td><td>7.56</td><td>1.26</td></tr>
<tr><td>8</td><td>(a | (~b)) & (c | d | (~e)) & ((~f) | g | h) & (i | j) & ((~b) | a | (~c)) & ((~d) | e) & (f | g | (~h)) & ((~i) | j)</td><td>16.64</td><td>1.47</td></tr>
<tr><td>9</td><td>((~a) | b | c) & ((~d) | e) & (f | g | (~h)) & ((~i) | j) & (a | (~b)) & ((~c) | d | e) & (f | (~g)) & ((~h) | i) & (j | a | (~b))</td><td>100.89</td><td>2.29</td></tr>
<tr><td>10</td><td>(~a) & (b | (~c)) & (d | e | (~f)) & ((~g) | h | i | j) & (a | (~b)) & (c | d | (~e)) & ((~h) | i) & (f | (~g) | (~h)) & (j | (~a) | b | (~c)) & ((~i) | (~j))</td><td>208.68</td><td>6.30</td></tr>
</table>

of steps of inference; therefore, the entered expression is $(a \to b)$ when $n = 1$. It follows that when $n = 6$, the logic expression is $(a \to b)\&(b \to c)\&(c \to d)\&(d \to e)\&(e \to f)\&(f \to g)$. This case is particularly important for machine proofs since mathematical proofs often contain hundreds of steps, many of which involve implications. All experiments were conducted on a personal MacBook Pro without GPU acceleration.

The new algorithm **BRP** shows a more controlled and gradual increase in computation time. In many cases, the number of intermediate terms in the reduction iteration is much smaller compared to the expansion terms, which leads to the speedup being significant.

To further test its performance, we use a second case involving horizontal clause expansion, with expressions in conjunctive normal form (CNF) randomly generated by large language models. Each expression is a conjunction of clauses built from variables "a" to "j" using various logical operators. This structure reflects typical Boolean conditions in software, SAT solving, and circuit verification. As shown in Table 3, unlike the brute-force method, **BRP** scales efficiently as the number of clauses increases from 6 to 10.

4 Conclusion and Future Research

The fast algorithm for Boole reduction in the framework of the Algebra of Boole has been successfully developed and implemented in Python. The program simplifies complex logic expressions to canonical forms, demonstrating its effectiveness. Specifically, the New Algorithm showed magnitudes of speedups in Boole reduction than the Brute-force approach. Potential applications include propositional logic, AI reasoning and integrated circuit designs.

Based on the success of this research, we hope to stimulate more research and algorithm innovation in the Algebra of Boole framework. Future developments could incorporate Boole Reduction into machine learning models, which could augment AI systems' reasoning capabilities and automate logic analysis.

Acknowledgements. I would like to thank my mentor, Dr. Lenore Blum, for valuable advice and discussions during the research process. I also appreciate Yueqing Luo for sharing his method of implementation and Dr. Marcus Jaiclin for encouraging me.

References

1. Complexity and Real Computation. Springer, New York (1998). https://doi.org/10.1007/978-1-4612-0701-6_23
2. Boole, G.: The mathematical analysis of logic. Macmillan (1847)
3. Brayton, R. K., Hachtel, G. D., McMullen, C., Sangiovanni-Vincentelli, A.: Logic minimization algorithms for VLSI synthesis, vol. 2. Springer Science & Business Media (1984)
4. Cook, S.A.: The complexity of theorem-proving procedures. In: Proceedings of the Third Annual ACM Symposium on Theory of Computing (STOC), pp. 151–158 (1971)
5. Darwiche, A.: Three modern roles for logic in AI. In: Proceedings of the 39th ACM SIGMOD-SIGACT-SIGAI Symposium on Principles of Database Systems (PODS'20). Association for Computing Machinery (2020)
6. Knuth, D.E.: Chapter 7.2.2.2: Satisfiability. In: The Art of Computer Programming, vol. 4B, Combinatorial algorithms, Part 2), pp. 185–369. Addison-Wesley Professional (2022)
7. Mano, M.M., Kime, C.: R. Logic and computer design fundamentals (4th new international ed.). Pearson Education Limited, p. 54 (2014)
8. McCarthy, J.: Programs with common sense. In: Proceedings of the Teddington Conference on the Mechanization of Thought Processes (1959)

9. Luo, Y.: Algebra of Boole (2024). https://github.com/shanyoumu461/Algebra-of-Boole
10. Russell, S., Norvig, P.: Artificial Intelligence: A Modern Approach, 3rd edn. Prentice-Hall, Upper Saddle River (2010)
11. Shannon, C.E.: A Symbolic Analysis of Relay and Switching Circuits. Trans. Am. Inst. Electr. Eng. **57**, 713–723 (1938)
12. Wildberger, N.J.: Boole reduction: a challenge for programmers — Math-Foundations 269 [Video]. (2019). YouTube. https://youtu.be/AJr44JgbKho?feature=shared

Specification and Verification

Logics for Kleene Algebra with Modal Operators: Kripke-Completeness and FMP

Yiheng Wang[1(✉)] and Yudi Ding[2]

[1] Institute of Logic and Cognition, Sun Yat-sen University, Guangzhou 510275, China
ianwang747@gmail.com

[2] Department of Philosophy, Xiamen University, Xiamen 361005, China

Abstract. This paper studies two kinds of logics for Kleene algebra with modal operators inspired by two different research traditions: positive modal logic and algebraic studies of rough set theory. We show the Kripke-completeness of some logics in the former approach using the canonical model method. We also prove the finite model property of some logics in the other using an algebraic proof-theoretical method.

Keywords: Kleene algebra with modal operators · Kripke-completeness · finite model property · algebraic rough set theory · positive modal logic

1 Introduction

A Kleene algebra[1] is a structure $(A, \wedge, \vee, \sim, 0, 1)$ where $(A, \wedge, \vee, 0, 1)$ is a bounded distributive lattice and $\sim$ is a Kleene negation: satisfying for any $a, b \in A$, (K1) $\sim(a \vee b) = \sim a \wedge \sim b$, (K2) $\sim\sim a = a$, (K3) $\sim 0 = 1$, and (K4) $a \wedge \sim a \leq b \vee \sim b$. If we drop (K4), one obtains a quasi-Boolean algebra (also known as De Morgan algebra, cf. [3,16]). Various algebraic and logical works have been conducted on this structure (cf. [5,6,11,12,14]). Kleene algebra can be regarded as the algebraic basis for the theory of inexact classes (cf. [6]). Kumar and Banerjee [12] also introduced rough set-theoretical semantics and representation for this structure. If modal operators $\Box, \Diamond$ are added, one obtains Kleene algebra with modal operators. However, there are two different ways of adding modal operators: one comes from the tradition of positive modal logic (cf. [9]); the other comes from the algebraic studies of rough set theory (cf. [17]). This paper will study two kinds of logics for Kleene algebra with modal operators arising from these two different but related approaches.

Y. Wang and Y. Ding—Both authors contributed equally to this work and should be considered as co-first authors.

[1] There is another "Kleene algebra" in the study of regular expressions and program semantics (cf. [19]). However, this paper uses this terminology to denote a particular extension of quasi-Boolean algebra, following the study tradition of [1,4,5,12].

M. Bonsangue and Y. Chen (Eds.): AILA 2025, CCIS 2668, pp. 203–210, 2026.
https://doi.org/10.1007/978-981-95-8262-4_16

The positive modal logic K_+ is K without negation [9]. Its algebraic counterpart, the positive modal algebra, is a bounded distributive lattice satisfying (P1)-(P3) in Definition 1. (P3)'s interaction axioms are essential for relational semantics. Consequently, the first modal extension of Kleene algebra enriches it with $\Box, \Diamond$ satisfying (P1)-(P3), defining a modal Kleene algebra (Definition 1). In algebra studies of rough set theory, modal extensions of quasi-Boolean algebras are used to model structures abstracted from applying rough set to knowledge representation [17]. The approximation space algebra induced from Pawlak's rough set yields the concept of topological quasi-Boolean algebra [2]: a quasi-Boolean algebra with $\Box, \Diamond$ satisfying (P1), (P2), (T) ($\Box a \leq a \leq \Diamond a$), and (4) ($\Box a \leq \Box\Box a$, $\Diamond\Diamond a \leq \Diamond a$). Dropping (T) and (4) gives a semi-topological quasi-Boolean algebra (cf. [18, Definition 2.3]). Since Kleene algebras extend quasi-Boolean algebras, their modal extension adds $\Box, \Diamond$ satisfying only (P1) and (P2), defining a semi-topological Kleene algebra (Sect. 3).

The contributions of this paper are twofold. On one hand, We establish relational semantics for modal Kleene algebra logics via compatibility frames (based on Dunn's perp semantics [8]), adding order-relation constraints (cf. Definition 3 (R1,R2)) to existing frame conditions for (K2)–(K4) [10,12]. Discrete duality is shown for KMK (cf. Theorem 1). Then we use the canonical model method to prove completeness for KMK and some extensions (cf. Theorem 3). On the other hand, we prove the finite model property (FMP) for logics of semi-topological Kleene algebra and its extensions (cf. Theorem 4), constructing finite counter-algebras via an algebraic proof-theoretical method (cf. e.g. [13]). We should clarify that $\Box$ and $\Diamond$ are not De Morgan duals in (1) (due to perp semantics), but are treated as duals in (2) since relational semantics are unavailable.

2 Logics for Modal Kleene Algebras

In this section, we introduce sequential logics for modal Kleene algebras. We then establish its relational semantics with discrete duality. By using the canonical model method, we obtain the Kripke-completeness for some logics.

Definition 1. *An algebra structure* $\mathbf{A} = (A, \wedge, \vee, \sim, \Box, \Diamond, 0, 1)$ *is a* modal Kleene algebra *(MKA) if* $(A, \wedge, \vee, \sim, 0, 1)$ *is a Kleene algebra and* $\Box, \Diamond$ *are unary operations satisfying the followings: for any* $a, b \in A$, (P1) $\Box 1 = 1$ *and* $\Diamond 0 = 0$, (P2) $\Box(a \wedge b) = \Box a \wedge \Box b$ *and* $\Diamond(a \vee b) = \Diamond a \vee \Diamond b$, (P3) $\Box a \wedge \Diamond b \leq \Diamond(a \wedge b)$ *and* $\Box(a \vee b) \leq \Box a \vee \Diamond b$. *Let* **MKA** *be the variety of all MKAs.*

The *set of formulas* $\mathscr{F}$ is defined as follows: $\mathscr{F} \ni \alpha ::= p \mid \bot \mid (\alpha_1 \wedge \alpha_2) \mid {\sim}\alpha \mid \Box\alpha \mid \Diamond\alpha$ where $p \in \mathbf{Var}$, a countable set of variables. Let $\top := {\sim}\bot$ and $\alpha_1 \vee \alpha_2 := {\sim}({\sim}\alpha_1 \wedge {\sim}\alpha_2)$. For $n \geq 0$ and $\ddagger \in \{\Box, \Diamond, \sim\}$, let $\ddagger^n\alpha$ be the formula defined by $\ddagger^0\alpha = \alpha$ and $\ddagger^{n+1}\alpha = \ddagger\ddagger^n\alpha$. A *basic sequent* is an expression of the form $\alpha \Rightarrow \beta$ where $\alpha, \beta \in \mathscr{F}$. Let s, t etc. denote any basic sequents, and $\mathcal{BS}$ denote the *set of all basic sequents*.

Definition 2. *A* modal Kleene sequential logic *(MKL) is a set* L *of basic sequents satisfying the following conditions:*

(1) *L contains all instances of the following axiom schemata:*

(ID) $\alpha \Rightarrow \alpha$ (⊤) $\alpha \Rightarrow \top$ (⊥) $\bot \Rightarrow \alpha$ (DIS) $\alpha \wedge (\beta \vee \gamma) \Rightarrow (\alpha \wedge \beta) \vee (\alpha \wedge \gamma)$ (KL) $\alpha \wedge {\sim}\alpha \Rightarrow \beta \vee {\sim}\beta$

(DN1) $\alpha \Rightarrow {\sim\sim}\alpha$ (DN2) ${\sim\sim}\alpha \Rightarrow \alpha$ ($\mathrm{K}_\Box$) $\Box\alpha \wedge \Box\beta \Rightarrow \Box(\alpha \wedge \beta)$ ($\mathrm{K}_\Diamond$) $\Diamond(\alpha \vee \beta) \Rightarrow \Diamond\alpha \vee \Diamond\beta$

($\mathrm{N}_\Box$) $\top \Rightarrow \Box\top$ ($\mathrm{N}_\Diamond$) $\Diamond\bot \Rightarrow \bot$ ($\mathrm{I}_\Box$) $\Box\alpha \wedge \Diamond\beta \Rightarrow \Diamond(\alpha \wedge \beta)$ ($\mathrm{I}_\Diamond$) $\Box(\alpha \vee \beta) \Rightarrow \Box\alpha \vee \Diamond\beta$

(2) *L is closed under the following rules: for* $i \in \{1, 2\}$,

$$\frac{\alpha_i \Rightarrow \beta}{\alpha_1 \wedge \alpha_2 \Rightarrow \beta}(\wedge\mathrm{L}) \quad \frac{\alpha \Rightarrow \beta_1 \quad \alpha \Rightarrow \beta_2}{\alpha \Rightarrow \beta_1 \wedge \beta_2}(\wedge\mathrm{R}) \quad \frac{\alpha \Rightarrow \beta}{{\sim}\beta \Rightarrow {\sim}\alpha}(\mathrm{CP}) \quad \frac{\alpha \Rightarrow \chi \quad \chi \Rightarrow \beta}{\alpha \Rightarrow \beta}(\mathrm{CUT})$$

$$\frac{{\sim}\alpha_1 \Rightarrow \beta \quad {\sim}\alpha_2 \Rightarrow \beta}{{\sim}(\alpha_1 \wedge \alpha_2) \Rightarrow \beta}({\sim}\wedge\mathrm{L}) \quad \frac{\alpha \Rightarrow {\sim}\beta_i}{\alpha \Rightarrow {\sim}(\beta_1 \wedge \beta_2)}({\sim}\wedge\mathrm{R}) \quad \frac{\alpha \Rightarrow \beta}{\Box\alpha \Rightarrow \Box\beta}(\mathrm{M}_\Box) \quad \frac{\alpha \Rightarrow \beta}{\Diamond\alpha \Rightarrow \Diamond\beta}(\mathrm{M}_\Diamond)$$

(3) *L is closed under substitution: if* $\alpha \Rightarrow \beta \in L$, *then* $\alpha^\sigma \Rightarrow \beta^\sigma \in L$ *for any* σ.

A basic sequent s is *derivable* in L (written $\vdash_L s$) if $s \in L$. We write $\alpha \Leftrightarrow \beta$ if $\vdash_L \alpha \Rightarrow \beta$ and $\vdash_L \beta \Rightarrow \alpha$. Let KMK be the smallest MKL. A MKL L is *consistent* if $L \neq \mathcal{BS}$.

Lemma 1. *For every MKL L, the following hold: (1)* $\vdash {\sim}(\alpha\wedge\beta) \Leftrightarrow {\sim}\alpha\vee{\sim}\beta$ *and* $\vdash {\sim}(\alpha\vee\beta) \Leftrightarrow {\sim}\alpha\wedge{\sim}\beta$. *(2)* $\vdash \alpha \Leftrightarrow {\sim\sim}\alpha$ *and* $\vdash \alpha\vee(\beta\wedge\gamma) \Leftrightarrow (\alpha\vee\beta)\wedge(\alpha\vee\gamma)$. *(3) If* $\vdash \alpha \Rightarrow \beta$, *then* $\vdash \Diamond\alpha \Rightarrow \Diamond\beta$ *and* $\vdash \Box\alpha \Rightarrow \Box\beta$. *(4)* $\vdash \Box\top \Leftrightarrow \top$ *and* $\vdash \Diamond\bot \Leftrightarrow \bot$. *(5)* $\vdash \Box(\alpha \wedge \beta) \Leftrightarrow \Box\alpha \wedge \Box\beta$ *and* $\vdash \Diamond(\alpha \vee \beta) \Leftrightarrow \Diamond\alpha \vee \Diamond\beta$.

Let $\mathbf{A}$ be a MKA. An *assignment* in $\mathbf{A}$ is a homomorphism $\theta : \mathscr{F} \to A$. A basic sequent $\alpha \Rightarrow \beta$ is *true* in $\mathbf{A}$ (written $\mathbf{A}, \theta \models \alpha \Rightarrow \beta$) for an assignment θ if $\theta(\alpha) \leq \theta(\beta)$ in $\mathbf{A}$. A basic sequent s is *valid* in $\mathbf{A}$ (written $\mathbf{A} \models s$) if it is true for all assignment. A basic sequent s is *valid* in a class of algebras (written $\mathbf{C} \models s$) if it is valid in every algebra of that class. Now we turn to relational semantics and Kripke-completeness. For any binary relations R and S, the *composition* of R and S is $S \circ R$ s.t. $(x, y) \in S \circ R$ iff there is a z, xRz and zSy.

Definition 3. *A* modal Kleene frame *is a* 4*-tuple* $\mathfrak{F} = (W, C, \leq, R)$ *where* $(W, \leq)$ *is a non-empty partially ordered set, and* C, R *are binary relations on* W *satisfying the following conditions:* (C1)$\forall w\forall u\forall w'\forall u'((w' \leq w \wedge u' \leq u \wedge wCu) \to w'Cu')$, (C2)$\forall w\forall u(wCu \to uCw)$, (C3)$\forall w\exists u(wCu \wedge \forall v(uCv \to v \leq w)$, (C4)$\forall w(wCw \vee \forall u(wCu \to u \leq w))$, (R1)$(R\circ \leq) \subseteq (\leq \circ R)$, *and* (R2)$(\leq \circ R^{-1}) \subseteq (R^{-1}\circ \leq)$.

For any $w \in W$, let $R(w) = \{u : wRu\}$ and $C(w) = \{u : wCu\}$, respectively. A *compatibility frame* is a triple $(W, \leq, C)$ satisfying (C1) (cf. [8]) Note that by (C3), $C(w) \neq \varnothing$ for any w. A valuation in $\mathfrak{F} = (W, C, \leq, R)$ is a function $V : Var \to UP(2^W)$ where $UP(2^W)$ is the set of all upward-closed subsets of W w.r.t. $\leq$. A *modal Kleene model* is a tuple $\mathfrak{M} = (\mathfrak{F}, V)$ where $\mathfrak{F}$ is a modal Kleene frame and V is a valuation. Clearly, V satisfies the *hereditary condition*: If $w \in V(p)$ and $w \leq u$, then $u \in V(p)$, for any $w, u \in W$. Homomorphically, V can be extended to $\mathscr{F}$ and the *truth set* for any formula is defined as follows: for any $w, u \in W$, $V(\bot) = \varnothing, V(\alpha \wedge \beta) = V(\alpha) \cap V(\beta), V({\sim}\alpha) =$

$\sim_C V(\alpha), V(\Box\alpha) = \Box_R V(\alpha), V(\Diamond\alpha) = \Diamond_R V(\alpha)$ where $\sim_C, \Box_R. \Diamond_R$ are defined as follows: $\sim_C(X) = \{w \in W : C(w) \cap X = \varnothing\}, \Box_R(X) = \{w \in W : R(w) \subseteq X\}, \Diamond_R(X) = \{w \in W : R(w) \cap X \neq \varnothing\}$. For any MKL-frame $\mathfrak{F}$, let $\mathfrak{F}^+ = (UP(2^W), \cap, \cup, \sim_C, \Box_R, \Diamond_R, \varnothing, W)$. Let $\mathfrak{M} = (\mathfrak{F}, V)$ be a modal Kleene model. A formula α is *true at w in M* (written $\mathfrak{M}, w \models \alpha$) if $w \in V(\alpha)$. For any basic sequent $\alpha \Rightarrow \beta$, it is *true at w in $\mathfrak{M}$* if $\mathfrak{M}, w \models \alpha$ implies $\mathfrak{M}, w \models \beta$ i.e. $w \notin V(\alpha)$ or $w \in V(\beta)$. Definitions related to validity shall follow naturally (cf. e.g. [9]). The *sequential theory of $\mathcal{K}$* is defined as the set $\mathsf{Th}(\mathcal{K}) = \{s \in \mathcal{BS} : \mathcal{K} \models s\}$. Let $\mathsf{Fr}(\mathcal{T}) = \{\mathfrak{F} : \mathfrak{F} \models \mathcal{T}\}$. A MKL L is *Kripke-complete* if $L = \mathsf{Th}(\mathsf{Fr}(L))$. Now we turn to the discrete duality. For any MKA $\mathbf{A}$, let $PF(A)$ ($PI(A)$) be the set of all prime filters (prime ideals) of $\mathbf{A}$. For any subset $B \subseteq A$, let $\ddagger^{-1}(B) = \{a : \ddagger a \in B\}$ and $\sim(B) = \{\sim a \in A : a \in B\}$ where $\ddagger \in \{\Box, \Diamond, \sim\}$. For any $F, G \in PF(A)$, let $(F, G) \in C_A$ iff $\sim^{-1}(F) \subseteq \overline{G}$ and $(F, G) \in R_A$ iff $\Box^{-1}(F) \subseteq G \subseteq \Diamond^{-1}(F)$. Let $\mathbf{A}_+ = (PF(A), C_A, \subseteq, R_A)$.

Lemma 2. *Let $(A, \wedge, \vee, \sim, \Box, \Diamond, 0, 1)$ be a MKA and $F \in PF(A)$. Then (1) $\Box a \in F$ iff for all $G \in PF(A)$, FR_AG implies $a \in G$; (2) $\Diamond a \in F$ iff there exists $G \in PF(A)$, FR_AG and $a \in G$.*

Proof. For (1), the left-to-right part is trivial. Conversely, suppose $\Box a \notin F$. Let I be the ideal generated by $\{a\} \cup \overline{\Diamond^{-1}(F)}$. Suppose $c \in \Box^{-1}(F) \cap I$, then $\Box c \in F$. Then $c \leq a \vee b$ for some $b \in \overline{\Diamond^{-1}(F)}$. Clearly $\Box c \leq \Box(a \vee b) \leq \Box a \vee \Diamond b$. Since $\Box a, \Diamond b \notin F$, $\Box a \vee \Diamond b \notin F$. Then $\Box c \notin F$, which is a contradiction. Thus $\Box^{-1}(F) \cap I = \varnothing$. By the Prime Filter Theorem for Bounded Distributive Lattice (cf. [7, pp. 235–236]), there is a $G \supseteq \Box^{-1}(F)$ s.t. $G \cap I = \varnothing$. Then for any $b \notin \Diamond^{-1}(F)$, $a \vee b \notin G$ and thus $a \notin G$. Therefore, there is a $G \in PF(A)$ s.t. $\Box^{-1}(F) \subseteq G \subseteq \Diamond^{-1}(F)$ and $a \notin G$. For (2), it can be treated similarly to (1) by $\Box a \wedge \Diamond b \leq \Diamond(a \wedge b)$.

Corollary 1. *(1) If $\Box^{-1}(F) \subseteq G$, then there is a $H \in PF(A)$ s.t. FR_AH and $H \subseteq G$; (2) If $G \subseteq \Diamond^{-1}(F)$, then there is a $H \in PF(A)$ s.t. FR_AH and $G \subseteq H$.*

Lemma 3. *The following hold: (1) $\mathfrak{F}^+$ is a MKA; (2) $\mathbf{A}_+$ is a MKL-frame.*

Theorem 1 (Discrete Duality). *(1) h is an embedding from $\mathbf{A}$ to $(\mathbf{A}_+)^+$ where $h(a) = \{F \in PF(A) : a \in F\}$. (2) k is an embedding from $\mathfrak{F}$ to $(\mathfrak{F}^+)_+$ where $k(w) = \{X \in UP(2^W) : w \in X\}$.*

Now we employ the canonical model method to show Kripke-completeness for KMK and some of its common modal extensions. For any MKL L, a set of formulas Γ is a *theory* of L if $\Gamma = \{\alpha \in \mathscr{F} : \Gamma \vdash_L \alpha\}$. Γ is *consistent* if $\bot \notin \Gamma$. Γ is a *prime theory* if it is a consistent theory and $\alpha \vee \beta \in \Gamma$ implies $\alpha \in \Gamma$ or $\beta \in \Gamma$. Let $PT(L)$ denote the set of all prime theories of L. Let $\ddagger^{-1}(\Gamma) = \{\alpha : \ddagger\alpha \in \Gamma\}$ where $\ddagger \in \{\Box, \Diamond, \sim\}$. A *dual theory* is a set of formulas $\Sigma = \{\alpha : \vdash \alpha \Rightarrow \bigvee \Delta\}$ where $\Delta \subseteq \Sigma$, a finite subset of Σ. Let L be a MKL, the *canonical model* of L is a 5-tuple $\mathfrak{M}^L = (W^L, \subseteq, C^L, R^L, V^L)$ defined as follows: for any $\Gamma, \Theta \in PT(L)$, (1) $W^L = PT(L)$, (2) $\Gamma C^L \Theta$ iff $\sim^{-1}(\Gamma) \subseteq \overline{\Theta}$, (3) $\Gamma R^L \Theta$ iff $\Box^{-1}(\Gamma) \subseteq \Theta \subseteq \Diamond^{-1}(\Gamma)$, and (4) $V^L(p) = \{\Gamma \in W^L : p \in \Gamma\}$ for any $p \in \mathbf{Var}$. The 4-tuple $\mathfrak{F}^L = (W^L, \subseteq, C^L, R^L)$ is the *canonical frame* of L.

Lemma 4. *For any $\Gamma \in PT(L)$, the followings hold: (1) $\Box\alpha \in \Gamma$ iff $\alpha \in \Theta$ for all $\Theta \in R^L(\Gamma)$; (2) $\Diamond\alpha \in \Gamma$ iff $\alpha \in \Theta$ for some $\Theta \in R^L(\Gamma)$; (3) If $\Box^{-1}(\Gamma) \subseteq \Theta$, then there is a $\Sigma \in PT(L)$ s.t. $\Gamma R^L \Sigma$ and $\Sigma \subseteq \Theta$; (4) If $\Theta \subseteq \Diamond^{-1}(\Gamma)$, then there is a $\Sigma \in PT(L)$ s.t. $\Gamma R^L \Sigma$ and $\Theta \subseteq \Sigma$.*

Lemma 5. *For any MKL L, the canonical frame $\mathfrak{F}^L$ is a MKL-frame.*

Lemma 6 (Truth Lemma). *For any formula $\alpha \in \mathscr{F}$, $\mathfrak{M}^L, \Gamma \models \alpha$ iff $\alpha \in \Gamma$.*

Theorem 2. *For any $\alpha \Rightarrow \beta$ and any MKL L, $\alpha \Rightarrow \beta \in L$ iff $\mathfrak{M}^L \models \alpha \Rightarrow \beta$.*

An MKL L is *canonical* if $\mathfrak{F}^L \models L$. A set of basic sequents $\mathcal{S}$ is *canonical* if for any MKL L, $\mathcal{S} \subseteq L$ implies L is canonical. Consider the following modal axioms: $(\mathrm{D}_\Box)$ $\top \Rightarrow {\sim}\Box\bot$; $(\mathrm{D}_\Diamond)$ $\top \Rightarrow \Diamond\top$; $(\mathrm{D}_\Box)$ $\Box p \Rightarrow p$; $(\mathrm{T}_\Diamond)$ $p \Rightarrow \Diamond p$; $(4_\Box)$ $\Box p \Rightarrow \Box\Box p$; $(4_\Diamond)$ $\Diamond\Diamond p \Rightarrow \Diamond p$; $(\mathrm{B}_\Box)$ $p \Rightarrow \Box\Diamond p$; $(\mathrm{B}_\Diamond)$ $\Diamond\Box p \Rightarrow p$; $(5_\Box)$ $\Diamond p \Rightarrow \Box\Diamond p$; $(5_\Diamond)$ $\Diamond\Box p \Rightarrow \Box p$. Further let $\mathsf{KMD} = \mathsf{KMK} \oplus (\mathrm{D}_\Box) \oplus (\mathrm{D}_\Diamond)$; $\mathsf{KMT} = \mathsf{KMK} \oplus (\mathrm{T}_\Box) \oplus (\mathrm{T}_\Diamond)$; $\mathsf{KM4} = \mathsf{KMK} \oplus (4_\Box) \oplus (4_\Diamond)$; $\mathsf{KMB} = \mathsf{KMK} \oplus (\mathrm{B}_\Box) \oplus (\mathrm{B}_\Diamond)$; $\mathsf{KM5} = \mathsf{KMK} \oplus (5_\Box) \oplus (5_\Diamond)$.

Lemma 7. *For any $\mathfrak{F} = (W, \leq, C, R)$, the followings hold: for any $w, u, v \in W$[2], (1) $\mathfrak{F} \models (\mathrm{D}_\Box) \wedge (\mathrm{D}_\Diamond)$ iff $R(w) \neq \varnothing$; (2) $\mathfrak{F} \models (\mathrm{T}_\Box) \wedge (\mathrm{T}_\Diamond)$ iff wRw; (3) $\mathfrak{F} \models (4_\Box) \wedge (4_\Diamond)$ iff wRu and uRv implies wRv; (4) $\mathfrak{F} \models (\mathrm{B}_\Box) \wedge (\mathrm{B}_\Diamond)$ iff wRu implies uRw; (5) $\mathfrak{F} \models (5_\Box) \wedge (5_\Diamond)$ iff wRu and wRv implies uRv or vRu.*

Theorem 3. KMK, KMD, KMT, KM4, KMB, *and* KM5 *are Kripke-complete.*

3 FMP for Logics of Semi-Topological Kleene Algebras

In this section, we move from the modal Kleene algebra to the semi-topological Kleene algebra. A *semi-topological Kleene algebra* (STKA) $(A, \wedge, \vee, {\sim}, \Diamond, 0, 1)$ is obtained by dropping (P3) of MKA defined in Definition 1. Let $\Box a := {\sim}\Diamond{\sim}a$ in any STKA and **STKA** be the variety of all STKAs. Let $\mathscr{F}' \ni \alpha ::= p \mid \bot \mid (\alpha_1 \wedge \alpha_2) \mid (\alpha_1 \vee \alpha_2) \mid {\sim}\alpha \mid \Diamond\alpha$ be the new language. Let $\top := {\sim}\bot$ and $\Box\alpha := {\sim}\Diamond{\sim}\alpha$. The smallest sequential logic for **STKA**, denoted by SK, is obtained from MKM by deleting $(\mathrm{I}_\Box)$ and $(\mathrm{I}_\Diamond)$[3]. Now we introduce a calculus equivalent to SK w.r.t. derivability but in a different style. We define the set of all formula structures $\mathscr{S}$ as: $\mathscr{S} \ni \circ^n(\alpha) ::= \alpha \mid \circ^n(\alpha)$ where $\alpha \in \mathscr{F}'$ and $n \geq 0$. Let $\circ^n(\alpha) = \circ(\circ^{n-1}(\alpha))$ and $\circ^0(\alpha) = \alpha$. A *sequent* is an expression of the form $\circ^n(\alpha) \Rightarrow \beta$ where $\circ^n(\alpha) \in \mathscr{S}$ and $\beta \in \mathscr{F}'$.

Definition 4. *The sequent calculus* GSK *for* **STKA** *consists of the following axioms and rules: for $n, m \geq 0$ and $i = \{1, 2\}$,*

$$(\mathrm{ID})\ \alpha \Rightarrow \alpha \quad (\mathrm{DIS})\ \alpha \wedge (\beta \vee \gamma) \Rightarrow (\alpha \wedge \beta) \vee (\alpha \wedge \gamma) \quad (\mathrm{KL})\ \alpha \wedge {\sim}\alpha \Rightarrow \beta \vee {\sim}\beta$$

$$(\top)\ \circ^n(\alpha) \Rightarrow \top \quad (\bot)\ \circ^n(\bot) \Rightarrow \beta \quad (\mathrm{DN1})\ \alpha \Rightarrow \neg\neg\alpha \quad (\mathrm{DN2})\ \neg\neg\alpha \Rightarrow \alpha$$

$$\frac{\alpha \Rightarrow \beta}{{\sim}\beta \Rightarrow {\sim}\alpha}(\mathrm{CP}) \quad \frac{\circ^n(\alpha_i) \Rightarrow \beta}{\circ^n(\alpha_1 \wedge \alpha_2) \Rightarrow \beta}(\wedge\Rightarrow) \quad \frac{\circ^n(\alpha) \Rightarrow \beta_1 \quad \circ^n(\alpha) \Rightarrow \beta_2}{\circ^n(\alpha) \Rightarrow \beta_1 \wedge \beta_2}(\Rightarrow\wedge) \quad \frac{\circ^n(\alpha_1) \Rightarrow \beta \quad \circ^n(\alpha_2) \Rightarrow \beta}{\circ^n(\alpha_1 \vee \alpha_2) \Rightarrow \beta}(\vee\Rightarrow)$$

$$\frac{\circ^n(\alpha) \Rightarrow \beta_i}{\circ^n(\alpha) \Rightarrow \beta_1 \vee \beta_2}(\Rightarrow\vee) \quad \frac{\circ^{n+1}(\alpha) \Rightarrow \beta}{\circ^n(\Diamond\alpha) \Rightarrow \beta}(\Diamond\Rightarrow) \quad \frac{\circ^n(\alpha) \Rightarrow \beta}{\circ^{n+1}(\alpha) \Rightarrow \Diamond\beta}(\Rightarrow\Diamond) \quad \frac{\circ^n(\alpha) \Rightarrow \beta \quad \circ^m(\beta) \Rightarrow \gamma}{\circ^{m+n}(\alpha) \Rightarrow \gamma}(\mathrm{Cut})$$

---

[2] Here $\mathfrak{F} \models (\mathrm{D}_\Box) \wedge (\mathrm{D}_\Diamond)$ means $\mathfrak{F} \models (\mathrm{D}_\Box)$ and $\mathfrak{F} \models (\mathrm{D}_\Diamond)$, and same for others.

[3] Since $\Box\alpha := {\sim}\Diamond{\sim}\alpha$, $(\mathrm{K}_\Box)$, $(\mathrm{N}_\Box)$, and $(\mathrm{M}_\Box)$ are actually redundant in SK.

The notations related to GSK are similar to those in Defintion 2. Observe that Lemma 1 also holds for GSK.

Lemma 8. *$\vdash_{\mathsf{GSK}} \alpha \Rightarrow \beta$ iff $\vdash_{\mathsf{SK}} \alpha \Rightarrow \beta$.*

Let $\mathbf{A} = (A, \sim, \Diamond)$ be a STKA. Similar to algebraic semantics for MKL, an assignment is a function $\theta : \mathscr{F}' \to \mathbf{A}$. A sequent $\vdash \circ^n(\alpha) \Rightarrow \beta$ is *true* in $\mathbf{A}$ with θ if $\Diamond^n\theta(\alpha) \leq \theta(\beta)$. The validity is defined accordingly. Observe that by an easy induction on the height of derivation, $\vdash \circ^n(\alpha) \Rightarrow \beta$ iff $\vdash \Diamond^n(\alpha) \Rightarrow \beta$. Let GSS4 be the S4-extensions of GSK by adding following rules: for $n \geq 0$,

$$\frac{\circ^{n+1}(\top) \Rightarrow \beta}{\circ^n(\top) \Rightarrow \beta}(\mathrm{D}) \quad \frac{\circ^{n+1}(\alpha) \Rightarrow \beta}{\circ^n(\alpha) \Rightarrow \beta}(\mathrm{T}) \quad \frac{\circ^{n+1}(\alpha) \Rightarrow \beta}{\circ^{n+2}(\alpha) \Rightarrow \beta}(4)$$

Let GSD, GST and GS4 be the D, T, and 4-extensions of GSK, respectively, obtained by adding the corresponding rule to GSK. We call the strongest algebra i.e. STKA satisfying $1 \leq \Diamond 1$, $a \leq \Diamond a$, and $\Diamond\Diamond a \leq \Diamond a$ the *topological Kleene algebra* (TKA).

Lemma 9. *(1) $\vdash_{\mathsf{GSD}} \top \Rightarrow \Diamond\top$; (2) $\vdash_{\mathsf{GST}} \alpha \Rightarrow \Diamond\alpha$; (3) $\vdash_{\mathsf{GS4}} \Diamond\Diamond\alpha \Rightarrow \Diamond\alpha$.*

Proof. We take (3) as an example. By ($\Rightarrow\Diamond$) on (ID), $\vdash \circ(\alpha) \Rightarrow \Diamond\alpha$. By rule (4), $\vdash \circ^2(\alpha) \Rightarrow \Diamond\alpha$. By ($\Diamond\Rightarrow$) twice, $\vdash \Diamond\Diamond\alpha \Rightarrow \Diamond\alpha$.

Now we show the FMP for GSK and its extensions with any combinations of D, T, and 4. Our proof strategy is to show that FMP holds for the strongest logic i.e. GSS4, then other weaker variants' proof can be obtained modularly by simply ignoring the irrelevant cases throughout the proof. We should show that if $\nvdash_{\mathsf{GSS4}} \circ^n(\alpha) \Rightarrow \beta$, then there is a finite TKA $\mathbf{A}$ s.t. $\mathbf{A} \not\models \circ^n(\alpha) \Rightarrow \beta$. For any set of formulas $\mathscr{T}$, a formula structure $\circ^n(\alpha)$ is a $\mathscr{T}$-formula structure if $\alpha \in \mathscr{T}$. Let $\mathscr{S}(\mathscr{T})$ be the set of all $\mathscr{T}$-formula structures. A sequent $\circ^n(\alpha) \Rightarrow \beta$ is a $\mathscr{T}$-sequent if $\alpha, \beta \in \mathscr{T}$. Let $\vdash \circ^n(\alpha) \Rightarrow_{\mathscr{T}} \beta$ denote the derivation of $\vdash \circ^n(\alpha) \Rightarrow \beta$ s.t. all sequents appearing in it are $\mathscr{T}$-sequents. For any set of formulas $\mathscr{T}$, let $c(\mathscr{T})$ denote the closure of $\mathscr{T}$ under $\{\bot, \wedge, \vee, \sim\}$ and taking subformulas. Throughout this section, let $\mathscr{T} = c(\mathscr{T})$.

Lemma 10 (Interpolation). *In GSS4, for any $n \geq 1, m \geq 0$, if $\vdash \circ^{m+n}(\alpha) \Rightarrow_{\mathscr{T}} \beta$, then there is a $\gamma \in \mathscr{T}$ s.t. $\vdash \circ^n(\alpha) \Rightarrow_{\mathscr{T}} \gamma$, $\vdash \circ^m(\gamma) \Rightarrow_{\mathscr{T}} \beta$, and $\vdash \circ(\gamma) \Rightarrow_{\mathscr{T}} \gamma$.*

Proof. Proofs are similar to [15, Lemma 5].

A formula $\alpha \in \mathscr{F}'$ is called a *letter* if $\alpha \in \mathbf{Var} \cup \{\top, \bot\}$ or $\alpha = \Diamond\beta$ for some $\beta \in \mathscr{F}'$. Let le be the set of all letters. A formula α is called a *literal* if $\alpha \in le$ or $\alpha = \sim\beta$ for some $\beta \in le$. Let li be the set of all literals. A formula is in *disjunctive normal form* (DNF) if it is of the form $\bigvee_{i \leq n} \bigwedge_{j \leq k} \varphi_{ij}$ where each $\varphi_{ij} \in li$. Let $\mathscr{T}_{li} \subseteq \mathscr{T}$ be the set of all literals in $\mathscr{T}$. $\mathscr{T}$ is *finitely based* if $\mathscr{T}_{li}$ is finite. Clearly, there is a DNF formula $\beta \in \mathscr{T}$ s.t. α is equivalent to β. Apart from the repetition, there exists a unique formula in DNF equivalent to α, which is denoted by $DNF_{\mathscr{T}}(\alpha)$. Let $DNF(\mathscr{T}) = \{DNF_{\mathscr{T}}(\alpha) \mid \alpha \in \mathscr{T}\}$. If $\mathscr{T}_{li}$

is finite, then $DNF(\mathscr{T})$ is finite. Observe that by Lemma 10, if $\vdash \circ^{n+m}(\alpha) \Rightarrow_{\mathscr{T}} \beta$, then there is a $\gamma \in DNF(\mathscr{T})$ s.t. $\vdash \circ^n(\alpha) \Rightarrow_{\mathscr{T}} \gamma$ and $\vdash \circ^m(\gamma) \Rightarrow_{\mathscr{T}} \beta$. Now we define an order on $\mathscr{S}(\mathscr{T})$: for any $\circ^n(\alpha), \circ^m(\beta) \in \mathscr{S}(\mathscr{T})$, $\circ^k(-)$, and $\varphi \in \mathscr{T}$:$\circ^n(\alpha) \trianglelefteq \circ^m(\beta)$ iff $\vdash \circ^k(\circ^m(\beta)) \Rightarrow_{\mathscr{T}} \varphi$ implies $\vdash \circ^k(\circ^n(\alpha)) \Rightarrow_{\mathscr{T}} \varphi$. Observe that $\trianglelefteq$ is a preorder i.e. reflexive and transitive. Let $\circ^n(\alpha) \approx_{\mathscr{T}} \circ^m(\beta)$ be $\circ^n(\alpha) \trianglelefteq \circ^m(\beta)$ and $\circ^m(\beta) \trianglelefteq \circ^n(\alpha)$. Clearly $\approx_{\mathscr{T}}$ is an equivalence relation. Let $[\alpha]_{\mathscr{T}} = \{\circ^m(\beta) \mid \circ^m(\beta) \approx_{\mathscr{T}} \alpha \;\&\; \circ^m(\beta) \in \mathscr{S}(\mathscr{T})\}$ and $[\mathscr{T}] = \{[\alpha]_{\mathscr{T}} \mid \alpha \in \mathscr{T})\}$. Since $[\alpha] = [DNF_{\mathscr{T}}(\alpha)]$ and the number of $[DNF_{\mathscr{T}}(\alpha)]$ is finite, $[\mathscr{T}]$ is finite.

Lemma 11. *For any $\circ(\alpha) \in \mathscr{S}(\mathscr{T})$, there is a $\beta \in DNF(\mathscr{T})$ s.t. $\circ(\alpha) \approx \beta$.*

Now we construct a quotient algebra. Let $\mathscr{T}$ be finitely based. The quotient algebra of $[\mathscr{T}]$ is a structure $\mathbf{Q} = ([\mathscr{T}], \wedge^\star, \vee^\star, \sim^\star, \Diamond^\star, \bot^\star, \top^\star)$ where operations $\bot^\star, \wedge^\star, \vee^\star, \sim^\star, \Diamond^\star$ in $[\mathscr{T}]$ are defined as: $\bot^\star = [\bot]_{\mathscr{T}}, \sim^\star[\alpha] = [\sim\alpha], [\alpha] \wedge^\star [\beta] = [\alpha \wedge \beta], [\alpha] \vee^\star [\beta] = [\alpha \vee \beta], \Diamond^\star[\alpha] = [\gamma]$ *s.t.* $\gamma \approx \circ(\alpha)$. where $\gamma = DNF_{\mathscr{T}}(\circ(\alpha))$. Let $[\alpha] \leq^\star [\beta]$ be defined as $[\alpha] \wedge^\star [\beta] = [\alpha]$ and $\top^* = \sim^* \bot^*$. By Lemma 11, $[\gamma]$ exists and is unique. Observe that the above operations are well-defined.

Lemma 12. *The followings are equivalent: (1) $\alpha \trianglelefteq \beta$; (2) $\vdash \alpha \Rightarrow_{\mathscr{T}} \beta$; (3) $[\alpha] \leq^\star [\beta]$.*

Lemma 13. *The following conditions hold for* $\mathbf{Q}$*: for any $[\alpha], [\beta], [\gamma] \in [\mathscr{T}]$,*

(1) $[\gamma] \leq^\star [\alpha] \wedge^\star [\beta]$ *iff* $[\gamma] \leq^\star [\alpha]$ *and* $[\gamma] \leq^\star [\beta]$.
(2) $[\alpha] \vee^\star [\beta] \leq^\star [\gamma]$ *iff* $[\alpha] \leq^\star [\gamma]$ *and* $[\beta] \leq^\star [\gamma]$.
(3) $[\alpha] \wedge^\star ([\beta] \vee^\star [\gamma]) = ([\alpha] \wedge^\star [\beta]) \vee^\star ([\alpha] \wedge^\star [\gamma])$.
(4) $\bot^\star \leq^\star [\alpha] \leq^\star \top^\star$, $\sim^\star\sim^\star[\alpha] = [\alpha]$, *and* $\sim^\star\bot^\star = \top^\star$.
(5) *If* $[\alpha] \leq^\star [\beta]$, *then* $\Diamond^\star[\alpha] \leq^\star \Diamond^\star[\beta]$.
(6) $\sim^\star([\alpha] \vee^\star [\beta]) = \sim^\star[\alpha] \wedge^\star \sim^\star[\beta]$ *and* $[\alpha] \wedge^\star \sim^\star[\alpha] \leq^\star [\beta] \vee^\star \sim^\star[\beta]$.
(7) $\Diamond^\star\bot^\star = \bot^\star$.
(8) $\Diamond^\star([\alpha] \vee [\beta]) = \Diamond^\star[\alpha] \vee \Diamond^\star[\beta]$.
(9) $[\alpha] \leq^\star \Diamond^\star[\alpha]$.
(10) $\top^\star \leq^\star \Diamond^\star\top^\star$.
(11) $\Diamond^\star\Diamond^\star[\alpha] \leq^\star \Diamond^\star[\alpha]$.

Proof. Items (1)-(4) and (6) are shown easily by Lemma 12 and Lemma 9. For (5), suppose $[\alpha] \leq^\star [\beta]$. Let $\Diamond^\star[\alpha] = [\gamma_1]$ and $\Diamond^\star[\beta] = [\gamma_2]$ s.t. $\circ(\alpha) \approx \gamma_1$ and $\circ(\beta) \approx \gamma_2$. By Lemma 12, $\vdash \alpha \Rightarrow_{\mathscr{T}} \beta$ and $\vdash \circ(\beta) \Rightarrow_{\mathscr{T}} \gamma_2$. By (Cut), $\vdash \circ(\alpha) \Rightarrow_{\mathscr{T}} \gamma_2$. Therefore, $\Diamond^\star[\alpha] \leq^\star \Diamond^\star[\beta]$. For (7), suppose $\Diamond^\star[\bot] = [\gamma]$ s.t. $\circ(\bot) \approx \gamma$. By ($\bot$), $\vdash \circ(\bot) \Rightarrow_{\mathscr{T}} \bot$. Then $\vdash \gamma \Rightarrow_{\mathscr{T}} \bot$ and by Lemma 12, $\Diamond^\star\bot^\star \leq^\star \bot^\star$. The other direction is easy to check. For (8), suppose $\Diamond^\star[\alpha] = [\theta_1]$, $\Diamond^\star[\beta] = [\theta_2]$, and $\Diamond^\star[\alpha \vee \beta] = [\theta_3]$ s.t. $\circ(\alpha) \approx \theta_1$, $\circ(\beta) \approx \theta_2$, and $\circ(\alpha \vee \beta) \approx \theta_3$. By Lemma 12, (i) $\vdash \circ(\alpha) \Rightarrow_{\mathscr{T}} \theta_1$, (ii) $\vdash \circ(\beta) \Rightarrow_{\mathscr{T}} \theta_2$, and (iii) $\vdash \circ(\alpha \vee \beta) \Rightarrow_{\mathscr{T}} \theta_3$. By ($\vee\Rightarrow$) and ($\Rightarrow\vee$) on (i) and (ii), $\vdash \circ(\alpha \vee \beta) \Rightarrow_{\mathscr{T}} \theta_1 \vee \theta_2$. Thus $\circ(\alpha \vee \beta) \trianglelefteq \theta_1 \vee \theta_2$. Since $\theta_3 \trianglelefteq \circ(\alpha \vee \beta)$ and $\trianglelefteq$ is transitive, $\theta_3 \trianglelefteq \theta_1 \vee \theta_2$. By Lemma 12, $\Diamond^\star([\alpha] \vee [\beta]) \leq^\star \Diamond^\star[\alpha] \vee \Diamond^\star[\beta]$. Conversely, by item (6) on $[\alpha] \leq^\star [\alpha] \vee [\beta]$, $\Diamond^\star[\alpha] \leq^\star \Diamond^\star([\alpha] \vee [\beta])$. Similarly one has $\Diamond^\star[\beta] \leq^\star \Diamond^\star([\alpha] \vee [\beta])$. By item (2), $\Diamond^\star[\alpha] \vee^\star \Diamond^\star[\beta] \leq^\star \Diamond^\star([\alpha] \vee [\beta])$. For (9), suppose $\Diamond^\star[\alpha] = [\gamma]$ s.t. $\circ(\alpha) \approx \gamma$. By Lemma 12, $\vdash \circ(\alpha) \Rightarrow_{\mathscr{T}} \gamma$. By (T), $\vdash \alpha \Rightarrow_{\mathscr{T}} \gamma$. By Lemma 12, $[\alpha] \leq^\star \Diamond^\star[\alpha]$. The proof of (10) is similar. For (11), suppose $\Diamond^\star[\alpha] = [\gamma_1]$ and $\Diamond^\star[\gamma_1] = [\gamma_2]$ s.t. $\circ(\alpha) \approx \gamma_1$ and $\circ(\gamma_1) \approx \gamma_2$. By Lemma 12, $\vdash \circ(\alpha) \Rightarrow_{\mathscr{T}} \gamma_1$. By the rule (4), $\vdash \circ^2(\alpha) \Rightarrow_{\mathscr{T}} \gamma_1$. Since $\circ(\alpha) \approx \gamma_1$ and $\circ(\gamma_1) \approx \gamma_2$, $\vdash \gamma_2 \Rightarrow_{\mathscr{T}} \gamma_1$. By Lemma 12, $\Diamond^\star\Diamond^\star[\alpha] \leq^\star \Diamond^\star[\alpha]$.

Corollary 2. *If $\mathscr{T}$ is finitely based,* $\mathbf{Q}$ *is a finite topological Kleene algebra.*

Lemma 14. *If* $\Diamond\alpha \in \mathscr{T}$, *then* $\Diamond^\star[\alpha] = [\Diamond\alpha]$.

The sequential logic of GSS4 is denoted as SS4, others are defined similarly.

Lemma 15. *If* $\nvdash_{\mathsf{GSS4}} \circ^n(\alpha) \Rightarrow \beta$, *then there is a finite topological Kleene algebra* $\mathbf{Q}$ *s.t.* $\mathbf{Q} \not\models \circ^n(\alpha) \Rightarrow \beta$.

Theorem 4. SK, SKD, SKT, SK4, SKD4, *and* SS4 *have FMP and are decidable.*

References

1. Balbes, R., Dwinger, P.: Distributive Lattices. University of Missouri Press (1977)
2. Banerjee, M., Chakraborty, M.K.: Rough sets through algebraic logic. Fund. Inform. **28**(3–4), 211–221 (1996)
3. Białynicki-Birula, A., Rasiowa, H.: On the representation of quasi-Boolean algebras. Bull. Polish Acad. Sci. **Cl. III 5**(3), 259–261 (1957)
4. Cignoli, R.: Boolean elements in łukasiewicz algebras i. In: Proceedings of the Japan Academy, pp. 670–675 (1965)
5. Cignoli, R.: The class of Kleene algebras satisfying an interpolation property and Nelson algebras. Algebra Universalis **23**, 262–292 (1986)
6. Cleave, J.P.: Quasi-Boolean algebras, empirical continuity and three-valued logic. Math. Log. Q. **22**(1), 481–500 (1976)
7. Davey, B.A., Priestley, H.A.: Introduction to Lattices and Order. Cambridge University Press (2002)
8. Dunn, J.M.: Star and perp: two treatments of negation. Philos. Perspect. **7**, 331–357 (1993)
9. Dunn, J.M.: Positive modal logic. Stud. Logica. **55**(2), 301–317 (1995)
10. Dunn, J.M., Zhou, C.: Negation in the context of gaggle theory. Stud. Logica. **80**, 235–264 (2005)
11. Kalman, J.A.: Lattices with involution. Trans. Am. Math. Soc. **87**(2), 485–491 (1958)
12. Kumar, A., Banerjee, M.: Kleene algebras and logic: Boolean and rough set representations, 3-valued, rough set and perp semantics. Stud. Logica. **105**(3), 439–469 (2017)
13. Lin, Z.: Non-associative Lambek calculus with modalities: interpolation, complexity and FEP. Logic J. IGPL **22**(3), 494–512 (2014)
14. Muškardin, V.: Representation theorem for finite quasi-Boolean algebras. Annales scientifiques de l'Université de Clermont. Mathématiques **60**(13), 117–128 (1976)
15. Peng, Y., Wang, Y.: On the finite model property of non-normal modal logics. In: International Workshop on Logic, Rationality and Interaction, pp. 207–221. Springer (2023). https://doi.org/10.1007/978-3-031-45558-2_16
16. Rasiowa, H.: An Algebraic Approach to Non-classical Logics. North-Holland Publishing Company, Amsterdam (1974)
17. Saha, A., Sen, J., Chakraborty, M.K.: Algebraic structures in the vicinity of pre-rough algebra and their logics I. Inf. Sci. **282**, 296–320 (2014)
18. Sardar, M.R., Chakraborty, M.K.: Rough set models of some abstract algebras close to pre-rough algebra. Inf. Sci. **621**, 104–118 (2023)
19. Shannon, C.E., McCarthy, J.: Automata Studies. Princeton University Press (1956)

Parameterized Dynamic Logic — Towards A Cyclic Logical Framework for General Program Specification and Verification

Yuanrui Zhang(✉)

College of Software, Nanjing University of Aeronautics and Astronautics, Nanjing, China
yuanruizhang@nuaa.edu.cn,zhangyrmath@126.com

Abstract. We present a theory of parameterized dynamic logic, namely DL_p, for specifying and reasoning about general program models based on their transitional behaviours. Different from most dynamic-logic theories that deal with regular expressions or a particular type of models, DL_p introduces a labelled system in which symbolic executions of general programs can be fully captured and derived. Our deduction approach is a cyclic one, tailored from previous work onto DL_p, in order to deal with potentially infinite derivations arose from symbolic executions of loop programs. The soundness of DL_p is formally analyzed and partially proved. We give an example of instantiations of DL_p in particular domains, showing the usage and potential of DL_p in practice. The cyclic proof system of DL_p is mechanized in Coq.

Keywords: Dynamic Logic · Program Deduction · Logical Framework · Cyclic Proof · Symbolic Execution

1 Introduction

Background and Motivations. Dynamic logic [16] is an extension of modal logic for reasoning about programs. Here, the term 'program' can mean an abstract formal model, not necessarily an explicit computer program. In dynamic logic, a program α is embedded into a modality $[\cdot]$ in a form of $[\alpha]\phi$, meaning that after all executions of α, formula ϕ holds. Formula $\phi \rightarrow [\alpha]\psi$ exactly captures partial correctness of programs expressed by triple $\{\phi\}\alpha\{\psi\}$ in Hoare logic [18]. With a dynamic form $[\alpha]\phi$ that mixes both programs and formulas, dynamic logic allows multiple modalities in a single formula, allowing expressing many complex program properties such as $[\alpha]\langle\beta\rangle\phi$ and $[\alpha]\psi \rightarrow \langle\beta\rangle\phi$, which cannot be directly captured in traditional Hoare logic. As one of popular logical formalisms, dynamic logic has been applied for many types of programs, such as process algebras [5], programming languages [4], synchronous systems [35], hybrid systems [27] and probabilistic systems [25]. Because of modality $\langle\cdot\rangle$, it is a natural candidate for unifying correctness and 'incorrectness' reasoning recently proposed and developed in work e.g. [24].

M. Bonsangue and Y. Chen (Eds.): AILA 2025, CCIS 2668, pp. 211–226, 2026.
https://doi.org/10.1007/978-981-95-8262-4_17

The programs of dynamic logics are usually (tailored) regular expressions with tests (e.g. [11,27]) or actual programming languages like Java [4]. The denotational semantics of these models is usually *compositional*, in the sense that the deductions of the logics mean to dissolve the syntactic structures of these models. For example, in propositional dynamic logic (PDL) [11], to prove a formula $[\alpha \cup \beta]\phi$, we prove both formulas $[\alpha]\phi$ and $[\beta]\phi$, where α and β are sub-regular-expressions of $\alpha \cup \beta$. This so-called 'divide-and-conquer' approach to program verification has brought numerous benefits, the most significant being its ability to scale verifications.

However, this typical we call *structure-based* reasoning heavily relies on programs' denotational semantics, thus brings two major drawbacks: (1) Firstly, the program models of a dynamic logic are usually in particular forms. Thus if applying the dynamic logic to a new type of programs, one needs to either perform a transformation from target programs into the programs of the dynamic logic so that existing inference rules can be utilized, or carefully design a set of particular rules to adapt the new programs' semantics. The former usually means losses of partial program structural information during the transformations, while the latter often demands a large amount of work. For example, Verifiable C [2], a famous program verifier for C programming language based on Hoare logic, used nearly 40,000 lines of Coq code to define the logic theory. (2) Secondly but importantly as well, some programs are naturally non-compositional or do not temporally provide a compositional semantics at some level of system design. Typical examples are neural networks [14], automata-based system models (e.g. a transition model of AADL [33]) and some programming languages (such as synchronous imperative programming languages Esterel [6] and Quartz [13]). For these models, one can only re-formalize their structures by additional transformation procedures so that structure-based reasoning is possible.

Recent years, there is a trend to unify different types of program models into a single logical framework by reasoning directly based on programs' transitional behaviours [9,17,20,22,29–31], which can in large scale compensate for the above two shortcomings. To our best knowledge, up to now there is only a few study (see Sect. 6 for a comparison) for dynamic-logic theories.

In this paper, we present a theory of parameterized dynamic logic (DL_p) to support a general approach for program verification in the framework based on dynamic logic. DL_p offers an abstract-leveled setting for describing a rich set of programs and formulas, and is empowered to support a *symbolic-execution-based* reasoning based on a set of program transitional behaviours (simply "program behaviours" below). This, on one hand, reduces the burden of developing different dynamic-logic theories for different programs; on the other, it saves the additional transformations in the derivations of non-compositional programs.

Illustration of Main Idea. Informally, in dynamic formula $[\alpha]\phi$ we treat program α and formula ϕ as 'parameters' that can be of arbitrary forms, and adopt a structure σ called "program configuration" to record current program status for programs' symbolic executions. So, a DL_p dynamic formula is of the form: $\sigma : [\alpha]\phi$, following a convention of labeled formulas [10].

To see how we can benefit from deriving a DL_p formula, consider a simple example. We prove a formula $\phi_1 =_{df} (x \geq 0 \to [x := x + 1]x > 0)$ in first-order dynamic logic [15] (FODL), where x is a variable ranging over the set of integer numbers. Intuitively, ϕ_1 means that if $x \geq 0$ holds, then $x > 0$ holds after the execution of the assignment $x := x+1$. In FODL, to derive formula ϕ_1, we apply the structural rule: $\dfrac{\phi[x/e]}{[x := e]\phi}{\scriptstyle (x:=e)}$ for assignment on formula $[x := x + 1]x > 0$ by substituting x of $x > 0$ with $x + 1$, and obtain $x + 1 > 0$. Formula ϕ_1 thus becomes $\phi_1' =_{df} (x \geq 0 \to x + 1 > 0)$, which is true for any integer number $x \in \mathbb{Z}$.

While in DL_p, formula ϕ_1 can be expressed as a form: $\psi_1 =_{df} (t \geq 0 \to \{x \mapsto t\} : [x := x+1]x > 0)$, where formula $[x := x+1]x > 0$ is labeled by configuration $\{x \mapsto t\}$, capturing the current program status with t a free variable, meaning "variable x has value t". With a configuration explicitly showing up, to derive formula ψ_1, we instead directly perform a program transition of $x := x + 1$ as: $(x := x + 1, \{x \mapsto t\}) \longrightarrow (\downarrow, \{x \mapsto t + 1\})$, which assign x's value with its current value added by 1. Here $\downarrow$ indicates a program termination. Formula ψ_1 thus becomes $\psi_1' =_{df} (t \geq 0 \to \{x \mapsto t + 1\} : x > 0)$, by ignoring the dynamic part '$[\downarrow]$' since $\downarrow$ behaves nothing. By applying configuration $\{x \mapsto t + 1\}$ on formula $x > 0$ (which means replacing variable x of $x > 0$ with its value $t + 1$ in $\{x \mapsto t + 1\}$), we obtain the same valid formula ϕ_1': $t \geq 0 \to t + 1 > 0$ (modulo the free variables x, t).

For many programs, transitions like $(x := x+1, \{x \mapsto t\}) \longrightarrow (\downarrow, \{x \mapsto t+1\})$ are natural from their operational semantics and can be easily formalized, while structural rules like $(x := e)$ would consume more efforts to design. And there might exists no structural rules in certain cases, as in Esterel programs illustrated in our online report [34].

Main Contributions. In this paper, after defining the logic, we propose a cyclic proof system for DL_p based on program behaviours. Cyclic proof approach (cf. [8]) provides a solution for reasoning about programs with explicit/implicit loop structures in DL_p formulas. Generally, it is a technique to ensure that a certain type of infinite proof trees can lead to a valid conclusion if it meets some certain conditions.

The main contributions of this paper are three folds: (1) We define the syntax and semantics of DL_p formulas. (2) We build a proof system for reasoning about DL_p formulas based on program behaviours. (3) We construct a sound cyclic preproof structure for DL_p and analyzes its soundness.

The rest of the paper is organized as follows. Section 2 defines the syntax and semantics of DL_p formulas. In Sect. 3, we propose a cyclic proof system for DL_p. In Sect. 4, we give an example of cyclic deductions of DL_p formulas. Section 5 analyzes the soundness of DL_p. Section 6 introduces related work.

2 Dynamic Logic DL_p

In this section, we firstly introduce the basic settings for the ingredients of DL_p; then we introduce the notion of program behaviours; lastly we formally define the syntax and semantics of DL_p formulas.

Programs, Configurations and Formulas. The construction of DL_p is based on a set **TA** of *terms* defined over a set *Var* of variables and a set Σ of signatures. In **TA**, we distinguish three subsets **Prog**, **Conf** and **Form**, representing the sets of programs, configurations and formulas respectively. $\mathbf{TA} \supseteq \mathbf{Prog} \cup \mathbf{Conf} \cup \mathbf{Form}$. We use $\equiv$ to represent the identical equivalence between two terms in **TA**. A function $f : \mathbf{TA} \to \mathbf{TA}$ is called *structural* (w.r.t. Σ) if it satisfies that for any $n-$ary signature $s_n \in \Sigma$ ($n \geq 0$, $0-$ary signature is a constant) and term $s_n(t_1, ..., t_n)$ with $t_1, ..., t_n \in \mathbf{TA}$, $f(s_n(t_1, ..., t_n)) \equiv s_n(f_1(t_1), ..., f_n(t_n))$ for some structural functions $f_1, ..., f_n : \mathbf{TA} \to \mathbf{TA}$. Naturally, we assume that a structural function always maps a term to a term with the same type: **Prog**, **Conf** and **Form**.

In **Prog**, there is one distinguished program $\downarrow$, called *termination*. It indicates a completion of executions of a program.

Program configurations have impacts on formulas. We assume that **Conf** is associated with a function $\mathfrak{I} : (\mathbf{Conf} \times \mathbf{Form}) \to \mathbf{Form}$, called *configuration interpretation*, that returns a formula by applying a configuration on a formula.

An *evaluation* $\rho : \mathbf{TA} \to \mathbf{TA}$ is a structural function that maps each formula $\phi \in \mathbf{Form}$ to a *proposition*—a special formula that has a boolean semantics of either truth (represented as 1) or falsehood (represented as 0). We denote the set of all propositions as **Prop**. $\mathbf{Prop} \subseteq \mathbf{Form}$. The boolean semantics of formulas is expressed by function $\mathfrak{T} : \mathbf{Prop} \to \{0, 1\}$. **Prop** forms the semantical domain as the basis for defining DL_p. An evaluation $\rho \in \mathbf{Eval}$ *satisfies* a formula $\phi \in \mathbf{Form}$, denoted by $\rho \models_{\mathfrak{T}} \phi$, if $\mathfrak{T}(\rho(\phi)) = 1$. A formula $\phi \in \mathbf{Form}$ is *valid*, denoted by $\models_{\mathfrak{T}} \phi$, if $\rho \models_{\mathfrak{T}} \phi$ for all $\rho \in \mathbf{Eval}$.

Example 1 (An Instantiation of Program Structures). Consider a *While* program *WP* as an example of an instantiation of structures **Prog**, **Conf** and $\mathfrak{I}$:

$$WP =_{df} \{while\ (n > 0)\ do\ s := s + n\ ;\ n := n - 1\ end\ \}.$$

Given an initial value of variables n, program *WP* computes the sum from n to 1 stored in variable s. A configuration σ_{WP} of *WP* is of the form: $\{x_1 \mapsto e_1, x_2 \mapsto e_2, ..., x_n \mapsto e_n\}$ ($n \geq 0$) as a variable storage that maps a variable x_i to a unique value of arithmetic expression e_i ($1 \leq i \leq n$). For example, $\{n \mapsto 5, s \mapsto 0\}$ denotes a configuration that maps n to 5 and s to 0. Formulas in this particular domain are first-order arithmetical formulas over integer numbers, with propositions are those "closed formulas" without free variables. The interpretation $\mathfrak{I}_{WP}(\sigma, \phi)$ is defined as a a substitution that replaces each free variable x of formula ϕ with its value-expression stored in σ. For instance, we have $\mathfrak{I}_{WP}(\{n \mapsto 5, s \mapsto 0\}, n > 0) = (5 > 0)$, which is true in the theory of integer numbers. An evaluation ρ_{WP} maps each variable to an integer number.

$\rho_{WP}(t)$ given a term t is defined in the usual sense that it replaces each free variable x of term t with an integer number $\rho_{WP}(x)$.

A formal definition of *While* programs is illustrated in Appendix B of [34].

Program Behaviours. A *program state* is a pair $(\alpha, \sigma) \in \mathbf{Prog} \times \mathbf{Conf}$ of programs and configurations. In **Form**, we assume a binary relation $(\alpha, \sigma) \longrightarrow (\alpha', \sigma')$ called a *program transition* between two program states (α, σ) and (α', σ'). For any evaluation $\rho \in \mathbf{Eval}$, proposition $\rho((\alpha, \sigma) \longrightarrow (\alpha', \sigma'))$ is assumed to be defined as: $\rho((\alpha, \sigma) \longrightarrow (\alpha', \sigma')) =_{df} \rho(\alpha, \sigma) \longrightarrow \rho(\alpha', \sigma')$. *Program behaviours*, denoted by Λ, is the set of all true program transitions:

$$\Lambda =_{df} \{(\alpha, \sigma) \longrightarrow (\alpha', \sigma') \mid \mathfrak{T}((\alpha, \sigma) \longrightarrow (\alpha', \sigma')) = 1\},$$

which is assumed to be *well-defined* in the sense that there is no true transitions of the form: $(\downarrow, \sigma) \longrightarrow ...$ from a terminal program.

A *path tr* over Λ is a finite or infinite sequence: $s_1 s_2 ... s_n ...$ $(n \geq 1)$, where for each pair (s_i, s_{i+1}) $(i \geq 1)$, $(s_i \longrightarrow s_{i+1}) \in \Lambda$ is a true program transition. A path is *terminal*, if it ends with program $\downarrow$ in the form of $(\alpha_1, \sigma_1)...(\downarrow, \sigma_n)$ $(n \geq 1)$. We call a path *minimum*, in the sense that in it there is no two identical program states. A state s is called *terminal*, if from s there is a terminal path over Λ.

In order to reason about termination of a program, in **Form** we assume a unary operator $(\alpha, \sigma) \Downarrow$ called the *termination* of a program state (α, σ). For an evaluation $\rho \in \mathbf{Eval}$, proposition $\rho((\alpha, \sigma) \Downarrow)$ is defined as: $\rho((\alpha, \sigma) \Downarrow) =_{df} (\rho(\alpha, \sigma)) \Downarrow$. $\mathfrak{T}((\alpha, \sigma) \Downarrow) =_{df} 1$ if there exists a terminal path over Λ starting from (α, σ). We use Ω to denote the set of all true program terminations: $\Omega =_{df} \{(\alpha, \sigma) \Downarrow \mid \mathfrak{T}((\alpha, \sigma) \Downarrow) = 1\}$.

For programming languages, usually, program behaviours Λ (also program terminations Ω) are defined as structural operational semantics [28] of Plotkin's style expressed as a set of rules, in a manner that a transition $\mathfrak{T}((\alpha, \sigma) \longrightarrow (\alpha', \sigma')) = 1$ only when it can be inferred according to these rules in a finite number of steps.

Example 2 (Examples of Program Behaviours). In Example 1, we have a program transition $(WP, \{n \mapsto 5, s \mapsto 0\}) \longrightarrow (WP', \{n \mapsto 5, s \mapsto 5\})$, where $WP' =_{df} n := n - 1 \ ; \ WP$, by executing assignment $s := s + n$. This transition is also a program behaviour, since it matches the operational semantics of $s := s + n$ (not shown in this paper, one can refer to Appendix B of [34]). However, transition $(WP, \{n \mapsto v, s \mapsto 0\}) \longrightarrow (WP', \{n \mapsto v, s \mapsto 5\})$ is not a proposition, because its truth value depends on whether $v > 0$ is true.

Syntax and Semantics of DL_p. Based on the assumed sets **Prog**, **Conf** and **Form**, we give the syntax of DL_p as follows.

Definition 1 (DL_p Formulas). *A parameterized dynamic logical (DL_p) formula ϕ is defined as follows in BNF form:*

$$\psi =_{df} F \mid \neg\psi \mid \psi \wedge \psi \mid [\alpha]\psi,$$
$$\phi =_{df} F \mid \sigma : \psi \mid \neg\phi \mid \phi \wedge \phi,$$

where $F \in \mathbf{Form}$, $\alpha \in \mathbf{Prog}$ *and* $\sigma \in \mathbf{Conf}$.

We denote the set of DL_p *formulas as* $\mathbf{DL_p}$.

σ and ϕ are called the *label* and the *unlabeled part* of formula $\sigma : \phi$ respectively. We call $[\alpha]$ the *dynamic part* of a formula, and call a DL_p formula having dynamic parts a *dynamic formula.* Intuitively, formula $[\alpha]\phi$ means that after all executions of program α, formula ϕ holds. $\langle\cdot\rangle$ is the dual operator of $[\cdot]$. Formula $\langle\alpha\rangle\phi$ can be written as $\neg[\alpha]\neg\phi$. Other formulas with logical connectives such as $\vee$ and $\rightarrow$ can be expressed by formulas with $\neg$ and $\wedge$ accordingly. Formula $\sigma : \phi$ means that ϕ holds under configuration σ, as σ has an impact on the semantics of formulas as indicated by interpretation $\mathfrak{I}$.

The semantics of a traditional dynamic logic is based on a Kripke structure [16], in which programs are interpreted as a set of world pairs and logical formulas are interpreted as a set of worlds. In DL_p, we define the semantics by extending ρ and $\mathfrak{T}$ to formulas $\mathbf{DL_p}$ and directly base on program behaviours Λ.

Definition 2 (Semantics of DL_p **Formulas).** *An evaluation* $\rho \in \mathbf{Eval}$ *structurally maps a* DL_p *formula* ϕ *into a proposition, whose truth value is defined inductively as follows by extending* $\mathfrak{T}$:

1. $\mathfrak{T}(\rho(F))$ *is already defined, if* $F \in \mathbf{Form}$;
2. $\mathfrak{T}(\rho(\sigma : F)) =_{df} 1$, *if* $F \in \mathbf{Form}$ *and* $\rho \models_{\mathfrak{T}} \mathfrak{I}(\sigma, F)$;
3. $\mathfrak{T}(\rho(\sigma : \neg\phi)) =_{df} \mathfrak{T}(\rho(\neg(\sigma : \phi)))$;
4. $\mathfrak{T}(\rho(\sigma : \phi_1 \wedge \phi_2)) =_{df} \mathfrak{T}(\rho((\sigma : \phi_1) \wedge (\sigma : \phi_2)))$;
5. $\mathfrak{T}(\rho(\sigma : [\alpha]\phi)) =_{df} 1$, *if for all terminal paths* $(\alpha_1, \sigma_1)...(\downarrow, \sigma_n)$ $(n \geq 1)$ *over* Λ *with* $(\alpha_1, \sigma_1) \equiv \rho(\alpha, \sigma)$, $\mathfrak{T}(\rho(\sigma_n : \phi)) = 1$;
6. $\mathfrak{T}(\rho(\neg\phi)) =_{df} 1$, *if* $\mathfrak{T}(\rho(\phi)) = 0$;
7. $\mathfrak{T}(\rho(\phi_1 \wedge \phi_2)) =_{df} 1$, *if both* $\mathfrak{T}(\rho(\phi_1)) = 1$ *and* $\mathfrak{T}(\rho(\phi_2)) = 1$;
8. $\mathfrak{T}(\rho(\phi)) =_{df} 0$ *for any* $\phi \in \mathbf{DL_p}$, *otherwise.*

For any $\phi \in \mathbf{DL_p}$, *write* $\rho \models_{\mathfrak{T}} \phi$ *if* $\mathfrak{T}(\rho(\phi)) = 1$, *or simply* $\rho \models \phi$.

Notice that in Definition 2 we do not specify $\rho(\phi)$ for a DL_p formula ϕ due to its generality. We only assume that ρ is structural.

According to the semantics of operator $\langle\cdot\rangle$, we have that $\mathfrak{T}(\rho(\langle\alpha\rangle\phi)) = 1$ iff there exists a terminal path $(\alpha_1, \sigma_1)...(\downarrow, \sigma_n)$ $(n \geq 1)$ over Λ with $(\alpha_1, \sigma_1) \equiv \rho(\alpha, \sigma)$ such that $\mathfrak{T}(\rho(\sigma_n : \phi)) = 1$.

A DL_p formula ϕ is called *valid*, if $\rho \models \phi$ for all evaluation $\rho \in \mathbf{Eval}$.

Example 3 (DL_p *Specifications).* A property of program *WP* (Example 1) is described as the following formula

$$v \geq 0 \rightarrow \sigma_1 : [WP]s = ((v+1)v)/2,$$

where $\sigma_1 =_{df} \{n \mapsto v, s \mapsto 0\}$ with v a free variable. This formula means that given an initial value $v \geq 0$, after executing *WP*, s equals to $((v+1)v)/2$, which is the sum of $1 + 2 + ... + v$. We will prove this formula in Sect. 4.

3 A Cyclic Proof System for DL_p

We propose a cyclic proof system for DL_p. In Sect. 3.1, we firstly propose a proof system P_{DLP} to support reasoning based on program behaviours. Then in Sect. 3.2 we construct a cyclic preproof structure for P_{DLP}, which support deriving infinite proof trees under certain soundness conditions.

3.1 A Proof System for DL_p

Sequent Calculus. We adopt sequents [12] as the basic deduction structure to carry logical formulas. A sequent is of the form: $\Gamma \Rightarrow \Delta$, which expresses the formula $\bigwedge_{\phi \in \Gamma} \phi \to \bigvee_{\psi \in \Delta} \psi$, meaning that if all formulas in Γ hold, then one of formulas in Δ holds.

The Proof System. The proof system P_{DLP} of DL_p relies on a pre-defined proof system $P_{\Lambda,\Omega}$ for deriving program behaviours Λ and terminations Ω. $P_{\Lambda,\Omega}$ is *sound* and *complete* w.r.t. Λ and Ω in the sense that for any transition $(\alpha_1, \sigma_1) \longrightarrow (\alpha_2, \sigma_2) \in$ **Prop** and termination $(\alpha, \sigma) \Downarrow \in$ **Prop**, $(\alpha_1, \sigma_1) \longrightarrow (\alpha_2, \sigma_2) \in \Lambda$ iff $\vdash_{P_{\Lambda,\Omega}} \cdot \Rightarrow (\alpha_1, \sigma_1) \longrightarrow (\alpha_2, \sigma_2)$, and $(\alpha, \sigma) \Downarrow \in \Omega$ iff $\vdash_{P_{\Lambda,\Omega}} \cdot \Rightarrow (\alpha, \sigma) \Downarrow$.

Note that in P_{DLP}, we usually assume that a formula does not contain a program transition or termination.

Table 1. Partial Inference Rules for Program Behaviours of *While* programs

$$\frac{}{\Gamma \Rightarrow (x := e, \sigma) \longrightarrow (\downarrow, \sigma^x_{\sigma^*(e)}), \Delta}\ (x{:=}e) \qquad \frac{\Gamma \Rightarrow (\alpha_1, \sigma) \longrightarrow (\alpha'_1, \sigma'), \Delta}{\Gamma \Rightarrow (\alpha_1; \alpha_2, \sigma) \longrightarrow (\alpha'_1; \alpha_2, \sigma'), \Delta}\ (;)$$

$$\frac{\Gamma \Rightarrow (\alpha_1, \sigma) \longrightarrow (\downarrow, \sigma'), \Delta}{\Gamma \Rightarrow (\alpha_1; \alpha_2, \sigma) \longrightarrow (\alpha_2, \sigma'), \Delta}\ (;\downarrow) \qquad \frac{\Gamma, \Im_{WP}(\sigma, \phi) \Rightarrow (\alpha, \sigma) \longrightarrow (\alpha', \sigma'), \Delta \quad \Gamma \Rightarrow \Im_{WP}(\sigma, \phi), \Delta}{\Gamma \Rightarrow (\mathit{while}\ \phi\ \mathit{do}\ \alpha\ \mathit{end}, \sigma) \longrightarrow (\alpha';\ \mathit{while}\ \phi\ \mathit{do}\ \alpha\ \mathit{end}, \sigma'), \Delta}\ (wh1)$$

$$\frac{\Gamma, \Im_{WP}(\sigma, \phi) \Rightarrow (\alpha, \sigma) \longrightarrow (\downarrow, \sigma'), \Delta \quad \Gamma \Rightarrow \Im_{WP}(\sigma, \phi), \Delta}{\Gamma \Rightarrow (\mathit{while}\ \phi\ \mathit{do}\ \alpha\ \mathit{end}, \sigma) \longrightarrow (\mathit{while}\ \phi\ \mathit{do}\ \alpha\ \mathit{end}, \sigma'), \Delta}\ (wh1\downarrow) \qquad \frac{\Gamma \Rightarrow \neg\Im_{WP}(\sigma, \phi), \Delta}{\Gamma \Rightarrow (\mathit{while}\ \phi\ \mathit{do}\ \alpha\ \mathit{end}, \sigma) \longrightarrow (\downarrow, \sigma), \Delta}\ (wh2)$$

Example 4. As an example, Table 1 displays a part of inference rules of the proof system $P_{\Lambda_{WP}, \Omega_{WP}}$ for the program behaviours Λ_{WP} of *While* programs. σ^x_e represents a configuration that store variable x as value e, while storing other variables as the same value as σ. $\sigma^*(e)$ is defined to return a term obtained by replacing each free variable x of e by the value of x in σ. See Appendix B of report [34] for a formal definition and for a proof system for program terminations Ω_{WP} of *While* programs.

Table 2 lists the primitive rules of P_{DLP}. Through P_{DLP}, a DL_p formula can be transformed into proof obligations as non-dynamic formulas, which can then be encoded and verified accordingly through, for example, an SAT/SMT checking procedure.

Table 2. Primitive Rules of Proof System P_{DLP}

$$\frac{\{\Gamma \Rightarrow \sigma' : [\alpha']\phi, \Delta\}_{(\alpha',\sigma')\in\Phi}}{\Gamma \Rightarrow \sigma : [\alpha]\phi, \Delta}\ {}^{1}([\alpha]),\quad \text{where } \Phi =_{df} \{(\alpha',\sigma') \mid \vdash_{P_{\Lambda,\Omega}} (\Gamma \Rightarrow (\alpha,\sigma) \longrightarrow (\alpha',\sigma'), \Delta)\}$$

$$\frac{\Gamma, \sigma' : [\alpha']\phi \Rightarrow \Delta}{\Gamma, \sigma : [\alpha]\phi \Rightarrow \Delta}\ {}^{1}([\alpha]2),\quad \text{if} \vdash_{P_{\Lambda,\Omega}} (\Gamma \Rightarrow (\alpha,\sigma) \longrightarrow (\alpha',\sigma'), \Delta)$$

$$\frac{}{\Gamma \Rightarrow \Delta}\ {}^{2}(Ter) \quad \Bigg| \quad \frac{\mathfrak{I}(\sigma,\phi)}{\sigma : \phi}\ {}^{3}(Int) \quad \Bigg| \quad \frac{\sigma : \phi}{\sigma : [\downarrow]\phi}\ ([\downarrow]) \quad \Bigg| \quad \frac{\Gamma \Rightarrow \Delta}{Sub(\Gamma) \Rightarrow Sub(\Delta)}\ {}^{4}(Sub) \quad \Bigg| \quad \frac{\neg(\sigma : \phi)}{\sigma : (\neg\phi)}\ (\sigma\neg) \quad \Bigg| \quad \frac{(\sigma : \phi) \wedge (\sigma : \psi)}{\sigma : (\phi \wedge \psi)}\ (\sigma\wedge)$$

$$\frac{}{\Gamma, \phi \Rightarrow \phi, \Delta}\ (ax) \quad \Bigg| \quad \frac{\Gamma \Rightarrow \phi, \Delta \quad \Gamma, \phi \Rightarrow \Delta}{\Gamma \Rightarrow \Delta}\ (Cut) \quad \Bigg| \quad \frac{\Gamma \Rightarrow \Delta}{\Gamma, \phi \Rightarrow \Delta}\ (Wk\ L) \quad \Bigg| \quad \frac{\Gamma \Rightarrow \Delta}{\Gamma \Rightarrow \phi, \Delta}\ (Wk\ R) \quad \Bigg| \quad \frac{\phi, \phi}{\phi}\ (Con)$$

$$\frac{\Gamma \Rightarrow \phi, \Delta}{\Gamma, \neg\phi \Rightarrow \Delta}\ (\neg L) \quad \Bigg| \quad \frac{\Gamma, \phi \Rightarrow \Delta}{\Gamma \Rightarrow \neg\phi, \Delta}\ (\neg R) \quad \Bigg| \quad \frac{\Gamma, \phi, \psi \Rightarrow \Delta}{\Gamma, \phi \wedge \psi \Rightarrow \Delta}\ (\wedge L) \quad \Bigg| \quad \frac{\Gamma \Rightarrow \phi, \Delta \quad \Gamma \Rightarrow \psi, \Delta}{\Gamma \Rightarrow \phi \wedge \psi, \Delta}\ (\wedge R)$$

[1] $\alpha \not\equiv \downarrow$. [2] for each ϕ in Γ or Δ, $\phi \in$ **Form**; $\Gamma \Rightarrow \Delta$ is valid. [3] $\phi \in$ **Form**. [4] *Sub* is by Definition 3.

In Table 2 we use a double-lined inference form: $\dfrac{\phi_1 \quad \dots \quad \phi_n}{\phi}$ to represent both rules $\dfrac{\Gamma \Rightarrow \phi_1, \Delta \quad \dots \quad \Gamma \Rightarrow \phi_n, \Delta}{\Gamma \Rightarrow \phi, \Delta}$ and $\dfrac{\Gamma, \phi_1 \Rightarrow \Delta \quad \dots \quad \Gamma, \phi_n \Rightarrow \Delta}{\Gamma, \phi \Rightarrow \Delta}$, provided any *contexts* Γ and Δ.

Target Pairs. In each rule of Table 2 except rule (*Sub*), we call a conclusion-premise (CP) pair (τ, τ') of formulas that are not in Γ and Δ a *target pair* of the rule. For instance, $(\sigma : [\alpha]\phi, \sigma' : [\alpha']\phi)$ is the target pair of rule $([\alpha]2)$, $(\neg\phi, \phi)$ is the target pair of rule $(\neg R)$.

Illustration of each rule is as follows.

Rule $([\alpha])$ and rule $([\alpha]2)$ ([34] displays its equivalent rule $(\langle\alpha\rangle)$) deal with dynamic parts of DL_p formulas based on program transitions. Both rules rely on the sub-proof-procedures of system $P_{\Lambda,\Omega}$. In rule $([\alpha])$, $\{...\}_{(\alpha',\sigma')\in\Phi}$ represents the collection of premises for all program states $(\alpha', \sigma') \in \Phi$. Notice that we assume that the system $P_{\Lambda,\Omega}$ only derives a finite set of transitions from (α, σ) (which is mostly the case in practice). So Φ is finite, and rule $([\alpha])$ only has a finite number of premises. When Φ is empty, the conclusion terminates. Intuitively, rule $([\alpha])$ says that to derive $[\alpha]\phi$ under configuration σ, we derive $[\alpha']\phi$ under configuration σ' for each transition from (α, σ) to (α', σ'). Compared to rule $([\alpha])$, rule $([\alpha]2)$ has only one premise for some (α', σ'). Intuitively, it says that if $[\alpha]\phi$ holds under configuration σ and if there is a transition $(\alpha, \sigma) \longrightarrow (\alpha', \sigma')$, then we have $[\alpha']\phi$ holds under σ'.

In rule (*Ter*), formula $\Gamma \Rightarrow \Delta$ is a non-dynamic formula. The introduction rule (*Int*) eliminates the label σ during the derivation. Rule $([\downarrow])$ deals with the situation when the program is a termination $\downarrow$. Its soundness is straightforward by the well-definedness of program behaviours Λ (Sect. 2). Rule (*Sub*) describes a specialization process (from premise to conclusion) for DL_p formulas. For a set A of formulas, $Sub(A) =_{df} \{Sub(\phi) \mid \phi \in A\}$, with *Sub* a function defined as follows in Definition 3. Intuitively, if formula $\Gamma \Rightarrow \Delta$ is valid, then its one of special cases $Sub(\Gamma) \Rightarrow Sub(\Delta)$ through an abstract version of substitutions *Sub* on formulas is valid. Rule (*Sub*) plays an important role in constructing a bud in a cyclic preproof structure (Sect. 3.2). See Sect. 4 as an example.

Definition 3 (Substitution). *A structural function* $\eta : \mathbf{TA} \to \mathbf{TA}$ *is called a 'substitution', if for any evaluation* $\rho \in \mathbf{Eval}$*, there exists a* $\rho' \in \mathbf{Eval}$ *such that* $\rho(\eta(\phi)) \equiv \rho'(\phi)$ *for each formula* $\phi \in \mathbf{DL_p}$.

Rules $(\sigma\neg)$ and $(\sigma\wedge)$ are for transforming labeled formulas. Their soundness are direct according to the semantics of labeled formulas (Definition 2). From rule (ax) to $(\sigma \wedge R)$ are the rules inherited from traditional first-order logic. The meanings of these rules are classic and are omitted in this paper.

The soundness of the rules in P_{DLP} is stated as follows.

Theorem 1. *All rules in* P_{DLP} *(Table 2) are sound.*

Following the above explanations, Theorem 1 can be proved directly according to the semantics of DL_p. See Appendix A of report [34] for more details.

3.2 Construction of A Cyclic Preproof Structure in P_{DLP}

In the proof system P_{DLP}, given a sequent $\Gamma \Rightarrow \Delta$, we expect a finite proof tree to prove $\Gamma \Rightarrow \Delta$. However, a branch of a proof tree does not always terminate. Because the process of symbolically executing a program via rule $([\alpha])$ or/and rule $([\alpha]2)$ might not stop. This is well known when a program has an explicit/implicit loop structure that may run infinitely. For example, a while program $W =_{df}$ *while true do* $x := x + 1$ *end* will proceed infinitely as the following transitions: $(W, \{x \mapsto 0\}) \longrightarrow (W, \{x \mapsto 1\}) \longrightarrow ....$

In this paper, we apply the cyclic proof approach (cf. [8]) to deal with a potential infinite proof tree in DL_p. Cyclic proof is a technique to ensure a valid conclusion of a special type of infinite proof trees, called 'preproof', under some certain conditions called "soundness conditions". Below we firstly introduce a preproof structure, then based on it we propose a 'cyclic' preproof—a structure that satisfies certain soundness conditions. Section 5 will explain why cyclic preproof can be sound.

Preproof and Derivation Traces. A *preproof* (cf. [8]) is an infinite proof tree expressed as a tree structure with finite nodes, in which there exist non-terminal leaf nodes, called *buds*. Each bud is identical to one of its ancestors in the tree. The ancestor identical to a bud N is called a *companion of* N.

A *derivation path* in a preproof is an infinite sequence of nodes $\nu_1\nu_2...\nu_m...$ $(m \geq 1)$ starting from the root node ν_1 of the preproof, where for each node pair (ν_i, ν_{i+1}) $(i \geq 1)$, ν_i is the conclusion and ν_{i+1} is a premise, of a rule.

A *derivation trace* over a derivation path $\mu_1\mu_2...\mu_k\nu_1\nu_2...\nu_m...$ $(k \geq 0, m \geq 1)$ is an infinite sequence $\tau_1\tau_2...\tau_m...$ of formulas starting from formula τ_1 in node ν_1 such that each pair (τ_i, τ_{i+1}) $(i \geq 1)$ is either (1) a target pair of a rule in Table 2 (except rule (Sub)); (2) or a pair $(Sub(\phi), \phi)$ of rule (Sub) for some formula ϕ; (3) or a CP pair of a rule satisfying $\tau_i \equiv \tau_{i+1}$ in Table 2.

Progressive Steps. A crucial prerequisite of defining cyclic preproofs is to introduce the notion of *(progressive) derivation traces* in a preproof of P_{DLP}.

Definition 4 (Progressive Step/Progressive Derivation Trace in DL_p). *In a preproof of P_{DLP}, given a derivation trace $\tau_1\tau_2...\tau_m...$ over a derivation path $...\nu_1\nu_2...\nu_m...$ ($m \geq 1$) starting from τ_1 in node ν_1, a formula pair (τ_i, τ_{i+1}) ($1 \leq i \leq m$) over (ν_i, ν_{i+1}) is called a "progressive step", if (τ_i, τ_{i+1}) is either (1) a target pair of an instance of rule ($[\alpha]$); (2) Or the target pair of an instance of rule ($[\alpha]2$), provided with an additional condition that $\vdash_{P_{\Lambda,\Omega}} (\Gamma \Rightarrow (\alpha', \sigma') \Downarrow, \Delta)$.*

If a derivation trace has an infinite number of progressive steps, we say that the trace is 'progressive'.

The additional condition of the instance of rule ($[\alpha]2$) is the key to prove the corresponding case in Lemma 1 of [34].

Cyclic Preproofs. We build a sound cyclic preproof structure as the following definition.

Definition 5 (A Cyclic Preproof for DL_p). *In P_{DLP}, a preproof is a 'cyclic' one, if there exists a progressive trace over every derivation path.*

Theorem 2 (Soundness of the Cyclic Preproof for DL_p). *Provided that $P_{\Lambda,\Omega}$ is sound, a cyclic preproof of P_{DLP} has a sound conclusion.*

Theorem 2 will be analyzed in Sect. 5.

Since DL_p is not a specific logic, it is impossible to discuss about its decidability, completeness or whether it is cut-free without any restrictions on sets **Prog**, **Conf** and **Form**. One of our future work will focus on analyzing under what restrictions, these properties can be obtained in a general sense.

4 Case Study: A Cyclic Deduction for While Programs

We give an example to show how a DL_p formula can be derived according to rules in Table 2. We prove the property given in Example 3, stated as the following sequent

$$\nu_1 =_{df} \cdot \Rightarrow v \geq 0 \rightarrow \sigma_1 : [WP](s = ((v+1)v)/2).$$

Table 3 shows the derivation. We omit all sub-proof-procedures in the proof system $P_{\Lambda_{WP},\Omega_{WP}}$ derived by the inference rules in Table 1 when deriving via rule ($[\alpha]$). We write term $t(x)$ if x is a variable that has free occurrences in t. Non-primitive rules ($\rightarrow R$) and ($\vee L$) can be derived by the rules for $\neg$ and $\wedge$ accordingly. The derivation from sequent 2 to 3 is according to rule $\dfrac{\Gamma \Rightarrow \Delta}{\Gamma[e/x] \Rightarrow \Delta[e/x]}{\scriptstyle (Sub)}$, where function $(\cdot)[e/x]$ is an instantiation of abstract substitution defined in Definition 3. Informally, for any formula ϕ, $\phi[e/x]$ substitutes each free variable x of ϕ with term e. We observe that sequent 2 can be writen as:

$$(v - m \geq 0)[0/m] \Rightarrow (\sigma_3(v) : [WP]\phi_1)[0/m],$$

as a special case of sequent 3. Intuitively, sequent 3 captures the situation after the mth loop ($m \geq 0$) of program WP. This step is crucial as starting from

Table 3. Derivations of Property ν_1

$$\dfrac{\dfrac{\dfrac{\dfrac{\dfrac{}{19}\,(Ter)}{4}\,(WkR)\quad \dfrac{\dfrac{\dfrac{\dfrac{\dfrac{\dfrac{\dfrac{18}{17}\,(WkL)}{16}\,(Sub)}{13}\,(WkL)\quad \dfrac{15}{14}\,(WkR)}{12}\,(Cut)}{11}\,([\alpha])}{6}\,([\alpha])\quad \dfrac{\dfrac{\dfrac{\dfrac{}{10}\,(Ter)}{9}\,(Int)}{8}\,([\downarrow])}{7}\,([\alpha])}{5}\,(\vee L)}{3}\,(Cut)}{2}\,(Sub)}{\nu_1 \colon 1}\,(\to)$$

Definitions of other symbols:

$WP =_{df} \{while\ (n > 0)\ do\ s := s + n\ ;\ n := n - 1\ end\ \}$

$\phi_1 =_{df} (s = ((v + 1)v)/2)$

$\sigma_1(v) =_{df} \{n \mapsto v, s \mapsto 0\}$

$\sigma_2(v) =_{df} \{n \mapsto v, s \mapsto 0\}$

$\sigma_3(v) =_{df} \{n \mapsto v - m, s \mapsto (2v - m + 1)m/2\}$

$\sigma_4(v) =_{df} \{n \mapsto v - m, s \mapsto (2v - (m + 1) + 1)(m + 1)/2\}$

$\sigma_5(v) =_{df} \{n \mapsto v - (m + 1), s \mapsto (2v - (m + 1) + 1)(m + 1)/2\}$

1:	$\cdot$	$\Rightarrow$	$v \geq 0 \to \sigma_1(v) : [WP]\phi_1$
2:	$v \geq 0$	$\Rightarrow$	$\sigma_1(v) : [WP]\phi_1$
3:	$v - m \geq 0$	$\Rightarrow$	$\underline{\sigma_3(v) : [WP]\phi_1}$
4:	$v - m \geq 0$	$\Rightarrow$	$\sigma_3(v) : [WP]\phi_1, v - m > 0 \vee v - m \leq 0$
19:	$v - m \geq 0$	$\Rightarrow$	$v - m > 0 \vee v - m \leq 0$
5:	$v - m \geq 0, v - m > 0 \vee v - m \leq 0$	$\Rightarrow$	$\underline{\sigma_3(v) : [WP]\phi_1}$
6:	$v - m \geq 0, v - m > 0$	$\Rightarrow$	$\underline{\sigma_3(v) : [WP]\phi_1}$
11:	$v - m \geq 0, v - m > 0$	$\Rightarrow$	$\underline{\sigma_4(v) : [n := n - 1;\ WP]\phi_1}$
12:	$v - m \geq 0, v - m > 0$	$\Rightarrow$	$\underline{\sigma_5(v) : [WP]\phi_1}$
13:	$\left\{\begin{array}{l} v - m \geq 0, v - m > 0, \\ v - (m + 1) \geq -1, v - (m + 1) \geq 0 \end{array}\right\}$	$\Rightarrow$	$\underline{\sigma_5(v) : [WP]\phi_1}$
16:	$v - (m + 1) \geq -1, v - (m + 1) \geq 0$	$\Rightarrow$	$\underline{\sigma_5(v) : [WP]\phi_1}$
17:	$v - m \geq -1, v - m \geq 0$	$\Rightarrow$	$\underline{\sigma_3(v) : [WP]\phi_1}$
18:	$v - m \geq 0$	$\Rightarrow$	$\underline{\sigma_3(v) : [WP]\phi_1}$
14:	$v - m \geq 0, v - m > 0$	$\Rightarrow$	$\sigma_5(v) : [WP]\phi_1, v - (m + 1) \geq -1, v - (m + 1) \geq 0$
15:	$v - m \geq 0, v - m > 0$	$\Rightarrow$	$v - (m + 1) \geq -1, v - (m + 1) \geq 0$
7:	$v - m \geq 0, v - m \leq 0$	$\Rightarrow$	$\sigma_3(v) : [WP]\phi_1$
8:	$v - m \geq 0, v - m \leq 0$	$\Rightarrow$	$\sigma_3(v) : [\downarrow]\phi_1$
9:	$v - m \geq 0, v - m \leq 0$	$\Rightarrow$	$\sigma_3(v) : (s = ((v + 1)v)/2)$
10:	$v - m \geq 0, v - m \leq 0$	$\Rightarrow$	$((2v - m + 1)m)/2 = ((v + 1)v)/2)$

sequent 3, we can find a bud node—18—that is identical to node 3. The derivation from sequent 3 to $\{4, 5\}$ provides a lemma: $v - m > 0 \vee v - m \leq 0$, which is obvious valid. Sequent 16 indicates the end of the $(m + 1)$th loop of program WP. From node 12 to 16, we rewrite the formulas on the left side into an obvious logical equivalent form in order to apply rule (Sub). From sequent 16 to 17 rule (Sub) is applied, with 16 can be written as:

$$(v - m \geq -1)[m + 1/m], (v - m \geq 0)[m + 1/m] \Rightarrow (\sigma_3 : [WP]\phi_1)[m + 1/m].$$

The whole proof tree is a cyclic preproof because the only derivation path: $1, 2, 3, 5, 6, 11, 12, 13, 16, 17, 18, 3, ...$ has a progressive derivation trace whose elements are underlined in Table 3.

Unlike traditional verifications of dynamic logic and Hoare logic, the derivations shown in Table 3 rely solely on the symbolic executions of while programs. In this approach, verifying a while loop reduces to selecting an appropriate configuration using rule (Sub). This eliminates the need for a dedicated rule to dissolve the while structure, as is typically required in classical Hoare logic.

Mechanization of DL_p. To further demonstrate its applicability we mechanize the theory of DL_p in Coq. We adopt the so-called "deep embedding" and currently have implemented the syntactic structure of DL_p as Coq objects and managed to perform the deduction of each rule in proof system P_{DLP}. The source code can be found in [1]. The semantics of DL_p and the soundness of DL_p has not been validated in Coq yet, which we attribute to one of our future work.

5 Soundness Analysis of Cyclic Proof System P_{DLP}

In this section, we analyze the soundness of the cyclic proof system P_{DLP} as stated as Theorem 2. By following a similar idea behind [7], we manage to prove the soundness for formulas in which the target formula $\sigma : [\alpha]\phi$ has only a single dynamic part $[\alpha]$. This case, however, already encompasses the full expressiveness of Hoare logic and is adequate for most practical applications of program verifications. Below we illustrate the main idea of the proof using the example given in Sect. 4. A complete proof can be found in [34].

Well-Foundedness. Given a set S and a partial-order relation $\preceq$ on S, $\preceq$ is called a *well-founded relation* over S, if for any element a in S, there is no infinite descent sequence: $a \succ a_1 \succ a_2 \succ ...$ in S. Set S is called a *well-founded* set w.r.t. $\preceq$.

Main Idea of Soundness Proof. We look for a type of well-founded sets under some partial-order relation $\preceq$ which are related to the truth values of dynamic formulas. For any dynamic formula τ, let its corresponding well-founded set be $C(\tau)$. This type of well-founded sets satisfies that for any pair (τ, τ') of a derivation trace in a derivation of DL_p formulas using rules in Table 2, we have $C(\tau) \succeq C(\tau')$; Moreover, if the derivation from τ to τ' is progressive (Definition 4), then $C(\tau) \succ C(\tau')$. This property is stated as Lemma 1 of [34].

The proof is conducted by contradiction. If the conclusion of a cyclic preproof is invalid, then there exists an *invalid derivation path* in which each node is invalid, and by Definition 5, there exists a progressive trace: $\tau_1\tau_2...\tau_n$ over the tail of the derivation path. By the property above, we can then obtain a sequence of well-founded sets: $C(\tau_1) \succeq C(\tau_2) \succeq ... \succeq C(\tau_n) \succeq ...$, in which due to the progressiveness of the derivation trace there are an infinite number of relation $\succ$ among these $\succeq$s. This violates the well-foundedness itself introduce above.

Illustrations in Our Example. In the example of *While* programs shown in this paper, given a formula $\sigma : [\alpha]\phi$, for any evaluation ρ, we consider a "counter-example" set $CT(\rho, \sigma : [\alpha]\phi)$ defined as the set of minimum paths of α that make $\sigma : [\alpha]\phi$ invalid, which is formally defined as follows:

$$CT(\rho, \sigma : [\alpha]\phi) =_{df} \{\rho(\alpha, \sigma)...(\downarrow, \sigma') \mid \rho \models \Gamma, \rho \not\models \sigma' : \phi\}.$$

Set $CT(\rho, \sigma : [\alpha]\phi)$ for any while program α is always finite. A relation $\preceq_m$ between two sets CT_1 and CT_2 is defined such that $CT_1 \preceq CT_2$ if each path of CT_1 is a suffix of a path in CT_2. And it is easy to prove that $\preceq_m$ is well-founded.

In the derivation shown in Sect. 4, if we assume the conclusion ν_1 is invalid, then by the soundness of each rule of Table 2, we can obtain (the only) one invalid derivation path: 1, 2, 3, 6, 11, 12, 13, 16, 17, 18, 1, ..., in which the derivation trace underlined in Table 2 is progressive. Starting from an evaluation ρ_0 that makes node 1 invalid, for each pair (τ, τ') of the derivation trace, we can prove that $CT(\rho, \tau) \succeq CT(\rho', \tau')$ for some ρ and ρ'. Especially, if the rule is $([\alpha])$, e.g., the pair over nodes (11, 12), we can prove that $CT(\rho, \tau) \succ CT(\rho', \tau')$, because each path of $CT(\rho', \tau')$, according to the meaning of rule $([\alpha])$, turns out to be a proper suffix of a path of $CT(\rho, \tau)$. This progressive derivation trace leads to the contradiction of the well-foundedness of relation $\preceq_m$.

In the proof given in [34], more restrictions on programs are needed to obtain a finite well-founded set C. One can find more details of the proof in [34].

6 Related Work

Previous work such as [9,29–31] in last decade addressed reasoning based on program behaviours using theories based on rewriting logic [21]. Matching logic [29] describes reachability between patterns, where a reachability rule $\varphi \Rightarrow \varphi'$ captures whether a pattern φ' is reachable from another pattern φ in a given pattern reachability system. Based on matching logic, one-path and all-paths reachability logics [30,31] were developed by enhancing the expressive power of the reachability rule. A more powerful matching μ-logic [9] was proposed by adding a least fixpoint μ-binder to matching logic.

Compared to these theories, the forms of dynamic logical formulas allow a direct description (without further encoding) of program properties, provided with the support of a proof system for efficiently deriving modalities. In terms of expressiveness, the semantics of modality $[\cdot]$ in dynamic logic cannot be fully captured by matching logic and one-path reachability logic, if the programs are non-deterministic.

[22] and [20] proposed a type of general program verification frameworks based on coinduction. A specification like $\sigma : [\alpha]\phi$ in DL_p was captured by a more general structure over mathematical sets. The deduction of a specification was realized through deductions over set relations, making use of a type of fixpoint theories over sets. While set theory may permit greater generality, logical forms like $[\alpha]\phi$ offer a clearer separation between programs and properties, and enables a more structured and manageable deduction process. In terms of expressiveness, the meaning of modality $\langle\cdot\rangle$ in DL_p cannot be directly expressed in the framework of [22].

The structure 'updates' adopted in work [3,4,26] are "delay substitutions" of variables and terms. It is a special case of the configurations in DL_p, if we take a configuration as a meta variable without explicit structures.

Cyclic proof approach firstly arose in [32] and was later developed in different logics [7,8]. [19] proposed a complete cyclic proof system for μ-calculus, which subsumes PDL [11] in its expressiveness. In [10], the authors proposed a complete labelled cyclic proof system for PDL. Both μ-calculus and PDL, as mentioned in Sect. 1, are logics designed for dissolving regular expressions as their program models. The labelled form of DL_p formula are alike in [10], but of a more general meaning and can be of arbitrary terms.

There has been some other work for generalizing the theories of dynamic logics, such as [17,23]. However, none of them allow general structures as in DL_p, nor adopt a similar approach for reasoning about programs. The logic proposed in [23], though for a general structure of monads, is still in explicit forms, thus is different from the design philosophy of DL_p. [17] modifies PDL by generalizing regular expressions as arbitrary programs. However, there the program behaviours are captured by pure program transitions with abstract actions, e.g. $\alpha \xrightarrow{a} \alpha'$. And yet no proof systems have been proposed and analyzed for the logic.

7 Conclusion and Future Work

As a summery, we claim that the theory of DL_p hopefully will become a candidate for unifying different dynamic-logic theories, to provide a convenient framework for reasoning based on symbolic executions directly. This is particularly important and has potentially many applications, as most of computer programs have operational semantics in their nature. Although an independent structure not built upon any other logical theories, DL_p actually provides a promising method for fast-prototyping program-verification infrastructures in general theorem provers like Coq or Isabelle. More investigations on this issue will be carried out in future.

Acknowledgment. This work is partially supported by the projects of National Science Foundation of China No. 62102329 and No. 62272397.

References

1. https://github.com/yrz5a/Coq-DLp.git
2. Appel, A.W., Dockins, R., et al.: Program Logics for Certified Compilers. Cambridge University Press (2014)
3. Beckert, B., Bruns, D.: Dynamic logic with trace semantics. In: Bonacina, M.P. (ed.) CADE 2013. LNCS (LNAI), vol. 7898, pp. 315–329. Springer, Heidelberg (2013). https://doi.org/10.1007/978-3-642-38574-2_22
4. Beckert, B., Klebanov, V., Weiß, B.: Dynamic logic for Java, pp. 49–106. Springer International Publishing (2016). https://doi.org/10.1007/978-3-319-49812-6_3
5. Benevides, M.R., Schechter, L.M.: A propositional dynamic logic for concurrent programs based on the π-calculus. In: M4M 2009, pp. 49–64. Elsevier (2010)
6. Berry, G., Gonthier, G.: The Esterel synchronous programming language: design, semantics, implementation. Sci. Comput. Program. **19**(2), 87–152 (1992)
7. Brotherston, J., Bornat, R., Calcagno, C.: Cyclic proofs of program termination in separation logic. SIGPLAN Not. **43**(1), 101–112 (2008)
8. Brotherston, J., Simpson, A.: Complete sequent calculi for induction and infinite descent. In: LICS 2007, pp. 51–62 (2007)
9. Chen, X., Rosu, G.: Matching *mu*-logic. In: LICS 2019, pp. 1–13. IEEE Computer Society (2019)

10. Docherty, S., Rowe, R.N.S.: A non-wellfounded, labelled proof system for propositional dynamic logic. In: Cerrito, S., Popescu, A. (eds.) TABLEAUX 2019. LNCS (LNAI), vol. 11714, pp. 335–352. Springer, Cham (2019). https://doi.org/10.1007/978-3-030-29026-9_19
11. Fischer, M.J., Ladner, R.E.: Propositional dynamic logic of regular programs. J. Comput. Syst. Sci. **18**(2), 194–211 (1979)
12. Gentzen, G.: Untersuchungen über das logische Schließen. Ph.D. thesis, NA Göttingen (1934)
13. Gesell, M., Schneider, K.: A Hoare calculus for the verification of synchronous languages. In: PLPV 2012, pp. 37–48. Association for Computing Machinery (2012)
14. Goodfellow, I.J., Bengio, Y., Courville, A.: Deep Learning. MIT Press (2016)
15. Harel, D. (ed.): First-Order Dynamic Logic. LNCS, vol. 68. Springer, Heidelberg (1979). https://doi.org/10.1007/3-540-09237-4
16. Harel, D., Kozen, D., Tiuryn, J.: Dynamic Logic. MIT Press (2000)
17. Hennicker, R., Wirsing, M.: A Generic Dynamic Logic with Applications to Interaction-Based Systems, pp. 172–187. Springer International Publishing (2019). https://doi.org/10.1007/978-3-030-30985-5_11
18. Hoare, C.A.R.: An axiomatic basis for computer programming. Commun. ACM **12**(10), 576–580 (1969)
19. Jungteerapanich, N.: A tableau system for the modal μ-calculus. In: TABLEAUX 2009, pp. 220–234. Springer, Berlin, Heidelberg (2009). https://doi.org/10.1007/978-3-642-02716-1_17
20. Li, X., Zhang, Q., Wang, G., Shi, Z., Guan, Y.: Reasoning about iteration and recursion uniformly based on big-step semantics. In: Qin, S., Woodcock, J., Zhang, W. (eds.) SETTA 2021. LNCS, vol. 13071, pp. 61–80. Springer, Cham (2021). https://doi.org/10.1007/978-3-030-91265-9_4
21. Meseguer, J.: Twenty years of rewriting logic. J. Logic Algebraic Program. **81**(7), 721–781 (2012)
22. Moore, B., Peña, L., Rosu, G.: Program verification by coinduction. In: Ahmed, A. (ed.) ESOP 2018. LNCS, vol. 10801, pp. 589–618. Springer, Cham (2018). https://doi.org/10.1007/978-3-319-89884-1_21
23. Mossakowski, T., Schröder, L., Goncharov, S.: A generic complete dynamic logic for reasoning about purity and effects. Formal Aspects Comput. **22**(3–4), 363–384 (2010)
24. O'Hearn, P.W.: Incorrectness logic. Proc. ACM Program. Lang. **4**(POPL) (2019)
25. Pardo, R., Johnsen, E.B., et al.: A specification logic for programs in the probabilistic guarded command language. In: ICTAC 2022, pp. 369–387. Springer-Verlag (2022). https://doi.org/10.1007/978-3-031-17715-6_24
26. Platzer, A.: Differential dynamic logic for verifying parametric hybrid systems. In: Olivetti, N. (ed.) TABLEAUX 2007. LNCS (LNAI), vol. 4548, pp. 216–232. Springer, Heidelberg (2007). https://doi.org/10.1007/978-3-540-73099-6_17
27. Platzer, A.: Logical foundations of cyber-physical systems. Springer (2018). https://doi.org/10.1007/978-3-319-63588-0
28. Plotkin, G.D.: A structural approach to operational semantics. Tech. Rep. DAIMI FN-19, University of Aarhus (1981)
29. Roşu, G., Ştefănescu, A.: Towards a unified theory of operational and axiomatic semantics. In: Czumaj, A., Mehlhorn, K., Pitts, A., Wattenhofer, R. (eds.) ICALP 2012. LNCS, vol. 7392, pp. 351–363. Springer, Heidelberg (2012). https://doi.org/10.1007/978-3-642-31585-5_33
30. Rosu, G., Stefanescu, A., Ciobâcá, S., Moore, B.M.: One-path reachability logic. In: LICS 2013, pp. 358–367 (2013)

31. Ştefănescu, A., Ciobâcă, Ş, Mereuta, R., Moore, B.M., Şerbănută, T.F., Roşu, G.: All-path reachability logic. In: Dowek, G. (ed.) RTA 2014. LNCS, vol. 8560, pp. 425–440. Springer, Cham (2014). https://doi.org/10.1007/978-3-319-08918-8_29
32. Stirling, C., Walker, D.: Local model checking in the modal mu-calculus. Theor. Comput. Sci. **89**(1), 161–177 (1991)
33. Yang, Z., Hu, K., et al.: From AADL to timed abstract state machines: a verified model transformation. J. Syst. Softw. **93**, 42–68 (2014)
34. Zhang, Y.: Parameterized dynamic logic — towards a cyclic logical framework for general program specification and verification (2024). https://arxiv.org/abs/2404.18098v4
35. Zhang, Y., Mallet, F., Liu, Z.: A dynamic logic for verification of synchronous models based on theorem proving. Front. Comput. Sci. **16**(4) (2022)

A Theory Repair Based Traffic Regulations Generalisation for Autonomous Vehicles

Yiwei Lu[1,2], Xue Li[3], Zhe Yu[1(✉)], Yuhui Lin[4], Burkhard Schafer[2], Alan Bundy[3], Andrew Ireland[4], and Zhe Lin[5]

[1] Institute of Logic and Cognition, Department of Philosophy, Sun Yat-sen University, Guangzhou, China
yuzh28@mail.sysu.cn
[2] School of Law, Old College, University of Edinburgh, Edinburgh, UK
Y.Lu-104@sms.ed.ac.uk, B.Schafer@ed.ac.uk
[3] School of Informatics, University of Edinburgh, Edinburgh, UK
{xue.shirley.li,A.Bundy}@ed.ac.uk
[4] School of Mathematical and Computer Sciences, Heriot-Watt University, Edinburgh, UK
{y.lin,ceeai}@hw.ac.uk
[5] Department of Philosophy, Xiamen University, Xiamen, China

Abstract. The development of AI products poses unique challenges to law reform, especially specific normative reform. In particular, some AI technologies like autonomous driving technologies blur the boundaries of these fundamental concepts of law, such as human beings, objects and behaviours. This gives rise to inconsistency and inapplicability of existing human-specific laws when turned to AI, such as irrational division of responsibility, conceptual ambiguities, conflicting guidance on behaviour, and conflicts with legislative intent. Considering the complexity and scale of the legal structure and how AI affects this structure, especially in a dynamic context, pure manual legal adjustments will naturally face difficulties in terms of accuracy and efficiency. This study therefore extended an automated theory repair system to design an intelligent legal aid system for the revision of driving rules in the context of automated driving and provided the code necessary to implement these functions.

Keywords: Abduction · Automated theory repair · Legal modification · Autonomous driving

1 Introduction

The continuous development of artificial intelligence technology has brought about entirely new pressures for fast legal change [7]. This is reflected, on the one hand, in the fact that pre-existing legal theories are challenged by ethical and fundamental assumptions, and, on the other hand, in the persistent difficulty of providing clear standards of conduct applicable to AI products [3]. For the development and manufacture of AI products, the impact of the second point may be even greater. This is because if avoiding the risk of additional violations is one of the most fundamental motivations for engineers and manufacturers to pursue legal compliance, then the lack of a clear code of

M. Bonsangue and Y. Chen (Eds.): AILA 2025, CCIS 2668, pp. 227–242, 2026.
https://doi.org/10.1007/978-981-95-8262-4_18

conduct will make it difficult to continue product design. For example, if it is not clear whether an autonomous vehicle (AV) should perform the actions that a driver should take while in motion, it will be difficult to design whether it should require children to fasten their seatbelts before starting, as human drivers do. In addition, without a clear code, producers would make different decisions and then end up with chaotic products that are potentially dangerous and harmful to users and society.

There are a number of difficulties common to the adaptation of any system of legal norms [24]. For one thing, the law is a multi-layered and complex structure. The relationships between legal norms are diverse, and changes to a single rule or norm are likely to have a knock-on effect on other norms, which places high demands on the precision of adjustment. For the other thing, the number of legal norms is extremely large, and the inconsistencies and uncertainties associated with any change are likely to be widespread. This makes even small-scale modifications of legal norms a costly exercise in checking and correcting.

Unfortunately, the characteristics of AI technology have an amplifying effect on the difficulties described above [10]. Serious incompatibilities arise when we try to apply existing human-specific legal norms to govern the behaviour of AI products, and we face additional challenges when we try to achieve consistency. At root, this is because AI products blur the law's basic assumptions about people, things, and behaviour. Whether we view them as subjects or instruments of behaviour, they trigger further inconsistencies. One immediate problem this creates is confusion between behaviour and the corresponding liability. For example, if we view an AV as a driving tool under current law, it would seem that it could be exempt from being fully responsible for the driving choices it controls and the passengers it affects. If we view it as a driver under current law, should it be the car's autonomous system that is responsible, or its designer or manufacturer, or the operator of some online platform?

In addition, current law presupposes that the subjects who read, understand, and practice it are human beings. This means that the expressions it adopts as well as the behaviours it prescribes are based on a common sense understanding of human beings, which includes but is not limited to human comprehension, human bodily and physical functions, and the behavioural ability and knowledge level of most people. When we apply such a legal system to the AI context, the first thing it brings is the difficulty of understanding and practicing. Artificial intelligence products may not have some of the common sense or associative abilities that humans need to understand legal concepts and rules, resulting in the inability to choose specific behaviours based on these norms. Just as a human can easily understand what it means to maintain an appropriate distance, an intelligent system may need more precise guidance on the concept of appropriateness. In response to this, a large body of research has attempted to address the problem in terms of changing the form of legal expression. For example, traffic laws are formally expressed and cut into the operating system of an AV to directly regulate its behaviour [2,23]. However, this would still face another problem, namely, that the characteristics of AI products change the original causal relationship between legal behaviours and outcomes. For example, for a human driver, the long-time use of video devices while driving can lead to distraction, resulting in danger. For an autonomous driving system, however, this may even be necessary to drive safely. Similarly, standards set against humans for a particular goal may not apply to AI like driving speed, driving time and so on.

The rapid evolution of AI technologies creates unprecedented pressure for legal adaptation, presenting a dual challenge: maintaining legal consistency while enabling efficient updates. Current approaches to rule generalization face significant limitations:

- Rule-based systems (e.g., LegalRuleML [19]) use static templates that lack flexibility for novel AI conflicts, requiring manual updates.
- Knowledge graph methods [1] effectively query existing norms but cannot generate new rules or resolve dynamic inconsistencies.
- LLM-based approaches often produce logically inconsistent outputs and lack verifiable reasoning chains for legal auditing [15].

Given these limitations, and the impracticality of relying solely on manual or fully automated methods, a hybrid approach is needed. Automated reasoning can generate logically consistent repair suggestions at scale, while human experts retain control over semantic validation and final decisions.

According to the previous analysis, this automated reasoning tool should have several characteristics: (1) It can express the characteristics of legal information and AI products. (2) The ability to detect problems between current legal systems and new features of AI products. (3) Able to give logical modification solutions while ensuring the legal intentions. Based on this, we chose to introduce and extend the ABC system [4,17]. And to better show how ABC works in this mission, we selected some British traffic rules (mainly from the Highway Code) as case studies. We analysed the types of adjustments needed to apply these rules to AVs and explored how the ABC method can be used to provide repair recommendations. The Highway Code is one of the legal guidance documents for obtaining a driving licence in the UK. If'driving like a human' is considered the minimum requirement for legal compliance for AVs, then testing and adapting traffic rules for human drivers can serve as a good example.

Next, we review related work and compare several existing methods with ABC. In Sect. 3, we summarize the key adjustments required when applying current traffic rules to autonomous vehicles. Subsequently, in Sect. 4, we introduce ABC and demonstrate how it generates reasonable repair suggestions for diverse issues. To further clarify the repair process, we present a case study in Sect. 5. Finally, we conclude the paper in Sect. 6.

2 Related Work

How to detect problems in existing theoretical frameworks has always been an important issue in the field of knowledge representation and reasoning. In the fields of semantic web and knowledge graphs, there are many methods for detecting conflicts in existing knowledge bases. This is especially true in subfields such as entity embedding and quality assessment [12,20]. However, effective methods for fixing these problems have rarely been proposed. Some existing methods that focus on theoretical repair have excessive requirements for data formats [8], or only provide limited types of modifications [17]. In a legal context, it is difficult to deal with the combination of expression forms and reasoning patterns. Some research requires a large amount of manual intervention in the reasoning process, which fails to meet efficiency requirements. More importantly, these methods treat the formal detection and removal of inconsistencies as the main or sole goal of theory modification, while ignoring the environment in which the modified theory will be applied. Legal adjustments need to consider the legislative intention and the underlying application logic, and consistency repair is only meaningful within this framework.

Some machine learning methods have been used to mine logical features to generate rules [14,21]. They can'create' concepts and predicates to a certain extent, but cannot modify logical relationships on demand. On the one hand, legal adjustments are relatively diverse, and creating independent concepts and rules for each new situation is not a way for law to self-repair. On the other hand, machine learning algorithms rely heavily on empirical data, but legal amendments are not a frequent occurrence, making it difficult to find a large amount of historical data for legal amendments in the same field. Moreover, past legal amendments have very limited reference value in terms of statistical probability regularity. Machine learning algorithms also find it difficult to break through the existing patterns in empirical data. Since laws are written in natural language, LLMs have some advantages in addressing this issue. However, they are not yet accurate in reasoning [11], and are therefore better at integrating and explaining existing legal information and structures than at making innovative changes. Furthermore, although LLMs can produce reasoning results that can be read directly, the reasoning process severely lacks the explainability valued by law. Current LLMs capable of providing so-called thought processes also focus on presenting the various factors that influence the reasoning results, rather than the complete logical process.

Based on the above discussion, the reason for introducing ABC in this research is primarily its ability to modify theories around a given goal. The ABC repair system can accept an input theory and a benchmark, and then repair the theory to make it consistent with the benchmark while satisfying the consistency requirement [4,17]. This satisfies the requirement for consistency in the legal adjustment process while protecting legal intention, and also enables the reasoning process to be interpreted from a legal perspective. Secondly, unlike machine learning-based systems, ABC is a logic-based automatic reasoning system. Therefore, it requires only a small amount of input data to function. Furthermore, symbolic reasoning based on formal representations is interpretable and strictly follows logical rules [13,18], which enables legal experts to reuse the reasoning results. ABC can provide repair solutions based on concept changes and logical relationship adjustments in more diverse ways[1] and can clearly trace the reasoning process and basis. All these features make ABC highly suitable for preliminary screening of legal adjustment solutions and significantly improve the efficiency of legal experts in considering logical consistency.

In previous research, ABC has been applied to model virtual bargaining in human coordination processes subject to communication constraints to generate repair solutions with better alternatives, thereby improving agreements [5]. In the field of software system maintenance, ABC has also been applied to root cause analysis [5]. It is used

[1] ABC's conceptual change include splitting/merging predicates, increasing and decreasing the arity of a predicate and introducing new predicates and constants.

to detect missing information and provide repair solutions to address these root causes. Furthermore, ABC has been used to correct erroneous analogies [6]; and to explore students' misunderstandings of arithmetic processes using repair solutions [22]. In these tasks, ABC demonstrates good performance in terms of reasoning accuracy, explainability, and adaptability to repair tasks.

3 Patterns of Conflicts

As mentioned above, in order to show more concretely how this system can give possible solutions for modifying existing legal norms to give clear guidance to autonomous vehicles, we select and analyse a series of traffic rules to summarise what types of problems and adjustments we need to handle. Firstly, we extract some main legal intentions from these rules, i.e., what effects these rules are essentially seeking. A list of legal intentions/responsibilities is shown below as a shown case:

1. Maintaining control of the vehicle;
2. Communicate necessary information to other road participants in a timely manner;
3. Protects public and private properties;
4. Keep oneself and other road participants moving properly and efficiently;
5. Protecting the lives of all other road participants;
6. Protecting the lives of drivers and passengers in special situations;
7. Prevention of possible accidents.

We consider legal intention as functions, i.e., taking target objects and scenarios to achieve certain properties. Problems arising when applying current legal rules to AVs could be understood as breaking/hampering the targeted functions. We manually extract 3 patterns of problems or needed adjustments surrounding the legal intentions as shown below. Conflicts between current traffic rules and autonomous could raise from one of or combinations of these 3 patterns:

Pattern 1. Prohibition from Legal intentions. The original legal intention is to avoid specific situations by prohibiting some actions. But the AVs have to or are expected to do them. **Cases:** Highway Code 149 and 150 (summarised): Drivers are prohibited from using handheld communication devices while driving. Hand-free communication devices should also be used on a limited basis without causing distraction. Viewing of any video device not related to driving is prohibited. Limited viewing of navigation and other related systems is permitted only if it does not cause distraction. This rule is to guarantee the driver focus on driving and road conditions. But for autonomous driving, communication devices, video sensors, and visualisation devices are the basis for safe driving. Prohibiting or partially prohibiting them could cause safety problems. And similar rules are but not limited to: Highway Code 148, 275.

Pattern 2. Instruction and suggestion from legal intentions. To realise given legal intentions, the law instructs or requires the driver to take certain actions. But these actions are unnecessary, impossible or even harmful for AVs. **Cases:** Highway Code 91 (summarised): Human drivers should take a break of at least 15 min every two hours when driving long distances. This instruction is to ensure the physical and mental state of human drivers and to avoid fatigue driving. But AVs don't get fatigued or need to take high-frequency breaks as humans do. Following this instruction would instead defeat the purpose of people applying autonomous driving. Similar rules are but not limited to: Highway Code 97, 160, 271.

Pattern 3. Unification and partition of legal subject. In current regulation, human drivers are considered as a unity of multiple legal subjects, while regulations assign multiple responsibilities to the single subject. However, in the case of AV, this is no longer the case. Part of the legal responsibilities, e.g. car control has been separated from the AI, while the others remain the legal subjects such as car owners or passengers. Moreover, we can further partition the legal subject in AI with subsystems, given that the main operation procedures of an AI is a loop of *sense*, *perceive*, *plan* and *act*. **Cases:** Highway Code 99 (summarised): Drivers should ensure that eligible children are using the corresponding safety facilities, such as seat belts and child seats. In an autonomous driving situation, where the vehicle has no physical function to ensure this move is made, the duty to detect and alert may be more appropriate. The responsibility for ensuring that children use safety facilities should perhaps be separated from the legal subject of the driver and attributed to the adults travelling with the child. Similar rules are but not limited to: Highway Code 89, 97, 228, 229.

Now we know the legal intentions and patterns violating these intentions when applying current traffic rules to autonomous vehicles. In the next section, we introduce the ABC system and demonstrate how it gives legal modification suggestions for different patterns for given legal intentions.

4 A Theory Repair Approach to Suggest Legal Regulation Generalisation

4.1 Theory Repair by ABC

The ABC repair system (ABC) is designed to repair formal logical theories, whose core mechanism resembles elements in regulation generalisation. It effectively addresses faults like inconsistencies, insufficiencies, and incompatibilities within a logical theory, as defined below. In these definitions, C denotes a conclusion, with P1 and P2 representing logical reasoning processes leading to C under a given theory.

- *Inconsistency*: the theory is self-contradictory w.r.t. the truth value of C [9].
- *Insufficiency*: when C is wanted, but it cannot be derived from the theory [17].
- *Incompatibility*: when C is unwanted, but it is derivable from the theory [17].

Based on the definitions of the three problems, we can correspond them or their combinations to the previously discussed patterns. The exact correspondence depends on the way we understand and model the contradiction. For example, in the case of autonomous vehicles having to make heavy use of communication and video devices, we can understand it as an incompatibility, i.e., we do not want the vehicle to lose focus on the road, but prohibiting the use of communication and video devices leads to this. We can also read it as an insufficiency, i.e., we want the vehicle to be able to pay attention to the road, but prohibiting the use of communication and video devices will not get that result. This modelling flexibility is also one of the strengths of ABC. It allows legal experts to condition their reasoning with their own inputs on their needs. For example, whether something is to be treated as an observed objective situation or a result that the law must ensure. We will also illustrate this point in a subsequent case.

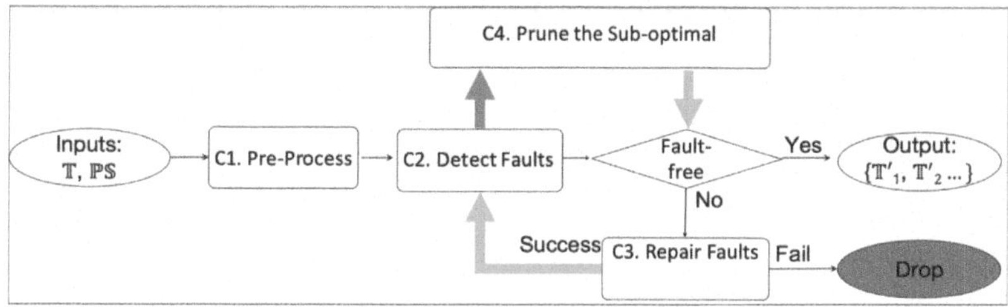

Fig. 1. Flowchart of ABC.

The flowchart of ABC is presented in Fig. 1. In this figure, green arrows indicate the sequential transfer of individual theories to the next process, while the blue arrow collects and transfers theories as a set. When a faulty theory is found to be irreparable, it is excluded from the repair process [16]. The inputs include the object theory $\mathbb{T}$ and a preferred structure $\mathbb{PS}$, where the former is subject to repair if faults are detected and the latter serves as the benchmark for evaluating the correctness of $\mathbb{T}$. When the theory is faulty,[2] ABC generates and outputs all possible repaired versions that meet the benchmark conditions. The code implementing the functionalities described in this research is available at: ABC_Datalog.

Table 1. Faults and their repair strategy in the ABC repair system.

Faults	Issue	Repair strategy
Inconsistency & Incompatibility	Exist the occurrences of proofs of C (P1s)	Break P1s
Insufficiency	Cannot find any proofs of C (P2s)	Build a P2

As we can see in Table 1, ABC has two main strategies for repair: breaking proofs for unwanted conclusions and constructing proofs for targeted ones. This supports repairing legal systems under given intentions like prohibition, instruction, requirement and so on. More importantly, ABC enables modifications that include adjustments to

[2] The original version of ABC addresses incompatibility and insufficiency and has since been extended to handle inconsistency. For simplicity, these aspects are uniformly referred to here as inconsistencies or faults, assuming that incompatibilities and insufficiencies represent inconsistencies between the theory and $\mathbb{PS}$.

the internal structure of the legal regulations, in addition to the addition and deletion of rules. Specifically, ABC has 11 operations that implement these two strategies for certain problems as shown in Fig. 2 and Fig. 3.

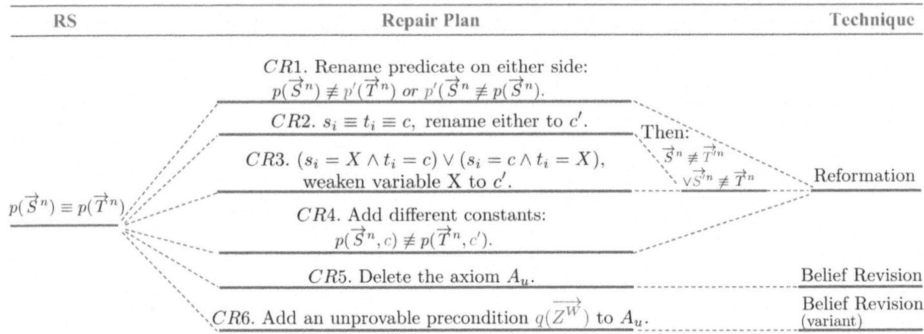

Fig. 2. Repairing operations for incompatibility and inconsistency.

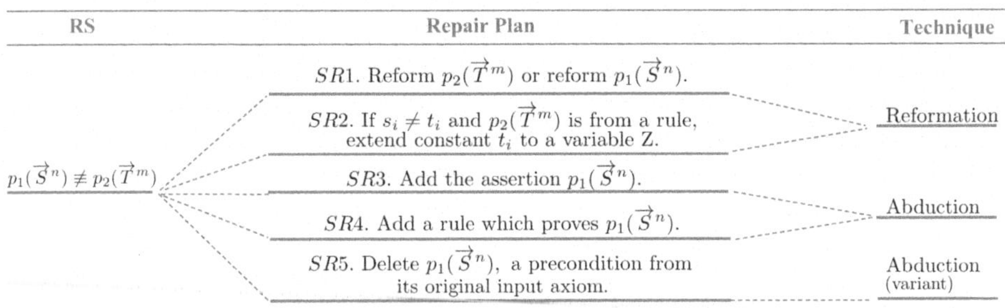

Fig. 3. Repairing operations for insufficiency.

To better understand these 11 operations, we categorize them into four types based on their logical methods (following [16]), as shown in Table 2. RC1 modifies the subject, object, or behavior relationship in a rule. For example, changing 'a citizen may drive an automobile' to 'a citizen may sit in an automobile'. RC2 alters the conditions of a rule, such as modifying 'a citizen may drive a car' to 'a citizen of adult age may drive a car'. RC3 adjusts the semantic scope of concepts or conditions, for instance changing 'male citizens of adult age may drive an automobile' to 'all citizens of adult age may drive an automobile'. Finally, RC4 represents the simplest form of legal modification - adding or deleting complete rules, like prohibiting autonomous car usage by adding: 'citizens are forbidden to use autonomous cars'. A more detailed correspondence between repair operations in ABC and legal modification methods can be found in Fig. 4.

Table 2. ABC's Repair categories and the corresponding practice in regulation generalisation.

Repair Categories	Example (old → (new)	Regulation Generalisation Practice.
RC1. Rename constant or predicate (CR1, CR2, SR1).	driver(D, C) → driver_dummy(D, C)	Change subject, object or relation.
RC2. Add/delete an argument of a predicate or a precondition of a rule (CR4, CR6, SR5).	driver(D, C) → driver(D, C, dummy)	Change applicable conditions or restrictions.
RC3. Generalise to broader individuals or restrict to specific individuals (SR2, CR3).	driver(D, C, dummy) → driver(D, C, X)	Extend to wider or restrict to narrower applicable range.
RC4. Delete or add an axiom (CR5, SR3, SR4).		Abandon or create a fact or a rule of regulation.

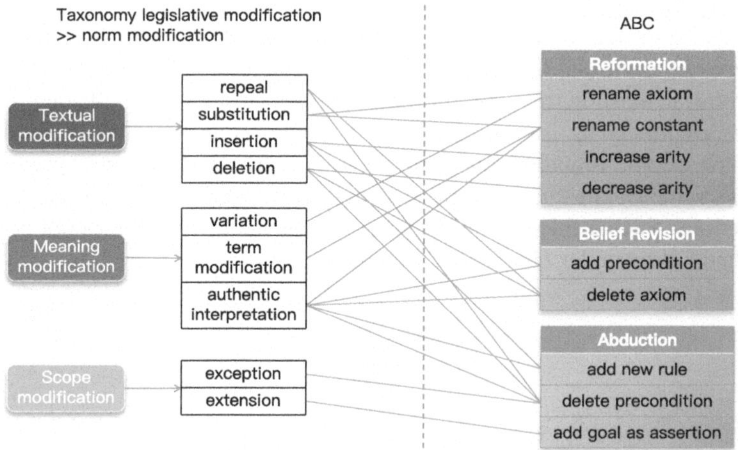

Fig. 4. A mapping of ABC repair operations with a legal modification account.

It is important to highlight that ABC's approach to repair is based on logical symbols rather than legal semantics. Therefore, it is entirely up to the legal experts to decide which logical solution is ultimately chosen and what legal semantics should be used for that logical solution. ABC merely provides suggestions to satisfy the logical targets, which are part and basis of requirements of legal modification.

To summarise, the workflow of ABC to give legal modification suggestions is shown in Fig. 5. The underlying strategy of applying ABC will be introduced with simplified examples for demonstration[3].

[3] In this section, all examples are simplified for demonstration without directly citing laws.

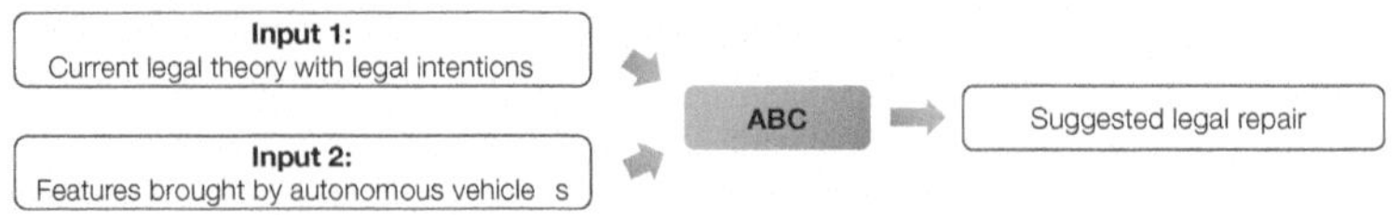

Fig. 5. Workflow of legal modification from ABC.

4.2 Automating Law for AV Formalisation

For formalising law for AVs, current laws (CLs) provide the main source of necessary information. The relationship between CL and future AV-specific regulations is shown in Fig. 6, where L_1 denotes parts of current laws (black) that are irrelevant for AVs, L_2 covers provisions that are relevant (blue) and may be directly retained or modified to suit AV contexts, and L_3 represents entirely new content that current laws do not address but that is required for AVs.

This paper uses Example 1 to clarify this structure. E-L1, which regulates driver fatigue, becomes irrelevant for fully autonomous vehicles and thus belongs to L_1. E-L2 illustrates how an existing rule—prohibiting drunk driving—could still apply if passengers in AVs are treated as drivers under certain conditions, requiring only modification to reflect AV-specific requirements (marked in red). E-L3 adds a new provision that autonomous vehicles must not perform system updates while driving, to prevent delays or malfunctions. Such a rule has no meaning for conventional vehicles but is essential for AVs, thus falling under L_3.

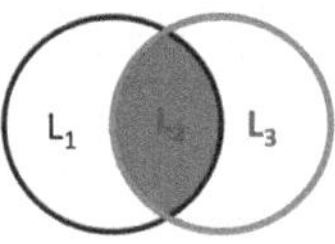

Fig. 6. Relationship between Current Laws and law for AVs.

Example 1

E-L1. You must not drive for more than 10 h in a day.
E-L2. Current drink-drive limit is 22 microgrammes of alcohol in 100 ml of breath.
E-L3. No operating system update while the vehicle is driving.

Accordingly, key tasks of formalising law for AV include reasoning about:

T1 what laws need to be added to deal with scenarios that only AVs experience?
T2 which parts of the current laws are to be revised due to their relevance but that they are inappropriate to AVs?
T3 what to remove when it is irrelevant to AVs?

Automating the law for AV formalisation can be understood as the task of automatically repairing current laws to meet a benchmark derived from expert decisions or simulation results of AV behaviour. Since the aim of this research is to support human legal experts in decision-making and ease their workload, the benchmark for ABC is assumed to rely primarily on characteristics observed during the AV design stage and in simulation tests.

Still using Example 1, when examining E-L1, one possible test is to simulate AV operation for X, $0 < X \leq 24$ hours per day, combined with safety tests designed to determine whether continuous driving remains acceptable. If all safety tests are passed when $X = 24$, it can be reasonably inferred that autonomous vehicles do not require restrictions on daily driving time, provided the hardware operates correctly and sufficient energy is available. Thus, E-L1 can be categorised under L_1. In a similar way, E-L2 can be verified by simulating scenarios that test the operator's blood alcohol limit. For E-L3, accident data from AV simulations can serve as evidence to inductively develop new legal provisions that prevent similar incidents.

Based on the above information and Fig. 5, the initial input in ABC comprises laws originally designed for human drivers and the specific characteristics of autonomous vehicles. The reasoning logic encoded as rules within both sources serves as the preliminary basis for deriving AV-specific legal provisions. Accordingly, these elements are first classified into one of the categories L_1, L_2, or L_3. The fundamental approach for this classification is outlined as follows:

C-L1. If corresponding rules are *not* involved in deriving any theorems from the theory representing simulations tests of the AV, those rules are probably not applicable to the AV so will be a candidate member of L_1.

C-L2. If corresponding rules are involved in deriving any theorems from the theory representing simulations tests of the AV, the laws represented by those rules are probably applicable to the AV so will be a candidate member of L_2.

C-L3. If some predicates from the theory representing system simulations never occur in rules representing laws, probably new rules need to be constructed, which is in class L_3, e.g., the new concept of operating system.

Note that using laws in L_1 and constructing laws for L_3 are more straightforward than operations for L_2 where a rule in L_2 is either directly taken or revised for AVs. The operation needed for a rule in L_2 depends on whether its conclusion violates legal principles, as discussed in Example 1.

Example for Revising the current law into law for AV. In this example, ABC detects the need to reform E-L2 based on simulation results. The input theory contains four axioms describing one should not drive when it is bigger than 0.22 in Scotland; $p1$ is allowed to drive in Scotland because of passing driving exams, although $p1$'s level of alcohol in the breath is 0.4. Here (A1) represents the current law corresponding to (E-L2). Then a simulation experiment is whether human operators of a certain alcohol level can pass driving exams under a certain level of alcohol[4]. The evidence from this simulation, highlighted in a purple background, is that $p1$'s alcohol in the breath is

[4] The definition of driving in AVs is not discussed here, i.e., the main user in the AV is assumed to be the "driver".

0.4 and $p1$ passed driving exams, given by A3. The $\mathscr{T}(\mathbb{PS})$ is the benchmark of the correctness of the law for the current simulation[5]: the conclusion of the rule should be a theorem from the input theory when its precondition is satisfied by the theory. In this example, it requires that one is allowed to drive in Scotland if passing the driving exams.

$$alcohol(X,Y,breath) \wedge Y > 0.22 \implies not(allow(driving,X,scotland)) \quad \text{(A1)}$$
$$\implies alcohol(p1,0.4,breath) \quad \text{(A2)}$$
$$\implies pass(p1,driving\_exams) \quad \text{(A3)}$$
$$\mathscr{T}(\mathbb{PS}) = \{pass(X,driving\_exams) \implies allow(driving,X,scotland)\} \quad \text{(PS1)}$$

The above theory is inconsistent because $p1$ is not permitted to drive according to (A1) and (A2), yet should be permitted under (A3) and $\mathscr{T}(\mathbb{PS})$. ABC can resolve this inconsistency in multiple ways. One possible repair is to adjust the precondition in A1 using the threshold specified in A2, as shown in (A1'), which is appropriate when a higher alcohol limit for autonomous vehicle users is desired. This revision implies that the law permits greater alcohol consumption for individuals using AVs, provided they do not become excessively intoxicated. Another repair option is to delete A1 entirely, which is suitable if the legal intention is to remove any alcohol concentration requirement for AV operation.

$$alcohol(X,Y,breath) \wedge Y > 0.4 \implies not(allow(driving(X,scotland))) \quad \text{(A1')}$$

It can be observed that ABC may generate numerous modification options within the confines of logical consistency. Heuristic algorithms could therefore play an important role in avoiding undesirable modifications. In the example above, protecting A2–A3 from alteration by ABC serves as a desirable heuristic, since they represent objective facts that are not intended to be revised.

In summary, the underlying idea of applying ABC to the task of legal revision is as follows: designers and developers of autonomous vehicles provide descriptive product characteristics derived from simulation tests, which are then input into ABC as benchmarks because they constitute objective facts about AVs. ABC subsequently tests these features with the aim of aligning existing laws with the realities of autonomous vehicles. When elements incompatible with AV operation are identified, ABC proposes modifications that maintain logical coherence. Legal experts then determine whether these proposals are appropriate and how they should be integrated into the broader legal framework.

5 Running Case

To better demonstrate the legal repair process of ABC, we formalise the situation below as a running case.

According to GB Domestic Rules: Drivers' hours, in order to avoid fatigued driving, drivers must not drive for more than 10 h in a single day for passenger vehicles and lorries that are not

[5] This is an extension of ABC that allows rules in the $\mathbb{PS}$ rather than just ground propositions.

required to comply with EU rules. At the same time, a rest period of at least 10 h is to be taken between every two working days. Now we assume that autonomous vehicles can work continuously and don't need to take breaks, which only refers to working status excluding maintaining or charging.

For simplicity, we formalise the illustrative example by giving all information as the input theory without a preferred structure, which allows ABC to detect and repair faults in the theory as inconsistencies[6]. To understand the formalised expressions below definitions could be referred to:

driver(X): X is a driver.
driving_time(X, Y, Z): Driver X has drived Y hours during Z hours.
fatigue_driving(X, Y, Z): Driver X is fatigue after driving Y hours during Z hours.
rest_time(X, Y, Z): Driver X is required to rest at lease Y hours after Z working hours.

The running case in ABC is formalised and performed as shown in Example 2 and Example 3.

Example 2 is the current legal system with new features brought by autonomous vehicles. Proposition(1) to (2) is the current rules for human drivers. (5) to (7) is the instantiation of new features, meaning a driver called av is driving without rest. (3) to (4) in blue is the new but inconsistent theory we want to add, i.e. the driver av won't get fatigue and don't need to rest.

Example 2 *Repaired fatigue driving theory.*

$$driver(X) \wedge driving\_time(X,Y,24) \wedge Y > 10 \implies fatigue\_driving(X,Y,24) \quad (1)$$
$$driver(X) \wedge rest\_time(X,Y,24) \wedge Y < 10 \implies rest\_required(X,Y,24) \quad (2)$$
$$driving\_time(av,Y,Z) \wedge fatigue\_driving(av,Y,Z) \implies \quad (3)$$
$$driver(av) \wedge rest\_time(av,Y,Z) \wedge rest\_required(av,Y,Z) \implies \quad (4)$$
$$\implies driving\_time(av,24,24) \quad (5)$$
$$\implies rest\_time(av,0,24) \quad (6)$$
$$\implies driver(av) \quad (7)$$

Example 3 *Repaired fatigue driving theory.*

$$driver(X,human) \wedge driving\_time(X,Y,24) \wedge Y > 10 \implies fatigue\_driving(X,Y,24) \quad (8)$$
$$driver(X,human) \wedge rest\_time(X,Y,24) \wedge Y < 10 \implies rest\_required(X,Y,24) \quad (9)$$
$$driving\_time(av,Y,Z) \wedge fatigue\_driving(av,Y,Z) \implies \quad (10)$$
$$driver(X,system) \wedge rest\_time(av,Y,Z) \wedge rest\_required(av,Y,Z) \implies \quad (11)$$
$$\implies driving\_time(av,24,24) \quad (12)$$
$$\implies rest\_time(av,0,24) \quad (13)$$
$$\implies driver(av,system) \quad (14)$$

[6] Alternatively, certain observations can be given as positive examples and negative examples in the preferred structure for which the corresponding faults will be insufficiencies and incompatibilities.

Example 3 is the repaired legal system. We can see in proposition (8), (9), (11) and (14) that the original predicate driver(X) has been added new conditions. The new predicate is driver(X, human) and driver(X,system) meaning driver X is human or a system. Now, if the driver is human, he has to follow the past rules, i.e. drive for limited times and take enough rest. But if the driver is an autonomous system, it can drive 24 h a day without rest.

We need to note that the semantics or names of human and system should be given by legal experts. ABC will give new predicate in format of driver(X,dummy1) and driver(X,dummy2). We have modelled the results of this process directly in the case. And, only one of the repair solutions that ABC will give is shown here. It could give all the options available that meet the requirements based on the filtering criteria. For example: increase the amount of continuous driving time allowed by law, add a direct rule to allow autonomous cars to drive for extended periods of time, etc. We have chosen to show one of the most common sense options here.

As we mentioned earlier, one of the strengths of ABC is its flexible modelling approach. In this example, we view the autonomous vehicle situation as an objective situation that conflicts with current regulations. From a legal perspective, it is possible that there is a legal intention desired to be artificially avoided or guaranteed. For example, legal experts believe that even autonomous vehicles should not be driven for more than 18 continuous hours for safety reasons. Alternatively, the law does not consider it acceptable to have autonomous vehicles on the road at this time. In this case, ABC users can add their intentions to the positive and negative examples in preferred structure and receive corresponding repair suggestions.

6 Conclusion and Future Work

In this paper, we summarise the types of inapplicability of existing traffic regulations to autonomous driving scenarios. We then introduce and expand the ABC system to help the law make modifications to these inapplications. Our findings demonstrate that ABC can automate suggestions for logical modifications while maintaining the intention of the law, with selection and semantic embedding by legal experts. This would certainly be helpful in adapting the law in the face of AI developments. Additionally, we have provided code to realize the functionalities described in this paper (ABC_Datalog).

In future work, we will extend this research in four key directions: (1) conducting quantitative benchmarking against existing methods (e.g., LegalRuleML, LLMs) to evaluate response time and logical consistency; (2) expanding the test case set to include domains such as data protection and financial regulation; (3) developing expert-in-the-loop interfaces with explainable reasoning outputs; and (4) integrating legal ontologies to support large-scale automated rule repair, validated through real-world regulatory case studies.

References

1. Aparicio, J.T., Arsenio, E., Santos, F., Henriques, R.: Using dynamic knowledge graphs to detect emerging communities of knowledge. Knowl.-Based Syst. **294** (2024)
2. Borgesa, G., Wüsta, C., Sasdellia, D., Margvelashvilia, S., Klier-Ringlea, S.: Making the implicit explicit: the potential of case law analysis for the formalization of legal. In: Proceedings of LN2FR 2022, pp. 66–75 (2022)
3. Brodsky, J.S.: Autonomous vehicle regulation: how an uncertain legal landscape may hit the brakes on self-driving cars. Berkeley Technol. Law J. **31**(2), 851–878 (2016)
4. Bundy, A., Li, X.: Representational change is integral to reasoning. Philos. Trans. Roy. Soc. A **381**(2251), 20220,052 (2023)
5. Bundy, A., Philalithis, E., Li, X.: Modelling virtual bargaining using logical representation change. In: Human-Like Machine Intelligence, pp. 68–89 (2021)
6. Cai, C.H., Bundy, A.: Repairing numerical equations in analogically blended theories using reformation. In: Proceedings of HLC 2022, pp. 18–23 (2022)
7. Carr, N.: As the role of the driver changes with autonomous vehicle technology, so, too, must the law change. St. Mary's Law J. **51**, 817–843 (2020)
8. Dimou, A., et al.: Assessing and refining mappingsto RDF to improve dataset quality. In: Arenas, M., et al. (eds.) ISWC 2015. LNCS, vol. 9367, pp. 133–149. Springer, Cham (2015). https://doi.org/10.1007/978-3-319-25010-6_8
9. Gärdenfors, P.: Belief Revision. Cambridge University Press, Cambridge (2003)
10. Hoffmann-Riem, W.: Artificial intelligence as a challenge for law and regulation. In: Regulating Artificial Intelligence, pp. 1–29 (2020)
11. Huang, J., et al.: Large language models cannot self-correct reasoning yet. arXiv preprint arXiv:2310.01798 (2023)
12. Idrissou, A., Van Harmelen, F., Van Den Besselaar, P.: Network metrics for assessing the quality of entity resolution between multiple datasets. Semant. Web **12**(1), 21–40 (2021)
13. Ilkou, E., Koutraki, M.: Symbolic vs sub-symbolic AI methods: friends or enemies? In: CIKM (Workshops), vol. 2699 (2020)
14. Jarvis, M.P., Nuzzo-Jones, G., Heffernan, N.T.: Applying machine learning techniques to rule generation in intelligent tutoring systems. In: Lester, J.C., Vicari, R.M., Paraguaçu, F. (eds.) ITS 2004. LNCS, vol. 3220, pp. 541–553. Springer, Heidelberg (2004). https://doi.org/10.1007/978-3-540-30139-4_51
15. Ji, Z., et al.: Survey of hallucination in natural language generation. ACM Comput. Surv. **55**(12), 1–38 (2023)
16. Li, X.: Automating the repair of faulty logical theories. Ph.D. thesis, The University of Edinburgh (2021)
17. Li, X., Bundy, A., Smaill, A.: ABC repair system for datalog-like theories. In: Proceedings of IC3K 2018 - Volume 2: KEOD, pp. 333–340 (2018)
18. Linardatos, P., Papastefanopoulos, V., Kotsiantis, S.: Explainable AI: a review of machine learning interpretability methods. Entropy **23**(1), 18 (2020)
19. Palmirani, M., Governatori, G., Rotolo, A., Tabet, S., Boley, H., Paschke, A.: LegalRuleML: XML-based rules and norms. In: Olken, F., Palmirani, M., Sottara, D. (eds.) RuleML 2011. LNCS, vol. 7018, pp. 298–312. Springer, Heidelberg (2011). https://doi.org/10.1007/978-3-642-24908-2_30
20. Raad, J., Beek, W., van Harmelen, F., Pernelle, N., Saïs, F.: Detecting erroneous identity links on the web using network metrics. In: Vrandečić, D., et al. (eds.) ISWC 2018. LNCS, vol. 11136, pp. 391–407. Springer, Cham (2018). https://doi.org/10.1007/978-3-030-00671-6_23

21. Schindler, C., Rausch, A.: Formal software architecture rule learning: a comparative investigation between large language models and inductive techniques. Electronics **13**(5) (2024)
22. Tang, J.: Arithmetic errors revisited: diagnosis and remediation of erroneous arithmetic performance as repair of faulty representations. Ph.D. thesis, School of Informatics, University of Edinburgh (2016)
23. Westhofen, L., Stierand, I., Becker, J.S., Möhlmann, E., Hagemann, W.: Towards a congruent interpretation of traffic rules for automated driving-experiences and challenges. In: Proceedings of LN2FR 2022, pp. 8–21 (2022)
24. Zander, M.: The Law-Making Process. Bloomsbury Publishing (2015)

Author Index

M. Bonsangue and Y. Chen (Eds.): AILA 2025, CCIS 2668, pp. 243–244, 2026.
https://doi.org/10.1007/978-981-95-8262-4

The manufacturer's authorised representative in the EU is Springer Nature Customer Service Centre GmbH, Europaplatz 3, 69115 Heidelberg, Germany. If you have any concerns regarding our products, please contact ProductSafety@springernature.com

Printed and bound by CPI Group (UK) Ltd, Croydon, CR0 4YY

07/07/2026

02160906-0004